"Fantini and colleagues exquisitely convey state-of-the [ ] Therapeutic Assessment with adults in this highly engrossing book that grounds specific TA methods in their theoretical, conceptual, and empirical bases. This is a valuable resource for every personality assessor, psychotherapist, assessment instructor, and student interested in the depth and impact of assessment interventions."

Radhika Krishnamurthy, *Clinical Psychology Professor at Florida Tech, and Former President of the Society for Personality Assessment*

"The authors sensitively illustrate, from first contact with an assessment client through to their summary session and beyond, how the assessor's role can facilitate transformative change. A decade-plus into my experience with Therapeutic Assessment, I found myself learning significantly from this volume, and grateful for the chance to further refine my approach."

Seth Grossman, *primary co-author of the MCMI-IV*

"This eagerly-awaited textbook comprehensively encapsulates the theory and practice of Therapeutic Assessment, the term created by Stephen E. Finn three decades ago to describe his unique assessment practice. This is essential reading for psychologists worldwide who want to advance their assessment skills and learn a proven method of helping clients change."

Noriko Nakamura, *Clinical Director, Asian-Pacific Center for Therapeutic Assessment, Tokyo*

Therapeutic Assessment with Adults

This book is a comprehensive guide to Therapeutic Assessment (TA) with adults, showing how to collaboratively engage clients in psychological testing to help them achieve major and long-lasting change.

This guide clearly lays out each step of TA with adults, including its rationale and detailed instructions on how to handle a range of clinical situations. Additionally, in part one, the authors fully describe the development of TA, its theoretical bases, and the most up-to-date research on the model. In the second part of the book, the authors describe the structure and techniques of TA, and illustrate each step with transcripts from a clinical case. Further clinical illustrations help the reader understand how to conduct a TA with different types of clients, including those from culturally diverse backgrounds.

This book is essential for all clinicians, therapists, and trainees working with adult clients; along with students in assessment courses.

Francesca Fantini, Ph.D., is a licensed psychologist. She is an Adjunct Professor at the Università Cattolica del Sacro Cuore (UCSC), Milan, Italy, where she teaches personality assessment. She is currently part of the scientific board of the European Center for Therapeutic Assessment at the same university and a board member of the Therapeutic Assessment Institute. She lectures in graduate and post-graduate courses on personality testing, collaborative use of tests, and Therapeutic Assessment in Italy and internationally. Dr. Fantini has published papers on Therapeutic Assessment with different kinds of clients (i.e., families with children, adult clients) and on the use of projective tests in multicultural assessment. She is one of the authors of the Italian adaptation of the Tell-Me-A-Story multicultural projective test (TEMAS).

Filippo Aschieri, Ph.D., is an Associate Professor at the Università Cattolica del Sacro Cuore (UCSC), Milan, Italy and is the International Coordinator of the Master in Systemic Psychology at University of Monterrey, Mexico. He received the Department Acknowledgement for high-quality research achievements (2015, 2019), the Martin Mayman Award for Distinguished Contribution to the Personality Assessment Literature from the Society for Personality Assessment (2013), and the Award for the integration of science and practice—Diagnosis and Assessment the *Journal of Contemporary Psychotherapy*, for the best article on personality assessment (2018). He is a board member of the Therapeutic Assessment Institute, Fellow of the Society for Personality Assessment, and the Director of the European Center for Therapeutic Assessment (ECTA) at UCSC, where he works as a clinician and supervisor. Since 2019 he serves as Scientific Director of the Specialization School in Integrated Psychotherapy—Sanicare, in Tuscany, Italy, in which students undertake a 4-year training program in TA with adult clients, families, and couples, and the relational-symbolic model for family intervention. In 2020, he was appointed Editor-in-Chief of *Rorschachiana* by the International Society for the Rorschach and Projective Methods.

Raja M. David, Psy.D., is a licensed psychologist in St. Paul, Minnesota, and the founder and owner of the Minnesota Center for Collaborative/Therapeutic Assessment. He was previously an Assistant Professor and Program Dean in the Doctoral Clinical Psychology program at the Minnesota School of Professional Psychology. In that role, he taught courses on therapy and assessment, and an elective course on Therapeutic Assessment (TA). In 2021, he authored a chapter on conducting the initial TA session for the *Oxford Handbook of Personality and Psychopathology Assessment, 2nd Ed.* (J. Mihura, Editor) and published an article in the Journal of Personality Assessment entitled *Virtual Delivery of Therapeutic Assessment: An Empirical Case Study*. Dr. David routinely conducts workshops on TA and has presented on the model at professional conferences, including twice being a plenary speaker at the International Collaborative/Therapeutic Assessment conference. In 2019, he recorded two podcasts on TA for the Testing Psychologist Podcast (*ww.thetestingpsychologist.com*) and in 2022 took on the role of editor for the *TA Connection*.

Hale Martin, Ph.D., is a Clinical Professor in the Graduate School of Professional Psychology at the University of Denver where he teaches assessment courses, including a course on Therapeutic Assessment. He teaches Therapeutic Assessment nationally and internationally and has published numerous chapters and articles on Therapeutic Assessment. He is also a licensed psychologist in Colorado and founder and director of the Colorado Center for Therapeutic Assessment as well as the Colorado Assessment Society, serving as its initial president for eight years and he still serves on the executive committee. He is a Fellow of the Society for Personality Assessment and a member of the Therapeutic Assessment Institute and on its Board of Directors. He is certified in adult Therapeutic Assessment and serves as Associate Editor of the *TA Connection*.

Stephen E. Finn, Ph.D., founder of the Center for Therapeutic Assessment, is a licensed clinical psychologist in practice in Austin, Texas, a Clinical Associate Professor of Psychology at the University of Texas at Austin, Senior Researcher and Director of Training at the European Center for Therapeutic Assessment at the Catholic University of Milan, Italy, and Director of Training at the Asian-Pacific Center for Therapeutic Assessment in Tokyo, Japan. He has published 90+ articles and chapters on psychological assessment, psychotherapy, and other topics in clinical psychology, and is the author of *In Our Clients' Shoes: Theory and Techniques of Therapeutic Assessment* (Erlbaum, 2007) and *A Manual for Using the MMPI-2 as a Therapeutic Intervention* (1996, University of Minnesota Press). Dr. Finn also co-edited, with Constance Fischer and Leonard Handler, *Collaborative/Therapeutic Assessment: A Casebook and Guide* (Wiley, 2012). In 2011 Dr. Finn was awarded the Bruno Klopfer Award from the Society of Personality Assessment for distinguished lifetime contributions to the field of personality assessment. In August 2017 he received the award for Distinguished Contributions to Assessment Psychology from Section IX (Assessment) of the Society for Clinical Psychology (Division 12 of the American Psychological Association). In 2018 he received the Carl Rogers Award for an outstanding contribution to theory and practice of humanistic psychology from the Society for Humanistic Psychology (Division 32 of the American Psychological Association).

Therapeutic Assessment with Adults

Using Psychological Testing to
Help Clients Change

**Francesca Fantini, Filippo Aschieri
Raja M. David, Hale Martin, and
Stephen. E. Finn**

Routledge
Taylor & Francis Group

NEW YORK AND LONDON

Cover image: wildpixel

First published 2022
by Routledge
605 Third Avenue, New York, NY 10158

and by Routledge
4 Park Square, Milton Park, Abingdon, Oxon, OX14 4RN

Routledge is an imprint of the Taylor & Francis Group, an informa business

© 2022 Francesca Fantini, Filippo Aschieri, Raja M. David, Hale Martin and Stephen. E. Finn

Library of Congress Cataloguing-in-Publication Data
Names: Fantini, Francesca, author.
Title: Therapeutic assessment with adults: using psychological testing to help clients change / Francesca Fantini, Ph.D., Filippo Aschieri, Ph.D., Raja M. David, Psy.D., Hale Martin, Ph.D., Stephen E. Finn, Ph.D.
Description: Abingdon, Oxon; New York, NY: Routledge, 2022. | Includes bibliographical references and index.
Identifiers: LCCN 2021058323 (print) | LCCN 2021058324 (ebook)
Subjects: LCSH: Psychodiagnostics. | Personality assessment. | Change (Psychology)
Classification: LCC RC469.F36 2022 (print) | LCC RC469 (ebook) | DDC 616.89/075--dc23/eng/20211220
LC record available at https://lccn.loc.gov/2021058323
LC ebook record available at https://lccn.loc.gov/2021058324

ISBN: 978-0-367-19492-5 (hbk)
ISBN: 978-0-367-19494-9 (pbk)
ISBN: 978-0-429-20279-7 (ebk)

DOI: 10.4324/9780429202797

Typeset in Times New Roman
by MPS Limited, Dehradun

To all our clients

Contents

Tables

Boxes

Figures

Foreword

October 25, 2006

Dear Chris,

I am writing with the results of the past 15 years of your career as a psychologist, so that you can have something to look on as you traverse the next decade and a half. I hope it will help you answer some of the questions that concern you as you navigate graduate school and your first experiences with patients. With hindsight, I think we were able to generate some preliminary but helpful answers to your questions, as well as some ideas about how you can continue to grow.

How do I decide what I want to do?

You enthusiastically listed the different possibilities within clinical psychology and described how you saw the presence of all of these possibilities as both an advantage and a challenge. You wanted to learn how to be competent at research and practice, to have expertise in personality and clinical psychology, and to conduct clinical assessment and psychotherapy. You also discussed the admiration and gratitude you had for your mentors and supervisors, and your wish to have a similar influence on future students and trainees. You said you wanted to "do it all," but you also felt external pressure to select, narrow, and specialize. You were told by trusted mentors that success in research meant cutting back on time spent doing clinical work, and that one's research must be programmatic. To be successful, you were told, people must know you as the person who does "X." But what, you asked, is my "X"?

In graduate school you learned that success in research creates opportunities to a greater degree than clinical experience, so your first priority was to establish a solid research record. But you also mentioned that, for you, it was equally important to pursue as many clinical experiences as possible, and that this came with an entirely different set of challenges. You said that it almost felt sneaky to take on extra cases that seemed interesting to you, as if you were betraying other peoples' expectations. You were developing the sense that you did not want to be in a place where caring about clinical practice had to feel sneaky, and an unpopular but genuine distaste for the radical version of "clinical science" that frames science and practice as somehow incompatible within the same person, and casts the former as more important.

As with your doctoral program, you would eventually choose an internship and a first job at institutions with a history of valuing research and practice equally. However, when you arrived as an assistant professor, you were again told that you can't do it all, that you would spread yourself too thin and burn out, that you should pick a specific focus, and that programmatic and fundable research was really the most important priority. When you expressed an interest in clinical licensure and supervision, you were looked upon with some skepticism, and asked whether you wanted to do assessment or psychotherapy. You stubbornly replied, "both...er, neither...um, are they really that different?"

I know it doesn't feel like it now, but it turns out you were trusting yourself. It felt confusing to receive messages about having to narrow your interests because this did not fit with the person you wanted to be—with the authentic version of yourself who you were becoming. You had an inner sense that there is a dialectic and often synergistic relationship between research and practice, assessment and psychotherapy, stability and change, security and growth. You tended to do well when you trusted that inner sense.

In fact, you already are doing it all! Right now, as a graduate student, you are conducting a trial with your advisor, Les Morey, to test whether a Therapeutic Assessment (TA) intervention can help suicidal patients engage better in a brief, manualized cognitive-behavioral treatment. In this context, you consulted with Steve Finn (what a thrill that was!). Remember being so impressed that Steve hadn't taken the path that others had chosen for him, but instead was impacting the world by mixing his interests and talents together in a way that was true to himself? That feeling was telling you something important. You have recently begun doing TAs with your own patients, learning first hand that assessment and therapy are not different strategies for different goals, but rather complementary foci that reinforce and strengthen one another. Over time, you will become even more confident in your belief that therapy without assessment is like a ship without a rudder, and assessment without therapy like a shipment without a harbor. Eventually, you will use TA as an organizing framework for your own teaching and clinical supervision, and you will help your students break down some of the unhelpful divisions in our field in their own work. You will even learn how to bring this integrative kind of thinking to a professorship without clinical responsibilities, first in California, and eventually in Switzerland (to be honest, that last bit is still a work in progress).

But the main point is this: You will never answer this question in the way you expected because it turns out to not be a helpful question for you. Instead, you will learn to reframe it. You will look back with regret about the times that you narrowed your goals because you thought someone else thought it was what you should do, and with gratitude to the times that you trusted yourself, attended to the guidance of good examples, and created your own path.

How do I establish an identity?

You spoke with passion about how much you value different theories of personality and psychotherapy and how fascinating it has been to learn about different personality tests. But you also expressed some surprise and frustration about how this variation has given way to cliquishness and campiness in mental health. In contrast to your fascination with how to put things together, in your experience of the field it felt like psychoanalytic and cognitive-behavioral camps were talking past one another, or that one had to decide whether self-report or performance-based tests were more valid, or whether to prefer the PAI or MMPI. You lamented how confusing this all was to you, given your assumption that humans are really complicated, psychology is really young, and nobody has all that much figured out.

In this context, you recalled a particularly impactful experience at a TA workshop at the Society for Personality Assessment. At one point, Steve Finn, the presenter, invited the audience to organize themselves into small groups to discuss a case with Rorschach and MMPI data. One group had only three people in it, and they invited you to join them. Those three people were—gulp—Joni Mihura, Dave Nichols, and Greg Meyer. To participate and be treated as an equal with these three luminaries, discussing the results of tests that they had mastered, observing the power of these instruments in their deft hands, and coupling the results with the TA framework to magnify your empathy for the person who had been tested, was formative for you. Let me tell you, the edge has not worn off. Recalling this workshop still brings a tear to my eye.

But why was it so important to you then, and why does it sustain such emotional resonance 15 years later? Looking back, this experience broke down the boundaries between different theoretical schools, different tests, different cliques. It showed the power of putting things together. Undergirding the exchange were the influences of the major theorists you loved—Sullivan's insight, Roger's empathy, Loevinger's iconoclasm, Meehl's rigor. It didn't matter what jargon we were using, or what tests answered which questions, or who came up with the cleverest interpretation. What mattered was that, with the right focus, personality assessment had become a powerful tool for understanding someone and helping them understand themselves.

You took away from that experience that TA is the kind of framework that provides a big enough tent for different models and tests and approaches to fit comfortably within you and your work. Another hero of yours, Jerry Wiggins, used funny words like "propaedeutic" and "ecumenical" to describe interpersonal theory. These words basically mean that it plays well with a variety of other theories, tests, and clinical techniques. TA is the same way (the connection between TA and interpersonal theory is described beautifully in Finn's chapter about Sullivan in his first TA book). Within the flexible framework of TA, the researcher/clinician/teacher/supervisor/patient does not feel compelled toward a rigid identity that must be declared and stamped for all time, but instead feels free to change, try different things, test new hypotheses, and learn from experience. Like identity itself, TA is not a stale box of answers, but a dynamic garden of becoming.

What should I actually do with patients?

Your last question is a tough one, and like the others, I suspect many other people in your shoes have felt the same way. You were troubled by a particular problem with almost all of the books you had read and workshops and classes in which you had participated. While they provided eloquent and comprehensive theories of behavior and intervention, helpful premises and guidelines for how to approach patients, and even specific techniques that could be generally applied for people with certain kinds of problems, these theories and models and guidelines were nevertheless divorced from *how* they should be applied in *specific* interactions with other human beings. You felt like you were missing something concrete and even felt some shame about this. If this was something people really needed, wouldn't there be lots of advice about it? Were you just dense?

After 15 years of practice, teaching, and supervision, I am more confident now than ever that you were not being dense, but rather that what you were looking for is hard (How did Rogers know to respond to Gloria, "You look to me like a pretty nice daughter"?). The anxiety of being a clinician exists not in the abstract, but in specific moments, when the patient says or does or feels or wants something and you must respond. Getting it wrong can mean becoming part of the problem rather than part of the solution. Delaying or letting the moment pass is a response with potentially negative consequences. It is reasonable to want an affirmative and specific framework that could help you feel secure about what to do in the moments that feel so critical. But even experts have a very difficult time providing such a framework because it is hard. That is why you had a difficult time finding what you were looking for.

This is also why it was so helpful to learn about TA. You came to realize that the same kind of flexible framework that helped you accommodate different roles and aspects of your identity can also provide the kinds of answers you were seeking about what to do in specific moments, in two different ways. First, integrating the underlying principle of TA regarding the central importance of reducing shame will help you see that any particular moment, as intense as it might be, is not critical, and to feel more comfortable with the fact that you will make mistakes like everyone else, and that reflecting on and talking about those mistakes with your patients can even be helpful. Second, you will learn that using TA as a framework for your research, practice, supervision, and consultation can help you become more competent in those moments when the interpersonal encounter is intense, and it feels like you must do something consequential. But keep in mind that this will continue to be hard, and the more support you have, the more you continue to work at it, the better.

That brings me to the good news. After more than two decades of producing the most important work at the intersection of personality assessment and psychotherapy, the team who developed TA into an international clinical phenomenon has now written a step-by-step manual for how to conduct the procedure in practice. Its chapters provide clear guidance about how to interact with patients when conducting a TA. This manual will not only serve as a tool for future studies testing the validity of TA as an intervention, but also as a framework that can help you in those moments when you want to do the right thing, whether you are conducting a TA, using some other clinical technique, or just trying to get through life as a social animal. The chapters are organized around the steps through which a TA unfolds. Within each chapter, you will find a systematic but flexible intervention framework, with a treasure of helpful tips and specific case examples. This book is going to be indispensable for anyone who wants to learn more about how to assess patients therapeutically. Perhaps more surprisingly, like you, people who read this book and incorporate its wisdom in their practice will also find that practicing TA is a powerful way to understand and accept themselves.

Sincerely
Chris Hopwood, PhD
Professor of Psychology
University of Zurich
October 25, 2021

Preface

It has been 25 years since Finn and Tonsager (1997) delineated the differences between traditional and therapeutic assessment and 15 years since Finn (2007) outlined the semi-structured model of Therapeutic Assessment (TA). Since then, numerous research papers, case studies, and books on TA have been published, and a recent multi-disciplinary database search yielded over 4,000 peer-reviewed journal articles pertaining to therapeutic assessment, collaborative assessment, or psychological assessment as a therapeutic intervention. The Therapeutic Assessment Institute (TAI) was established in 2015 to coordinate research and training in TA, and at least several thousand clinicians around the world have attended practical seminars on TA with adults, children, adolescents, and couples. At the time we write, the TA community has just held its third international conference, and 32 psychologists in 6 countries are fully certified in at least one model of TA. Truly, the explosion of interest in collaborative and Therapeutic Assessment is striking and also heartening for those of us who believe deeply in the TA model.

While all these developments are encouraging, one thing that has been lacking till now is a comprehensive definitive text on TA with adults—a "manual" if you will—that clearly lays out each step of the semi-structured model with its rationale and detailed instructions on how to handle a range of clinical situations. This book fills this gap. After studying this volume, even beginning clinicians should have a working understanding of how to operationalize TA with adult clients and can begin practicing the model with tests they know well and that have proven validity. We also review the growing research on TA with adults and discuss why TA works from different theoretical points of view. This information will aid those readers who are called upon to explain TA to referral sources, clients, employers, third-party payers, and other stakeholders in the psychological assessment process.

The authors of this book are all certified in TA with adults (and include the original developer of TA), have worked with TA clinically for years with a variety of clients, and are all actively involved in teaching TA to graduate students and professionals around the world. Thus, we have drawn on these experiences to anticipate questions, quandaries, and blocks encountered by TA practitioners, and to address them throughout the book. Although we do not assume to have foreseen all the issues that may arise, we have tried to model how to apply the core values, theory, and "deep structure" of TA to address a variety of challenges. Also, as you will read at numerous places in this book, we *strongly* encourage you to take the steps and techniques we have laid out and adapt them to your own clients and clinical setting. Not only is this type of flexibility "permitted" in TA, but it is also an essential aspect of collaborating with clients. No single TA with an adult is exactly like another, and TA is still an open model that is growing and changing. We eagerly anticipate learning from your experiences and innovations as you practice TA.

As you will also read, we believe TA is best practiced in a community, and this book would not exist without the support we have received from many individuals who have supported us in its development. We cannot thank them all, but especially we want to recognize our colleagues in the TA community for their inspiration and collaboration over the years as TA has developed. Many people formulated innovations in TA that we have incorporated into this book. We are also grateful to Hal Richardson for his careful work on the artwork in this volume. And finally, our sincere thanks to "Emma" for letting us share her story with you all and for the courage she showed during her TA.

If this book is your first in-depth exposure to TA, we hope you will be touched, fascinated, and inspired by how empathically based, respectful, collaborative assessment can have a major impact on clients and assessors alike. Therapeutic Assessment is still a "best-kept secret" in many clinical settings in the world, and our greatest wish is that this book will reach people who have not previously heard of TA or studied it in detail. And please, if you are inspired by this book, we invite you to help us spread the word about the power of TA.

Part I

Theoretical Bases, Development, and Research on Therapeutic Assessment

1   How Can a Psychological Assessment Be Therapeutic?

Dear Emma,

As promised, in this letter I have written down the results of the testing that we put together in our last meeting so that you will have something to look back on. I believe we came to important understandings of your questions that will be helpful to you as you move ahead with your life. I hope this letter will serve as a good point of reference for the things we spoke about. As we agreed, I am also sending a copy of this letter to Jeanne, your therapist.

First, I want to reiterate how much I enjoyed working with you and getting to know you. Thank you for trusting me enough to collaborate in this important work we did. I also want to thank you for all the effort you put into the testing. I know I asked you to do a lot, but you always worked hard, even though you sometimes had had a hard day, and sometimes our work touched on difficult issues. I believe your willingness to extend yourself in difficult areas is a good sign for your future endeavors. I want to do the best I can to summarize the answers to the questions you asked of the assessment.

[…]

Why have I never been able to maintain a long-term position in a career I am passionate about, like teaching?

Your self-doubt and fears make it difficult to commit passionately to a career—even if you suspect you would succeed. Some of your fears may stem from being very averse to anger and the threat of rage, especially when it is directed at you by an unhappy boss, a disgruntled co-worker, or a dissatisfied parent.

Maintaining a solid career would also require some ability to be appropriately adversarial. As strange as that may sound, sometimes just having the confidence to stand up for yourself, if need be, causes others to treat you better. It's like you have a sign on your back that says, "I am friendly, but I can protect myself, so don't mess with me." As you mentioned in one of our sessions, your anger (and also its close cousins: Irritation, resentfulness, dissatisfaction, etc.) may "come out sideways," without you even being aware of it. If this happens, it can also interfere with work relationships.

[…]

Again, Emma, it was a great pleasure to work with you. I was touched by your honesty in the face of your fears and your earnest efforts to understand and improve. It is clear you have done a lot of work on yourself, and this is the best sign that you

DOI: 10.4324/9780429202797-2

will continue to grow and become the best version of yourself. I hope this testing is helpful in your future work.

Best wishes for a bright future,
Hale

If you have no previous exposure to TA and have been trained in traditional clinical psychological testing, the preceding letter may startle you or even make you uneasy. Some people in our field are concerned about the very idea of writing a letter to a client about test results, especially given that such a procedure has not been mentioned in well-known assessment textbooks (e.g., Anastasi, 1988; Maloney & Ward, 1976; Sattler, 1988; Tallent, 1992). The content of the letter to Emma also often generates questions in clinicians unfamiliar with TA: "Why does the clinician reveal his own emotional reactions to the client?" "Doesn't the conversational tone make the report less professional?" and "Couldn't a letter like this disrupt the relationship between the referring therapist, Jeanne, and the client Emma?" We will address these concerns later in the book. But for now, we ask you to look beyond your initial reaction to this written feedback to get a deeper sense of TA itself, as it embraces a different set of goals and processes.

What is Therapeutic Assessment

TA is a semi-structured intervention designed by Stephen E. Finn, who provided assessment and therapy to many types of clients in different settings for over twenty years as he developed this model. TA incorporates the use of psychological testing and addresses the goals of a traditional assessment (i.e., assessing clients' psychological functioning to understand their presenting problems, identifying a diagnosis, planning subsequent treatment) but it also goes further. Clinicians practicing TA build a collaborative and therapeutic relationship with clients, and use specific techniques and methods to help them reach a more accurate and compassionate understanding of themselves. At the end of a TA, clients often feel more hopeful and have improved self-esteem, and their daily functioning may be enhanced to the point that they do not need subsequent treatment. In other cases, TA helps clients better understand why and how they should continue treatment. The research shows that these clients are more likely to follow through with clinicians' recommendations than those who undergo a traditional assessment and that they show greater alliance with treatment professionals and a greater rate of change in psychotherapy than clients who have not taken part in TA (see Chapter 3 for a summary of research on the efficacy of TA with different types of clients).

TA can be useful as a therapeutic intervention or as a first step before therapy begins. Given its flexible nature as a brief intervention grounded in assessment procedures, clinicians can employ it as a method of consultation when other interventions have been less successful. Treatment professionals at an impasse with their clients may refer them for a TA with an assessor who then helps answer questions posed by both the referring professional and the client about how to make more progress. In these situations, an assessor conducts a TA with the client while keeping the referring professional involved in ways that will be described in Chapters 4–11. As a result, TA can provide new ways of understanding clients' struggles and the reasons for treatment impasses that often lead to a positive shift for clients, treating professionals, and the treatment process.

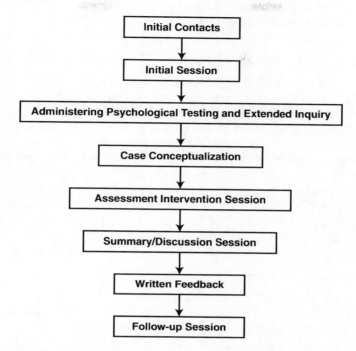

Figure 1.1 Steps of Therapeutic Assessment with an Adult Client.

Last, when clients—or clients and referring professionals—are curious about how clients are doing at the end of an intervention or after a period of no intervention, an assessor can use TA to look at how certain variables of interest (e.g., levels of anxiety and depression) have shifted and also delineate areas where more work could be done.

To achieve its goals, TA is structured around eight steps (see Figure 1.1) that will be described in Chapters 4–11 of this book. A TA begins with the first contact with a client (see Chapter 4), which often happens by phone. This is an important moment as the clinician begins relating to the client and sharing information about TA. Then, during the first session (see Chapter 5), the assessor continues to build a therapeutic relationship with the client while collecting their goals for the assessment, framed as "Assessment Questions" (AQs) to be answered by the end of the TA. Addressing the AQs becomes the agreed-upon goal of the TA, and the client and assessor collaborate on this joint project throughout the assessment process. To fulfill this goal, the clinician and client spend several sessions completing and discussing selected psychological tests and engaging in activities that help answer the AQs (see Chapters 6, 7, 8). Finally, the clinician and client discuss the results of the testing and jointly construct answers to the client's AQs during the Summary/Discussion Session (see Chapter 9), and eventually a Follow-up Session (see Chapter 11). Before the follow-up, the clinician sends the client a written report, typically in the form of an individualized letter, similar to the one presented at the beginning of this chapter (see Chapter 10). The structure of TA was designed to meet clients' needs by using specific theoretical lenses, and was developed based on client input, research, and years of clinical experience. The theoretical lenses

TA assessors most commonly use frame how we understand why most clients are searching for psychological help and how best to respond to them.

Common Features of Clients Undergoing a Therapeutic Assessment

The extract of Emma's feedback letter (see Chapter 10 for the complete text) provides an example of the possible questions that might motivate a client to ask for a TA. In the 30 years since its initial description in a publication by Finn and Tonsager (1992), many clients have undergone a TA with questions mirroring those that bring clients to traditional assessment or psychotherapy. They wonder, for example, how to make relevant choices in their lives ("Should I go to medical school?"), how to find more satisfaction ("Why am I so unfulfilled even though I have a good job and a lovely family?"), how to change behaviors and symptoms that concern them ("How can I stop cutting myself?" "Why do I drink so much?"), and how to solve problems in close relationships ("How can I get over the death of my mother?" "Why haven't I been able to have a successful long-term relationship?").

Clients' Narratives

In TA, we see all "voluntary" clients (i.e., self-referred or agreeing to be referred by a mental health professional) as sharing a common feature: Their narratives (or stories) about themselves—their identity, goals, or relationships—generally are not accurate, useful, or satisfactory. We define a narrative as the "internalized, evolving story of the self that each person crafts to provide their life with a sense of purpose and unity" (Adler, 2012, p. 367). Personal narratives are created through human beings' never-ending work of elaborating and making meaning of their life experiences to create a "map" for themselves about the world and others. Narratives help people understand and navigate the world and are essential for adapting to various environments. Typically, we create personal narratives during childhood, and they reflect our early life contexts, but all of us continue to elaborate (and potentially revise) our narratives throughout our lives.

Narratives may vary in how accurate, coherent, useful, and self-compassionate they are at different points during a person's life. Adverse childhood experiences may lead people to develop self-blaming narratives or narratives devoid of self-compassion. For example, children who are neglected by their parents often develop a deep sense of being unlovable, and this explains why their parents did not provide better care. Over time, and especially if there are no other adults to care for these children in meaningful ways, they may develop a narrative in which they themselves are flawed ("I am a bad person, and my feelings and needs are excessive") and their identity may be permeated by shame ("I am so damaged that I cannot be loved and accepted"). Frequently these narratives are not conscious, yet they are still expressed in how the person behaves in relationships and in the world.

Many people who grow up in difficult life circumstances and who develop inaccurate and negative self-narratives (i.e., ones lacking in self-compassion) cannot appreciate the impact their experiences had on them. We all only know the lives that we have led, and cannot understand how things might have been (or still could be) different if our environments were different. As a result, we "take ourselves personally" and attribute our problems to "personal" or "global" causes. Such individuals may develop a self-narrative that asserts, "I am not intelligent," rather than "Learning is difficult for me because lifelong depression has made it hard to concentrate and remember things." The latter thought takes context into account, and thus is likely to be more realistic and compassionate. There is a saying that TA assessors often use to capture this issue: "A fish doesn't know it is wet." In short, our self-narratives are limited by our restricted perspectives. It is impossible for the individual above to know what learning would have been like if he had not been depressed. Moreover, these negative, personal narratives were often logical in the past because (1) they fit with the views of important people in our lives (e.g., neglectful or abusive caregivers) and (2) they protected us from overwhelming feelings (e.g., anger, grief, longing) for which we had no support. Importantly, it can be tempting to retain these old narratives later in adulthood, since a different, more accurate view of ourselves might threaten our important current relationships or arouse painful feelings of grief. We understand clients' request for a TA, or other kinds of psychological help, as a result of a painful mismatch between their usual ways of perceiving themselves and reacting to the world, which were once adaptive, and their current goals and desires to grow and achieve greater life satisfaction. Many clients who seek a TA report feeling "stuck," in part because their old narratives no longer help them face the challenges and demands of their world.

For example, Sandra was a 30-year-old Italian woman, who identified as heterosexual and struggled to understand why it was so difficult to form and maintain close relationships with male partners. She desired such connections but was unaware of how her deep-seated and implicit fear of abandonment was damaging interpersonal exchanges. Sandra's explicit wish ("I want to find a partner and feel loved") conflicted with her experience of being let down with no warning by multiple partners. She reported that at times her partners would say they felt "kept at arm's length" by her, but she found such feedback surprising and difficult to understand. What was not apparent to Sandra, but was evident from her performance-based testing and Early Memories Procedure (EMP; Bruhn, 1992a, b), was that her distance-creating behaviors with intimate partners resulted from a strong self-blaming narrative that she developed early in life. Her self-narrative could be worded as, "Deep-down I am bad, and I do not want any potential partner to really know me and discover that." Sandra developed this narrative in a family with harsh, cold parents. In this context, young Sandra assumed that the reason she did not receive affection or comfort was because she did not deserve it due to her "flaws." This explanation, despite being painful at a certain level, was useful to Sandra to make sense of her experiences, and it preserved a view of her parents as benign, which protected her sense of safety.

During her TA, Sandra and the assessor talked about her Rorschach (R-PAS; Meyer et al., 2011), which included four Morbid responses. Sandra realized that the "smashed butterfly" and the "wounded animals" she saw in the cards represented her deep sense of being "flawed" and "damaged." While discussing this realization, the assessor helped her connect this self-view to her early relational experiences, as captured in her EMP responses. Together, they came to understand how Sandra learned to blame herself for negative experiences where she was "smashed" or "hit," even though she had no responsibility for what occurred and no ability to change her parents' behaviors. This example begins to demonstrate what will be further elaborated upon, since during Sandra's TA the clinician actively and collaboratively used information from the testing to help Sandra become more aware of, and to co-edit, her pre-existing narrative. That co-editing process helps clients build a more integrated, accurate, and compassionate understanding of the past and present. Sandra's self-narrative shifted to, "As a child,

I was neglected by my parents, and I learned to think about myself as bad and not lovable. I am now beginning to see that my needs are legitimate, and I am worthy of love. I hope to find a partner who is more attuned and generous than my parents were, and who can love me, if I open up to him."

Clients' Need for Self-verification

People's narratives do not change easily. This becomes especially clear when we meet clients who are suffering because of their inaccurate or self-blaming narratives, but who cannot change their views of themselves (and the world) even when we gently or firmly point out that there are various ways to interpret what we see. We understand this phenomenon as an individual's need for self-verification, as described by William Swann in his self-verification theory (Swann, 1997). According to Swann, all people share a strong desire to have the way they see themselves confirmed by others. This desire influences us all, whether our views of ourselves are predominantly positive or negative. Once people become confident in how they view themselves, they will "screen in" information consistent with their self-views and "screen out" information that is contradictory. They will also seek life contexts where their self-views are confirmed and avoid those where they are challenged. For example, if a female client sees herself as sociable and agreeable, she will actively search for situations where she can meet new people and she will act confidently and expect to be well received by others. Furthermore, she will seek out friends and partners who enjoy her way of socializing and avoid those who do not, or who see her differently (e.g., as too dramatic and superficial) than she sees herself. Another example would be a young man who sees himself as stupid (even if this is not true) because his parents and siblings were geniuses. According to self-verification theory, the man might act lighthearted and silly when he is with his friends so that they will continue to view him as less intelligent than others in their group. In other words, he will behave in ways that make it likely that his inaccurate self-view is confirmed. But, you may ask, why would he continue to reinforce a belief that is painful to him?

Self-verification theory asserts that when people receive feedback about themselves that is congruent with what they already think and believe, they feel competent, in control, and have a sense that the world is a predictable place. This perception is powerful and can greatly reduce anxiety (Swann, 1997). On the contrary, when individuals cannot disregard or ignore new information that challenges their self-views, they may feel very anxious. If the new idea conflicts with a fundamental belief about themselves and they also have a fragile sense of self, they may even fall into a "disintegration experience." The experience of disintegration has been described by the founding father of self-psychology, Heinz Kohut (1984). Kohut wrote about the great emotional distress, disorientation, and fear that can result when an individual is unable to refute evidence that some central and tightly held belief about the self is wrong. As this is a primary concern during the Assessment Intervention Session (AIS; see Chapter 8) and the Summary/Discussion Session (see Chapter 9), the concept of disintegration anxiety is further discussed there.

Understandably, individuals will work hard to avoid falling into such a disorganizing experience, and thus they do not welcome and integrate information that diverges from their pre-existing self-views. Studies based on self-verification theory have shown that people accept or reject positive feedback depending on how coherent it is with their own pre-existing views of themselves (Schroeder et al., 1993). Many of us have experienced this when paying a compliment to someone with low self-esteem. Such people often react by looking both happy and distressed, then reject the compliment and "explain away" the positive feedback and why it is not true. Connected to these ideas are studies that have shown that feedback congruent with one's self-representation is remembered better than incongruent feedback, whether positive or negative (Swann et al., 1992). The need for self-verification also seems to have consequences for our choice of romantic partners. Giesler et al., (1996) discovered that people are more likely to develop long-term and stable relationships with partners who confirm the way they see themselves, even if it is negative.

The concept of self-verification helps us understand what is traditionally called "resistance" in psychotherapy. Therapists have used terms like resistance and "repetition compulsion" to explain why clients reject sensible advice and positive feedback and continue to act in ways that appear to increase their suffering. Calling a client "resistant" often implies a therapist's frustration with a client: "If only the client would accept what I say, then things will go better." In contrast, self-verification theory suggests that the more we provide clients feedback about themselves that is incongruent with their self-views, the more likely they are to reject it (Giesler et al., 1996). This is particularly true if we are using psychological tests as the basis of our feedback. In fact, the nature of these instruments—their "scientific" essence, their reliance on scores and norms—can create an "aura" of validity that ends up activating our clients' self-protective reactions, which we then interpret as "resistance" to changing their views (Finn & Martin, 2013). To avoid this risk, TA assessors focus on understanding and mirroring the pre-existing self-narratives clients already hold, and on affirming whatever aspects of those narratives are an accurate and useful to the client's future developmental progress. This is a fundamental part of our endeavor to create a fruitful alliance with our clients, by giving them the experience of having an attentive other (the assessor) who acknowledges the importance of their own perspective before introducing new information. Once clients' needs for self-verification have been met, they are more open to new, less-congruent information.

Clients' Epistemic Hypervigilance

Epistemic hypervigilance (EH) is another concept that can be used to characterize clients who access mental health services. This is especially true of clients with personality or psychotic disorders but it is also commonly seen in clients with a history of relational trauma. EH is characterized by a pervasive distrust of others and an inability to learn from social experiences; typically, it results from early relationships that were traumatic, or in which caregivers failed to provide an attuned response to the child's needs (Fonagy, et al., 2017a, b; Kamphuis & Finn, 2019). In short, if our earliest caregivers are untrustworthy, we become confused about who we can trust. This can lead to rigid views of the world and ourselves. Signs that clients are struggling with EH may emerge in the first session of a TA, when they ask questions like, "Why do I keep making the same mistakes again and again with people?" or "Why do I keep choosing partners who are bad for me?"

As various authors have stressed (e.g., Fonagy et al., 2017a, b; Sperber et al., 2010), it is vitally important that human beings learn from those around them and use that information to modify their ideas and beliefs in a flexible way. The ability to learn from others allows us to assimilate a lot of information quickly (by oral transmission of knowledge), without having to experience in person all that is important for our survival, adaptation, and development. However, such learning is only possible when we believe the communication we receive from others to be authentic and personally relevant. When this occurs, we are in a position of epistemic trust (ET; Fonagy & Allison, 2014). ET is a fundamental evolutionary resource, allowing infants to absorb a huge amount of information and strategies that is transmitted by a culture, primarily via caregivers. ET continues to function throughout our lives, helping us integrate the information we need in order to adapt to new contexts and new encounters.

To be adaptive, ET has to be balanced with healthy epistemic mistrust (EM; Fonagy & Alison, 2014) or epistemic vigilance (EV; Fonagy et al., 2017a, b). These terms refer to a set of skills individuals use to judge whether a person communicating certain content has our best interests in mind or is trying to mislead us in order to gain some advantage (Sperber et al., 2010). People with good intentions who give us relevant and generalizable information eventually become *deferential sources* (Wilson & Sperber, 2012), whom we tend to believe. If someone is unknown to us or has an obvious conflict of interest (e.g., a car salesman), EM helps us to be skeptical about such communication. Two factors lead us to consider new information as meaningful: first, we view the communicator as a reliable source of information; second, we perceive the information to be coherent, logical, and fitting with our pre-existing beliefs. If new information is too divergent from important pre-existing beliefs, we are likely to reject it, even if it comes from a deferential source (Sperber et al., 2010). These ideas align with our previous discussion of self-verification theory.

Fonagy and others (Fonagy et al., 2017b) assert that adverse life experiences can damage a person's capacity for ET to the point that they enter a state of EH. When this occurs, individuals no longer use information communicated by others in their social environment to update their pre-existing knowledge. Therefore, persons with EH have difficulty using other people as sources of new and relevant information. As a result, such individuals tend to be cognitively rigid and develop problems in interpersonal relationships. Similar early interpersonal experiences can also lead to epistemic hypovigilance, where individuals trust others too easily or choose who to trust based on variables (e.g., appearance, race, political party) that may not necessarily be indicative of trustworthiness. In fact, many people with personality disorders show a cyclical pattern of exhibiting epistemic hypovigilance, shifting to epistemic hypervigilance, and finally returning once more to trusting too easily (see Kamphuis & Finn, 2019). In TA we have called this problem the "broken trust meter."

EH is a barrier for psychological treatment, as it blocks clients from seeing the therapist as a benevolent figure and leads them to distrust the authenticity of the information communicated by that professional. Therapists characterize these clients as "hard to reach" (Fonagy et al., 2017a, b). Fonagy and colleagues, however, emphasize that this inflexibility and skepticism is a useful strategy for individuals with a vulnerable sense of self, because it protects them from being emotionally overwhelmed. Such individuals are likely to feel threatened by information that challenges their pre-existing beliefs and are at risk for an overwhelming negative emotional reaction if such information "gets through" (Fonagy et al., 2015).

To help clients with EH successfully restore their capacity for ET, the clinician needs to overcome their hypervigilance and earn the role of a deferential source of information. The clinician accomplishes this goal by seeing the world from the client's perspective, therefore validating the client's subjective experience as worthy of consideration (i.e., by the therapist *mentalizing* the client–see Box 1.1). By this technique, clients feel seen and understood, and as a result, they can open their minds to the clinician's communication. This is the first step toward trusting other people and the social world again (Fonagy & Allison, 2014). The clinician accomplishes this successful communication by using non-verbal signals (i.e., *ostensive cues*) to recognize the client explicitly as an individual with meaningful intentions (Fonagy et al., 2015). A clinician can also look to demonstrate that they are not always putting their own personal needs first; for example, by waiving the fee for a session the client missed because of an emergency beyond their control.

Box 1.1   What is Mentalizing?

Peter Fonagy introduced the term *mentalization* in 1989 to help explain the psychological difficulties many clients, particularly those struggling with personality disorders, experience. *Mentalization* is the ability to understand that our own and others' behaviors result from inner psychological states and mental processes. Our ability to mentalize helps us regulate our emotions and guide our behaviors. For example, we are less likely to get angry and react aggressively to a friend's harsh tone of voice, if we understand that this tone is due to internal turmoil over a personal crisis and has little or nothing to do with us.

The ability to mentalize in adulthood appears to have its roots in positive early experiences where a child's main caregivers could interpret behavioral and emotional signals correctly (e.g., understand a baby is crying because of hunger), respond in a timely fashion (e.g., feed the baby within a brief time), and promote mutuality in the relationship. For example, a baby may be distressed about being alone. The caregiver notices and responds by initiating a game of "peek-a-boo." The baby responds by turning towards the caregiver, smiling, and laughing. Over time, a child in a relationship with an attuned and attentive caregiver who can accurately interpret their mental states (i.e., mentalize the child) learns to see the caregiver as a person who can also be trusted to transmit accurate and relevant information and knowledge. The caregiver becomes a deferential source of information about the child and the world. This process is facilitated by the species-specific sensitivity of the child toward certain nonverbal behavioral signals, called *ostensive cues*, which catch the child's attention and help the child focus, listen to, and incorporate the communication that follows the signals. Examples of these signals include eye-contact, taking turns, and being called by name (Fonagy et al., 2015).

Fonagy and his colleagues hypothesize that most clients with mental disorders experienced primary relationships lacking the qualities described above. As a result, these clients never developed an ability to read and understand others' intentions accurately, which led to difficulty regulating their emotions and relating to others. They suggest that clients who struggle with mentalization are also more vulnerable to stressors and particularly to trauma. Such individuals often have difficulty putting potentially traumatic events into perspective; instead, they tend to be overwhelmed by negative events and "to take them personally" or offer an irrational explanation (e.g., superstitions). This failure to mentalize predisposes such individuals to suffer persistent negative effects resulting from the event and to have their self-image defined by the negative event (e.g., "This unexpected loss is another sign of me being a failure"). Finally, since they lack the capacity to make sense of the event through an understanding of others' internal states, such individuals tend to focus instead on external appearances that could be misleading. For example, if a group of people witnesses a car accident, and a person who cannot mentalize observes a lack of strong reactions in people around them, rather than interpreting this as a sign that others are in shock, they may instead conclude they are the only one overwhelmed by the event and thus "weak." These tendencies, all related to an impaired ability to mentalize, limit an individual's resilience when faced with a potentially traumatic event and the negative impact that trauma will have on the self.

Kamphuis and Finn (2019) described the implications of EH and ET for TA, and the assessor's work of mentalizing the client. In TA, clinicians promote ET in their clients by using valid assessment tools to gain a meaningful understanding of clients' inner worlds in a brief time. This understanding then helps the clinician read clients' needs accurately and respond in attuned ways. Furthermore, collecting AQs at the beginning of a TA (see Chapter 5) promotes clients' subjective expression of needs and signals that the client's goals are the focus of all subsequent work. The testing phase and the Extended Inquiry (EI; see Chapter 6) anchor the TA findings to the client's questions, hence signaling to them that the information obtained from the testing applies to their individual agendas. In this way, the AQs are ostensive cues, increasing a client's openness to new learning. Furthermore, the EI and the AIS (see Chapter 8) prioritize learning that comes from clients' insights and experiences in session. This allows them to feel they are authoring "in first person" new understandings about what is confusing them in the present. The collaborative discussion of the TA results during the Summary/Discussion Session (see Chapter 9) develops ET yet further, because the clinician first introduces information that confirms and reinforces clients' pre-existing narratives, and only afterwards provides new information. Last, the final communication, written in language the client can comprehend (see Chapter 10), demonstrates that the clinician has considered the client's perspective and summarized the information discussed in a way that they can use in the future.

Clients' Attachment System

Clients' struggles to revise their narratives and trust others is frequently due to their vulnerability to feelings of fear or to perceived threat. Threat and fear normally activate the attachment system, an innate psychobiological system whose goal is to protect humans from danger (see Box 1.2). Thus, many clients seeking psychological services have difficulties based on attachment.

More specifically, while clients often desire and welcome their first encounter with a clinician, they may also perceive the meeting as a potentially dangerous event, in

Box 1.2   Attachment

Attachment theory, initially proposed by Bowlby (1958), asserts that humans (similar to other primates) developed through evolution an inherent, biological set of behaviors to protect themselves from danger. This inborn set of responses is called the *attachment system*. (Other intrinsic behavioral systems include the *caregiving system*, the *exploratory system*, the *affiliative system*, and the *sexual system*.) Bowlby proposed that the attachment system is activated by: (a) Actual environmental threats that endanger a person's survival; (b) indirect "clues of danger" (such as darkness, loud noises, isolation), which increase the likelihood of risk; and (c) attachment-related threats, such as real or expected separation from or loss of an attachment figure (1973, 1969/1982).

During childhood, the attachment system initiates relatively simple behaviors in the child (crying) to signal distress to the attachment figure (parent), stimulating that figure to respond in a timely and appropriate fashion to restore safety. Over time, the child's repeated experience of being soothed (or not) by the attachment figure is internalized and leads to the creation of Internalized Working Models (IWMs). IWMs are mental "maps" of how an individual expects close, protective relationships are going to work. They primarily emerge from memories of early attachment figures and what occurred when help was needed, but they can also be influenced by close relationships later in life. IWMs shape the strategies used by an individual to reach a sense of safety.

A *Secure attachment status* results from relational experiences in which, the communication between caregiver and child was collaborative and attuned. Repeated positive experiences of effective synchronization lead an individual to develop an expectation that, when they need care and protection, a supportive other will respond in a timely way to address their needs. The internalization and generalization of such IWMs allow securely attached people to see themselves as competent and worthy, and to see others as generally trustworthy. Their primary attachment strategy when facing difficult situations is to seek proximity and support from attachment figures (such as a spouse) and to reflect upon their inner states (i.e., mentalize). Secure attachment allows individuals to process negative emotions, give them a coherent meaning, regulate their intensity, effectively cope with problems, and actively seek support.

Bowlby (1980) identified three primary attachment-related defensive processes, prevalent in patterns of attachment that are insecure: (1) Deactivation, (2) Cognitive Disconnection, and (3) Segregated Systems. These strategies aim to restore an individual's sense of safety when they perceive an actual or feared threat.

Deactivation shifts the individual's attention from the threat, focusing instead on problem solving and achievement. Deactivation "shuts down" the attachment system by excluding the kind of distressing information, events, or emotions that would activate it, before those stressors reach a conscious level (George & West, 2011). During an assessment, clients who predominantly use deactivation to manage attachment insecurity will often ask why they have not had successful intimate relationships, despite being very accomplished in their careers.

Cognitive Disconnection splits distressing emotions related to the activation of the attachment system from the thoughts and cognitions typically connected to them. With the attachment system aroused, the individual feels distressed but cannot pinpoint the true origin of their painful emotions. This strategy leaves a person to "dwell so insistently on the details of his own reactions and suffering that he has no time to consider what the interpersonal situation for his reactions may really be" (Bowlby, 1980, p. 65). Since the individual is not conscious of its source, the distress tends not to be addressed effectively. Hence, an individual is often caught in the impossible task of trying to find a solution to a hyper-activated attachment system (i.e., increased anxiety, anger, shame, sadness, fear) without having the information necessary to resolve the problem in an adaptive way. Assessment clients who rely on cognitive disconnection to manage attachment threats will sometimes present with anxiety, depression, or physical complaints that make little sense and that have not responded to various forms of treatment.

Segregated systems is an attachment defense that develops when an individual cannot resolve a dual desire both to approach and to withdraw from a caregiver, or when the individual faces persistent mixed signals about safety and attachment with no relief (Reisz et al., 2018). A classic example is the person with an unpredictable attachment figure, who is either comforting or abusive at different times. This kind of early attachment trauma can lead to the development of incompatible models and expectations of attachment relationships that are *segregated* from each other in the mind, meaning they are not in awareness at the same time. When situational cues elicit the segregated experiences, memories, and emotions, they can seep through and cause the individual to behave abnormally (Bowlby, 1980). A client with segregated systems might seek an assessment asking, "Why do I suddenly feel terrified when I start to feel close to someone?" or "Why do my romantic partners tell me they feel like they are dating two different people?"

which they will disclose their vulnerabilities to a stranger who may judge, condemn, shame, or reject them. Clients will be particularly wary if they have already developed negative expectations about others and relationships (e.g., "If people really get to know how I am, they will run the other way"). Such concerns are based on clients' previous adverse experiences with primary caregivers and other adults who guided their development. Clients' fear of being rejected, judged, or shamed, will likely activate their attachment system (i.e., danger-signaling) which then inhibits their ability to be curious about themselves and explore new ways of thinking about problems, thereby creating an obstacle to the therapeutic process. Attachment researchers have explained how the attachment system and the *exploratory system* (i.e., the inborn desire to seek novelty and discover new things) are reciprocally activated. When one biological system is "turned on" the other is "turned off." This becomes logical when we remember that fear and the resulting behaviors used to seek safety (e.g., turning to what is familiar, moving closer to an attachment figure or a familiar place, avoiding things and people that are strange and new) have an evolutionary priority; they are in place to protect humans from danger and to promote their survival. Therefore, activation of the attachment system generally deactivates or inhibits exploration and the search for novelty, and "only when relief is attained and a sense of attachment security is restored can the individual deploy attention and energy to [...] exploration" (Mikulincer & Shaver, 2007, p. 16). Such mechanisms apply not only to physical dangers but also to emotional ones, such as those clients face at the beginning of an encounter with a clinician. For these reasons, in TA, we pay a great deal of attention to establishing safety in our relationship with the client, recognizing that security is a precondition for self-disclosure, self-exploration, and therefore therapeutic change (Aschieri et al., 2016).

As seen through the lens of attachment theory, the success of encounters (especially the first) between clinicians and clients may depend on the clinician's ability to manage three semi-independent processes that regulate the attachment system and create a sense of safety: (1) emotional attunement, (2) collaborative communication, and (3) the repair of disruptions (Stern, 2004).

Emotional attunement is a relational process that allows the participants in an interpersonal exchange to share their mental states and feel a reciprocal understanding of their affects and emotions. When emotional attunement is attained within the therapeutic relationship, it has the potential to soothe negative emotions and enhance positive ones, eventually allowing clients to regulate their emotional arousal and to reflect on their inner states more effectively (Trewarthen & Hubley, 1978).

Collaborative communication refers to verbal and nonverbal communication cues that are unique to the relationship between client and assessor. Through collaborative communication, partners signal to each other the uniqueness of their relationship, by inventing and using signals meaningful only to each other. A "private language" is born that shows the special connection these two people have. Verbal examples of collaborative communication include specific words that capture a client's experience. For example, a client and assessor might adopt the phrase "the grey under the surface" to refer to depressive feelings outside of the client's awareness. Other metaphors may include shared experiences during a test or the client's test responses. For example, a client might see "two ducks" on an area of a Rorschach card where most people see two humans. Later, the assessor references this test response as an example of the client's idiosyncratic perceptions, and in future sessions, the client and assessor use "seeing ducks" as shorthand for the client misperceiving a situation. Non-verbal examples of collaborative communication include the behavioral rituals that the assessor and client develop during the therapeutic process, from the way they shake hands when they meet in the waiting room to facial expressions or tones of voice that have a distinct meaning in the relationship.

Repairing disruptions in the therapeutic relationship is an essential aspect of successful psychological interventions (Safran & Muran, 2000). Empathic breaks are inevitable in every intimate relationship, including between clinician and client. As with mother-infant dyads, conjunction and disjunction dynamics in a therapeutic process are messy and fraught with the potential for "missteps, apologies, tries, retries, match-ups, and missteps again" (Tronick & Beeghly, 2011, p. 112). What differentiates healthy relationships from problematic ones is a timely effort to repair the disruptions as soon as they emerge. How does a clinician repairs disruptions to a relationship with a client? The clinician must be attuned to signs that a disruption has occurred. For example, an assessor may notice that in response to a certain question, a client falls silent and looks at the floor—a telltale sign of shame (Gilbert & Andrews, 1998). The assessor could then either change the topic briefly, making a mental note of the client's reaction or apologize and assure the client it is okay not to answer the question. If the client recovers and resumes eye contact, the assessor may judge that a successful repair has occurred.

Clients' Dilemma of Change

To build further on the theories presented above, it may be said that for a psychological assessment to be therapeutic, clients–with the help of the clinician–must develop curiosity about themselves. Clients ideally move from a position of EH to a state of ET, balanced with healthy EV, and take in new information to develop more compassionate, accurate, and useful narratives about themselves and their relationships. They also need to access healthier and more secure, dyadic, and integrated ways of regulating their emotions. This is no simple task. Therefore it is not surprising that, despite being motivated by a desire to change for the better, to fulfill their desires and aspirations, and to decrease problematic emotional states and symptomatic behaviors, many clients seem to reject relationships, information, and opportunities that could help them achieve these goals. The possibility for change comes with costs not easily paid.

Dilemma of change is a term introduced by Peggy Papp in 1983 to capture a client's internal conflict between a desire to change and a fear of change. The concept of dilemma of change frames the pros and cons of a client's process of questioning areas of their lives or psychological functioning, that while restricting them from reaching important goals, also protect them from dreaded outcomes, most often the risks of being overwhelmed by intolerable emotions or disrupting important relationships. Understanding clients' dilemmas of change can help clinicians find compassion for behaviors that appear dysfunctional or self-destructive and that do not easily respond to psychological interventions. Whereas other psychological theories talk about "repetition compulsion" or of clients being "resistant," an understanding of the dilemma of change helps clinicians to have more empathy for their clients and to locate "tipping points" on which to focus interventions. Finally, when assessors recognize and label clients' dilemmas of change, it often alleviates shame and sets the stage for forward progress.

Returning to Sandra, her dilemma of change can be understood as follows. On the one hand, she could continue relating to partners as she has in the past, keeping them at a distance, at the cost of a successful intimate relationship (ultimately leaving her alone and unsatisfied), but with the advantage of being protected from feeling a deep sense of being unworthy and unlovable. In this way, Sandra could also avoid feeling anger or even hatred for her parents, who were largely responsible for the way she felt about herself. On the other hand, Sandra could stop distancing potential partners and risk more emotional intimacy in hopes of creating a deeper and more rewarding bond, but, if she did so, she would inevitably arouse painful underlying feelings of shame and unworthiness. These feelings remained outside of Sandra's awareness; she could not face them alone, due to the risk of becoming overwhelmed and falling into a disintegration experience. Importantly, if Sandra felt and came to understand her deep shame, she would also be compelled to revise her family history and her (at least partially) idealized view of her parents, putting herself at the double risk of being overwhelmed by feelings of both anger and despair.

A dilemma of change like this is accompanied by powerful, difficult emotions around both choices. How would Sandra feel about herself if she were to face another relational failure due to her difficulty with intimacy? Alternatively, what would it mean for Sandra to realize that her parents had not cared for her as she needed, and that this has left her feeling unworthy of love and incapable of signaling her own needs to partners as an adult? Sadness, feeling like a failure, anger, regret, and grief are all potentially overwhelming emotions that Sandra would need to traverse to find a way out of this dilemma. Given these entanglements, clients will actively avoid such emotions if, like Sandra, they expect no one to support them or to help "hold" these feelings. Often, the only way clients can tolerate the distressing emotions they face while resolving their dilemmas of change is with the skilled emotional support of a clinician, who helps them develop viable "third ways" to sort out their inner conflicts in a productive and therapeutic manner. With Sandra, for example, the clinician helped find a "third way" by conducting a TA. Since Sandra struggled to face her underlying negative feelings alone, the clinician offered support as a benevolent, responsive, and attuned listener. Thanks to this, Sandra could access and express her pain connected to the experience of being rejected and abandoned, without being traumatized by these feelings. This experience taught Sandra that there was indeed a way out of her dilemma of change.

Why Are Psychological Tests Useful?

Psychological testing is critical to helping us meet the many goals we have described above. Testing helps us understand clients' struggles and resources by allowing us to view our clients according to specific psychological dimensions (e.g., level of depression, general intelligence, thought disturbance) or categories (e.g., Major Depression, Posttraumatic Stress Disorder, Social Anxiety Disorder). In addition, the tests are occasions to engage clients in meaningful discussions about their test behaviors, responses, and results—and how those relate to daily problems in living—which can lead to therapeutic change through processes that will be described in the next section.

Understanding Clients' Struggles and Resources: The Utility of Psychological Tests in Accurately Mapping Clients' Psychological Functioning

Over the past two decades, some authors have described a decline and marginalization of psychological assessment in graduate training programs (Handler & Smith, 2013; Stedman et al., 2001) and in professional psychologists' practices (Wright & Hopwood, 2016). This phenomenon seems to be related to several factors, such as increased demand for psychotherapy and decreased demand for assessment, and the promulgation of manualized treatment models tailored to diagnoses and symptoms, rather than underlying psychological processes (Evans & Finn, 2017; Smith, 2016). Despite this trend, Meyer et al. (2001) in their comprehensive review of the validity and reliability of psychological testing, concluded that (a) psychological test validity is strong and compelling, (b) psychological test validity is comparable with medical test validity, (c) distinct assessment methods provide unique sources of information, and (d) clinicians who rely only on interviews are likely to develop incomplete understandings of their clients. Evans and Finn (2017) also stressed that "clinical judgment blended with the psychometric support from different types of psychological tests, each with its own strengths, weaknesses, and method variance, has been shown to produce the most reliable and valid measurement of psychopathology" (p. 176). These statements reflect the view shared by other scholars and professionals that psychological assessment is still a centerpiece of professional psychology (Bornstein, 2017; Smith, 2016). In TA, we strongly believe that psychological tests, in addition to interviews, are precious tools for understanding our clients' psychological functioning and dilemmas of change.

Although in some situations a single test may address a client's needs well (e.g., the Minnesota Multiphasic Personality Inventory-3 to gain a quick assessment of a client's level of depression and anxiety; MMPI-3; Ben-Porath & Tellegen, 2020), in recent years Multi-Method Assessment (MMA) has been preferred in an effort to increase the accuracy with which we understand our clients (Meyer et al., 2001; Hopwood & Bornstein, 2014). MMA involves a combination of different assessment methods, such as the joint use of a broadband self-report personality inventory and a performance-based personality test such as the Rorschach, the use of formal assessment instruments and a clinical interview, or the use of a clinical interview and direct observation of the client. MMA asserts that different methods of measurement allow us to understand a single dimension or construct (such as a client's depression), more accurately since no single method can capture all the different aspects of that dimension. Each measurement method (i.e., interview, self-report, performance-based test, observer report) can only describe the construct in question within the limits of its particular way of looking at that construct (Meyer, 2018). Specifically, the information offered by self-report tests will be limited by a client's awareness of, and ability to report, behaviors, thoughts, or feelings connected to depression, while performance-based tests will provide information about implicit psychological processes connected to depression rather than observable behaviors. The complex construct of our client's "depression" lives in a reality layer that we can only estimate through our limited assessment tools, and "the map *is not* the territory it represents" (Korzybski, 1933, p. 58). This point of view—that knowledge is always perspectival—is fundamental in TA.

The task for assessors is then to integrate the findings from the different methods, which is challenging because different assessment modalities often produce discrepant findings. Meyer (2018) proposed that the way clients score differently or consistently across different tests might represent their "personality signatures" (see also Mischel, 2004). Depending on their specific features, different tests create more or less structured, familiar, interpersonal, and emotionally arousing situations. Therefore, the way clients respond to and interact with these different test situations often resembles how they respond in different life contexts with similar features. Finn (1996, 2007) developed a model for interpreting congruent and divergent results for the Minnesota Multiphasic Personality Inventory (MMPI-2; Butcher et al., 1989) and the Rorschach, two of the most frequently used self-report and performance-based personality assessment instruments (Ready & Veague, 2014). The model considers the level of disturbance shown respectively by the two tests and interprets potential discrepancies as being connected to clients' differing levels of awareness about their psychological functioning and the way their personality features show up in the specific contexts created by the tests. Finn's model can be adapted to convergence/divergence patterns between almost all self-report and performance-based tests and is highly compatible with Bornstein's (2002) widely accepted "process dissociation" test interpretation model.

Using test results to describe the specific "personality signature" of clients and inferring from their scores on different tests how they may struggle in real life are at the core of what TA clinicians refer to as case conceptualization (see Chapter 7). The case conceptualization allows clinicians to understand accurately clients' psychological functioning, their dilemmas of change, and what might reduce the forces restraining them from change. Additionally, a good case conceptualization is a precondition for assessors to answer clients' AQs meaningfully and fulfill clients' goals for their assessments.

Understanding Clients' Struggles and Resources: Input from Evolutionary Psychology and Interpersonal Neurobiology

Numerous findings from evolutionary psychology as well as neurobiological research support the idea that emotions are sources of essential information that promote the survival of the human species when accurately understood. *Primary emotions* are genetically-based, adaptive responses that serve to indicate that meaningful change has occurred in the environment (e.g., feeling fear is connected to the emergence of a danger; Prinz, 2004). *Secondary emotions*, such as shame and embarrassment, are equally important and result from the way the people in our environment respond to us when we display primary emotions. For example, if we are rejected as a child whenever we show anger, we may come to feel shame in situations that elicit anger. The awareness of our emotions in distinct moments and across different contexts and the ability to access different emotional states that are useful and relevant to various situations are both essential to individual mental health and are connected to "emotion regulation."

Emotion regulation refers to "how we try to influence which emotions we have, when we have them, and how we experience and express these emotions" (Gross, 2008, p. 497; see Box 1.3).

Box 1.3   Emotional Regulation

According to Gross (2008, 2015) the more typical ways to regulate emotions are:

a   Selecting contexts in which different emotions may arise (e.g., by preferring contexts that promote positive emotions).
b   Actively influencing our emotional response with a situation (e.g., by telling a joke when an unexpected problem arises to decrease feelings of anxiety).
c   Directing our attention toward specific aspects of a situation (e.g., comforting ourselves after failing an exam by remembering that most of the class failed it too).
d   Revising our understanding of a problem (e.g., an adolescent, frustrated by his mother's efforts to control his time studying, may come to see his mother's behavior as a useful tool that helps him focus on his studies; this new way of considering his mother's actions would more likely replace his frustration with gratitude).

e   Modulating their emotional responses (e.g., counting to ten before insulting someone).

While some emotion regulation strategies promote adjustment and well-being, others (e.g., emotional avoidance, rumination, and suppression of emotion) can have psychopathological outcomes (Aldao et al., 2010).

One fairly frequent problem with emotion regulation seen in clients seeking psychological care has been called "split-off" or "dissociated" affect states (Fosha, 2000). By this term, we mean that certain clients appear to be unaware of and blocked from expressing one or more primary or secondary emotions (e.g., anger, sadness, fear, shame). As a result, these people do not feel as most would in certain situations, and thus cannot take appropriate action. Often, the life difficulties that prompt clients to seek a TA are related to split-off affects. For example, a client may ask, "Why have I not been more successful at work?" and careful interviewing reveals they do not promote themselves at work or in other competitive contexts and have even suggested they be passed over for promotions. Psychological testing may reveal this client to have split-off emotions of anger and positive entitlement, rendering the client incapable of being appropriately assertive and positively competitive at work and in other contexts.

How do split-off affect states develop? Typically, from interpersonal learning or unresolved trauma. For example, the client mentioned earlier may have grown up with an angry, abusive father who terrified the whole family with his rages and a submissive, unassertive mother who was unable to protect herself or her children. In that context, the client understandably may have learned to ignore or bury their own anger, because (1) it would have been dangerous to feel and express it, for them and for the whole family, (2) they followed their mother's model, and (3) they were directly or indirectly rewarded (e.g., their mother praised their patience; their father directed his anger towards other, more rebellious siblings). Emotions split-off in such traumatic contexts are often dissociated, completely out of consciousness and no longer available to serve adaptive functions. Alternatively, such emotions can sometimes be unintegrated without being completely dissociated; so they can frighten clients by "popping up" in uncontrolled and surprising ways leading clients to block them when they can. However, split-off emotions are not always due to severe individual or familial trauma. For example, the client mentioned earlier may have been raised in a culture where anger, assertiveness, and competition were taboo; whenever the client expressed these natural emotions as a child, they were shamed or punished. We know that shame and anxiety become "attached" (through classical conditioning) to the forbidden emotion, so that if it ever arises, it is avoided or suppressed (Aschieri et al., 2016). In this way, diverse cultures develop their own signatures of forbidden or split-off emotions (De Leersnyder et al., 2013).

As mentioned earlier, many emotional states can be dissociated, leading to a host of distinct problems in living. Imagine a traumatized mother who becomes overwhelmed and withdraws whenever her child expresses fear. Over time, to protect the attachment bond, the child becomes conditioned to suppress or ignore the physiological sensations of fear, avoids situations where they might feel fear, or plunges into dangerous situations with no awareness that they are putting themselves at risk. As an adult, this client might seek an assessment asking, "Why do I keep making bad choices and doing things that hurt me in the end?" As this implies, split-off affects do not just disappear but continue to influence the development of individuals, in severe cases even leading to "vertical splits" (Goldberg, 1999), in which the same person seems to embody wildly different personalities à la Dr. Jekyll and Mr. Hyde, or dissociative identity disorder, in which whole personalities are independent of and have no awareness of the others. In less severe instances, split-off affects are associated with a wide variety of mental/emotional problems, including character disorders and addictions.

Recent brain studies have shown that the right hemisphere, which has dense reciprocal neural connections to specific subcortical nuclei (e.g., the amygdala), plays a fundamental role in processing emotions, attachment, and traumatic experiences (see Schore 2009 for a summary). Since dissociated affect states and implicit self-views are processed primarily in the right hemisphere, they are difficult to access through language (e.g., by simply asking clients in interviews for their conscious representations of themselves). This is another reason psychological tests can be valuable sources of information for understanding clients. In fact, all standardized self-report and performance-based tests give information about clients' emotional awareness, emotional expression, and emotional regulation. In particular, and depending on the context, extremely low scores on self-report tests may indicate dissociated affect states, since they signify affects or emotions less present in the individual than normally expected. For example, if a man whose wife of 30 years has just died shows no signs of depression or emotional distress on relevant self-report tests, we might question his ability to be aware of and to express sadness and depression. Discrepancies between sources of information (e.g., between self-report and performance-based tests, between interviews and tests, between observations and interviews) are often extremely useful in identifying split-off affect states. To return to our example, if the man mentioned earlier showed signs of negative affective states on a performance-based test like the Rorschach (e.g., above-average scores of Morbid Contents, Aromatic Colors, and Diffuse Shading), this suggests that depression and sadness may be dissociated affect states, as these scores are behaviorally associated with depression while being inconsistent with the man's self-report. Finn (2012) hypothesized that performance-based personality tests access such split-off states because they tap areas of the brain governed by the right hemisphere and the subcortical nuclei (Asari et al., 2008; Bucheim et al., 2008).

Identifying clients' split-off affect states can help clinicians and clients understand clients' dilemmas of change. Furthermore, if a clinician can safely make a client aware of split-off affects, and the client can then recognize, own, and reintegrate them, the client will have new options with which to approach their life problems. In the following chapter, we discuss how to conduct a TA to help clients become aware of split-off affects, tie them to their problems in living, and begin to reintegrate such emotions into their personalities (see Chapters 6 and 8).

Why Are Psychological Tests Used Collaboratively in Therapeutic Assessment?

Constance Fischer (1985/1994, 2000) pioneered the theory and practice of using psychological tests collaboratively. According to Fischer, when clients and assessors collaborate, or "co-labor," around the meaning of tests responses and scores and how they apply to clients' lives, both parties benefit immensely. In the collaboration, assessors create an individualized and useful understanding of a particular client using various assessment instruments, and the client is given a new perspective with which to think about their current life struggles. In this process, the meaning of test responses and scores emerges from both (1) the assessors' knowledge of research, psychometrics, and various psychological theories, and (2) clients' knowledge of their personal lives, background, and behaviors in different contexts. In Fischer's view, assessors are experts on tests and theories, while clients are experts on their own lives; thus, the collaborative work of understanding test results represents a middle ground between assessors and clients' knowledge.

The collaboration between assessor and client unfolds in several ways. The assessor typically provides small bits of information derived from test scores or results (scaffolding) and allows the client to confirm, reformulate, or reject the new information on the basis of their self-knowledge. Clients advance the process with their spontaneous observations and insights, which assessors then tie to the meaning of test scores or to a certain theory about human functioning. At its core, collaborative assessment is a joint meaning-making process that positively reinforces clients' active participation both by interpreting their own results and by contributing their own insights and associations. Furthermore, the client's disagreements with typical test interpretations are powerful occasions to explore unexpected meanings arising from the tests and potential blocks or mistrust toward the assessment or the assessor. Collaboratively working with tests significantly increases the likelihood of clients feeling heard, attended to, and cared for.

Some authors describe collaboration as a way to compare and incorporate the information coming from various sources, which creates different "stories" about the client (Aschieri, 2012, Aschieri et al., 2010). In a collaborative assessment, these "stories" are typically (1) ones told by the client based on information and accounts from their everyday lives ("stories with personal meanings"); (2) ones created by the clinician after comparing a client's test scores with normative samples ("stories written with numbers"); and (3) ones that emerge from the new observations and joint experiences that assessor and client share during the unfolding of the assessment ("stories written by four hands"; Aschieri, 2012, p. 361).

According to Fischer (1985/1994, 2000), assessor and client work collaboratively during various steps of the assessment. In the beginning, they can discuss and agree upon the client's goals for the assessment, and subsequently, after tests have been administered and results have emerged, they can share observations and ideas about the client's experiences and behaviors. During the assessment, they create a shared language, especially through the clinician's active efforts to incorporate the client's way of describing their subjective experience. Client and assessor are attentive to test behaviors and experiences that resemble the client's usual ways of being in the world, especially if those are costly or problematic. Then they search for new ways of being that "branch off" from these old ones, but are less detrimental. Finally, clients and assessors also collaborate on assessment reports. Clients are actively encouraged to write comments and to share any disagreements, and these are provided to any future readers of the report.

In recent decades, many studies and theoretical developments in clinical assessment have supported the idea that the collaborative use of tests provides more valid and contextualized information than does a traditional, non-collaborative assessment, and that collaboration allows the assessment to become a therapeutic experience for clients. We will summarize some of these recent developments.

The Collaborative Use of Tests Yields More Valid Information

It is well established that clients' attitudes when completing psychological tests have a powerful impact on the validity of test results (Meyer, 1996, 1997). For this reason, many tests have specific scales or indicators to assess how clients are responding. For example, the MMPI-2 and MMPI-2-RF (Ben-Porath & Tellegen, 2008/2011) assess clients' response coherence and tendency to over-report or under-report symptoms, and the R-PAS assesses clients' engagement with the Rorschach and indicates the presence of a defensive stance that might hinder relevant information emerging from the coding.

Collaborating with clients during an assessment is a very effective way to maximize the likelihood of collecting valid and reliable test protocols. In fact, when assessors and clients agree on clients' goals for the assessment (see Chapter 5), clients are more likely to be open and engaged during the testing, anticipating the tests will help to serve their goals. Furthermore, engaging clients as active participants and "experts" in understanding their own testing, along with the clinician's willingness to discuss non-defensively clients' reservations about participating in the assessment, support the creation of a trusting relationship. As a result, clients are overall more engaged in the testing, and even guarded clients become progressively more open in their test responses as their trust in the clinician and the assessment process grows.

Although test scores may indicate that a protocol is "invalid" according to traditional interpretation guidelines (e.g., over-reporting or under-reporting on the MMPI-2-RF or constricted or guarded Rorschach protocols), clinicians practicing TA are taught to regard such results as crucial information that help us understand clients' dilemmas of change, or clients' reactions to the assessment or the assessor (Finn, 1999). Because we consider assessment to be an interpersonal process, we believe test results not only indicate stable features of clients' personalities, but also reflect specific assessment contexts, and clients' reactions to assessors' behaviors or personas (Aschieri, 2012). For example, a very high L (Lie) scale on the MMPI-2 (typically suggesting that the client tried to present themselves in a virtuous light) may—depending on other test scores and observations—suggest to a TA assessor that the client is afraid of being rejected or judged by the assessor. This would raise the question of whether the client felt safe enough in the assessment process to begin the testing phase. In such a situation, the assessor would approach the client, ask for their thoughts about the L Scale elevation, and see if the hypothesis about the client fearing rejection seemed true. If so, the assessor would explore the client's fears: Does the client fear rejection in other contexts or is the fear specific to the context of the assessment? Does the client feel conflicted about the assessment, partly willing to disclose and partly fearing the consequences? This kind of exploration can potentially increase the accuracy of the assessor's interpretation of the client's high L score. Lastly, the assessor might work with the client to discover something that might increase their sense of safety with the assessor and the assessment (e.g., further discussing limits of confidentiality). If this work succeeds, the client might be more open when responding to subsequent tests, thereby providing more valid and useful results;

if not, the assessor might acknowledge the client's dilemma and consider whether the TA should continue.

The Collaborative Use of Tests Yields More Contextualized Information

Different scholars have maintained that psychological tests are most useful when they frame, reflect, and help explain clients' functioning in particular life contexts (Fischer, 1985/1994; Mischel, 2004; Fischer & Finn, 2014). Fischer (1985/1994; 2000) pointed out that clients often seek psychological assessments with over-generalized descriptions of their struggles, such as, "I am always depressed," and that these broad generalizations may show up in their testing as well (e.g., high scores on multiple self-report scales related to depression). Such generalities are at least partially inaccurate, as humans are fluid beings with a certain flexibility in interacting with their environment not static assemblies of traits and patterns. The work of the clinician is to help clients reflect on their everyday-life experiences and the different situations they encounter, so that more useful, contextualized understandings may emerge. For example, a clinician and client may discover that the client becomes sleepy, unmotivated, and sad when studying their medical school coursework, but feels happy and energetic when building their toy model rockets. Understanding these contextual elements of the client's "depression" not only helps the assessor to interpret the client's test responses and scores but also empowers the client to recognize life factors that could affect their depression. The client might realize they never wanted to study medicine and did so only because of family pressure. This insight might help the client define new options: deciding to pursue another course of study, for example, or finding their own personal reasons for being a physician. These types of breakthroughs become possible when clinician and client collaborate to explore the specific contexts in which a certain problem emerges.

Fischer and Finn (2014) developed the term "life validity" to capture this type of collaborative interpretation of test results. Life validity is a form of construct validity focused on the extent to which clients *themselves* can see and affirm that their tests responses and scores connect to their life contexts; in other words, a test score has life validity when a client can relate it to their daily life. In TA, and specifically through the EI (see Chapter 6), clinicians support clients in exploring their test responses and behaviors. In this way, clients develop their own connections between the features of a test (e.g., anxiety-provoking, requiring specific cognitive or interpersonal skills), their experience during the test administration, and their life experiences in contexts with similar features. Additionally, when a test result lacks life validity, clinicians can consider whether: (1) The test result is inaccurate, 2) the client's context or cultural background changes how the test score should be interpreted, or 3) the client is unwilling to disclose a specific aspect of their personal life. In any of these instances, the assessor's case conceptualization must evolve. (See Chapter 7).

The Collaborative Use of Tests Helps Make Psychological Assessment a Therapeutic Experience for Clients

In TA, tests are viewed as "empathy magnifiers" (Finn, 2007), meaning that they can help clinicians "get in clients' shoes" and identify clients' current self-narratives, coping strategies, strengths, and dilemmas of change. Test results enhance the empathic capacity of clinicians, which allows them to better mentalize their clients and to design therapeutic interventions tailored to their specific needs. By collaborating with them in the testing phases, assessors create transformative experiences for clients through several processes we will now describe.

The Collaborative Use of Tests Creates a Context for the Client to Feel Seen and Understood

Kohut (1971, 1977, 1982) stressed that clients need to be "accurately seen" by clinicians to develop a coherent self. Similarly, Linehan (1993) suggested that therapists' accurate perception and mirroring of their clients allows clients to regulate their emotions better and reinforces their own identities, strengthening the therapeutic relationship. Mirroring is a ubiquitous therapeutic tool, which can be defined as the clinician's ability to identify, label, and accurately describe clients' states of mind. Mirroring requires "the therapist's sensitive ability and willingness to understand the client's thoughts, feelings, and struggles from the client's point of view" (Rogers, 1980, p. 85). In TA, clinicians use tests to increase how accurately they can mirror clients' struggles and strengths (Aschieri et al., 2016). When we collaborate with clients and discuss their test responses during the EI, the client's contributions allow us "get in their shoes" which then helps them feel mirrored (Finn, 2009). As a result, many of our clients—even those who have worked previously with excellent therapists—report that they "have never felt so understood" as they have during a TA. As Finn (2009) wrote, "people all have a longing to be seen, deeply understood, and accepted for who they are" (p. 22). For these reasons, the collaborative use of tests can be very therapeutic for clients.

The Collaborative Use of Tests Fosters Clients' Self-efficacy and Hope

As Fischer (1985/1994) highlighted, many clients who seek clinical services feel "acted upon" and helpless vis-à-vis their life struggles. They do not see themselves as authors of their own lives, and traditional assessment can reinforce this sense of powerlessness by enacting a relationship where an "expert psychologist" pronounces the "Truth" about who the client "really" is. In TA, the collaborative use of tests fosters clients' self-efficacy in showing them their input is essential to the assessor interpreting the test results. Additionally, when assessors sensitively "scaffold" clients' new understandings, clients often feel that they have achieved insights on their own, which increases their sense of feeling competent (Kamphuis & Finn, 2019). Finally, as clients explore new ways of approaching tests (which directly apply to parallel life situations) with support from assessors, they gain confidence that they can solve their problems. All these experiences strengthen clients' self-efficacy and also engender hope.

The Collaborative Use of Tests Helps Restore Epistemic Trust in Clients

According to Fonagy and Allison (2014), feeling understood by a therapist and feeling regarded as an active agent whose thoughts and feelings are worthy of consideration greatly affect a client's trust in the therapist and the information that they are trying to convey during therapy. This experience is fundamental if clients are to regard the new information as personally relevant and generalizable or to change their previously rigid IWM. As clients come to trust the clinician, they generalize this experience and learn to use social communication to continue adapting to their environments (Fonagy et al., 2015).

As detailed by Kamphuis and Finn (2019), collaborative assessment is a powerful aid in restoring ET. First, when assessors and clients work together to define clients' goals at the beginning of a TA (see Chapter 5), this promotes clients' subjective expression of needs and signals that the assessment is focused on their agendas. Clients feel they are treated as an intentional agent with their own needs and points of view, which is essential to decreasing EH. EH continues to decrease as clinicians collaborate with clients in discussing their tests responses and results (see especially Chapter 6). Such discussions create the opportunity for "bottom-up" learning, which arises from clients' experiences and allows clients to author "in the first person" new understandings about their present struggles; for example, "After seeing all those smashed animals in the Rorschach, I am starting to think that I feel 'smashed' by what happened to me in my family." When clients are recognized as experts on their own lives, they are more open to "top down" learning, which stems from assessors' expertise on tests and psychological theories ("The smashed animals on your Rorschach receive a certain score, and research suggests such scores point to how deep down you might view yourself as damaged, and that you might have more depressive feelings than most people.")

The Collaborative Use of Tests Provides Clients with Relevant Pieces of Information to Update Their Narratives

We have described how clients' narratives about themselves and their relationships are often inaccurate, incoherent, and self-blaming. A collaborative discussion of clients' test results and responses helps them discover new and significant pieces of knowledge with which to update their narratives while helping them avoid the risk of falling into a disintegration experience. As described in the sections above, the new knowledge arises from integrating information from various sources: the personal stories told by the clients, the stories written with the test numbers, and the stories written by clinician and client together (Aschieri, 2012). Some case examples follow.

AN INACCURATE NARRATIVE

James asked for a TA to understand why he could not reach orgasm during sex with his girlfriend, Sarah. Due to his sexual difficulties, James had wondered if he was still in love with Sarah. During the first session, James' narrative about both his sexual problem and intimate relationships was: "When people are in love with each other, they do not have problems in their sexual performance. Since I am having problems, this might mean I don't love Sarah, so, I should consider breaking up with her." However, James' narrative did not accurately map onto his own experience, as he came to realize while discussing one of his stories for the Thematic Apperception Test (TAT; Murray, 1943). Card 3BM of the TAT is a picture of a person huddled next to a couch. While creating a story for this card, James said: "I see this man; he is desperate, probably thinking of suicide." During the EI, the clinician asked James if the man in the card seemed connected to him. James disclosed that he had recently been feeling desperate and had thought about suicide (this information had not emerged earlier in the assessment). The clinician asked James if he saw any connection between his emotional pain and his sexual problem. With the clinician's support, James realized that his negative feelings (which stemmed from factors outside his intimate relationship) were hindering his ability to engage fully in sex with Sarah. He understood that his sexual problem was due not to a lack of love for Sarah, but to his depression, which showed up in other test results. James developed a more accurate narrative about his difficulties through the collaborative discussion of the test data.

AN INCOHERENT NARRATIVE

Amelia, was a 45 year old, successful manager at an insurance company. She asked for a TA because she was dissatisfied with her boyfriend Javier, and she wondered if he was the "right one" for her. Amelia complained to the assessor about Javier's poor treatment of her and about his dependency on his mother. Since Javier was not interested in participating in a couple's TA, the assessor began an individual TA with Amelia. During the first session, she described how during the previous 12 years, she moved to five different cities because of her job. She stated that she had to adapt to different situations but did not resent it, and in fact, had acclimated successfully. She mentioned in passing that not having a consistent partner during those years had been "a little hard" for her. Through the discussions and MMPI-2-RF results, the clinician developed the impression that part of Amelia's narrative was: "I am a strong woman, capable of relying on myself to adapt to the many changes in my life. Even though I would like to have a stable partner, that is not fundamental to my well-being." However, this narrative did not fit with Amelia's loyalty towards Javier, who did not treat her well nor protect her from his mother's demeaning comments. Amelia's past intimate relationships seemed to have been characterized by her tendency to stay attached to partners who did not care enough for her. Furthermore, on a self-report test related to couple attachment, Amelia described herself as longing for intimacy and fearful of abandonment by her partners.

Amelia's responses to the EMP helped explain how these incoherent self-narratives—the strong independent woman and the woman who longed for intimacy—had been created. During her childhood, Amelia was repeatedly let down by caregivers, and she learned to take care of herself and avoid relying on others. However, Amelia still needed to be loved and cared for. As a result, at the time of the TA, Amelia was in a relationship that was unsatisfying, but she could not ask Javier for what she needed, because she feared being let down and abandoned again. The collaborative discussion of the EMP during the EI helped Amelia realize how important it was for her to find someone who would love and take care of her. She also began to recognize how she contributed to her relationship dissatisfaction by not expressing her wants and needs. As a result, Amelia identified a new therapy goal: To build awareness of her needs in her intimate relationship and to develop an ability to express those needs to Javier.

A SELF-BLAMING NARRATIVE

Ben (Finn, 2012) was referred for a TA because of risky sexual behavior. His MMPI-2 (code type 4-7) was consistent with a vicious cycle that Ben described. He would engage in unsafe sexual encounters (e.g., having unprotected sex with a stranger), and then fall into a state of intense shame and self-recrimination. To escape these painful emotions, he would then act out again sexually, as this provided temporary relief from his suffering. From the interview and MMPI-2 results, it was clear that Ben's narrative was very self-blaming, and that he felt deep shame for being unable to stop his dangerous sexual behavior. From the Rorschach and the EMP, the assessor conceptualized Ben's dilemma of change: Ben had developed a very negative view of himself during a deprived childhood with a severely depressed mother and absent father. However, he felt loyal to his mother and family, and did not want to connect his bad feelings about himself to his early experiences. The sexual acting out gave Ben both a reasonable focus for his shame and some occasional relief from those feeling. Ben would need a new understanding of his intolerable self-hatred and depression, and new ways to handle these feelings, in order to curb his risky sexual behaviors. The assessor executed an AIS, during which Ben monitored sexual feelings as he created stories for selected TAT cards. Both the assessor and Ben noticed that when his stories involved characters who were alone and depressed, his desire to act out sexually increased. Furthermore, Ben realized he related to the lonely children in his stories and he was able to acknowledge the difficulties in his childhood while maintaining a view of his parents as "good people" who "did their best." The assessor led collaborative conversation that was part of the AIS helped Ben connect his sexual behavior with his loneliness and depression. As Ben's understanding of these factors increased, so did his ability to forgive himself. His new, more accurate, and compassionate self-narrative paved the way for an effective psychotherapy experience, where his depression, self-blame, and compulsive sexual behavior were targeted.

The Collaborative Use of Tests Creates Opportunities for Improving Clients' Emotion Regulation

As described earlier, many clients referred for psychological assessment have difficulties both with being aware of certain emotions and expressing them in modulated ways. During a TA, assessors' collaborative use of tests creates occasions to improve clients' emotion regulation skills by facilitating emotional expression within the client-assessor relationship. With a clinician's support, such experiences help clients develop greater emotional awareness and they begin to integrate split-off affects.

How do tests help with this process? Many psychological tests (e.g., the TAT and Rorschach) are emotionally arousing, because of their potent visual and imaginary stimuli or because the testing process itself mirrors past situations that were emotionally difficult for the client (e.g., completing a cognitive achievement test while being watched and "rated" by an authority figure who knows the "right" answer). Thus, certain psychological tests create an experience of affect exposure (McCullough et al., 2003), and both client and assessor can observe and discuss how the client responds. While administering tests, assessors observe whether the client experiences or expresses emotions typically elicited by the test stimuli. For example, when given a TAT card that typically pulls for anger and conflict, watching to see whether the client creates a story incorporating those elements. If not, this is an opportunity for the assessor and client to begin exploring if there are suppressed or split-off emotions. A different client who struggles with certain subtests on a cognitive measure may get angry and start demeaning the assessor for making them feel inadequate. When such emotions and behaviors arise, client and assessor can discuss what it is like for the client to feel inadequate and lose their temper, and what helps in such situations. The supportive, curious, non-judgmental stance of the clinician creates the context for clients to feel and verbalize unintegrated emotions. Such experiences help clients begin to integrate split-off emotions and also provide a map, of sorts, for how they can work on those issues in the future.

How TA Aligns with Diversity Sensitive Approaches to Assessment

As has been increasingly recognized of late, all clients who present for a psychological assessment are embedded in a cultural context inextricably tied to their ways of dealing with stress, problems in living, expression of emotions, views of relationships, and perceptions of mental health. Traditional psychological assessment has been justifiably criticized for not adequately considering the influence of culture on test scores and assessment processes (e.g., Aschieri, 2016; Smith & Krishnamurthy, 2018). However, there have been some notable exceptions—as far back as 30 years ago—of psychologists who championed a culture-centered approach to assessment (e.g., Dana, 1993, 1997). While professional organizations have been attentive to the development of multicultural competency for the past two decades (American Psychological Association, 1993, 2003), only recently have there been more focused efforts as it relates to assessment (e.g., Brabender & Mihura, 2016; Smith & Krishnamurthy, 2018) Recently, the Black Lives Matter, Me Too, GLBTQ, and related social justice movements in the United States and around the world have further raised awareness of the importance of race, gender, gender identity, sexual orientation, ethnicity, religion, immigrant status, economic background, and physical challenges when working with assessment clients. We wholeheartedly agree that understanding clients' contexts is essential for an accurate and useful case conceptualization, and we can identify many examples where failure to consider diversity elements led to biased interpretations of test scores and over-pathologization of clients' lives. Consider these scenarios, based on actual clients:

Tamara, 19, an African American student at a prestigious US university, sought a psychological assessment because of generalized anxiety and feelings of insecurity about her academic achievement. The assessor, a White middle-aged man, asked Tamara to complete an MMPI-3; after noting Tamara's elevated scores on the Self-Doubt and Inefficacy scales, he told Tamara she needed to work on her self-esteem and recommended cognitive-behavioral therapy, never considering the implications of Tamara's status as the only Black person in most of her classes or what supports were available to her when she entered the university.

Liam, a 30-year-old gay man, wanted to understand why he had not yet managed a long-term intimate relationship, even though he made friends quickly and found it easy to date. When the assessor, a heterosexual woman, collected background information on Liam's previous relationships, she commented that Liam "certainly had had a lot of casual sex." She wondered aloud if this might have gotten in the way of him finding longer-term intimacy. When the assessor then asked Liam to fill out the MMPI-3, the results came back suggesting a pattern of defensive responding. The assessor accordingly concluded Liam had problems "being vulnerable" with others.

Cecilia, a 40-year-old Filipino woman, had left her three young children with her parents in the Philippines and immigrated to Italy to earn money for the family. She was referred for an assessment by her physician, who was concerned that Cecilia might be clinically depressed. The assessor asked Cecilia to complete the Beck Depression Inventory 2nd Edition (BDI2), and based on her elevated score, suggested to the referring physician that Cecilia be put on antidepressant medication. The psychologist provided no other recommendations or considered how Cecilia's separation from her children might be causing her to grieve.

Each of these examples shows how assessors can reach erroneous or incomplete conclusions and send potentially damaging messages to clients when they fail to consider important aspects of clients' cultural contexts. Tamara's assessor attributed her difficulties to an individual-difference variable ("low self-esteem"), rather than taking into account how intimidating it might be for Tamara to be the only Black person in her classes at a prestigious, mainly White university. John's assessor judged a normal behavior of gay males (lots of sexual encounters) as a sign of deeper psychological issues, and then interpreted John's understandable self-protective test response as a sign of psychopathology rather than a result of the assessor-client interaction. While Cecilia's assessor may have concluded correctly that she was depressed and might benefit from anti-depressant medication, she failed to appreciate how leaving her children and moving to Italy might have affected Cecilia emotionally, and how other interventions (e.g., a support group of immigrant parents in similar situations) might also have been useful.

As various authors (Aschieri, 2016; Fantini, 2016; Smith, 2016; Martin, 2018; Rosenberg et al., 2012) have agreed, the principles and practices of TA are particularly suited to diversity sensitive psychological assessment for several reasons:

1 TA is client-centered, and the focus and procedures of a TA are adapted to each client, thereby allowing for and respecting diverse cultural contexts. As Martin (2018) wrote: "… [in TA] we seek to intimately understand the client's world and the forces that have acted on the client. We do this by inquiring, listening, and believing the client" (p. 290).

2 Because they are essential collaborators at every step, clients from minority cultures feel more empowered in a TA than in traditional psychological assessment, and they are more willing to share sensitive information with the assessor. We remain committed to being life-long learners about client diversity factors and lean on our values of openness, humility, and respect, which allows clients to share about their culture and life experiences.

3 TA emphasizes the importance of the assessor-client relationship, which provides a way for both to dialogue about real cultural differences. As Rosenberg et al., (2012) wrote: "…[in TA] bridging the wide gap between cultures and overcoming cultural mistrust starts in building the assessor-client relationship and taking both world views into account as a way to create meaning from the assessment results" (p. 223).

4 TA assessors believe that no test result or score has a fixed, immutable meaning, and that test results can be understood only through a joint assessor-client dialogue. This approach minimizes the possibility of an assessor imposing an inaccurate, culturally insensitive meaning to test scores, and aligns with best practices when considering ecological aspects of the client's life (Cimbora & Krishnamurthy, 2018; Claus-Ehlers et al., 2019).

5 Finally, the practice of TA emphasizes the importance of clinician self-reflection. This often occurs as we consider our test data and conversations with the client,

and about their diversity elements and our own, and we consider how they may be comingling and influencing each other. This aligns with best practices when working with diverse individuals (Baca & Smith, 2018; Pope et al., 2021).

Limitations and Contraindications for Therapeutic Assessment

To date, TA has proved effective with adult clients experiencing various mental health issues and problematic behaviors. Participants in TA research have included clients in residential treatment for substance abuse; college students seeking counseling for depression, anxiety, and interpersonal problems; outpatient clients with borderline personality disorder and suicidal ideation; and clients with chronic pain (see Chapter 2 for a complete review of research findings on TA). These studies have documented the positive impact of TA on clients' symptoms, self-esteem, alliance with providers, and treatment satisfaction (as compared to traditional assessment and other credible interventions).

Given the research, the potential contraindications for TA are not related to the nature or severity of clients' psychopathology. Rather, the major factors to consider when deciding whether and how a TA should be implemented with a client concern the context in which the intervention might take place. As a general principle, assessors decide if participation in a TA protects the client's best interests, is likely to yield valid conclusion about the issues at the center for the referral question, and whether TA is the most cost-effective way to meet the goals of the assessment. TA is not always suitable with clients who are in a state of acute crisis. For example, clients who are experiencing significant family violence, or clients who are actively psychotic, should priortize first-tier interventions to safeguard their psychological and physical wellbeing. A TA would only be viable after these factors have been addressed. Second, TA should be avoided when the results might not be used in the client's best interests. For example, during a child-custody assessment, assessors should evaluate if the deep self-exploration facilitated by TA might be detrimental to a client's court case. If a TA were to commence in such a situation, the assessor and client should know the potential risks (there is evidence that TA can be useful in parent coordination after custody issues have been settled [Evans, 2012]). Third, TA is not the best choice when the reasons for an assessment can be answered with traditional, non-collaborative test procedures. For example, when an assessment is requested for straightforward classification purposes (e.g., IQ level), to determine eligibility (e.g., selection assessment for entering the police force), or for descriptive diagnoses based on the DSM 5.0 (American Psychiatric Association, 2013). In such situations, it likely will be more cost-effective for clinicians to perform a traditional, non-collaborative assessment. Importantly, even in these instances where a TA is not advisable, assessors can still apply the core values of TA—respect, humility, compassion, openness, and curiosity—and this will benefit both them and their clients.

Conclusions

TA is an integrative therapeutic approach that combines the collaborative use of psychological tests with sound and effective techniques to build alliance, help clients mentalize and rewrite their core narratives, integrate split-off affect states, restore ET, and practice new, more adaptive behaviors with support from a professional. Similar to what occurs with other psychological services, the extent to which clients change during a TA varies and depends on factors such as the client's presenting problems, the levels of psychopathology and resilience, the clinician's skills, and the context of the intervention. As a result, we, as clinicians, experience the unfolding of each TA in various ways. Some clients discover the answers to their questions quickly and use the TA to build new narratives about themselves. In these TAs, clients seem able to process emotions related to their new realizations and then fine-tune their behaviors and coping strategies based on the new narratives constructed during the process. These "life-changing" assessments are most likely to happen with clients who have the ability to reflect on and be curious about themselves, and who can build a trusting relationship with the clinician in a brief time span. In other situations, TA is an occasion for clients to experience emotional support from a professional who validates their experience, while both identifying answers to their AQs and a path forward for continued growth. This is often the expereince for clients who hold more rigid narratives, feel threatened by new information, and are less capable of building an alliance with the clinician. For these clients, important changes to their narratives may happen during a subsequent long-term treatment, and behavioral changes should not be expected (or even aspired to) during the TA. For these clients, the positive experience with the assessor, and the clarification of their dilemma of change, may help reduce shame and increase their motivation for additional psychological services, which may be sufficient in helping them move forward.

In most instances, during a TA clients show some areas of functioning that remain stable (because they do not experience any problems in those domains or because the assessors judged the clients were not ready to address those issues, or both), some areas that show signifcant change (often those connected with their AQs), and some areas that clients see as connected to their problems, but which they have mixed feelings about changing. The major task of the assessor in all TAs is to contain their own desires to see a change in clients in order to feel effective, helpful, and capable, and to respectfully and humbly put clients at the center of their own change process.

In this chapter, we reviewed the basic theories and assumptions that form the foundation of TA. In Chapter 2, we will review the history and development of TA and in Chapter 3, we summarize the most relevant and up-to-date research on TA. From Chapter 4 to Chapter 11, we guide assessors and clinicians through each step of TA with adult clients. Finally, in Chapter 12, we address how to learn, market, and bill for a TA, followed by a summary in Chapter 13.

References

Adler, J. M. (2012). Living into the story: Agency and coherence in a longitudinal study of narrative identity development and mental health over the course of psychotherapy. *Journal of Personality and Social Psychology, 102*(2), 367–389.

American Psychiatric Association. (2013). *Diagnostic and statistical manual of mental disorders* (5th ed.). Author.

American Psychological Association. (1993). Guidelines for providers of psychological services to ethnic, linguistic, and culturally diverse populations. *American Psychologist, 48*(1), 45–48.

American Psychological Association. (2003). Guidelines on multicultural education, training, research, practice, and organizational change for Psychologists. *American Psychologist, 58*(5), 377–402.

Anastasi, A. (1988). *Psychological testing*. Macmillan.

Aldao, A., Nolen-Hoeksema, S., & Schweizer, S. (2010). Emotion regulation strategies and psychopathology: A meta-analysis. *Clinical Psychology Review, 30*, 217–237.

Asari, T., Konishi, S., Jimura, K., Chkazoe, J., Nakamura, N., & Miyashita, Y. (2008). Amygdalar enlargement associated with unique perception. *Cortex, 30*, 1–6.

Aschieri, F. (2012). Epistemological and ethical challenges in standardized testing and collaborative assessment. *Journal of Humanistic Psychology, 52*(3), 350–368.

Aschieri, F. (2016). Shame as a cultural artifact: A call for reflexivity and self-awareness in personality assessment. *Journal of Personality Assessment, 98*(6), 567–575.

Aschieri, F., Fantini, F., & Smith, J. D. (2016). Collaborative/Therapeutic Assessment: Procedures to enhance client outcomes. In S. Maltzmann (Ed.), *Oxford handbook of treatment processes and outcomes in counseling psychology* (pp. 241–269). Oxford University Press.

Aschieri, F., Finn, S. E., & Bevilacqua, P. (2010). Therapeutic Assessment and epistemological triangulation. In V. Cigoli & M. Gennari (Eds.), *Close relationships and community psychology: An international perspective* (pp. 241–253). Franco Angeli.

Baca, L. & Smith, S. R. (2018). The role of self-reflection and self-assessment in the psychological assessment process. In S. R. Smith & R. Krishnamurthy (Eds.), *Diversity-sensitive personality assessment* (pp. 3–22). Routledge.

Ben-Porath, Y. S., & Tellegen, A. (2008/2011). *MMPI-2-RF (Minnesota Multiphasic Personality Inventory-2 Restructured Form): Manual for administration, scoring, and interpretation*. University of Minnesota Press.

Ben-Porath, Y. S., & Tellegen, A. (2020). *Minnesota Multiphasic Personality Inventory-3 (MMPI-3): Manual for administration, scoring, and interpretation*. University of Minnesota Press.

Bornstein, R. F. (2002). A process dissociation approach to objective-projective test score interrelationships. *Journal of Personality Assessment, 78*, 47–68.

Bornstein, R. F. (2017). Evidence-based psychological assessment. *Journal of Personality Assessment, 99*(4), 435–445.

Bowlby, J. (1958). The nature of the child's tie to his mother. *The International Journal of Psychoanalysis, 39*, 350–373.

Bowlby, J. (1969/1982). *Attachment and loss. Attachment* (2nd ed., Vol. 1). Basic Books.

Bowlby, J. (1973). *Attachment and loss. Vol. 2: Separation: Anxiety and anger*. Basic Books.

Bowlby, J. (1980). *Attachment and Loss. Vol. 3: Loss, sadness and depression*. Basic Books.

Brabender, V. M. & Mihura, J. L. (Eds.). (2016). *Handbook of gender and sexuality in psychological assessment*. Routledge.

Bruhn, A. R. (1992a). The Early Memories Procedure: A projective test of autobiographical memory (Part I). *Journal of Personality Assessment, 58*, 1–15.

Bruhn, A. R. (1992b). The Early Memories Procedure: A projective test of autobiographical memory (Part II). *Journal of Personality Assessment, 58*, 326–346.

Bucheim, A., Erk, S., George, C., Kächele, H., Kircher, T., Martius, P., et al. (2008). Neural correlates of attachment dysregulation in borderline personality disorder using functional magnetic resonance imaging. *Psychiatry Research: Neuroimaging, 163*, 223–235.

Butcher, J. N., Dahlstrom, W. G., Graham, J. R., Tellegen, A., & Kaemmer, B. (1989). *Minnesota Multiphasic Personality Inventory-2 (MMPI-2): Manual for administration and scoring*. University of Minnesota Press.

Cimbora, D. M. & Krishnamurthy, R. (2018). The importance of client context. In S. R. Smith & R. Krishnamurthy (Eds.), *Diversity-sensitive personality assessment* (pp. 43–56). Routledge.

Clauss-Ehlers, C. S., Chiriboga, D. A., Hunter, S. J., Roysircar, G., & Tummala-Narra, P. (2019). APA Multicultural Guidelines executive summary: Ecological approach to context, identity, and intersectionality. *American Psychologist, 74*(2), 232–244.

Dana, R. H. (1993). *Multicultural assessment perspectives for professional psychology.* Allyn & Bacon.

Dana, R. H. (1997). *Understanding cultural identity in intervention and assessment.* Sage.

De Leersnyder, J. D., Boiger, M., & Mesquita, B. (2013). Cultural regulation of emotion: Individual, relational, and structural sources. *Frontiers in Psychology, 4*(55).

Evans, F. B. (2012). Therapeutic assessment alternative to custody evaluations: An adolescent whose parents could not stop fighting. In S. E. Finn, C. T. Fischer, and L. Handler (Eds.), *Collaborative/Therapeutic Assessment: A casebook and guide* (pp. 357–378). Wiley.

Evans, B. F., & Finn, S. E. (2017). Training and consultation in psychological assessment with professional psychologists: Suggestions for enhancing the profession and individual practices. *Journal of Personality Assessment, 99,* 175–185.

Fantini, F. (2016). Family traditions, cultural values and the assessor's countertransference: Therapeutic Assessment of a young Sicilian woman. *Journal of Personality Assessment, 98*(6), 576–584.

Finn, S. E. (1996). Assessment feedback integrating MMPI–2 and Rorschach findings. *Journal of Personality Assessment, 67*(3), 543–557.

Finn, S. E. (1999, March). *Giving feedback to clients about "defensive" test protocols: Guidelines from Therapeutic Assessment.* Paper presented at the annual meeting of the Society for Personality Assessment, New Orleans, LA. Reprinted as Chapter 6 in Finn, S. E. (2007). *In our clients' shoes: Theory and techniques of Therapeutic Assessment* (pp. 55–64). Mahwah, NJ: Erlbaum.

Finn, S. E. (2007). *In our clients' shoes: Theory and techniques of Therapeutic Assessment* Erlbaum.

Finn, S. E. (2009). The many faces of empathy in experiential, person-centered, collaborative assessment. *Journal of Personality Assessment, 91*(1), 20–23.

Finn, S. E. (2012). Implications of recent research in neurobiology for psychological assessment. *Journal of Personality Assessment, 94*(5), 440–449.

Finn, S. E., & Martin, H. (2013). Therapeutic assessment: Using psychological testing as brief therapy. In K. F. Geisinger, B. A. Bracken, J. F. Carlson, J. C. Hansen, N. R. Kuncel, S. P. Reise, M. C. Rodriguez (Eds.), *APA handbook of testing and assessment in psychology*, Vol. 2: Testing and assessment in clinical and counseling psychology (pp. 453–465). American Psychological Association.

Finn, S. E., & Tonsager, S. E. (1992). The therapeutic effects of providing MMPI-2 test feedback to college students awaiting psychotherapy. *Psychological Assessment, 4,* 278–287.

Fischer, C. (1985/94). *Individualizing psychological assessment.* Routledge. (Originally published by Brooks Cole).

Fischer, C. (2000). Collaborative, individualized assessment. *Journal of Personality Assessment, 74,* 2–14.

Fischer, C. T., & Finn, S. E. (2014). Developing the life meaning of psychological test data: Collaborative and therapeutic approaches. In Archer, R. P., & Smith. S. R. (Eds.), *Personality assessment, 2nd edition* (pp. 401–431). Routledge.

Fonagy, P. (1989). On tolerating mental states: Theory of mind in borderline patients. *Bulletin of the Anna Freud Centre, 12,* 91–115.

Fonagy, P., & Allison, E. (2014). The role of mentalizing and epistemic trust in the psychotherapeutic relationship. *Psychotherapy, 51,* 372–380.

Fonagy, P., Luyten, P., & Allison, E. (2015). Epistemic petrification and the restoration of epistemic trust: A new conceptualization of borderline personality disorder and its psychosocial treatment. *Journal of Personality Disorders, 29,* 575–609.

Fonagy, P., Luyten, P., Allison, E., & Campbell, C. (2017a). What we have changed our minds about: Part 1. Borderline personality as a limitation of resilience. *Borderline Personality and Emotional Dysregulation, 4*(11).

Fonagy, P., Luyten, P., Allison, E., & Campbell, C. (2017b). What we have changed our minds about: Part 2. Borderline personality, epistemic trust, and the developmental significance of social communication. *Borderline Personality and Emotional Dysregulation, 4*(9).

Fosha, D. (2000). *The transforming power of affect: A model for accelerated change.* Basic Books.

George, C., & West, M. (2011). The adult attachment projective picture system: Integrating attachment into clinical assessment. *Journal of Personality Assessment, 93*(5), 407–416.

Giesler, R. B., Josephs, R. A., & Swann, W. B. (1996). Self-verification in clinical depression: The desire for negative evaluation. *Journal of Abnormal Psychology, 105*(3), 358–368.

Gilbert, P. & Andrews, B. (1998). (Eds.), *Shame: Interpersonal behavior, psychopathology, and culture.* Oxford University Press.

Goldberg, A. (1999). *Being of two minds: The vertical split in psychoanalysis and psychotherapy.* Routledge.

Gross, J. J. (2008). Emotion regulation. In M. Lewis, J. M. Haviland-Jones, and L. F. Barrett (Eds.), *Handbook of emotions* (3rd Ed) (pp. 497–512). Guilford.

Gross, J. J. (2015). Emotion regulation: Current status and future prospects. *Psychological Inquiry, 26*(1), 1–26.

Handler, L., & Smith, J. D. (2013). Education and training in psychological assessment. In J. R. Graham, J. A. Naglieri, & I. B. Weiner (Eds.), *Handbook of psychology: Assessment psychology* (pp. 211–238). John Wiley & Sons, Inc.

Hopwood, C. J. & Bornstein, R. F. (2014). *Multimethod clinical assessment of personality and psychopathology.* Guilford Press.

Kamphuis, J. H., & Finn, S. E. (2019). Therapeutic Assessment in personality disorders: Toward the restoration of epistemic trust. *Journal of Personality Assessment, 101*(6), 662–674.

Kohut, H. (1971). *The analysis of the self.* International Universities Press.

Kohut, H. (1977). *The restoration of the self.* International Universities Press.

Kohut, H. (1982). Introspection, empathy, and mental health. *International Journal of Psychoanalysis, 63*, 395–408.

Kohut, H. (1984). *How does analysis cure?* University of Chicago Press.

Korzybski, A. (1933). *Science and Sanity: An Introduction to Non-Aristotelian Systems and General Semantics.* Institute of General Semantics.

Linehan, M. M. (1993). *Cognitive-behavioral treatment of borderline personality disorder.* Guilford Press.

Maloney, M. P., & Ward, M. P. (1976). *Psychological assessment: A conceptual approach.* Oxford University Press.

Martin, H. (2018). Collaborative/Therapeutic Assessment and diversity: The complexity of being human. In S. R. Smith & R. Krishnamurthy (Eds.), *Diversity-sensitive personality assessment* (pp. 278–293). Routledge.

McCullough, L., Kuhn, N., Andrews, S., Kaplan, A., Wolf, J., & Hurley C. (2003). *Treating affect phobia: A manual for short-term dynamic psychotherapy.* The Guilford Press.

Meyer, G. J., Finn, S. E., Eyde, L. D., Kay, G. G., Moreland, K. L., Dies, R. R., Eisman, E. J., Kubiszyn, T. W., & Reed, G. M. (2001). Psychological testing and psychological assessment: A review of evidence and issues. *American Psychologist, 56*, 128–165.

Meyer, G. (2018, March). *On methods of knowing in psychology.* Keynote address at the annual meeting of the Society for Personality Assessment.

Meyer, G. J. (1996). The Rorschach and MMPI: Toward a more scientifically differentiated understanding of cross-method assessment. *Journal of Personality Assessment, 67*, 558–578.

Meyer, G. J. (1997). On the integration of personality assessment methods: The Rorschach and MMPI-2. *Journal of Personality Assessment, 68*, 297–330.

Meyer, G. J., Viglione, D. J., Mihura, J. L., Erard, R. E., & Erdberg, P. (2011). *Rorschach Performance Assessment System: Administration, coding, interpretation, and technical manual.* Rorschach Performance Assessment System.

Mikulincer, M., & Shaver, P. R. (2007). *Attachment in adulthood: Structure, dynamics, and change.* Guilford Press.

Mischel, W. (2004). Toward an integrative science of the person. *Annual Review of Psychology, 55,* 1–22.

Murray, H. A. (1943). *Thematic Apperception Test manual.* Harvard University Press.

Papp, P. (1983). *The process of change.* Guilford Press.

Pope, K. S., Vasquez, M. J. T., Chevez-Dueñas, N. Y., & Adames, H. Y. (2021). *Ethics in psychotherapy and counseling: A practical guide,* 6th Edition. Wiley.

Prinz, J. (2004). Which emotions are basic? In D. Evans and P. Cruse (Eds.), *Emotion, evolution, and rationality* (pp. 1–19). Oxford University Press.

Ready, R. E., & Veague, H. B. (2014). Training in psychological assessment: Current practices of clinical psychology programs. *Professional Psychology: Research and Practice, 45,* 278–282.

Reisz, S., Duschinsky, R., & Siegel, D. J. (2018). Disorganized attachment and defense: Exploring John Bowlby's unpublished reflections. *Attachment & Human Development, 20*(2), 107–134.

Rogers, C. R. (1980). *A way of being.* Houghton Mifflin.

Rosenberg, A., Almeida, A., & Macdonald, H. (2012). Crossing the cultural divide: Issues in translation, mistrust, and co-creation of meaning in cross-cultural Therapeutic Assessment. *Journal of Personality Assessment, 94,* 223–231.

Safran, J. D. & Muran, J. C. (2000). *Negotiating the therapeutic alliance: A relational treatment guide.* Guilford.

Sattler, J. M. (1988). *Assessment of children* (3rd ed.). Jerome M. Sattler.

Schore, A. (2009). Right brain affect regulation: An essential mechanism of development, trauma, dissociation, and psychotherapy. In Fosha, D., Solomon, M., & Siegel, D. (Eds.), *The healing power of emotions: Integrating relationships, body, and mind. A dialogue among scientists and clinicians* (pp. 112–144). Norton.

Schroeder, D. G., Hahn, E. D., Finn, S. E., & Swann, W. B. Jr. (1993, June). *Personality feedback has more impact when mildly discrepant from self-views.* Paper presented at the fifth annual convention of the American Psychological Society, Chicago, IL.

Smith, J. D. (2016). Introduction to the special section on cultural considerations in collaborative and Therapeutic Assessment. *Journal of Personality Assessment, 98*(6), 563–566.

Smith, S. R., & Krishnamurthy, R. (Eds.) (2018). *Diversity-sensitive personality assessment.* Routledge.

Sperber, D., Clement, F., Heitz, C., Mascaro, O., Mercier, H., Origgi, G., & Wilson, D. (2010). Epistemic vigilance. *Mind & Language, 25*(4), 359–393.

Stedman, J. M., Hatch, J. P., & Schoenfeld, L. S. (2001). The current status of psychological assessment training in graduate and professional schools. *Journal of Personality Assessment, 77*(3), 398–407.

Stern, D. N. (2004). *The present moment: In psychotherapy and everyday life.* W. W. Norton & Co.

Swann, W. B. (1997). The trouble with change: Self-verification and allegiance to the self. *Psychological Science, 8,* 177–180.

Swann, W. B., Stein-Seroussi, A., & Giesler, R. B. (1992). Why people self-verify. *Journal of Personality and Social Psychology, 62*(3), 392–401.

Swann, W. B., Wenzlaff, R. M., Krull, D. S., & Pelham, B. W. (1992). The allure of negative feedback: Self-verification strivings among depressed persons. *Journal of Abnormal Psychology, 101,* 293–306.

Tallent, N. (1992). *The practice of psychological assessment.* Pearson College Division.

Trewarthen, C., & Hubley, P. (1978). Secondary Intersubjectivity: Confidence, confiding and acts of meaning in the first year. In A. Lock (Ed.), *Action, gesture and symbol,* (pp. 183–229). Academic Press.

Tronick, E., & Beeghly, M. (2011). Infants' meaning making and the development of mental health problems. *American Psychologist, 66,* 107–119.

Wilson, D., & Sperber, D. (2012). *Meaning and relevance.* Cambridge University Press.

Wright, A. G., & Hopwood, C. J. (2016). Advancing the assessment of dynamic psychological processes. *Assessment, 23*(4), 399–403.

2 Development of Therapeutic Assessment

Critiques of Psychological Assessment

Tests, as occasions to work collaboratively with clients to promote their growth, have a long history, dating back to the mid-1900s. At that time, the history of collaborative assessment began amidst a conflict that divided psychologists between those who valued psychological assessment's utility and those who criticized it. The arguments against psychological assessment were summarized later by Sugarman (1978). Critiques included both the assessment procedures and the personality of assessors, who were seen as professionals acting out pathological identifications. In some publications, assessment procedures were criticized because they broke down the person into meaningless bits of information, failing to frame the meaning of clients' behaviors in their real-life contexts (Nadolsky, 1966, 1969; Leary, 1970). Appelbaum (1976) and Shectman (1979) maintained that testing was fundamentally redundant and unnatural, as it provided, in the best circumstance, nothing more than the same information that psychotherapy yields. However, contrary to psychotherapy, the assessment did so in an artificial environment. According to other psychologists, assessments measured people's behaviors but failed to assess the meaning they attributed to their behaviors (Munter, 1975; Jourard, 1968). There were also those who saw these issues as connected to the assessor's personality or professional style, and some argued that testing was used defensively to avoid personal connection with clients (Appelbaum, 1976; Brown, 1972; Shevrin & Shectman, 1973). Munter (1975) believed that the assessor's interest in diagnosis was the result of their identification with the aggressor. In this view, an assessment simply emphasized negative aspects of people's functioning and represented a socially acceptable way to stigmatize some people (Szasz, 1960). Finally, Brown (1972) criticized assessments because psychological reports contained overly abstract and intellectualized concepts, failing to capture clients' subjectivity and experienced reality. All these critiques were also influenced by the paternalistic stance of many assessors. Such a stance was well captured by Brodsky (1972), who noticed that clients, who should partner in the evaluation process since it affects their welfare, rarely had access to their own files. The underlying rationale was that the evaluator knew what was best for them.

Precursors of Therapeutic Assessment

Between the 1950s and 1970s, various authors proposed innovative ideas regarding how to think about and practice psychological assessment. Although these authors did

DOI: 10.4324/9780429202797-3

not have a direct impact on Finn's development of Therapeutic Assessment (TA) during the 1990s, they collectively contributed to some of the shifting views of psychological assessment. With their publications and work, they created a favorable context for the later development of collaborative and therapeutic approaches to assessment.

In 1953, Luborsky argued in favor of using psychological testing to engage clients in their treatment. He assessed medical students who were applying to the Menninger School of Psychiatry, and were generally well-functioning and educated. Through his clinical experiences, he began to appreciate the potential of actively engaging clients in the assessment process. He developed several procedures that currently could be identified as examples of Extended Inquiries (EI, see Chapter 6). For instance, he proposed ways to discuss Thematic Apperception Test (TAT; Murray, 1943) stories with clients and promoted clients' active interpretation of a story's meaning. He asked clients, "Please try to interpret these stories by telling me what they show about things you have done in the past and, especially, what they show about what you are like as a person" (Luborsky, 1953, p. 217). With less psychologically sophisticated clients, he suggested reviewing the TAT stories with the client by saying, "You know, when a person makes up a story, he can't help telling something about himself. Take this story of yours and tell me some of the ways you put yourself into it" or "What do you suppose I can learn about you from this story you told?" (p. 218).

A similar approach of engaging clients in a respectful and collaborative use of testing was advocated by Harrower (1956). She helped clients make sense of and use their responses to projective materials to improve their well-being and psychological functioning, similar to what happens during the EI. In particular, the discussion of Rorschach responses in psychotherapy was encouraged to "elicit and trigger key areas of [the client's] conflicts. Much as a fragment of a dream will lead to a whole constellation of important associative ideas, so a key Rorschach response can be used to elicit important material" (p. 75). Harrower encouraged assessors to build a personal connection with the client and believed that if clinicians allowed themselves to delve deeply into the client's production, tests could be powerful tools to increase clients' self-awareness. Such beliefs led her to use tests creatively and she stated that "there is no one correct way of using any of these tests, nor is there one prescribed sequence, nor need that all tests be used with each case" (ibid.). These aspects are similar to Finn's view of testing as a way for assessors to "get in their clients' shoes," increasing their understanding of how clients experiences their world (Finn, 2007).

Almost ten years later, Baker (1964) advocated for the use of testing in a therapeutic manner as a way of working with severely disturbed clients. He first addressed the typical critique psychotherapists made of assessors, namely that their interpretations of test results could be unsafe or emotionally upsetting for clients, unlike the more cautious interpretations made in psychotherapy. Baker agreed that there was a risk of provoking pain and damaging clients through test interpretations, but argued that this was only true if the assessor was not skilled at discussing tests results in a safe way with clients. He maintained that "the supportiveness of the atmosphere in which the data are discussed is one of the most important features in working with patients of varying ego strength" (p. 6). He also encouraged clinicians to communicate with clients about test results, but the language should be jargon-free. Test interpretations must be attuned to the client's defenses, and assessors should dose (scaffold) the information according to what the client is able to process. To build the assessor-client relationship, the assessor should focus on (1) mirroring and responding to the healthy needs of clients during the assessment; (2) promoting a positive emotional atmosphere; (3) engaging clients as co-observers of their own test data; and (4) checking what kind of impact the discussion is having on the client and the assessment process. These elements are similar to core features of TA as we also believe in both creating a safe emotional environment and in the importance of not overwhelming clients with information they are not able to process. (Level 3 Information as described below.)

Other psychologists during this era were also providing guidance about how best to discuss test results with clients. Richman (1967) noted that "clinical psychologists have been concerned about the proper presentation of their test results to everyone but the patient" (p. 63). He was critical of the psychological assessment literature, which was focused only on how to report test results to different professionals, and not directly to the client. In his view, "The client emerges as a rather weak being, while the psychologist accepts the magical image of himself as someone in charge of great and dangerous secrets" (p. 63).

Richman (1967) introduced the idea that the risk of harming clients was related to how test results were presented. He recommended explaining to clients that clinicians could make mistakes in scoring and interpreting the test results, and that the client's collaboration in judging the accuracy of the assessment feedback was valued and appreciated. After using this approach with many clients, Richman concluded that its success depended on the client's desire to know the assessment results and the dissatisfaction they felt with some part of their life, which motivated them to voluntarily seek "help and advice" (p. 68).

A few years later, without mentioning Richman's thinking regarding how to cultivate clients' collaboration and curiosity, Mosak and Gushurst (1972) wrote about the importance of this goal. According to these authors, clinicians should inform clients "about the nature and purpose of the testing" (p. 541). They also believed in the importance of addressing clients' expectations, hopes, and fears before the assessment feedback is provided, in order to prevent clients' potential negative reactions. They also stressed that feedback to the clients should only include information that clients were interested in hearing.

These authors also summarized the advantages of creating a collaborative context to discuss the client's test results before beginning therapy (Mosak & Gushurst, 1972). They argued that discussing test results promotes trust in the clinician, as their knowledge of tests suggests that "the therapist is trained, conscientious, and scientific: He does not guess at the problem, he studies it" (p. 541). They also believed that the connections between test data and real-life examples would stimulate client self-awareness. Further, providing test feedback, indirectly communicates the clinician's trust in the client's ability to process it and this builds hope in their "ability to comprehend and tolerate information that may, in some respects, be unfavorable or unpleasant" (p. 542). Importantly, when the clinician respects the client when they disagree with findings, "the therapist [assessor] demonstrates his recognition of the patient's intelligence and self-knowledge" (p. 542). These ideas are in concert with many foundational TA concepts, such as promoting the client's view that the assessor is a reliable source of important information and seeing clients as experts of their own life.

Finally, Craddick (1975) stressed that a collaborative and trusting relationship with the client was crucial if tests were to be used as transformative tools with clients.

Clinicians' trust in the client is enhanced when there are no secondary gains for the client from the assessment process or reasons why testing could be used against the client by referring professionals. He advocated for exploration with the client of their reasons for participating in an assessment and believed that clients' goals for the assessment should be framed as assessment questions. In his practice, he first collected clients' assessment questions. Next, he talked with clients about their test responses, asking them to expand on their meaning, and then discussed results with clients and third parties (both individually and, when necessary, together). He also integrated the client's disagreements into the written report for third parties.

Constance Fischer: A Human Science Approach to Psychological Assessment

The changes in the assessment practice previously described were accompanied by a revision of the philosophical view of testing and psychological assessment. A fundamental author in this regard was Constance Fischer (1970), who criticized the prevailing reductionist philosophy of science applied in the assessment field and advocated for a shift to a "human science" perspective. She highlighted that causal determinism, which prevailed in the assessment field, led psychologists to consider human motives and needs as "real" stances existing "within" people, which could be analyzed by abstinent and neutral observers (i.e., assessors), who could understand clients objectively. Fischer believed that this perspective should be abandoned, as it was leading to much of the criticism about testing and assessment. Instead, she advocated for replacing causal determinism with a human science perspective as a foundation of psychological assessment. She believed that such a shift could lead to positive modifications in the assessment practice, by acknowledging the role of the clinician's subjectivity and of the relationship between clinician and client. This shift would also allow assessors to consider the influence of context in the emergence of the phenomena that were observed during the assessment sessions and through the assessment results. From Fischer's perspective, the clinician and the client's joint observations about the client's way of responding to the test materials would become valuable information. She also described how different tests can trigger different behaviors in clients, as happens in different real-life contexts, and those should be taken into consideration when interpreting test results.

In some of her papers (1977, 1979), Fischer used phenomenology (Heidegger, 1962; Husserl, 1962) as a framework for her approach to testing. She strived to use descriptions rather than definitions, to value understanding more than explaining, and to intervene rather than passively observe. Assessors, in this framework, engage clients in exploring the relationship among the test data, the client's interpretations, and the goals of the assessment. During this exploration, clinician and client would go through a hermeneutic circle (Fischer, 2000), linking test results to the client's subjective feelings and opinions and to the shared experiences and observations developed during the assessment. In this way, they would together unpack meanings multiple times, seeing and checking different options in each iteration.

Fischer is the seminal author of collaborative assessment. Her work has been highly influential to the development of TA theory and techniques, to the extent that Finn himself has described TA as semi-structured form of collaborative assessment (Finn, 2007). Fischer provided a solid philosophical framework that was welcomed by assessors who felt that psychological assessment did not need to be a cold, aloof application of standardized procedures in a laboratory setting. She also influenced assessment practices, identifying multiple ways to help clients connect their test performances to relevant aspects of their daily lives. Moreover, she designed ways to support clients in finding behavioral alternatives to approach the test demands, which could then be implemented in their lives outside the assessor's office. Fischer, through her writings and her personal connection with Stephen Finn, represented a source of inspiration for the core ideas of TA (Finn, personal communication, 2019).

Leonard Handler: A Pioneer of Therapeutic Assessment

Leonard Handler was a clinical psychologist, researcher, and faculty member at the University of Tennessee, who focused much of his work on the integration of assessment and therapy (Handler, 2010). In the 1960s, he began working as an assessor and therapist at the Dearborn VA Hospital outpatient clinic, where he spent time discussing with clients their responses to tests through a variety of "Testing of the Limits" techniques borrowed from Bruno Klopfer's approach to the Rorschach. Later in his career, he started calling this set of techniques the "extended inquiry," a term that now defines one of the fundamental steps of TA (Finn & Smith, 2016; see Chapter 6).

In his assessments, Handler was also interested in knowing the client's background, thoughts, and feelings, in contrast to the VA policy that was "for the social worker to obtain the patient's history, the psychologist to do the testing, and the psychiatrist to make the final decision concerning ward placement" (Handler, 2010, p. 6). Handler also believed that continuing to work in therapy with assessment clients would be more beneficial to them than transferring them to a new therapist. Such an approach was innovative in a time when it was commonly believed that the relationship developed with the client during an assessment could impair subsequent treatment if done by the same professional.

Handler developed a friendship with Stephen Finn and Connie Fischer and became an active member of the Collaborative and Therapeutic Assessment community for almost 15 years (Finn & Smith, 2016). In this community of clinicians, teachers, and researchers interested in Collaborative Assessment and TA theories and practices, Handler found fertile ground for his trust in the value and wisdom of the client, his desire to use tests in alternative ways when it was helpful to clients, and his belief in the therapeutic power of psychological tests.

Stephen E. Finn: The Development of Therapeutic Assessment

In his 2007 book, Stephen Finn described the process by which he developed TA. The first important step toward the development of the model was Finn's observation that at times assessments could have a positive impact on clients, which made him curious about how to make this happen more often (Finn & Tonsager, 2002). Since Finn had witnessed clients responding therapeutically to test feedback, he first focused on the last step of TA, the Summary/Discussion Session (see Chapter 9). The challenges of sharing with clients relevant information about their test results prompted Finn (1996) to develop an empirically researched strategy to organize test findings called the "Levels of Information." Finn's heuristic was based on self-verification theory (Swann, 1997; see Chapter 1), which posits that people are more willing to take in information that confirms their preexisting self-views or schemas (even when this information is negative), and less willing to accept feedback that contradicts these views. In Finn's extrapolation from this theory, Level 1 Information is assessment data that is familiar to the client and congruent with their existing self-views. Level 2 Information differs somewhat from clients' current self-views, but does not produce undue anxiety and does not mobilize the client's defenses when shared. Level 3 Information significantly differs from clients' current self-views and, without proper preparation, will raise clients' anxiety, resulting in a rejection of the findings or, worse, a disintegration experience (see Chapters 1 and 8). Often, clients are not ready to integrate Level 3 Information at the end of an assessment. In fact, it requires a strong therapeutic alliance and time to prepare clients to accept feedback that is significantly discrepant from their self-views. To increase the likelihood of clients accepting Level 3 Information, Finn proposed that assessors should always start the discussion of the test results by providing Level 1 Information, followed by Level 2 Information, and–when necessary and only if clients are open to learning more–eventually Level 3 Information.

Collecting Assessment Questions (AQs; see Chapter 5) at the beginning of the assessment process was the second step that Finn (2007) included in the TA model. He realized that some aspects of clients' narratives were more open to change than others and that collecting clients' AQs could help assessors identify and understand where these narratives were more flexible and modifiable. Finn understood that asking clients about the areas of their lives (i.e., the parts of their narratives) that they had doubts about also prepared clients to eventually attend to and integrate Level 3 Information. Importantly, collecting clients' AQs at the beginning of a TA had the power to both decrease their anxiety about the assessment and increase their curiosity.

Subsequently, Finn added to the TA model the use of an individualized written feedback TA letter that summarizes the assessment results and the answers to the client's AQs (see Chapter 10). This letter was sent to the client after the oral feedback that took place during the Summary/Discussion Session. The benefits of using individualized letters were later supported in a study by Lance and Krishnamurthy (2003), who concluded that providing clients with both oral and written feedback was more beneficial to clients than solely providing one type of feedback.

Finn (2007) then formalized the principles for selecting and administering standardized tests and transforming them into therapeutic experiences. He understood that clients were more prone to engage fully in an assessment when the choice of the testing reflected their major concerns (i.e., their AQs), meaning that the tests were face valid for the client. While test administration always followed standardized procedures, after each test, Finn engaged clients in expanding and reflecting on their test responses and connecting them to their AQs and their lives outside the assessment. Here he integrated Handler's "Extended Inquiry," mentioned above.

Another unique element included by Finn in the assessment process was the Assessment Intervention Session (AIS; see Chapter 8). Finn was inspired to add this type of session by the examples of the creative and transformative application of tests used by Fischer (1985/1994), who often abandoned the standardized procedures of testing to help clients find viable new pathways and change for the better. While Finn wanted to have a therapeutic impact on clients, he also did not want to lose valuable nomothetic data obtained by using tests in standardized ways. He also did not want to limit the effectiveness of tests as authoritative sources of useful information for clients. Hence, Finn postponed the use of test materials as means of therapeutic interventions until after the standardized testing phase was completed. He also developed the AIS to help clients who arrived at the end of the assessment still unable to assimilate Level 3 Information. For this reason, the AIS happens after the standardized testing is completed and before the discussion of the test results. In this session, the assessor plans an activity using test materials to "re-create" in the room the key problematic issues or behaviors identified in the test results. During the AIS, the assessor works to help clients explore these issues and, once the client gains insight, support them in practicing novel solutions. In this way, the AIS helps assessors prepare clients to understand and assimilate the answers to their AQs that will be discussed in the Summary/Discussion Session.

The last element of TA formalized by Finn (2007) was the Follow-up Session (see Chapter 11). This step was incorporated after several clients, mainly those who did not attend further treatment after the TA, requested a session several months after receiving the feedback letter. Finn's experience was that these "single" sessions had the potential to bolster the changes that clients achieved during and after the TA, and provided an opportunity for clients to further enhance the developing, new narrative.

In conclusion, TA is the synthesis of over 70 years of thinking and experimentation on how to use tests in creative and beneficial ways for clients. The shifts in the professional and scientific context during the second half of the 1990s and the beginning of the 2000s created a favorable path for Finn to elaborate and expand several techniques for using tests collaboratively and therapeutically with clients and to provide a comprehensive theory for their use.

References

Appelbaum, S. A. (1976). The dangerous edge of insight. *Psychotherapy: Theory, Research & Practice, 13*(3), 202–206. doi: 10.1037/h0088340

Baker, G. (1964). A therapeutic application of psychodiagnostic test results. *Journal of Projective Techniques & Personality Assessment, 28*(1), 3–8.

Brodsky, S. L. (1972). Shared results and open files with the client. *Professional Psychology, 3*(4), 36.

Brown, E. C. (1972). Assessment from a humanistic perspective. *Psychotherapy: Theory, Research, and Practice, 9,* 103–106.

Craddick, R. A. (1975). Sharing oneself in the assessment procedure. *Professional Psychology, 6*(3), 279–282. doi: 10.1037/0735-7028.6.3.279

Finn, S. E. (1996). *Manual for using the MMPI-2 as a therapeutic intervention.* University of Minnesota Press.

Finn, S. E. (2007). *In our clients' shoes: Theory and techniques of Therapeutic Assessment.* Erlbaum.

Finn, S. E., & Smith, J. D. (2016). Leonard Handler's enduring contributions to Therapeutic Assessment. *The TA Connection, 4*(1), 18–23.

Finn, S. E., & Tonsager, M. E. (2002). How Therapeutic Assessment became humanistic. *The Humanistic Psychologist, 30*(1–2), 10–22. doi: 10.1080/08873267.2002.9977019

Fischer, C. (1970). The testee as co-evaluator. *Journal of Counseling Psychology, 17,* 70–76.

Fischer, C. (1977). Historical relations of psychology as an object-science and subject-science: Toward psychology as a human science. *Journal of the History of the Behavioral Sciences, 13,* 369–378.

Fischer, C. (1979). Individualized assessment and phenomenological psychology. *Journal of Personality Assessment, 43,* 115–122.

Fischer, C. (1985/94). *Individualizing psychological assessment.* Routledge. (Originally published by Brooks Cole.)

Fischer, C. (2000). Collaborative, individualized assessment. *Journal of Personality Assessment, 74,* 2–14.

Handler, L. (2010). A psychologist grows in Brooklyn: Reflections from the past. *Journal of Personality Assessment, 85*(1), 1–16.

Harrower, M. (1956). Projective counseling—a psychotherapeutic technique. *American Journal of Psychotherapy, 10,* 74–86.

Heidegger, M. (1962). *Being and Time.* Blackwell Publishing.

Husserl, E. (1962). *Ideas: General introduction to pure phenomenology.* Collier. (Original work published 1913)

Jourard, S. (1968). *Disclosing man to himself.* Van Nostrand Reinhold.

Lance, B. R., & Krishnamurthy, R. (2003). *A comparison of the effectiveness of three modes of MMPI-2 test feedback.* In A. Caldwell (Chair), "MMPI-2/MMPI-A." Paper presented at the Annual Meeting of the Society for Personality Assessment, San Francisco, CA.

Leary, T. (1970). The diagnosis of behavior and the diagnosis of experience. In A. Mahler (Ed.). *New approaches to personality classification.* Columbia University Press.

Luborsky, L. (1953). Self-interpretation of the TAT as a clinical technique. *Journal of Projective Techniques, 17,* 217–223.

Mosak, H. H., & Gushurst, R. S. (1972). Some therapeutic uses of psychologic testing. *American Journal of Psychotherapy, 26*(4), 539–546.

Munter, P. O. (1975). Psychobiographical assessment. *Journal of Personality Assessment, 39*(4), 424–428. doi: 10.1207/s15327752jpa3904_18

Murray, H. A. (1943). *Thematic Apperception Test Manual.* Harvard University Press.

Nadolsky, J. (1966). Diagnosis in rehabilitation counseling: An existential approach. *Rehabilitation Literature, 33,* 66–75.

Nadolsky, J. (1969). The existential in vocational evaluation. *Journal of Rehabilitation, 35*(3), 22–24.

Richman, J. (1967). Reporting diagnostic test results to patients and their families. *Journal of Projective Techniques and Personality Assessment, 31*(3), 62–70.

Shectman, F. (1979). Problems in communicating psychological understanding: Why won't they listen to me? *American Psychologist, 34*(9), 781–790. doi: 10.1037/0003-066X.34.9.781

Shevrin, H., & Shectman, F. (1973). The diagnostic process in psychiatric evaluations. *Bulletin of the Menninger Clinic, 37*(5), 451–494.

Sugarman, A. (1978). Is psychodiagnostic assessment humanistic? *Journal of Personality Assessment, 42*(1), 11–21. doi: 10.1207/s15327752jpa4201_2

Swann, W. B. (1997). The trouble with change: Self-verification and allegiance to the self. *Psychological Science, 8,* 177–180.

Szasz, T. S. (1960). The myth of mental illness. *American Psychologist, 15*(2), 113–118.

3   Research on Therapeutic Assessment

Therapeutic Assessment (TA) is described by Finn (2007) as a semi-structured model of assessment and intervention based on several steps (see Chapter 2). Despite the clarity of the model's definition, its implementation in clinical practice and research has at times been confusing and difficult to evaluate. The literature on using psychological tests in a therapeutic manner has focused not only on TA as developed by Finn (2007; see, for example, Aschieri & Smith, 2012) but more frequently on adapted, shorter versions of TA. For example, Finn and Tonsager (1992) is widely cited as one of the original studies on TA, and they examined the effects of collecting clients' Assessment Questions (AQs) and conducting a collaborative feedback session. Collecting AQs and being collaborative during the final discussion are steps in the TA model, but there are also steps that were not studied as part of Finn and Tonsager's research. This same abbreviated version of TA was also examined by other researchers such as Newman and Greenway (1997) and Essig and Kelly (2013).

In organizing and presenting the research on TA in this chapter, we considered variabiliities in the model's application as described above, and established criteria to determine which studies included full TAs that followed the model and which did not.

With these considerations in mind, we grouped our summary of the research into five sections. In the first section, we summarize published studies comparing what we define as a full TA, which is consistent with the choices of Durosini and Aschieri (2021), and a control condition. Studies with a full TA included:

1   The administration of at least one standardized test/psychological measure.
2   An individualized, collaborative feedback session with clients.
3   At least one additional TA element among the following: (a) Collection of clients' AQs, (b) Extended Inquiry (EI), (c) Assessment Intervention Session (AIS), (d) feedback planned according to Finn's levels of information, (e) written feedback in the form of a letter, or (f) interaction with the client's larger system (e.g., the referring professional).

The second section includes studies that focused on various aspects of TA, but the application of the model does not meet the criteria described above. To increase consistency in the presentation of this research we focus on between-group differences on dependent variables measured at the last data point of the study. We made this choice because many studies comparing TA with other conditions track the outcome variables at different points in time (e.g., at the onset of the treatment, at the end, and after a follow-up period). In the third section, we present repeated-measures quasi-

DOI: 10.4324/9780429202797-4

experimental single case studies and aggregated single case studies on TA. The fourth section includes qualitative research on TA. Last, we summarize the findings from a recent meta-analysis by Durosini and Aschieri (2021).

TA Compared to Control Conditions

The studies summarized in this section show the efficacy of TA, or of single aspects of it, in improving client's symptomatology, self-esteem, and psychological functioning, and variables related to client-clinician alliance.

Comparing TA and Control Conditions on Variables Related to Individual Psychological Functioning and Alliance with Professionals

Two early studies compared TA to a supportive therapy intervention with university students asking for psychological counseling; both showed that TA significantly reduced client-reported symptomatology and increased self-esteem in the TA group compared with the control group (Finn & Tonsager, 1992; Newman & Greenway, 1997). In a different study, the addition of TA to a manualized cognitive-behavioral treatment for borderline personality disorder (BPD) produced a moderate to large significant decrease in the affective instability and suicidal ideation of clients with BPD compared to a control group who received only the BPD treatment (Morey et al., 2010).

Studies comparing TA with traditional information-gathering models of assessment have found that TA produced greater engagement, higher levels of agreement on treatment goals and tasks, stronger alliance with the assessor, better compliance with treatment recommendations, and a stronger therapeutic alliance with the therapist in subsequent outpatient psychotherapy (Ackerman et al., 2000; Hilsenroth et al., 2002, 2004).

TA with adults in an inpatient treatment program for substance use disorders was compared to a control group who only participated in an initial session, testing, and one-month follow-up session (Blonigen et al., 2015). Participants in the TA group showed a moderately higher treatment satisfaction and perception of program support. Also, their relationships with peers improved, as did the overall alliance with the program.

A few studies have tested variables related to both individual functioning and to therapeutic alliance. Essig and Kelly (2013) compared TA and a traditional assessment with clients at a career counseling service at a large Midwestern university in the United States. The results showed that both conditions were equally helpful in increasing the client's decision-making and confidence, and in decreasing their anxiety. Furthermore, participants in the TA condition had a higher level of awareness of both their professional strengths and preferences, when compared to participants in the traditional assessment condition.

De Saeger et al. (2014) compared TA with a goal-focused intervention designed to motivate clients with severe personality disorders to attend subsequent treatment. Compared to the control group, participants receiving TA had greater levels of satisfaction, and higher expectations that the treatment they were about to receive would be helpful. They also had a greater awareness of the topics to address in that subsequent treatment. These clients showed a marginally stronger therapeutic alliance with the TA clinician, when compared with the clients-clinician alliance in the control condition. However, the TA procedure did not lead to decreased symptom severity or these severely disturbed clients.

Comparing Selected Aspects of TA and Control Conditions

Three studies tested the effect of providing individualized oral and/or written feedback to university students compared either to (1) a general discussion about the test instrument used in the study (Allen et al., 2003) or (2) no feedback (Aldea et al., 2010; Schnabel et al., 2016). In two of the studies, results showed that participants receiving individualized feedback rated the relationship with the assessor as more positive (Allen et al., 2003; Aldea et al., 2010). Participants also had a higher level of satisfaction with the feedback (Allen et al., 2003) and lower levels of distress and emotional reactivity than the control group (Aldea et al., 2010). The clients who participated in a collaborative assessment also reported better self-understanding and, to a lesser degree, better self-esteem and self-competence because of the feedback (Allen et al., 2003). The third study focused on how individualized feedback impacted students' intercultural competence and readiness to change, and the authors found that such feedback produced large, statistically significant differences in intercultural competence, self-confidence, and self-understanding (Schnabel et al., 2016).

Another study focused on three groups of adults in inpatient psychiatric treatment, all of whom received the usual group therapy, medication management, and psychoeducation. One group received only this standard treatment, one group also had supportive individual counseling, and another group also participated in a brief TA. The results indicated superior outcomes for patients receiving TA in terms of satisfaction with treatment and alliance with professionals (Little & Smith, 2008).

Table 3.1 provides more details of the features of each study and the research results.

Repeated-Measures Quasi-Experimental Single-Case Studies

Single-case quasi-experiments on TA—where clients are formally tracked over time and time series analysis is used to assess significant changes—have played a significant role in TA research. Published single-cases have involved various types of clients and issues, such as a young adult female with academic, self-esteem, and interpersonal problems (Aschieri & Smith, 2012), a middle-aged woman experiencing anxiety and depressive symptoms following successful treatment for stage IV melanoma (Smith & George, 2012), a client who received a diagnosis of complex post-traumatic stress disorder (CPTSD; Tarocchi et al., 2013), a client diagnosed with persistent complicated bereavement disorder (PCBD) associated with major depressive disorder (MDD) and post-traumatic stress disorder (PTSD; Durosini et al., 2017), and a university student reporting emotional disconnection and difficulties expressing anger (Fantini & Smith, 2018). All these clients participated in research using a time-series analysis design, where they regularly rated individualized variables connected to their difficulties, such as anxiety, loneliness, distress, despair, anger, and emotional disconnection. In each study, the ratings were collected during a baseline-period before the TA, during the TA, and for several days or weeks after the end of the TA. Some

Table 3.1 Studies on Variables Related to Individual Symptoms, Self-esteem, and Therapeutic Alliance: TA Compared to Control Conditions

Authors	Participants	TA/experimental condition	Control condition	Results
Ackerman et al. (2000)	Clients at an outpatient university-based community clinic.	First session: Interview and testing. Second session: Interview and testing. Clients completed additional testing between second and third sessions. Third session: Discussion of the test results with an individualized, collaborative feedback.	First session: Semi-structured interview. Second session: Testing (Additional session: Some clients did additional testing). Fourth session: Feedback.	Less likely premature termination of subsequent treatment ($d = .42$) in the TA group compared to the control group.
Blonigen et al. (2015)	Clients with a substance use disorder in an inpatient treatment program.	First session: Clients' AQs and testing. Second session: Discussion of the test results and answers to AQs. Third session: 1-month follow-up.	Short intervention. First session: Collection of background information and self-report testing. Second session: 1-month follow-up, discussion of the test results and answers to AQs.	Moderate to large higher ratings of satisfaction and alliance with the treatment program (d from .50 to .74) in the TA group compared to the control group. Longer (but not statistically significant) retention in the program for the TA group ($d = .26$).
De Saeger 2014)	Clients in both inpatient and outpatient units with personality disorders in a specialized clinic for PD treatment.	First session: Clients' AQs and testing. Second session: Testing. Third session: Assessment Intervention Session (AIS). Fourth session: Discussion	First session: Enhancement of motivation for treatment and psycho-education. Second session: Discussion of the client's main problem. Third session: Focus on clients' dilemmas of change. Fourth session: Reframing of	Moderate to large higher ratings on new awareness, satisfaction, and expectation for further treatment (d from .39 to 67) in the TA group compared to the control group. No differences in symptom change between the conditions.

(Continued)

Table 3.1 (Continued)

Authors	Participants	TA/experimental condition	Control condition	Results
		of the test results and answer to AQs.	the presenting problem and subsequent goal setting.	
Essig & Kelly (2013)	Outpatient clients seeking career counseling at a university counseling center.	First session: Clients' AQs and testing. Second session: Discussion of the test results and answer to AQs.	First session: Interview to gather information about career indecision and testing. Second session: Standardized feedback.	Larger reduction in career choice anxiety ($d = .56$), small to large improvements in self-efficacy and vocational identity ($d = .26$ and .65) in the TA condition compared to control condition.
Finn & Tonsager (1992)	Outpatient college students at the University of Texas Counseling and Mental Health Center.	First session: Clients' AQs and testing. Second session: Discussion of the test results and answer to AQs. Third session: 2-week follow-up.	First session: Brief interview to discuss the client's current concerns and testing. Second session: Further discussion of the client's concerns. Third session: 2-week follow-up.	Larger reduction in client-reported symptomatology and more hope ($d = .85$ and .68), moderately higher self-esteem ($d = .45$) and better relationship with the assessor ($d = .27$) in the TA group compared to the control group.
Hilsenroth et al. (2002)	Clients of two university-based outpatient community clinics.	First session: Interview and testing. Second session: Interview and testing. Clients completed additional testing between second and third sessions. Third session: Discussion of the test results with individualized, collaborative feedback.	First session: Interview. Second session: Testing. Third session: Feedback.	Clients in the TA group rated moderately higher scores on total alliance ($d = .51$), agreement on goals and tasks ($d = .66$) and bond ($d = .50$) compared to the control group. Clinicians in the TA group rated their clients significantly higher on shared goals ($d = .80$), bond ($d = .74$), and working alliance ($d = .69$).
Hilsenroth et al. (2004)	Follow-up and re-analysis of data from Hilsenroth et al. 2002.	Same as above.	Same as above.	Clients in the experimental group had a significantly stronger therapeutic alliance in subsequent psychotherapy

				Results
Newman & Greenway (1997)	Outpatient college students at the Monash University Counseling Service.	First session: Clients' AQs and testing. Second session: Discussion of the test results and answers to AQs.	First session: Interview on presenting problems, client's AQs and testing. Second session: Additional testing. Third session (after measurement of dependent variables): Discussion of the test results and answers to AQs.	($d = .52$), with alliance components ranging from $d = .17$ for collaboration to $d = .66$ for agreement on goals and tasks of treatment. Significant increase in self-esteem ($d = .26$) and increased reduction in self-reported symptoms and distress ($d = .44$) after 2 weeks follow-up in the TA condition compared to the control group.
Morey et al. (2010)	Adult outpatients with BPD diagnosis and suicidal intention at the Texas A&M University Psychology Clinic.	First session: Clients' AQs and testing. Second session: Discussion of the test results and answers to AQs. Five sessions of Manual Assisted Cognitive Therapy (MACT).	First session: Client introduction to the MACT. Five sessions of a MACT.	Moderate to large significant decrease in various measures of affective instability (d from .21 to 1.09) and suicidality (d from .44 to 1.48) in TA combined with therapy compared to only therapy. No differences in treatment retention over a six-week period between the two conditions.

Notes: d = Cohen's d. To increase the effect size consistency of the client's reported ratings among studies, we referred to Table 1, Durosini and Aschieri (2021); PD = personality disorders; AQs = Assessment Questions; BPD = borderline personality disorder.

clients started therapy right after the TA and continued the ratings for a period during their post-TA treatment.

The analyses in all these studies revealed significant improvements, in some cases starting with the beginning of the TA (Aschieri & Smith, 2012; Smith & George, 2012; Tarocchi et al., 2013). When clients continued the ratings during a post-TA treatment, the results showed that improvements were maintained during the subsequent therapy (Smith & George, 2012; Tarocchi et al., 2013). Interestingly, in other cases, TA did not produce a linear decrease in symptoms, but instead a transient period of worsening due to clients' increased emotional awareness during the process, which was then followed by some improvement (Durosini et al., 2017; Fantini & Smith, 2018). Table 3.2 provides more details about each study and the research results.

Smith et al. (2014) published the only aggregated, repeated-measures single-case experiment with adults, involving ten participants. In this research, all clients were in ongoing psychotherapy, all suffered from internalizing symptoms (e.g., anxiety, depression), and all were referred for TA by their psychotherapists. The authors examined the effectiveness of TA in reducing their symptomatic distress and improving the processes and outcomes of the psychotherapy. The participants rated their individualized presenting problems daily during the baseline, TA intervention, and follow-up period. The results indicated that participation in a mid-therapy consultation using TA coincided with a significant reduction in clients' symptomatic distress, with significant improvements occurring for the majority of the participants. Furthermore, the joint feedback to clients and referring therapists was followed by a significant increase in the working alliance between the clients and therapists, compared to their alliance ratings prior to the TA. This study suggests that clients who complete a TA during psychotherapy can greatly improve their rate of change during their treatment.

Qualitative Studies of TA

Two qualitative studies explored individual's subjective experience of TA. Smith and Egan (2017) focused on doctoral students' experiences of learning TA and of conducting a brief TA in the context of a required course in personality assessment, while also exploring the experiences of the clients whom the students assessed. At the end of the course, students responded to open-ended questions about their experience with the course and how they experienced the TAs they conducted. Clients were students from a separate graduate program who were invited to use a TA to work on their current interpersonal and mental health concerns. At the end of the TA, they also responded to open-ended questions about their experience. Assessors' responses were coded using content analysis. Clients' responses were coded according to the four content areas reflected in the Assessment Questionnaire (AQ; Finn et al., 2000; see Chapter 10). Smith and Egan found that student assessors unanimously stressed the utility of TA in their work with clients. Ninety percent of the respondents began to consider personality assessment as a humanistic, collaborative, and ethical professional endeavor, 80% described TA as a rewarding, enjoyable, and helpful experience, and 60% mentioned the congruence of TA with their egalitarian values and professional and personal identities. Students also identified specific difficulties implementing TA, such as time management challenges and containing feedback that could overwhelm clients. The student assessors also came to realize that they needed a

Table 3.2 Summary of Repeated-Measures Single-case Studies

Authors	Client's description, presenting problems, and background information	Structure of the TA	Qualitative description of the effect of TA on client	Measures of outcome and process
Aschieri & Smith (2012)	Client: A young adult female. Presenting problems: Academic problems, low self-esteem, and loneliness. The client blamed herself for her problems, yet could acknowledge that one of her main issues was how hard she was on herself. Background information: At the onset of the assessment, the client was living alone in an apartment far from home.	The TA included: 1 Collection of AQs. 2 Administration and EI of Rorschach and the EMP. 3 Summary/Discussion Session. 4 Follow-up Session, two months after the previous session. No formal AIS was included. The TA (up to the Summary/ Discussion session) was completed in 28 days.	The client's self-blaming narrative shifted towards a more compassionate narrative about her struggles. The client realized that she was repeatedly abandoned by her parents as a child and coped by blaming herself, rather than accurately seeing her parents as failing to protect her and provide appropriate nurturing. The client initially felt alone and incapable of feeling affection and receiving it. At the Follow-up Session, the client showed up with a vivacious puppy. She also had made connections with new friends and moved into a new house, which she shared with another student.	The client showed improvements on a composite measure of functioning, which included daily ratings of anxiety, loneliness, recognition of love for herself, recognition of love from others, and the degree to which she was hard on herself ($r = -.46$). Further, an analysis of the slope of her symptomatology ratings over time revealed a significant trajectory of improvement that began with the first session of the TA ($r = .58$).
Smith & George (2012)	Client: A middle-aged woman. Presenting problems: The client lamented anxiety and depressive symptoms, felt incapable of "moving forward" and complained about her emotional volatility, which was in stark contrast to the emotional sturdiness she had felt before	The TA included: 1 Collection of AQs. 2 Over a two-week period, there was a collection of background information, which was used as baseline data. 3 Administration of the EMP and EI.	Through the TA, the client had a growth-enhancing experience of using interpersonal support to contain and soothe her psychological pain and discomfort. This proved to be important since the AAP revealed an unresolved (disorganized) attachment status. The client disclosed that in	The client had a significant reduction in her symptoms immediately after she began the TA ($r = -.61$). The improvements the client experienced during the assessment were maintained during the subsequent four months of biweekly psychotherapy, but the

(Continued)

Table 3.2 (Continued)

Authors	Client's description, presenting problems, and background information	Structure of the TA	Qualitative description of the effect of TA on client	Measures of outcome and process
	cancer. Background information: The client was seeking a TA after the successful treatment of stage IV melanoma.	4 Administration of the AAP and EI. 5 AIS. 6 Summary/Discussion Session. The client was given a TA letter and a Follow-up Session occurred during the psychotherapy that began immediately after the Summary/Discussion Session.	addition to suffering with the trauma related to having cancer and receiving medical treatment, she also experienced familial trauma in childhood. The TA helped the client develop a more coherent and compassionate story about herself, as a sturdy woman with a complicated past that she tried to set aside, but that was flooding her with unresolved and unintegrated feelings due to her medical conditions.	woman did not continue to improve during this period. Although change occurred early in this case, the authors stressed that long-term treatment helped avoid a relapse of the client's symptoms.
Tarocchi, Aschieri, Fantini, & Smith (2013)	Client: A 37-year-old woman. Presenting problems: The client had Complex Post-traumatic Stress Disorder. At the time of the assessment she felt desperate, fatigued, unable to contend with her own expectations in life, and she viewed herself as a failure without hope for the future. Background information: Her past experiences included an abusive father, running away from a non-protective family environment at 14 years of	The TA included: 1 Collection of AQs. 2 Administration of the MMPI-2. 3 Administration of the EMP and EI (2 sessions). 4 Administration and EI on the AAP and Rorschach (three sessions). 5 Summary/Discussion Session. 6 Follow-up Session, 51 days after the Summary/Discussion Session. The TA (up to the Summary/Discussion Session) was completed in 48 days.	The TA helped the client see how her early traumas were connected to her current situation. The client realized she needed to explore feelings connected to the trauma and her relationship with the perpetrator, that she could not previously process for the sake of maintaining dependency on the abuser.	In comparison with baseline, participation in this TA coincided with significant improvements in the client's self-reported level of loneliness ($r = .51$) and despair ($r = .71$). The change in anxiety was moderate but not significant ($r = .37$). However, the composite score, reflecting overall distress, was significantly reduced ($r = .64$). The results also indicated that the effects were maintained during a two-month follow-up

age, occasional use of heroin, becoming a mother at 17 years of age while dating an unstable and violent partner.

period, which was followed by psychotherapy with the assessor.

Durosini, Tarocchi, & Aschieri (2017)

Client: An adult man. Presenting problems: The client received a diagnosis of Persistent Complicated Bereavement Disorder (PCBD) associated with major depressive disorder (MDD) and Post-Traumatic Stress Disorder (PTSD). Background information: The client was married for 25 years with two adolescent children. He did not report psychological or relational problems until the death of his mother, six years prior to the assessment, and of his father one year before the assessment. Both parents died from heart attacks. At the time of the TA he had left his home without providing an explanation to his family, and lamented he could only live in a "ball" that isolated him from others.

The TA included:
1 Collection of AQs.
2 Administration and EI of the MMPI-2-RF (2 sessions).
3 Administration and EI of the EMP (2 sessions).
4 AIS.
5 Summary/Discussion Session.
6 Follow-up Session, 42 days after the Summary/Discussion Session. The TA (up to the Summary/Discussion Session) was completed in 46 days.

The client understood he did not feel worthy of his daughter's love and, by leaving his home, he tried to protect his family from the pain they might have felt when he would have died. He also drew a connection between the "ball" state and its role as a shield against the intolerable pain of his depression. The EMP discussion and the AIS helped the client to process the losses he experienced as a child, and he was able to use the assessor's support to work through feeling sad and powerless. It could be speculated that while emotional numbing protected him from being overwhelmed by loss and despair, it also hindered his grief process. As painful as it was, at the Follow-up Session the client was less depressed and trending steadily toward improvement.

Results suggested a reverse "U" shaped trajectory, in which the assessment did not produce a linear decrease in symptoms, but a transient period of worsening from baseline to intervention ($r = .48$), due to increased emotional awareness during the intervention, followed by moderate improvement (from comparison between intervention and follow up, $r = -.37$).

(Continued)

Table 3.2 (Continued)

Authors	Client's description, presenting problems, and background information	Structure of the TA	Qualitative description of the effect of TA on client	Measures of outcome and process
Fantini & Smith (2018)	Client: A female university student. Presenting problems: Anger management (with her mother), lack of motivation, feeling distant from others, and detached from her emotions. Background information: One year before the assessment, the client learned, eavesdropping on a conversation between her parents, that her mother was dating another man. Despite feeling furious at her mother, the client pretended nothing happened in her family and went on to successfully pass her exams until her parents separated. After the separation, the father became depressed, the mother acted cheerfully, and no one talked about the changes that occurred.	The TA included: 1 Collection of AQs. 2 Administration of the MMPI-2-RF and EI. 3 Administration of the Rorschach and EI. 4 Administration of the EMP and EI. 5 Summary/Discussion Session. 6 Follow-up session, 21 days after the Summary/Discussion Session. The TA (up to the Summary/Discussion Session) was completed in 28 days.	The client was stuck in the bargaining stage of grief for her parents' separation. The EI of her Rorschach responses allowed the client to recognize her use of avoidant strategies in order to protect herself from the risk of losing control of her anger. In order to progress to the acceptance stage, the client would have had to enter a stage of depression. However, perceiving, exploring, and expressing negative emotions was difficult for her based on her Rorschach. Subsequent psychotherapy might have helped her to better recognize and articulate her emotions in a way that she could not do at the time of the assessment.	Results suggested a reverse "U" shaped trajectory, with a peak of symptomatic distress during the week after the EI on the Rorschach compared to previous average ratings ($r = .81$). That EI discussion helped the client enter into contact with the previously dissociated affect states. At the follow-up, the distress returned to similar levels to those present at the baseline ($r = -.73$). However, in the meantime the client learned to use other strategies to regulate her emotions, suggesting an improvement in her wellbeing.

Notes: AQs = Assessment Questions; AIS = Assessment Intervention Session; EMP = Early Memories Procedure (Bruhn, 1992a, b); AAP = Adult Attachment Projective System (George & West, 2012); MMPI-2 = Minnesota Multiphasic Inventory – 2nd Edition (Butcher et al., 2001); MMPI-2-RF = Minnesota Multiphasic Inventory – 2 Revised Form (Ben-Porath & Tellegen, 2008).

more sophisticated theoretical background to be helpful to the clients. All ten clients appreciated the positive and accurate mirroring and the quality of the relationship with the assessor as well as the assessment itself. Eight participants stated that they reached a new understanding about themselves and understood how the assessment results related to their lives. While only present in a small portion of the responses, eight participants identified negative feelings connected to discussing childhood memories and to the pace of the assessment.

De Saeger et al. (2016) qualitatively explored ten clients' experience of a TA; all were participants in a published randomized control trial (De Saeger et al., 2014—described above). De Saeger conducted in-depth interviews of clients focused on memorable, specific, positive, and negative aspects of their TAs. Interviews were transcribed and analyzed using the Consensual Qualitative Research design (CQR; Hill, 2012; Hill et al., 1997). The primary themes identified in clients' responses included (a) positive relational aspects, (b) new insights into personal dynamics, (c) a sense of empowerment, and (d) validation of self as related to the experience of TA. Positive relational aspects included warm, kind, and pleasant memories of the assessor, and positive feelings about the assessor-client working relationship. In some of the interviews, participants compared the collaboration, equality, and validation they found in the TA experience with their previous treatment experiences, which were described in more negative terms. Assessors' interest in the subjective experiences of patients and the egalitarian atmosphere of TA stood out as fundamental ingredients of the positive relational experience. New insights about personal functioning included understanding intrapsychic dynamics, relational patterns, and the role of shame in hindering clients' abilities to effectively use others for support. TA gave clients a sense of empowerment, promoting their readiness to change and increasing their sense of being actively involved in their treatments. Participants felt validated by the assessors' sincere feedback in the sessions, during the test feedback, and through the narrative report. Interestingly, negative experiences were not directly connected to the TA but to the larger setting in which the TAs took place. For example, many clients were eager to begin treatment immediately after their TAs but were placed on a wait list before they could begin psychotherapy. This and other negative experiences highlight the importance of TA assessors being aware of how their assessments fit in the settings where clients are being served. If possible, assessors will want to ensure that the structure of the treatment setting is consistent with TA's core values.

Meta-analysis of TA

Durosini and Aschieri (2021) conducted a meta-analysis of research on TA, and included only studies in which the TA intervention met the specific criteria previously described in this chapter. A literature search yielded nine studies, containing 491 participants ($N = 220$ in the TA group and $N = 271$ in the control group), and 42 dependent variables. The main outcomes were the treatment process, clients' symptoms, and clients' personal growth. Based on the study characteristics, moderators of TA effectiveness were (1) year of publication, (2) quality of the study, (3) the number of TA elements included, (4) the length of the TA, (5) whether the assessors received supervision, (6) the type of client (i.e., outpatient or inpatient), and (7) whether TA was used as a standalone intervention or was delivered along with other treatments. For treatment process, the random effects three-level analysis showed a statistically significant, medium-to-large effect size equal to $d = 0.47$ (95% CI [0.33; 0.60]; $p < .001$). This suggests that TA increases variables such as therapeutic alliance, clients' desire to change and trust in treatment, and treatment retention. Regarding change in clients' symptoms, analyses revealed that TA had a statistically significant, small-to-moderate mean effect size ($d = .35$, 95% CI [.06; .65]; $p = .022$); furthermore, the moderator analysis showed that TA lead to even more decrease in symptoms when it was combined with another treatment modality. Finally, for clients' personal growth, analysis showed a statistically significant small-to-moderate effect size ($d = .38$, 95% CI [.06; .71]; $p = .028$), suggesting that TA positively affects variables such as self-esteem, self-awareness, and empathy for others.

Durosini and Aschieri concluded that:

> The meta-analysis revealed a moderate to large effect of TA on the clients' perceptions of treatment utility and alliance (*treatment process*) and a moderate effect of TA on the clients' level of symptom severity (*clients' symptoms*) and on the clients' growth during the assessment (*clients' growth*). These results were attained in three or fewer sessions, including one session for the administration of testing, which does not include any active therapeutic ingredient. Effects of such a short intervention are not influenced by such potentially important variables as the overall length of the TA, supervision, or the typology of clients. The only significant moderating variable was the addition of TA to another treatment. This suggests that TA allows clients to benefit more from the other treatment, or that they enter into the other treatment feeling better already better and continue to improve their condition (pp. 969–970).

Having reviewed the published studies on TA with adults clients, we know turn to explain how the research answers three questions about TA: To what extent is TA effective? Which type of clients benefit the most from TA? What is it about TA that makes it therapeutic?

To What Extent is TA Effective?

Results of the meta-analysis, between-group comparisons, and repeated measures single-case studies support the efficacy of TA on dimensions connected with symptomatic distress, problematic behaviors, self-enhancement (i.e., increased self-esteem), and motivation for treatment and alliance with the assessor and subsequent therapists. Changes are moderate to large. The number of TA sessions used in these studies ranged from two to eight. Also, in most of the between-group comparisons, the TA intervention included only the formulation of AQs and collaborative feedback, rather than the complete TA model. All these results suggest that TA can be an effective brief intervention for many clients and that the benefit to them may occur more rapidly than other types of psychotherapeutic intervention. We wholeheartedly agree with what Poston and Hanson (2010) concluded:

> Clinicians should familiarize themselves with therapeutic models of assessment … [and] seek out continuing-education training related to these models. Those who engage in assessment and testing as usual may miss out, it seems, on a golden opportunity to effect client change and enhance clinically important treatment processes (p. 210).

Which type of clients most benefit from TA? TA has proved to be effective with various types of patients in different settings. These include clients receiving outpatient care presenting with various diagnoses, clients in residential treatment for substance abuse, and clients in inpatient settings. The clients who have benefited have had various mental health issues such as unresolved childhood trauma, suicidal risk, and other comorbid conditions.

Between-group comparisons suggest clients show moderate changes after a TA, while single case studies add valuable information regarding two trajectories of change. For clients suffering from acute distress who are emotionally dysregulated, TA has a cumulative effect, and their well-being and self-efficacy increases across sessions (Smith, 2013). For some clients whose problems in living are connected to repressed emotions and rigid defense mechanisms, participation in a TA may temporarily increase their subjective distress while they experience previously dissociated affective states, but this distress is typically resolved by the end of the assessment.

What is it about TA that Makes it Therapeutic?

Unfortunately, there is limited information from published studies to answer this question. Based on Durosini and Aschieri's (2021) meta-analysis and De Saeger et al.'s (2016) qualitative study, it appears that more than the actual steps of TA, what affects clients is how assessors express the underlying values and principles of the model. When test results are used to serve the client's goals, and assessment sessions are characterized by collaboration, respect, and equality, clients feel a stronger relationship with the assessor and experience a different kind of respect and validation that may not be present in other treatment experiences. Based on clients' comments, it also seems that new insights are possible because shame and previous traumatic experiences are actively addressed by an active, caring assessor who uses psychological tests to re-conceptualize the clients' needs and promote their development.

Single-case and qualitative studies highlight several features of successful TAs and what makes them therapeutic. First, the collection of individualized AQs increases clients' investment in the process and leads to a more active and less defended stance toward the information derived from the testing. Second, when new information from the assessment is provided within a warm and respectful relational framework, this leads to a deepening of clients' emotions and an increase in their self-awareness. Third, in TA, clients' defenses and resistance to change are seen as adaptive mechanisms that clients developed to adjust to their environments. This understanding, which is evident in TA practitioners' goal of finding compassion for clients' dilemmas of change, reduces the likelihood of clients having a negative reaction to the process, and it increases client participation. Taken together, these mechanisms allow clients to make the best use of the new information derived from the TA. They also are able to develop a better capacity to balance epistemic mistrust and epistemic trust with the clinician, and by extension, this helps them take in accurate and relevant information from other important people in their lives.

References

Ackerman, S. J., Hilsenroth, M. J., Baity, M. R., & Blagys, M. D. (2000). Interaction of therapeutic process and alliance during psychological assessment. *Journal of Personality Assessment, 75,* 82–109. doi: 10.1207/S15327752JPA7501_7.

Aldea, M. A., Rice, K. G., Gormley, B., & Rojas, A. (2010). Telling perfectionists about their perfectionism: Effects of providing feedback on emotional reactivity and psychological symptoms. *Behavior Research and Therapy, 48,* 1194–1203. doi: 10.1016/j.brat.2010.09.003.

Allen, A., Montgomery, M., Tubman, J., Frazier, L., & Escovar, L. (2003). The effects of assessment feedback on rapport-building and self-enhancement processes. *Journal of Mental Health Counseling, 25,* 165–181.

Aschieri, F., & Smith, J. D. (2012). The effectiveness of therapeutic assessment with an adult client: A single–case study using a time–series design. *Journal of Personality Assessment, 94,* 1–11.

Ben-Porath, Y. S. , & Tellegen, A. (2008). *MMPI-2: Restructured Form (MMPI-2-RF) manual for administration.* University of Minnesota Press.

Blonigen, D. M., Timko, C., Jacob, T., & Moos, R. H. (2015). Patient-centered feedback on the results of personality testing increases early engagement in residential substance use disorder treatment: a pilot randomized controlled trial. *Addiction Science & Clinical Practice, 10,* 9. doi: 10.1186/s13722-015-0030-9.

Bruhn, A. R. (1992a). The Early Memories Procedure: A projective test of autobiographical memory (Part I). *Journal of Personality Assessment, 58,* 1–15.

Bruhn, A. R. (1992b). The Early Memories Procedure: A projective test of autobiographical memory (Part II). *Journal of Personality Assessment, 58,* 326–346.

Butcher, J. N., Graham, J. R., Ben-Porath, Y. S., Tellegen, A., Dahlstrom, W. G. , & Kaemmer, B. (2001). *Minnesota Multiphasic Personality Inventory-2: Manual for administration, scoring, and interpretation,* revised edition. University of Minnesota Press.

De Saeger, H., Kamphuis, J. H., Finn, S. E., Smith, J. D., Verheul, R., van Busschbach, J. J., Feenstra, D. J., & Horn, E. K. (2014). Therapeutic Assessment promotes treatment readiness but does not affect symptom change in patients with personality disorders: Findings from a randomized clinical trial. *Psychological Assessment, 26,* 474–483. doi: 10.1037/a0035667.

De Saeger, H., Bartak, A., Eder, E. E., & Kamphuis, J. H. (2016). Memorable experiences in Therapeutic Assessment: Inviting the patient's perspective following a pretreatment randomized controlled trial. *Journal of Personality Assessment, 98*(5), 472–479. doi: 10.1080/00223891. 2015.1136314.

Durosini, I., & Aschieri, F. (2021). Therapeutic assessment efficacy: A meta-analysis. *Psychological Assessment, 33*(10), 962–972. doi: 10.1037/pas0001038.

Durosini, I., Tarocchi, A., & Aschieri, F. (2017). Therapeutic Assessment with a client with persistent complex bereavement disorder: A single-case time-series design. *Clinical Case Studies, 16*(4), 295–312. 10.1177/1534650117693942.

Essig, G. N., & Kelly, K. R. (2013). Comparison of the effectiveness of two assessment feedback models in reducing career indecision. *Journal of Career Assessment, 21,* 519–536. doi:10. 1177/1069072712475283.

Fantini, F., & Smith, J. D. (2018). Using R-PAS in the Therapeutic Assessment of a university student with emotional disconnection. In J. Mihura & G. J. Meyer (Eds.), *Using the Rorschach Performance Assessment System (R-PAS)* (pp. 138–157). Guilford Press.

Finn, S. E. (2007). *In our clients' shoes: Theory and techniques of Therapeutic Assessment,* Lawrence Erlbaum Associates.

Finn, S. E., Schroeder, D. G., & Tonsager, M. E. (2000). *The Assessment Questionnaire-2 (AQ-2): A measure of clients' experiences with psychological assessment.* Unpublished manuscript, Center for Therapeutic Assessment.

Finn, S. E., & Tonsager, M. E. (1992). Therapeutic effects of providing MMPI-2 test feedback to college students awaiting psychotherapy. *Psychological Assessment, 4*, 278–287. doi: 10.1037/1040-3590.4.3.278.

George, C. , & West, M. L. (2012). *The Adult Attachment Projective Picture System: Attachment theory and assessment in adults.* Guilford Press.

Herman, J. L. (1992). Complex PTSD: A syndrome in survivors of prolonged and repeated trauma. *Journal of Traumatic Stress, 5*, 377–391. doi: 10.1002/jts.2490050305.

Hill, C. E. (Ed.). (2012). *Consensual qualitative research: A practical resource for investigating social science phenomena.* American Psychological Association.

Hill, C. E., Thompson, B. J., & Williams, E. N. (1997). A guide to conducting consensual qualitative research. *The Counseling Psychologist, 25*, 517–572. doi: 10.1177/0011000097254001.

Hilsenroth, M. J., Ackerman, S. J., Clemence, A. J., Strassle, C. G., & Handler, L. (2002). Effects of structured clinician training on patient and therapist perspectives of alliance early in psychotherapy. *Psychotherapy: Theory, Research, Practice, Training, 39*(4), 309–323. doi: 10.1037/0033-3204.39.4.309.

Hilsenroth, M. J., Peters, E. J., & Ackerman, S. J. (2004). The development of therapeutic alliance during psychology assessment: Patient and therapist perspectives across treatment. *Journal of Personality Assessment, 83*, 331–344. doi: 10.1207/s15327752jpa8303_14.

Little, J. A., & Smith, S. R. (2008). *Collaborative assessment, supportive psychotherapy, or treatment as usual: An analysis of ultra-brief individualized intervention with psychiatric inpatients.* Paper presented at the annual meeting of the Society for Personality Assessment, Chicago, IL.

Morey, L. C., Lowmaster, S. E., & Hopwood, C. J. (2010). A pilot study of manual-assisted cognitive therapy with a therapeutic assessment augmentation for borderline personality disorder. *Psychiatry Research, 178*, 531–535. doi: 10.1016/j.psychres.2010.04.055.

Newman, M. L., & Greenway, P. (1997). Therapeutic effects of providing MMPI-2 test feedback to clients at a university counseling service: A collaborative approach. *Psychological Assessment, 9*(2), 122–131. doi: 10.1037/1040-3590.9.2.122.

Poston, J. M., & Hanson, W. M. (2010). Meta-analysis of psychological assessment as a therapeutic intervention. *Psychological Assessment, 22*, 203–212. doi: 10.1037/a0018679.

Schnabel, D. B. L., Kelava, A., & van de Vijver, F. (2016). The effects of using collaborative assessment with students going abroad: Intercultural competence development, self-understanding, self-confidence, and stages of change. *Journal of College Student Development, 57*(1), 79–94. doi: 10.1353/csd.2016.0000.

Smith, J. D. (2013). The Anatomy of Change in Therapeutic Assessment: A review of Recent Single-Case Time-Series Studies. *TA Connection, 1*(1), 2–6.

Smith, J. D., & Egan, K. N. (2017). Trainee and client experiences of Therapeutic Assessment in a required graduate course: A qualitative analysis. *Journal of Personality Assessment, 99*(2), 126–135. doi: 10.1080/00223891.2015.1077336.

Smith, J. D., Eichler, W. C., Norman, K. R., & Smith, S. R. (2014). The effectiveness of a therapeutic model of assessment for psychotherapy consultation: A pragmatic replicated single-case study. *Journal of Personality Assessment, 97*(3), 261–270. doi: 10.1080/00223891.2014.955917.

Smith, J. D., & George, C. (2012). Therapeutic Assessment case study: Treatment of a woman diagnosed with metastatic cancer and attachment trauma. *Journal of Personality Assessment, 94*(4), 331–344.

Tarocchi, A., Aschieri, F., Fantini, F., & Smith, J. D. (2013). Therapeutic Assessment of complex trauma: A single-case time-series study. *Clinical Case Studies, 12*(3), 228–245. doi: 10.1177/1534650113479442.

Part II

Steps of Therapeutic Assessment with Adult Clients

As described in Part I, Therapeutic Assessment (TA) is a semi-structured intervention aimed at helping clients better understand themselves and their struggles and move forward from stuck places in their lives. A full TA is structured around eight key steps (see Figure 1.1 in Chapter 1), and these will be extensively described in the following chapters. This eight-step model is designed to best meet the needs of clients with an array of problems and adverse life conditions, and the full model is a powerful intervention—especially with difficult clients (e.g., De Saeger et al., 2014). We believe if you incorporate each step of the TA model, this increases the probability of a significant therapeutic impact on your clients' lives.

However, from its inception, Finn and others have emphasized that TA is a semi-structured approach, and that it is possible, and even necessary, to adapt the model (Finn, 2007; Finn et al., 2012). For example, it is not always possible to conduct a full TA because of time or money limitations. This may be especially true in mental health settings where clinicians only have a few sessions with each client, which is insufficient for a full TA. In private practices, clinicians may meet clients who do not have the financial resources to pay for a full TA. In these situations, we encourage assessors to adapt the TA model and choose those steps that fit best for both clients and the work setting. As described in Chapter 3, there is evidence that even a brief TA of two to three sessions can have a considerable therapeutic impact (see Durosini & Aschieri, 2021).

So, as you implement TA with clients, use some parts of TA in your work, even if you are unable to practice the full model. We are convinced that clinicians who incorporate the core values of TA and adopt even a few of the TA techniques will see a considerable improvement in their client outcomes.

DOI: 10.4324/9780429202797-5

4 Initial Contact

Building the Relationship and Providing Informed Consent for TA

The first contact is a starting place for building the therapeutic relationship that is at the core of TA (Finn, 2007). Many relational processes, which more fully unfold during the first session, begin when an individual takes the step of contacting a clinician to ask for help. The potential challenges of building a therapeutic alliance and ways to address them within TA will be more thoroughly explained in Chapter 5, as they primarily apply to the work of the first session. However, an important goal of the first contact with the client is to set the relational frame that will be continued throughout the TA.

Our experience is that potential clients contact us in different ways to inquire about the services we provide or to check our availability for a first session. For simplicity's sake, in this chapter by "first contact" we refer to the first phone call that happens when a client wants to set up an appointment or explore whether a TA is a suitable match. Although other means of communication might be viable entry points to TA, the most common method is a phone call, and a 15–20 minute conversation is often adequate. The in vivo interaction on the phone, with its load of paraverbal information and spontaneous conversation, allows the clinician to begin to understand the client and build a connection. However, the processes we describe can also apply to other types of initial interactions with future clients, such as an in-person or virtual (e.g., Skype or Zoom) meeting.

The Relational Frame: Client Anxiety, Capacity for Trust, and the Clinician's Goals

We see humans as having an inborn need to feel seen, understood, and accepted (Rogers, 1961). All individuals asking for psychological help feel hope about having these needs met, but might also fear judgment and rejection. This is particularly true if such adverse experiences have characterized their past relationships or they have experienced social stigma around mental health issues. If a client has had negative experiences with mental health professionals, they might fear that something similar will happen with the assessor. Such negative expectations work as restraining forces to the client's desire to access help and so make it difficult for many people to take the first step of contacting a clinician.[1] Clients commonly tell us during the unfolding of a TA or a therapy session that they had been contemplating asking for help for some time before actually doing it. Thus, many clients are likely to approach the step

DOI: 10.4324/9780429202797-6

of contacting us with anxiety, some to the point of being hypervigilant about who we are, what we do, and in what ways we can or cannot help. Even if clients have already collected information about us from other sources, their fears might still motivate them to keep a close eye on us to decide whether it is worth the risk of scheduling a first appointment, or if it is safer to disengage.

Clients who have epistemic hypervigilance (EH, Fonagy et al., 2017a, b), as described in Chapter 1, are unlikely to tell us a lot about themselves on the phone before they know us and we pass their relational tests (see Chapter 5). However, if they express some distress while explaining why they are searching for help, we respond in an attuned manner to show that we are attentive listeners who are ready to put ourselves in their shoes. This is the beginning of our work to create an alliance with clients by becoming a trusted other (see Chapter 1, regarding building epistemic trust). Furthermore, we have an ethical obligation to share enough information about our work during the first contact so that clients can make an informed decision (American Psychological Association, 2017). Besides being ethical, clients who have difficulties with trust benefit from developing a strong understanding of what will occur during a TA, as this lowers their anxiety. While some clients directly ask questions about us and our work, others who are more inhibited might not do so, but they still benefit from receiving the same information.

On the other side of the continuum, some potential clients are highly trusting individuals, who approach the first contact with unwarranted openness, or hypovigilance, much like they approach other new relationships. These clients enter the first contact with overly optimistic expectations, hoping that testing alone may solve their problems. Such people rely on their loosely structured or even vague expectations about what is going to happen, and often feel hurt or disappointed when reality turns out to differ from what they thought (Sperber et al., 2010). When they feel betrayed, such individuals typically close up and become hypervigilant or end the relationship. These are clients who tell us at the start of the first call about their trauma history, but if we let them do so, they may feel hurt and let down when they discover we cannot meet them for an appointment until a month later.

In countries where the professional guidelines for psychologists are less structured, providing information during a call about the costs of an assessment or a session might not be a requirement. However, by not sharing this information during the first phone call, clinicians may end up colluding with the hypovigilance of some clients. Later, the client might feel exploited when they are in our office and understand our fee, judging it as too expensive. Therefore, besides our ethical and legal requirements, overly trusting clients benefit from hearing information that allows them to have realistic expectations about our work.

Between the two ends of the continuum (hypervigilance and hypovigilance), there are multiple degrees of vigilance and trust that future clients may exercise regarding us as potential helpers. Within the limits of the first contact, we balance responding to our client's needs for attuned listening with efficient structuring of the phone conversation to provide the required information about a TA. Attending to these objectives is an important step in building a trusting relationship with our potential future client.

Holding the following goals in mind helps us manage the first phone contact in specific ways: (a) To give the clients a first, albeit limited, experience of our way of relating to them; (b) to provide basic information such as cost, the length of a TA, and the potential benefits and risks, so that we align with the ethical and legal requirements of our country; (c) to determine if a TA is appropriate for the client; (d) to schedule the first appointment and increase the likelihood of the client attending the session; and (e) to develop some initial hypotheses and understanding of the client's presenting problem, while determining if we have the needed competencies to work with this client.

It takes a considerable level of clinical skill to successfully manage the relational dynamics and the complex goals of the first phone call. Therefore, we encourage clinicians practicing TA to organize their practice so that they conduct the first conversation and do not delegate it to others, such as an administrative assistant, colleague, or trainee. We know that in certain settings this may not be possible. However, delegating the first contact to others results in a missed opportunity to begin forming a collaborative relationship with the client.

Primary Topics of Discussion for the First Contact in TA

To fulfill the goals listed above, there are topics we make sure we discuss during the first contact with potential clients (See Table 4.1) We take notes during the conversation and capture our impressions after the call ends. In this way, we begin to consider potential questions the client is trying to answer and how best to approach the first session (Finn & Martin, 2013).

Table 4.1 Primary Areas of Discussion During the First Contact

---

1 What the client is hoping to figure out through an assessment.
2 Explaining the TA process.
3 Describing ways the client can learn more about TA through an information sheet or website.
4 Exploring whether a client has participated in psychological testing in the past.
5 Explaining how we will connect with referring professionals (RPs).
6 Providing informed consent about our process and fees, and scheduling the first session.
7 Allowing the client time to ask questions about TA and us.

What the Client is Hoping to Figure Out Through an Assessment

As already mentioned, we ask potential clients why they are seeking help and listen carefully to their explanations. As they speak, we consider whether TA is a good match for their needs and look for moments to validate any distress they express. Here is an example:

Sam:	Good morning. My name is Sam, and I got your number from a friend. I would like to schedule a session.
Assessor:	Sure, I have some availability. But first, tell me a bit about what you are looking for.
Sam:	I am searching for psychological help to overcome some problems with intimate relationships. I heard about you from a friend who met with you and was happy with the results. I am not sure if an assessment or therapy would be a good way to start.[2]

Assessor: I see. Can you help me understand what you mean by problems with intimate relationships?

Sam: I have been wondering about this for a while. I have a hard time keeping partners, and I am fed up with being let down by them.

Assessor: I imagine that is hard. [*The assessor mirrors the emotion expressed by the client*].

Sam: Yes. That's why I decided to search for a psychologist.

Assessor: Do you currently have a partner and if so, are you having problems? [*The assessor wonders whether Sam needs an individual TA or if he would be better served through a couple's TA or another intervention for couples*].

Sam: No, I am alone at the moment.

Assessor: Okay. Let me tell you about the way I work so you have a better understanding of what we might do together…

In the example, the clinician validated the client's experience, collected some data to decide that a TA may be appropriate, and provided information so the client could make an informed choice. During this exchange, the assessor wondered whether a couple's TA may be more appropriate, and if Sam had indicated he was in a relationship, the assessor would have explored this possibility with him. The distress Sam expressed about his relationship difficulties provided the clinician an opportunity to mirror his feelings. While it was only a brief moment, we have found that even a single empathic comment builds connection so that the client feels less anxious and more open to engaging in a TA.

Explaining the TA Process

Often, individuals searching for psychological help do not know about TA. Clients asking for an assessment may expect to meet for a limited time to complete psychological tests and are not aware how a TA could be more beneficial. Other clients do not even understand the distinction between psychological assessments and psychotherapy. Therefore, we offer a brief description of what we do in a TA, providing enough detail to help the client understand that engaging in the process might be a good way to address their goals. We explain how during the first session, we will help them form questions about themselves and their difficulties that will be addressed by the assessment. Next, we describe how psychological tests will be administered and explored, and, eventually, there will be a discussion session during which the test data is reviewed and the client's questions are answered. When clients respond positively to the idea of a TA, we ask them to think about questions we can explore during the first meeting. Encouraging the client to consider questions puts them in an active position that promotes their curiosity, and it helps them understand that the work centers on their personal concerns. Building a collaborative relationship is further described in Chapter 5 but begins in these early moments of connection with the client, and our interpersonal stance fosters clients' motivation to engage in the process openly (Kamphuis & Finn, 2019). What follows is an example that continues the previous dialogue:

Assessor: Okay, let me explain what a TA is like. In this approach, we use interviews and testing to answer the questions you have about your problems, your relationships, or things in your life you'd like to better understand. For example, you might want to have a question about what you mentioned earlier regarding your difficulty keeping partners.

Sam: Um...maybe there's something wrong with how I relate to partners, something that I do, and I do not even realize I am doing it...

Assessor: I'm not sure yet as we are just getting to know each other, but if that is what is happening, I can see how it would be confusing. These are the kinds of things we can talk about in our first meeting, so that we clearly identify your questions. After that meeting, I'll choose tests that will help us find answers to those questions, and we'll work together to see what we can figure out. I am an expert on tests, but you are an expert on your life, and I hope that if we put our expertise together, we can help you find the next steps that will help with your intimate relationships.

Ways Clients Can Learn More About TA Through an Information Sheet or Website

We tell the client that we will send an information sheet after the phone call with more information about TA and our work (see Box 4.1). Many assessors also have websites that contain this information, and we guide the client to those. The information we provide on the phone and the information sheet are ways we help clients develop a better understanding of how we work and what a TA will be like. This often lowers client anxiety, thus supporting them to get to the first session with more trust and less hypervigilance.[3]

Box 4.1   Client Assessment Information Sheet

Given individual differences, it is best for clinicians to develop their own information sheet about their work, regardless of whether it is TA or other kinds of psychological assessment. Generally, the information sheet includes the assessor's approach to assessment, which may include the common questions addressed and the type of client they typically evaluate. Below are topics we have found to be useful in an information sheet about TA:

1   What psychological assessment is and how the information collected is used.
2   What TA is and how it differs from a traditional assessment.
3   The procedures/steps in a TA.
4   The typical cost of TA and how that is determined.
5   Potential benefits and risks.
6   Practical information (address, office hours, parking).

Exploring Whether a Client Has Participated in Testing in the Past

During the first phone contact, we ask if the client has had previous experiences with psychological testing, especially if the client plans to use health insurance. Some clients may have already used insurance for testing, and if they participate in more testing, it is possible that it might not be covered. With such clients, we encourage them to check with their insurance company to ensure additional testing will be covered. There are a few other reasons we may ask about previous testing experiences, although in countries where health insurance is not used this topic could be postponed to the first session. First, if a client has recently completed testing, we are likely to obtain those test results and integrate them into our work. A client may have completed a Personality Assessment Inventory (PAI; Morey, 1996) and obtaining that test profile could be helpful in understanding the client and may lead us to pick a different measure if additional self-report data would be helpful. Second, we ask the client about their past assessment experience to understand their mindset as they approach a TA. A client may say, "It was positive, and I learned a lot about how my learning issues impact my work performance, but I'm still struggling with my mood." For such a client we explain how we will ensure that those additional areas of concern will be targeted, and during the first session, we inquire further about the parts of that assessment experience that were beneficial, so that we can employ similar tactics. However, some clients may have had a negative experience with testing, and when this occurs, we ask about what made it negative, validate their concerns, and if warranted apologize on behalf of the field. This effort aligns with our goals of building a connection with the client and repairing a relationship disruption (Finn, 2012), which is elaborated in Chapter 5.

Explaining How We Will Connect with Referring Professionals (RPs)

If there is an RP involved, we ask clients during the call whether they are willing to sign a release of information and if they agree that the information gathered can be shared with the RP. During this part of the conversation, the assessor also describes how RPs are typically involved during a TA. We explain that the TA will address the RP and client's areas of uncertainty and goals and the assessor will have ongoing contact with the RP. We also share that if both client and RP agree, the Summary/Discussion Session will be held at the RP's office. In this way, the RP also hears directly from the assessor about the test results and answers to the questions.

Providing Informed Consent About Our Process and Fees, and Scheduling the First Session

In alignment with the goal of providing informed consent and setting clear expectations, we provide practical information about our work such as our fee, office location, and whether we have availability limitations. Among this practical information, there is a kind that is not negotiable (i.e., our office location), but another kind that might be more open for discussion, for example, in some settings, the fee we charge or our hours of service. Sometimes clients try to negotiate these aspects of our practice, for example, by asking us to reduce our fee.[4] If this happens, we carry on a productive conversation with the client, being flexible if possible, without sacrificing our payment requirements and our free time. Here is an example of such a discussion:

Client: I am definitely interested. How many interviews and testing sessions will we schedule?

Assessor: Well, it's hard to say now. A TA with an adult usually is five to eight sessions. However, the first time we meet we will explore your questions, and depending on what and how many there are, I will be able to be more precise.

Client: You know, my insurance will not cover all these sessions, so I need to keep the cost down. What is your fee?

Assessor: My fee is X and includes the time I spend for our discussions, the coding and interpretation of your testing, the cost of the test materials, and the letter I will write you at the end of the assessment about the results.

Client: Mhm…I am not sure I can afford that…I am a working student and I do not want to ask my parents for help.

Assessor: I understand. Well, there are a couple of things we can consider together. Most TAs I conduct usually cost between X and Y, so you are likely to be in that cost range. However, it is possible to limit our work and still have a helpful experience. I suggest we meet and see whether we can limit the goals of our work to fewer sessions. For example, if we agree on only one or two questions connected to what you are trying to figure out, we might have fewer sessions. It also depends on what you are dealing with and what you hope to figure out. Sometimes, just one test can help a lot in answering a person's questions, and in other cases, one test provides a limited amount of information and if we have additional tests, we increase the likelihood of this process being useful to you.

Client: That makes sense. Let's schedule a first appointment and we can figure this out then.

Allowing the Client Time to Ask Questions About TA and Us

Finally, we always provide time for the client to ask questions about the TA process and us as clinicians. This is in alignment with our collaborative interpersonal stance, and we ensure that the client understands the process before the first meeting. If they have questions about us, we answer in a brief and concise way, which builds the relationship and curiosity, all of which foster epistemic trust (ET; Kamphuis & Finn, 2019). The information we provide about ourselves is done so in a professional manner, and this practice aligns with the growing research on the role of self-disclosure in building rapport (Hill et al., 2018). Many clients have no questions about us, but those that do typically inquire about our work experience, and providing this information lets the client know that we value their capacity to make an informed decision about entering into a TA (Finn, 1996).

Decision-making During the First Phone Contact

During the first phone contact, there are often different decisions that we consider with the client.

Does this Client Need a TA or Is a Traditional Evaluation or Therapy More Appropriate?

Sometimes we are contacted by people who are seeking help but are considering the traditional, information-gathering approach of assessment, typically at the recommendation of another professional. This is often the case when a client is looking to determine if they qualify for a diagnosis and identify the best treatment. With such clients, we help weigh the decision of whether a traditional evaluation or a TA would be best; this requires us to explain TA and the pros and cons of each choice. Sometimes, a traditional assessment has the advantage of requiring less time and money than a TA, but the client may not be aware of the limitations of a traditional assessment. Therefore, we explain the TA model in a way that allows the client to consider their choice. We often share some or all of the benefits of completing a TA, such as (a) the advantage of exploring various kinds of questions that are relevant to the client, and not just a diagnostic question; (b) the opportunity to get deep and meaningful answers to their questions with personalized suggestions; (c) the benefit of a personalized letter that summarizes in understandable language what we learned together, instead of a traditional report that is often more useful for communication among mental health professionals; and (d) the likelihood, that as a result of the TA, the client will feel more hopeful and their problems may get better (Durosini & Aschieri 2021). We explain that to get these benefits, it takes time to talk about the client's goals for the assessment and to explore the meaning of the test results and how they relate to the client's life. However, as described below, sometimes a traditional evaluation would be best for the client, and in these situations, we provide the information the client needs so they can make an informed choice.

Other clients may contact us asking for therapy or, as mentioned, psychological help without knowing exactly what they want. When this happens, we help clients make an informed choice by educating them about the psychological services we provide, and the advantages and potential disadvantages of each service. For example, psychotherapy does not require an upfront commitment on the part of clients, but it can take some time for them to feel that they are making progress. TA can be a good way to start addressing problems, especially if clients are not exactly clear on their goals, but it does require a short-term commitment (e.g., 6-8 weeks). If they need additional services, TA will end with a clear picture of the reasons for the client's difficulties, which helps focus subsequent therapy on the most salient issues. Describing the TA process and listing its benefits, as well as those of other approaches, helps clients understand their choices. It also helps them see that while we believe strongly in TA, we want them to choose what is best to meet their needs.

Finally, there are some clients who will feel uncertain about the best way to proceed by the end of the phone call. With such clients, having a first session to continue the conversation and help them make a decision is likely best. Some of these clients may have had past negative experiences with testing which contributes to their uncertainty, and they may believe that psychological tests are ways to label people and over pathologize them. Other clients may feel uncertain about whether a TA, traditional assessment, or therapy are the best ways to proceed, and sorting this out may not be possible during a call. Provided the clinician conducts TAs, traditional evaluations, and therapy, we may continue the discussion in the first session, and help the client weigh their choices then.

Is the Adult TA Model Appropriate for This Client, or Would It Be More Appropriate to Use Another TA Model?

Depending on the client's problem, we might need to determine which TA model is best. For example, if there is a couple's problem and the client's partner agrees to take part, we would structure a TA following the model for couples (Finn, 2015; Aschieri et al., in press). Another example might be a young adult with issues related to their parents or who still lives in the family home. In these instances, we consider if it would be better to structure the TA following the adolescent model (see Tharinger et al., 2013).

This decision is important to offer the best approach, and also to help us determine if we have the expertise to work with that client. Some TA assesors only see adults, while others learn the other models and work with children, adolescents, or couples. The possibility of a different model depends on our assessment of the problem and also whether the client can involve other people in the TA. It is possible that the client rules out involving others and the assessor agrees to an individual TA, with an understanding that the absence of the partner or parents may limit the efficacy. At other times, the client might not be inclined to involve others, but then later reconsiders when they realize that the best way to address their questions is to include them. Typically, the best option is including the other individuals at the beginning of the TA. However, if the client does not agree, it might be possible to involve other people once the TA begins. Importantly, if the client chooses another TA model, we discuss the impact on cost, given that will lead to additional sessions.

Does the Client Require a Referral to Another Professional?

Sometimes we realize we cannot offer competent services to the person contacting us. If the client is a young adult with academic difficulties at college, we may realize that they are dealing with a potential learning disorder. If we are not competent in the assessment of learning disabilities, we refer the client to another professional. At other times, we might have personal issues that interfere with treating certain types of clients. For example, if we are dealing with a recent loss, and the client is struggling with grief, we know that a TA with that client will require us to support them in their grief work. We consider what we are dealing with and whether we can work with such a client. By gathering data about the client's issues, we obtain the information we need to determine if another clinician is more appropriate.

How Much Will the TA Cost the Client?

We address how to bill for a TA in Chapter 12, but TA is a skilled intervention, as much as other kinds of psychotherapy, so it is important to charge accordingly (Evans & Finn, 2017). The complexity of the process and the highly individualized oral and written communication provided at the end make it very different than traditional evaluations in terms of time, skills, and effort required of the clinician. Given the length and complexity of a TA depends on the client's goals for the assessment, it might not be possible to know during the first phone call how much to charge. Therefore, we explain our fee for the first session, provide the client with a general sense of how much the TA will cost (often by quoting a price range), and after the first session provide an estimate for the entire TA. Given our goal of being transparent with clients and our ethical requirements, we provide an estimate of the total cost so they have an understanding of their potential monetary responsibility.

Working with Different Client Issues During the First Phone Call

There are several challenges we may face during a first contact and we explain these and how to manage them.

Two types of clients may challenge our capacity to hold limits. The first type is clients who start a long conversation on the phone. They might tell us a lot about their presenting problems or tell us about a previous experience with a mental health professional, or other related topics. If we do not contain these clients, we end up conducting a free therapy session, with no agreement on how to proceed (TA vs. traditional assessment vs. therapy) and what the process will be like. There might be clinical reasons the client behaves this way related to their inability to use healthy mistrust when entering new relationships. For other clients, their verbosity may be a defense against getting in contact with underlying emotions. Yet others are cognitively disorganized and this comes through in the first contact. In each of these instances, letting clients speak, especially in the absence of a structured and agreed-upon context, does not serve them well. For the sake of building a connection, we allow the client to speak freely to some extent and then help contain their emotions. The challenge is to avoid falling into a rescuer role or not being able to maintain our boundaries and protect our own and our client's interests (Finn, 2014). To prevent this mistake, we take a balanced stance, and we gently but firmly contain the client. We may say, "I understand this is very important to you, and I can see why. I want to devote the right amount of time and attention to talk about it, but I can't do it right now on the phone. So, I propose we postpone part of this discussion to our first meeting."

The second type of client challenges aspects of our practice, such as our fee or the times we are available for appointments. This is likely to be particularly relevant in settings where these aspects of a practice are under less standard regulations and are open for negotiation. These clients may lament that we cost too much and ask us to reduce our fee or might push us to schedule an appointment in the evening later than we are available. Again, the challenge is not falling into a rescuer role and agreeing to their requests, with the risk of later feeling unsatisfied or exploited (Finn, 2014). The amount of flexibility we apply to these requests depends, in part, on our awareness of how our personal needs are related to these aspects of our practice. For example, we consider how much work is necessary to conduct a full TA, and what fee is appropriate. As described, TA is designed to be a semi-structured approach that can be modified, and for some clients a brief TA may be adequate, and thus cost less. However, we also explain how a brief TA may be less fulfilling. If we consider adjusting our schedule to see a client outside of our normal schedule, we ask ourselves what we are sacrificing. Again, when flexibility is not possible, we gently but firmly hold to our limits and explain the reasons a TA is expensive but still a good option or state that we cannot change our schedule.

Sometimes, these types of requests might be a way for clients to unconsciously test us (see Chapter 5, Box 6, on Control-Mastery Theory for relational tests made by clients). Seen from this perspective, their pushing of our limits might be a way to test our capacity to set limits without being harsh or shaming, thus balancing the protection of our needs and the care we feel for them. If we demonstrate our ability to do so, these clients might feel reassured and begin to see us as trustworthy figures.

Working with a Referring Professional

Clients are often referred for a TA by other mental health professionals to clarify things they feel uncertain about or to determine how best to proceed with treatment. The model works well as consultation to psychotherapy, and to answer questions that referring professionals (RP) might have (e.g., "What is the most appropriate diagnosis for this client?"). In such cases, the initial contact between the client and the assessor should occur after contact with the RP, if possible. When RPs ask a clinician to conduct a TA, the assessor approaches the request mindful of three elements: (1) What the RP knows about TA, (2) how best to engage the RP as a collaborator, and (3) how the RP's feelings of vulnerability may contribute to challenges collaborating with them (Aschieri et al., 2018; Finn, 2007).

Educating RPs About TA

Similar to future clients, RPs also differ in how much they know about TA. Some RPs know the model well and refer clients to TA assessors because they appreciate the benefit to them and their clients. Other RPs have not heard of TA and are more familiar with the traditional model of assessment. With these RPs, we explain how TA works and how the process might benefit their client. We provide much of the same information we provide to clients about the model and often share our client information sheet, or some professionals create a separate sheet for RPs. Importantly, we invite collaboration and explain how we will remain in contact throughout the process. This is often a significant difference for RPs when compared to a traditional evaluation. Many RPs have had the experience of referring their clients for a psychological assessment and they were never contacted by the assessor. We find that RPs new to TA welcome the opportunity to collaborate and share their impressions of the client, and appreciate the consistent communication that occurs. During this initial stage of educating the RP, we let them know that if the client and RP agree, our preference is to conduct the Summary/Discussion Session at their office.

Building a Collaborative Relationship with the RP

To set the stage for collaboration with the RP, we discuss how the decision was made to refer for a TA (Finn, 2007; Fischer, 1985/1994). The assessor helps the RP to formulate their Assessment Questions (AQs), which will be addressed along with the client's AQs (see Chapter 5). Examples of RPs' questions might be: "Why is Olivia so resistant to the idea of leaving her abusive husband?" or "Is there anything I should change in my therapy with Juan to make treatment of his compulsions more useful?" RPs' questions usually are focused on areas they are curious about regarding the client's psychological functioning, or aspects of the treatment and the therapeutic relationship. While discussing the RP's AQs, the assessor asks about their level of comfort in sharing their questions with the client and offers to help refine the language. For example, an RP may ask, "To what extent can Nick overcome the break-up with his boyfriend, given his dependent personality?" The assessor worked with the RP to edit the question, and the RP agreed to ask, "How can I best help Nick with his pain regarding the break-up with his boyfriend, and support him in becoming more independent?" In our experience, helping RPs re-word their questions so we can share them with clients involves replacing psycho-logical jargon with words the client will understand, and the language conveys the concern the RP has for their client.

However, sometimes RPs do not feel comfortable sharing their AQs with clients, or the concerns they have might be hurtful for the client to hear and they cannot be made less so through editing. This may happen, for example, when RPs suspect a severe diagnosis that the client has no awareness of. In these cases, the assessor may agree to keep the RP's questions as an assessment goal, while not sharing them explicitly with the client. While this kind of arrangement might be appropriate in some circumstances to avoid harming a client, it may also indicate a more complicated start of a TA. The assessor may wonder if this is a sign of an issue in the RP and client's relationship, which blocks the RP's ability to be more honest with the client.

When RPs have had previous experience with TA, they may be a resource for ex-plaining what TA is to their clients before referring them. This often makes our first contact with the client smoother, as they already have some of the information we typically share, and they may be less on guard because of the trust they have in their therapist. Even in these situations, we take time during the phone call to ask about clients' understanding of the TA process, to check for potential misunderstandings, and we send the information sheet. In our initial contacts with the RPs, we may also suggest that they help the client think about AQs. In this way, the client can also use the RPs as support for taking an active stance from the very beginning of the TA.

Lastly, the assessor and the RP address the limits of confidentiality, which are defined by the release of information that the assessor will ask the client to sign, as described above.

Working with the RP's Sense of Vulnerability

As mentioned, RPs often request a TA when they feel that therapy is not proceeding as expected, and sometimes when their clients feel discouraged or unsatisfied. In this situation, asking for help from another colleague may be challenging for an RP, since it potentially raises questions about their competency. This may be particularly true if the RP is a master's level clinician, and the assessor has a doctorate, given the power differences that can occur with these different degrees. We remain aware of the RP's potential feeling of vulnerability, and we work with any expressions of shame directly and openly. For example, we reassure the RP that it is a common experience for mental health professionals to feel stuck with certain clients, and, if appropriate, share how the assessor has had this experience with some of their own clients.

In addition, sometimes conducting a TA as consultation to therapy brings unique demands. This might be true when the RP has a different background from the as-sessor. For example, differences in language, theoretical orientation, training, and culture of the profession play a role in shaping different views of the client's diffi-culties. We keep ourselves grounded by relying on TA values and remain curious about the RP's perspective. In this way, assessors work toward collaborating with the RP while considering their vulnerability, thus avoiding the risk of disruptions or polarizations that will be a disservice to the client. Assessors may feel supported by remembering that the RP's request for consultation is one of facing a dilemma that could be worded as: "If I accept a new way of seeing my client, I may feel that my previous way of seeing them was wrong/bad/useless; if I do not accept a new way of seeing my client, I may continue to feel that my current way of working with them may be not effective, and thus potentially wrong/bad/useless." When working with RPs who face this dilemma, assessors maintain a collaborative stance, so RPs do not feel judged as "bad," while potentially addressing the need to change their way of seeing the client or treating them. In the following chapters, we will illustrate how to cultivate the relationship with RPs throughout a TA.

Clinical Case: Initial Contact with Emma

We next introduce you to Emma, who was assessed by one of the authors, Hale Martin, at the Colorado Center for Collaborative Assessment. The case description is written in the first person by Hale, and we have altered identifying information to protect Emma's privacy.

Emma was a 49-year-old woman who was referred for a TA by her highly experienced therapist Jeanne, who felt that their work had been floundering from the beginning. Jeanne had been working weekly with Emma for two years, and although Emma was pleasant and cooperative and seemed to be working hard, Jeanne felt there had been little sustained direction or progress or even any clear understanding of the fundamental issues. Jeanne saw Emma as an enigma—and that was rare in her vast experience. She wondered why she had not been able to develop enough understanding to be helpful. What was she missing? She noted that Emma's behaviors in the room were a bit unusual, noting that her eye squinting, head tilt, and some grimaces were odd, causing Jeanne to consider some underlying organic basis to Emma's life-long struggles. Jeanne was familiar with TA and had discussed with Emma that a psychological assessment might help their work together, and Emma was open to that possibility. When Hale spoke with Jeanne, she developed two questions for the TA that she did not mind sharing with Emma:

1   What am I missing that is impeding therapy with Emma?
2   Is there something organic underlying Emma's problems?

My first contact with Emma was by phone. We talked for 10 minutes about her interest in doing a psychological assessment, and she was excited by the prospect. I explained my approach was TA and told her that we would work together to answer important questions about her life that we would formulate in our first meeting. I then suggested she think about what questions captured the burning issues that she needed to be addressed to move forward in her life. She quickly responded: "Can I make a living on my own? Is there something holding me back? And can I retrain my brain to be more efficient?" I responded that those sounded like important questions and gave her a brief explanation of what our work would entail. I also gave Emma the Therapeutic Assessment Institute website address to provide her with further information. I told her the cost of the assessment, and she told me that her sister Tessa was the trustee of her father's estate and controlled the family's money and, thus, she would have to approve money for the assessment. She gave me Tessa's phone number and asked me to call her to explain TA and its value, to see if money could be directed toward it. This, along with her quick first question about her ability to make a living, made me curious about how independent Emma was and if it would be helpful to involve the family in the assessment. Throughout the phone conversation, Emma was pleasant, grateful, and agreeable, but also seemed a little disorganized and overwhelmed. We agreed I would contact Tessa to explain to her what the assessment would entail and to discuss the cost.

My conversation with Tessa was also very pleasant and agreeable but seemed calmer and more organized than that I had with Emma. Tessa came across as a caring sister with great concern about Emma. She confirmed that Emma had had a tough time after their father's death four years previously but added that, actually, Emma had had a tough time since childhood. Tessa mentioned that Emma had struggled with compulsive and hoarding behaviors as a child and adolescent that had gotten in the way of her friendships, and that as an adult, Emma had been unable to be consistently self-sufficient. As their father approached his death, he had asked Tessa to make sure Emma was taken care of. Their mother had recently been diagnosed with Alzheimer's disease and had been moved from the family home to an assisted living unit. For financial reasons, the family had decided to sell the home where Emma now lived alone, and Tessa was concerned how Emma would manage on her own. She wondered if Emma needed public assistance to survive and hoped the assessment would give insight into that question. I explained to Tessa that because Emma was an adult, the results of the assessment would be provided only to Emma unless she gave written consent to release information to others. Tessa agreed to that and expressed confidence Emma would consent. We discussed whether Tessa being involved might be helpful to the assessment. She offered to participate in any way that would be useful but agreed that it was Emma's decision. After we discussed the TA, Tessa decided it seemed like a promising idea and consented to paying for it out of their family funds.

Reflections After the Initial Contacts

After these phone discussions, I felt intrigued. I wondered what might be going on that caused a seasoned therapist like Jeanne to be confused enough to seek an assessment of her client after two years of therapy. I also wondered what caused Tessa to think that Emma might need public assistance. I hypothesized that there likely were some substantial problems that would take a lot of sorting out. Because I was not an expert in neuropsychology, I hoped I had enough knowledge of it to recognize any needs for neuropsychological testing, and I knew I could rely on consultation with a colleague in that area, if needed. I also thought back about agreeing to call Tessa rather than have Emma arrange for Tessa to call me, as I typically would have. What led me to alter my usual approach? I was curious about this and realized that something about Emma led me to feel the need to take care of her. I noted this for future consideration. However, overall, it seemed that Emma was very interested in the assessment and that we likely would be able to develop a good working relationship. I looked forward to meeting with Emma to pursue a better understanding of how a TA might help her.

Notes

1 Andrade and colleagues (2014) found that 4,583 respondents in an international survey (38.5% of a larger sample of subjects who met the criteria for a DSM-IV diagnosis) reported no use of mental health services, although they all subjectively perceived the need for some

kind of treatment. When asked why they did not use services albeit needing them, the vast majority (96.3%) of respondents reported at least one attitudinal barrier, among which the most common one by far was wanting to handle the problem alone. The authors linked the desire to handle the problem by oneself to self-stigma and diagnostic label avoidance. Factors such as public attitudes toward mental illness or fear of being discriminated against in the workplace for revealing a mental illness or psychiatric treatment were also influential elements that restrained people from disclosing their own mental health history and gaining access to adequate care.

2 Depending on the country, clients may not have knowledge about psychological assessments, therapy, and the differences between them before talking to a professional. In the United States, it is common for clients to specifically ask for an assessment or therapy. In other countries, it is common for potential clients to ask for psychological help that is not further specified. Therefore, the initial contact is less of a discussion about whether testing or therapy is best, and more the clinician's choice of what to propose to address the client's concerns.

3 The combination of having a clinician managing the first phone call and sending an information sheet right after, reduced the rates of clients not showing up at the first session at counseling service for university students coordinated by one of the authors, compared to a previous organization where an assistant managed the phone call and scheduling, and no information sheet was sent to the potential client.

4 Negotiating the cost of an assessment with a client may be less likely in some settings where fees are set by workplace or health insurance policies. However, private practice fees are often subject to fewer restrictions and are more open to negotiation.

References

American Psychological Association. (2017). *Ethical principles of psychologists and code of conduct* (2002, amended effective June 1, 2010, and January 1, 2017).

Andrade, L. H., Alonso, J., et al. (2014). Barriers to mental health treatment: Results from the WHO World Mental Health (WMH) Surveys. *Psychological Medicine, 44*(6), 1303–1317. doi: 10.1017/S0033291713001943.

Aschieri, F., Caputo, C., & Righetti, T. (in press). Therapeutic Assessment with Couples (TA-C). In J. Mihura (Ed.), *The Oxford handbook of personality and psychopathology assessment* (2nd ed.). Oxford University Press.

Aschieri, F., Fantini, F., & Finn, S. E. (2018). Incorporation of Therapeutic Assessment into treatment with clients in mental health programming. In J. N. Butcher & J. M. Hooley (Eds.), *APA handbook of psychopathology: Understanding, assessing, and treating adult mental disorders* (pp. 631–642). American Psychological Association.

De Saeger, H., Kamphuis, J. H., Finn, S. E., Smith, J. D., Verheul, R., van Busschbach, J. J., Feenstra, D. J., & Horn, E. K. (2014). Therapeutic Assessment promotes treatment readiness but does not affect symptom change in patients with personality disorders: Findings from a randomized clinical trial. *Psychological Assessment, 26*, 474–483. doi: 10.1037/a0035667.

Durosini, I., & Aschieri, F. (2021). Therapeutic Assessment efficacy: A meta-analysis. *Psychological Assessment*. Advance online publication. doi: 10.1037/pas0001038.

Evans, F. B. & Finn S. E. (2017). Training and consultation in psychological assessment with professional psychologists: Suggestions for enhancing the profession and individual practices. *Journal of Personality Assessment, 99*(2), 175–185. doi: 10.1080/00223891.2016.1187156.

Finn, S. E. (1996). *Manual for using the MMPI-2 as a therapeutic intervention*. University of Minnesota Press.

Finn, S. E. (2007). *In our clients' shoes: Theory and techniques of Therapeutic Assessment*. Taylor & Francis Group.

Finn, S. E. (2012). Implications of recent research in neurobiology for psychological assessment. *Journal of Personality Assessment, 94*(5), 440–449.

Finn, S. E. (2014). *Learning to navigate the Karpman's triangle: The healing potential of assessing traumatized clients.* Paper presented at the annual meeting of the Society for Personality Assessment, Arlington, VA.

Finn, S. E. (2015). Therapeutic Assessment with couples, *Pratiques Psychologiques, 21*(4), 345–373.

Finn, S. E., Fischer, C. T., & Handler, L. (Eds.) (2012). *Collaborative/Therapeutic Assessment: A casebook and guide.* John Wiley & Sons, Inc.

Finn, S. E., & Martin, H. (2013). Therapeutic Assessment: Using psychological assessment as brief therapy. In K. F. Geisinger, B. A. Bracken, J. F. Carlson, J. I. C. Hansen, N. R. Kuncel, S. P. Reise, & M. C. Rodriguez (Eds.), *APA handbook of testing and assessment in psychology, Vol. 2: Testing and assessment in clinical and counseling psychology* (pp. 453–465). American Psychological Association.

Fischer, C. (1985/1994). *Individualizing psychological assessment.* Lawrence Erlbaum & Associates.

Fonagy, P., Luyten, P., Allison, E., & Campbell, C. (2017a). What we have changed our minds about: Part I. Borderline personality as a limitation of resilience. *Borderline Personality and Emotional Dysregulation, 4*(11), doi: 10.1186=s40479-017-0061-9.

Fonagy, P., Luyten, P., Allison, E., & Campbell, C. (2017b). What we have changed our minds about: Part 2. Borderline personality, epistemic trust, and the developmental significance of social communication. *Borderline Personality and Emotional Dysregulation, 4*(9), doi: 10.1186/s40479-017-0062-8.

Hill, C. E., Knox, S., & Pinto-Coelho, K. (2018). Therapist self-disclosure and immediacy: A qualitative meta-analysis. *Psychotherapy, 55*(4), 445–460.

Kamphuis, J. H. & Finn, S. E. (2019). Therapeutic Assessment in personality disorders: Toward the restoration of epistemic trust. *Journal of Personality Assessment, 101*(6), 662-674, doi: 10.1080/00223891.2018.1476360.

Morey, L. C. (1996). *An interpretive guide to the Personality Assessment Inventory.* Psychological Assessment Resources, Inc.

Rogers, C. R. (1961). *On becoming a person.* Houghton Mifflin.

Sperber, D., Clement, F., Heitz, C., Mascaro, O., Mercier, H., Origgi, G., & Wilson, D. (2010). Epistemic vigilance. *Mind & Language, 25*(4), 359–393.

Tharinger, D. J., Gentry, L. B., & Finn, S. E. (2013). Therapeutic Assessment with adolescents and their parents: A comprehensive model. In D. H. Saklofske, C. R. Reynolds & V. L. Schwean (Eds.), *Oxford handbook of child psychological assessment* (pp. 385–420). Oxford University Press.

5   Initial Session

The first encounter with a client is an important moment in a therapeutic process and requires complex clinical skills to address the different needs and challenges that the client and the context bring. Since Therapeutic Assessment (TA) is a therapeutic intervention, the multifaceted issue of how to begin relating with clients in order to create a positive alliance is crucial. To be successful in this endeavor, during the first session we pursue these main goals: (1) Building a trusting therapeutic relationship and helping the client feel secure about the process, and (2) collecting and refining the client's Assessment Questions (AQs), which capture their goals for the TA and guide the subsequent steps.

Creating a Therapeutic Relationship with the Client: Helping Them Regulate Their Attachment System and Building Epistemic Trust

As described in Chapter 1, when clients come to the first session, their attachment system is likely to be activated given they are entering into a new relationship and endeavor. That activation may make it difficult for them to be curious, open to exploring new behaviors, and capable of thinking about themselves and their world in new ways. Furthermore, many clients seeking mental health services have an insecure attachment status (i.e., they have e dismissive, preoccupied, or unresolved attachment status; Bakermans-Kranenburg & van IJzendoorn, 2009; Riem et al., 2019). We are likely to see the activation of attachment-related defenses with these individuals. These may include *deactivation* ("shutting down" the attachment system by shifting attention from emotion to intellectual topics) or *cognitive disconnection* (feeling distressed but maintaining its source out of consciousness with thinking that is derailed; George & West, 2012). The activation of these defenses generally lowers the client's awareness of their emotional states, or their ability to produce accurate and coherent accounts of themselves and their struggles. For some of these clients, we can also see that they are in a state of epistemic hypervigilance (EH), which hinders their capacity to regard the information coming from us as relevant and generalizable (Fonagy et al., 2017a, b). Therefore, they are limited in their capacity to learn from the TA and grow and change.

These initial challenges have the potential to impact the efficacy of a TA. For this reason, from the beginning of a TA it is important to create a relational context that supports the client in regulating their attachment system, and helps them restore their capacity for epistemic trust (ET). We accomplish these goals through interventions during which the client feels accurately seen and understood (i.e., the clinician

DOI: 10.4324/9780429202797-7

mentalizing the client). We will describe three areas of focus that help regulate the client's attachment system, promote client curiosity, and increase ET (Kamphuis & Finn, 2019).

Emotional Attunement

Emotional attunement as described in Chapter 1 is the process of sharing mental states and a reciprocal understanding of emotions. It is a concept derived from research on infant emotion regulation and what transpires between caregiver and child through implicit processes that are mainly emotional and procedural (Tronick et al., 1998). During mother-child interactions, the child's behaviors communicate information to their caregiver about their internal state (e.g., intentions, affects, and arousal level). In response, the caregiver helps regulate the infant. The caregiver responds to the child in a sensitive and timely fashion, so that the child's emotions and reactions are acknowledged, reflected (mirrored), and enhanced when positive, or soothed when negative. The child then responds to the caregiver's signals, which becomes a "dance" of sorts, and the caregiver and child mutually regulate each other.

The concept of emotional attunement has been translated to the therapist-client relationship. The therapist mentalizes the client's emotional state, leading to attuned non-verbal and verbal communications, which helps regulate the client's emotions (Beebe et al., 2005). Through this process, the client comes to experience a unique shared interpersonal state with the therapist (Tronick et al., 1998), which also has the potential for soothing negative emotions and enhancing positive ones.

Depending on the client's attachment system and their predominant attachment defenses, an attuned response from the clinician may look quite different from one client to another. In general, dismissing clients, also described as over-regulated, tend to be organized in their presentation, but appear cut-off from their emotions, withdrawn, or "up in their heads" (George & West, 2012). They often focus on what is "right," instead of on what they feel or desire. Their prevalent attachment defense is deactivation, through which they manage their fear of intimacy. Emotional attunement with these clients often initially involves a cautious approach, listening carefully and asking questions on a more cognitive level, allowing for the gradual development of the connection and emotional deepening. Our general attitude might be less active and we "sit back" with such clients, as a more intimate first approach would risk fueling their fear of intimacy and strengthening their defenses.

In contrast, we might meet under-regulated clients who generally have a preoccupied or unresolved attachment status. These clients often appear anxious and disorganized, and have difficulty telling a coherent narrative about themselves. For example, they may talk about sad topics without appearing sad, but laughing instead. They also tend to be more emotionally labile and dramatic in their emotional display. They manage their fears by displacing the focus of their attention (George & West, 2012). With such clients, an attuned response from the assessor ("sitting forward") includes both reflecting their emotions and taking an active approach in "containing" and structuring their somewhat disorganized discourse. For example, when we notice the client's thinking is becoming derailed or tangential, we gently but firmly focus the conversation by guiding them back to the goals for the assessment or to relevant aspects of their personal history. In this way, we signal our active presence and help them gradually reconnect with the emotions behind their defenses. Clients with an unresolved attachment status, besides being disorganized and confused in their presentation, might also be more difficult to attune with, because they may appear to want a connection; however, our countertransference might include feeling "blocked" or held at a distance. These clients require a flexible approach, including both structuring the conversation and not pushing for too much intimacy.

Accurate Mirroring

With all clients, we find opportunities during the first session to mirror their emotional state, although in general, somewhat more with under-regulated clients than with over-regulated ones. As mentioned, mirroring refers to the clinician's work of identifying, labeling, and accurately describing the client's state of mind (Rogers, 1980; Linehan, 1993). We mirror the client's inner states in the here and now interaction ("I see how desperate you are"). We may also mirror them more tentatively, helping clients gain awareness of their own emotions ("From what you said, I guess the heaviness you feel on your chest may be related to your sense of helplessness"). At the same time, we while mirroring our clients' emotional states, we also validate by using our knowledge of their history ("Given your previous experiences with this man, no wonder you are suspicious of him"), or we link them to universal human experiences ("I see you were overwhelmed by sadness, but everybody would have felt the same in those conditions"; Aschieri et al., 2016).

When this type of assessor reflection is performed authentically and targets emotions at the surface of the client's awareness, we communicate an accurate understanding of the client's present affective state. In turn, this helps the client become more aware of their emotional arousal and is part of our work of mentalizing the client, which allows them to flex their ET and builds their sense of safety with us (Kamphuis & Finn, 2019). We have also helped them regulate their attachment system when this works as we hope.

Collaborative Communication

The term collaborative communication refers to a set of verbal and nonverbal means of communication unique to the relationship in which they develop (Siegel, 1999). In the first session, collaborative communication overlaps with emotional attunement, particularly as related to non-verbal communication. We synchronize body posture, facial expressions, and paraverbalizations (e.g., "oh" "mhm") in response to the client. We also flexibly adapt our level of energy, body posture, rate of speech, or use of pauses, to what best fits each client. Every clinician has their own personality and style that leads to consistency in their way of approaching clients, but they also need to modify their style in accordance with the client in front of them. So, with some clients we are quieter and pause more in response to their comments, while with other clients we energize ourselves, as they bring energy into the room. Over time, effective synchronization might also lead to us developing our own non-verbal rituals with a client (e.g., at the beginning of every session we offer candy to a client who has come to appreciate the gesture).

Collaboration is also a central feature of TA with regard to the verbal aspects of communication and helps build trust (Finn, 2012). In the first session, we are attentive to our client's language, and in particular to the spontaneous use of certain words, images, or metaphors that they use (e.g., a client talking about their lack of assertiveness as "not being self-confident," or a client referring to his experience of feeling attracted to women other than his wife as his "demons"). By adopting the client's language, we enter into their world, giving importance to their perspective and way of communicating. All these efforts help us understand the client's subjective experience more deeply (Fischer, 1985/1994).

However, using a collaborative communication style is more than just modeling our language on the clients. Rather, it is an interactive and bidirectional process, in which the clinician takes an active role. We may propose terms or images to describe the client's subjective experience and then we listen carefully to see if the client adopts our suggestion or drops it. If the client adopts a term proposed by us, that may become part of our relationship's shared and unique language. However, if the client does not use that language, it likely means that they do not feel it is a meaningful way to describe their experience. In this case, we do not continue to use those words, as our goal is to find ways to describe the client's world so that they feel seen and understood, and they will begin trusting us (Finn, 2012).

Last, we often use words that convey our desire to work collaboratively with the client. At its simplest, words such as "collaborate" and "together" help the client understand that we are working with them in a partnership. Assessors also speak in the first person to build and mold the relationship further. We may say, "Today *we'll* be identifying the questions you hope to get answered, and *we'll collaborate together* to figure those out and refine them." At the end of the session, we may say, "I think you have some great questions, and I'm sure *we* can work *together* over the coming sessions to identify answers."

Repairing Disruptions

All interactions, beginning from those between caregiver and child, move from co-ordinated (or synchronous) to mis-coordinated (or disrupted) states and back again. "The mis-coordinated states ... represent normal events. They occur when one of the partners fails to accurately appreciate the meaning of the other's emotional display [or the meaning of a concept or message that is communicated] and in turn reacts inappropriately" (Tronick et al., 1998, p. 294).

During the first session, miscoordination between our clients and us may arise in various situations. These may be small disruptions that create mild emotional reactions in the client, for example, a partially inaccurate attempt to mirror their emotions. A clinician may say, "It seems that situation made you angry," to which the client replies, "No, not angry. I'd say I felt more nervous." A similar situation may be an attempt to redirect the conversation that the client resists (e.g., *Clinician*: "Can we go back to what you were saying ..." *Client*: "Sure, but first let me finish telling you this ...").

However, there are also instances when the disruption generates anxiety, shame, or distress in the client. These may be moments when we inadvertently violated the client's privacy by inquiring about areas of their life that they did not feel safe discussing.

Other times such disruptions may be caused by our failure to accurately read their signals of discomfort, and proceeded with the interview without acknowledging their feelings.

Because a disruption is an interactive process, it can only be acknowledged after considering the client's reaction to our behaviors. Even though we make all possible efforts to stay attuned to each client, our exchanges will inevitably be unsynchronized at times, especially during a first session where we have limited information about each other. Given this, we are attentive to the inevitable disruptions and then make an appropriate repair.

The repair of a disruption can be defined as the transition from a mis-coordinated state to a coordinated state (Safran & Muran, 2000). It is a mutually regulated process during which we adjust our behavior in response to the client's signals, to repair the miscoordination. We notice the client's discomfort and use that information to make an attuned response. Their signals are likely to include nonverbal behaviors such as rigid facial expressions, diminished eye contact, interruption in the flow of speech, or directing the conversation away from an emotionally charged topic. In some instances, our response happens naturally, as might occur when we do not accurately mirror the client's emotional state with our language, but we quickly adopt the term the client used to correct us in describing their experience. A different example would be when we try to interrupt a client to return to a previous topic that we think is more significant, but the client insists on finishing what they were talking about, and we let them do so.

On occasion, a disruption may produce greater distress in a client or be hurtful. When more significant disruptions occur, we pause and discuss what happened, taking time to clarify both our misperception and their experience. When appropriate, we apologize and sincerely explain how our behaviors were unhelpful (e.g., "I am sorry I did not pause earlier when you were starting to feel uncomfortable. I was so focused on understanding that issue and didn't realize how difficult it was for you. I'll try harder to be attentive to any other moments of discomfort you experience.") When the client experiences a sincere and complete repair from us, that often results in a stronger alliance and increases positive emotions about the relationship (Safran & Muran, 2000).

Active Listening

The term "active listening" refers to skills such as eye contact, leaning forward, head nods, facial expressions of curiosity or attunement to the emotions that are expressed in the moment, and short verbal acknowledgments (i.e., "yes," "uh huh"; Miller & Rollnick, 2002). When we use these skills, we demonstrate involvement and interest in what the client discusses. Active listening behaviors are part of the cues we use to explicitly recognize the client as a person with a perspective that is important to us, which helps build a trusting relationship. As active listeners, we might also reflect what the client said by paraphrasing (e.g., "What I'm hearing is ...," and "Sounds like you are saying ..."). In this way, we communicate to the client that we both accurately understand their perspective and we are attuned to them. Additionally, when we are inaccurate, we give clients the opportunity to correct us and improve our understanding of them.

The case of Emma at the end of this chapter illustrates the work of building an alliance with an under-regulated client in the first session of a TA. What follows is a case that demonstrates the use of emotional attunement, collaborative communication, mirroring, repair of disruptions, and active listening, in the first session with an over-regulated man.

Kendrick was a 46-year-old male referred for a TA by his couple's therapist. Kendrick and his wife had a few couple's sessions before the therapist decided to refer him for a TA. The therapist explained to Kendrick how the TA process would unfold, and the assessor conducted an initial phone call as described in Chapter 4. Kendrick was fairly quiet on the phone but agreed to engage in a TA. When Kendrick arrived in the assessor's office, it was evident from his rigid and closed posture that he felt uneasy. What follows is the first exchange between Kendrick and the assessor after some initial small talk that the assessor used to help Kendrick feel more comfortable. The assessor is initially taken aback by discovering that Kendrick does not understand why he was asked to do testing given the discussion that occurred on the phone.

Kendrick: My couple's therapist wanted me to do this ... and I am here.

Assessor: Yes. I had a chance to speak with her. She said she told you to come here to do some testing to help with the couple's therapy that you're doing with your wife. (Kendrick became a little bit fidgety on the couch) *[Kendrick's distressed reaction suggests that a rupture potentially occurred. The assessor failed to recognize the difficult emotional state Kendrick was in, which he contributed to by his statement that he was "told" to do the TA].*

Kendrick: She asked me to come and see you, but truly I don't understand how much this could help.

Assessor: I see, you don't understand ... she didn't talk to you about why she wanted you to do this? *[The assessor emotionally attunes to the client by paraphrasing what he said].*

Kendrick: No, I guess it is something that she and my wife hope might help.

Assessor: Okay, well, let me just explain a little bit. Your therapist asked me to do some testing with you that might help with the couple's therapy that you and your wife are doing. What I want to do today is talk about the testing and have us get to know each other a little bit. Does that seem okay to you? *[The assessor responds in a collaborative way to Kendrick's confusion by clarifying the goals for the session].*

Kendrick: "Mhm." (Nods imperceptibly and starts nervously pinching his hands) *[Although Kendrick seemed to verbally agree in response to the assessor's question, he also appeared to be feeling more discomfort].*

Assessor: So, mainly what I'd like to do today is see what questions you'd like to get answered for yourself through the testing. *[The assessor moves too quickly and makes another rupture by not recognizing the signals that Kendrick is becoming more uncomfortable. Kendrick is not sure he wants to be there, but the assessor is asking him to open up his curiosity and identify questions about himself].*

Kendrick: I don't have any questions.

Assessor: I see, you don't have any questions ... *[The assessor is taken aback and tries to attune to Kendrick by echoing what he said].*

Kendrick:	I don't even understand why I need testing.
Assessor:	So, Dr. White just asked you to come and ... you ... *[The assessor tries to collaboratively engage him in clarifying the context of the referral].*
Kendrick:	(Sighs) I told my wife Michelle that I would try therapy ... which I don't really understand the need for ... and the couple's therapist suggested this testing, and I don't understand that much either. I told Michelle that I'd give it a try, and I'm giving it a try.
Assessor:	I can see that ... you're giving it a try even if you don't understand how this could be helpful. Can you talk with me a little bit about what got you and Michelle into couple's therapy? *[The assessor keeps trying to attune better to Kendrick, by mirroring his effort and engaging him in clarifying the context].*
Kendrick:	My wife Michelle.
Assessor:	Your wife Michelle, okay.
Kendrick:	She's been very depressed and says that we have severe problems in our marriage ... I didn't feel that and it came as a surprise to me ...
Assessor:	Uh-huh ... *[Active listening].*
Kendrick:	I tried to make things better at home and she just keeps getting more depressed ... it's been going on for months. So she suggested couple's therapy. I've never been in therapy, and I have a lot of reservations about it.
Assessor:	So it sounds like this is all pretty confusing for you. *[The assessor attunes to Kendrick by mirroring his emotions].*
Kendrick:	Pretty much! *[Kendrick's reaction signals that the attunement was accurate].* I haven't seen the need for therapy, and I don't really know where the therapist is trying to go in the therapy.
Assessor:	Aha ... It must be very confusing to do something you don't want to do and be uncertain about where it's headed. So, from your point of view, was it more your wife's problem with her depression? *[The assessor mirrors Kendrick's emotional state and engages him collaboratively in explaining his perspective about the problematic issue that brought him to the TA. At the same time the assessor is paraphrasing what he said].*
Kendrick:	Yes because I am perfectly satisfied in our marriage. I see it as a pretty good partnership ... my wife does not.
Assessor:	Aha ... Michelle does not ... but from your point of view things are going pretty well except for Michelle's depression. *[By reflecting Kendrick's message., the assessor strengthens the collaborative construction of a shared understanding of Kendrick's point of view].*
Kendrick:	Yes. And we have always gotten along well and I thought that we were doing ok. *[Kendrick expresses more emotion in his response, reacting to the successful attunement by the assessor].* We have a nice home life. A nice home and I really didn't see any problems.
Assessor:	Why did Michelle say she is unhappy with your relationship? *[The assessor's choice of words for this question is based on the effort to collaboratively adopt Kendrick's point of view].*
Kendrick:	I don't understand much about that, and she says this is part of the problem, that ... it's not that I ignore the problems, I don't see the problems. It's hard for me to say what Michelle is upset about, that's why we are in counseling.

Assessor: Aha ... to understand why you don't see things the same way. And do you have any ideas about why the therapist wanted you to come for the testing?

Kendrick: No.

Assessor: No. Okay. So this is all pretty confusing for you. *[The assessor attunes to Kendrick by mirroring his emotional state].*(Kendrick nods and seems much more relaxed).

Assessor: Okay. I see that and appreciate you letting me know how you are feeling about meeting. I also appreciate your willingness to come even though this wasn't your idea. Would it be helpful if I explain a bit further about what I do?

Kendrick: Sure.

Assessor: I specialize in using psychological tests to help people understand themselves better, and areas of their life where they feel confused, uncertain, or stuck. Typically, during this session, I work with clients to identify questions about themselves they hope to get answered through the tests and I'm hoping that by the time you leave today we can come up with a few questions about things you don't understand and which are confusing to you, that I can use the testing to help answer. *[The assessor tries to reframe the process as a collaborative enterprise].*

From that moment on, Kendrick appeared more relaxed and focused on finding personal goals for the TA. He eventually came up with the following AQs: "Why do I not see problems that others see?," "Why am I always so tired?," and "Do I need therapy?"

Dealing with Clients' Shame[1]

Shame is a very painful emotional experience that is often accompanied by intense feelings of helplessness and confusion. When present, people often have thoughts about being "bad," worthless, or damaged, and the impulse to hide, disappear, escape, apologize, and self-punish (Dearing & Tagney, 2011; See Box 5.1).

Box 5.1   Shame

A shame experience in childhood is typically created when the child displays a certain behavior (e.g., putting their hands in the kitty litter box, or reaching for a sharp knife) and looks back at the caregiver, anticipating an attuned and positive mirroring. The caregiver, however, responds with verbal and non-verbal manifestations of disgust, horror, anger, or fear (i.e., facial expression, hand gestures, "no!") due to the negative evaluation of the child's behavior. The child, as a result, will experience shame, which decreases the likelihood of them engaging in such behaviors in the future. In such situations, shame is adaptive, in that it decreases the likelihood of dangerous or socially unacceptable behaviors (Schore, 1998).

   In adulthood, individuals may feel shame when they experience a misattuned response from another person in the form of anger, punishment, disapproval, rejection, or exclusion. A shame reaction is most likely if the misattuned response is from an important person or it occurs in the presence of others. In these instances, shame becomes an in-the-moment experience (state) resulting from the individual feeling that they violated a standard or have fallen short of an important goal. If certain behaviors, emotions, and urges are repeatedly shamed or punished, they will become associated with shame in the individual, even when others are not present (Dearing & Tagney, 2011). In turn, those parts of themselves will be inhibited. This process is especially powerful and has pervasive consequences when specific emotions or their expression are deemed unacceptable in a social environment. When this occurs, they become "split-off," which means these affects become dissociated; they do not completely disappear, but they become mostly unavailable to the person as a means to react to various situations in their life contexts and are possibly expressed indirectly, or in very specific situations. For example, when children grow up in an environment where anger and its behavioral expressions are not tolerated and are repeatedly shamed, as adults these individuals may not be able to express anger and defend themselves in situations where they would need to do so. They may not be able to set limits with others regarding respecting their personal boundaries and needs. This will potentially cause them to be victims in situations or relationships where they will not have the capability to defend themselves and protect their needs. Such individuals might express anger with their children indirectly in the form of disappointment, or other passive-aggressive behaviors. And possibly, under very specific contexts, such individuals may explode in rage, only to be horrified and ashamed afterwards, leading to even more dissociation of anger.

The dissociation of affective states and the connected behavioral systems can potentially lead to various problems in an individual's personality functioning. When such adults had a childhood in which they experienced harsh punishments without repair they may experience overwhelming shame. They may have a sense of being "bad," "broken," or unlovable, and this may become a core part of their identity (shame as a trait). A core narrative of oneself as defective is more likely to develop if many different emotions and behaviors were punished, especially developmentally normal ones (e.g., anger, sadness, sexual urges, dependency needs).

Shame as a core feature of the individual's identity (trait) is relevant in a therapeutic framework, as it is often associated with important clinical phenomena, such as low self-esteem, depression, anxiety, distrust, addictions, eating disorders, personality disorders, and suicide. Core shame is therefore a potential feature of the clients we meet in TA, and something we want to detect, if present, to have an accurate understanding of our clients and intervene in a therapeutic way. Sometimes, when clients have a good level of awareness related to this aspect of their self-narrative, shame as a trait may already be evident in the first session through the words they use to describe themselves (e.g., "I am not good," or "No one can love me the way I am"). Such clients may even develop an AQ related to these parts of their being, such as, "Why is my self-esteem so low?" or "Why am I so hard on myself?" However, when shame is at an implicit level of the client's self-narrative or when the client has structured character defenses against shame, it may not be evident in the early phases of TA and is more likely to show up in the test results.

Shame as an in-the-moment experience (state) may be an important aspect of the first session, as clients are in the vulnerable position of opening up about their difficulties and may feel a sense of failure, or believe they will be seen as weak or defective. Since shame is an emotion created interpersonally and reinforced by the presence of others, the way we respond to the client's shame is critical in intensifying or regulating their emotional state. For example, there is some evidence that "interpersonally distant" or authoritarian therapists may generate and reinforce shame in clients (e.g., Ackerman & Hilsenroth, 2001).

In general, to heal shame, a person must expose the shameful behavior, thought, emotion, or impulse to others, and be seen, accepted, and possibly appreciated (Dearing & Tagney, 2011). It is therefore critical that in the first session, as well as in other phases of TA, the clinician is able to recognize and respond therapeutically to signs of the client falling into a state of shame. There are various behavioral signs of the emergence of shame: blushing, turning pale, looking down or to the side, covering the eyes, the face, or the mouth, or a slumped body posture and lowered head. Other clients may have a difficult time sitting still, and they may laugh or smile anxiously, pick at their clothes or skin, and possibly cry. Such behavioral displays are more common than verbal statements, but the ashamed client might also say things like, "I feel ridiculous/stupid/dumb/weak," or use other self-critical language (Dearing & Tagney, 2011).

Below we describe ways of intervening with shame, but it is important to underline that these interventions are most beneficial when they are part of a therapeutic relationship that is supportive, validating, empathically attuned, and collaborative. Therefore, shame is best addressed when we can build a connection based on the relational qualities described above, and when we respect the ways clients are coping. We stay close to the TA value of humility and remind ourselves that clients are "more simply human than otherwise" (Sullivan, 1953, p. 4). Additionally, specific interventions to heal shame are most effective when we can first sit with clients' distress—listening, accepting, and mirroring their shame. If we intervene too quickly to move clients out of shame, we run the risk of making clients feel there is something wrong with their shame (i.e., shame about shame). Therefore, we first display compassion for the old shameful narrative before trying to intervene (e.g., "I understand why you came to feel shame about this … do you mind if I ask a few questions?" or "I know most people might judge what you're saying, so it makes sense that you are ashamed, but I think about what you told me in a slightly different way. May I share my thoughts?").

When we recognize one or more of the indicators of shame, we can intervene therapeutically in various ways. What we choose to do depends on our understanding of the particular client and what is contributing to their shame. Among the possible interventions for shame, we will focus on three we find most beneficial: *reframing, confronting shame,* and *judicious therapist self-disclosure.*

Reframing

To reframe means "to change the conceptual and/or emotional setting or viewpoint in relation to which a situation is experienced and to place it in another frame which fits the 'facts' of the same concrete situation equally well or even better, and thereby changes its entire meaning" (Watzlawick et al., 1974; p. 94). As a therapeutic response to shame, reframing helps clients think differently about whatever is causing them to feel shame. Typically, when people feel shame, they "take themselves too personally." By presenting alternative, contextualized explanations, we help clients recognize that their behaviors and feelings reflect factors beyond their control, and are not solely based on their conscious choices or personality features. Reframing shame often involves highlighting situational, contextual, biological, or systemic factors that influenced, or are still influencing, the client's "shameful" behavior. When reframing is successful, clients begin to develop a more accurate and compassionate story about themselves and the issue producing shame.

To be successful, reframing requires us to consider alternative stories about the client's behaviors or difficulties, and is most successful when the client is open to incorporating new stories into their pre-existing narrative. Given the latter, reframing is easier when we are familiar with the client's situation and we have a trusting relationship, as often is the case in later stages of a TA. However, in the first session, the relationship built through the alliance-building process described and the exploration of the information the client shares, may form the basis for effective reframing. We refer to our knowledge of psychopathology, trauma, attachment, and other psychological theories and facts to "scientifically" support the validity of the new story we present to the client.

For example, during the first session of her TA, Julie, a 40-year-old woman, met with a female assessor, and they discussed her fatigue since giving birth to her second child. Julie described difficulties keeping up with work and household responsibilities, and taking care of her 4-year-old child and the newborn. Julie's baby was waking up several times a night, and each time it was difficult to get him back to sleep. As Julie was breastfeeding, she was primarily responsible for the baby at night, although her husband supported her in other ways such as helping around the house. After the clinician validated and mirrored her feelings of exhaustion, Julie suddenly fell into shame and, while avoiding eye contact and wiping away tears, reluctantly disclosed that several times at night she had imagined killing her baby. The clinician intervened immediately by saying that she understood how Julie might be horrified by such thoughts, and they were common for mothers with certain types of babies. The clinician went on to clarify that infants have different temperaments, and it sounded like Julie's child was difficult to soothe. The clinician stressed that children with this kind of temperament are normally harder to relate to, and often leave parents feeling powerless and desperate. Julie was relieved by this information, looked less ashamed, and was suddenly curious to know more about how an infant's temperament impacts parenting.

Confronting or Contradicting Shame

A second shame intervention we commonly use is contradicting clients' negative stories emphatically and directly with the aim of interrupting the in-the-moment experience of shame. This intervention is useful when a client makes reference to what we might be thinking or how we might be seeing them. Some examples follow.

Client: I know this sounds horrible, but I sometimes wish my parents were dead.
Clinician: No, that isn't horrible. They have been abusive to you for years and you feel trapped by your financial dependence on them.

OR

Client: You'll probably think I'm completely irresponsible, but if I could I would just walk away from my job.

Clinician: I don't think that means you're irresponsible at all. It simply tells me how you don't see many other options to address how unhappy you are.

OR

Client: I know this sounds crazy, but I sometimes feel like I know what other people are feeling before they do.

Clinician: I don't think you're crazy. The testing shows you are a highly sensitive person and it's quite possible you perceive others' emotions before they are aware of them.

We are honest and authoritative, and provide an explanation while avoiding overly positive statements that will feel false to the client (e.g., "You were so courageous!"). To be most effective, this intervention is often combined with reframing, as illustrated in the examples. We contradict the client's shame forcefully, and provide a viable explanation for our different point of view. If the client persists in experiencing shame, we expand our intervention. For example, returning to the example of Julie above, in a subsequent session when talking about her baby Julie burst into tears and disclosed her fear that the clinician was judging her: "You must think I am a terrible mother." The clinician offered her a tissue, and gently asked Julie to look at her face. She then asked, "Do you see any sign on my face that I am thinking you are not a good mother?" Julie said "No." The clinician continued, "Again, I don't think that you are a bad mother. I think you have a baby who is difficult-to-soothe." After further talking about the baby's temperament, Julie felt relief and talked more freely about her experiences and that she felt dismissed by her mother, husband, and sister when she told them how distressed she was about her baby. Julie's trust in the clinician grew and her shame decreased, allowing them to discuss her feelings of loneliness, and how the relationship challenges contributed to her distress and fatigue.

Judicious Therapist Self-Disclosure

The third commonly used shame intervention is clinician self-disclosure. This technique can be extremely effective in decreasing client's isolation and sense of shame, but we use it with some caveats (Knox & Hill, 2003). With judicious self-disclosure, we reveal that we can personally relate to the client's struggles (e.g., "I've struggled with that in my life, too," "When I was your age, I did the very same thing"). The self-disclosure must be brief, concise, and match the client's situation. It should not pull the attention towards us too much, nor should it impact the client's view of us as a competent helper. For these reasons we would not disclose things like, "I struggle with drugs and alcohol also" or "I also have been in an inpatient hospital." Rather, our self-disclosures emphasize our common humanity with the client regarding a specific life experience or a similar emotion or process. For example, "I've had days I regretted having children too" or "I've had my own struggles in life." The self-disclosure is made ONLY when the client is manifesting shame and is brief, and we understand that when therapists self-disclose too much, that undermines the client's trust in the clinician (Knox & Hill, 2003). Importantly, we only self-disclose when we can be authentic about the topic, and it is an area of our life that is resolved. If the topic is a current source of shame for the clinician, it would be better *not* to self-disclose and to use a different shame intervention.

Returning to Julie's first session, instead of the first two interventions, the clinician could have used self-disclosure when she saw Julie experiencing shame. For example, the clinician could have shared that when her second child was born, she also felt powerless and angry. She could have added that she remembered how hard it was to keep up with multiple demands and to soothe her child at night, and that she also felt mentally and physically exhausted. By sincerely and deeply joining Julie around how difficult it is to be a mother when you do not have enough support, the clinician helps "carry" Julie's distress and provides hope. This highlights another potential benefit of judicious self-disclosure: It gives clients the opportunity to see that even a professional can experience the same problem (or aspects of it), and successfully get through it.

In conclusion, interventions that help clients with shame during the first session are important for building a therapeutic relationship. Shame makes people feel painfully different and "bad" in other people's eyes and their own (whether such narratives are accurate or not). Failing to intervene when shame is present can strengthen those feelings, as clinicians risk being seen as silently agreeing with the client's self-criticism. However, recall that the practice of early interventions to modify clients' self-narratives, or counteract other affective states, is less common during the first session compared to later in a TA. Thus, the ideas presented in this section are also applied during other steps of the TA. In the first session, the main goals include learning about the client's narrative about themselves and the world and communicating that we understand those narratives and appreciate their importance. In this way, clients come to feel seen and understood by the clinician and develop a relationship that allows them to increase their ET, so that they eventually assimilate new information (Kamphuis & Finn, 2019).

Collecting Assessment Questions (AQs)

The second goal of the first session is to help clients identify and frame AQs that capture in their own words the things they have wondered about themselves, their relationships, or aspects of their lives that they find concerning. Once formalized, the client's AQs guide the subsequent phases of the process, since the goal of the assessment is to collaboratively discover answers to their questions.

Collecting AQs is both a result and an instrument of our work of building a secure and trusting relationship with the client through the processes discussed above. The more we successfully build an alliance with the client, the more the client's attachment system will regulate, activating the exploratory system and curiosity about the self. This helps client step back from their problems and formulate questions that capture what they want to learn. Simultaneously, by asking clients to formulate questions, and by collecting the AQs in their own words, we signal to them that we take their agenda seriously. When clients are active participants in the process, the alliance is strengthened.

Asking clients to put into words their AQs is also a way to define the TA contract, since the AQs signal the boundaries we use to inquire about their life. Involving clients as active participants and respecting those boundaries are important, as that lowers client anxiety and fosters their trust in us, building their motivation to engage in the process in an open and honest fashion. In addition, since the AQs will guide the subsequent phases of the TA, they are consistently referenced to explain and justify the relevance of what occurs in each session. This further helps us establish a safe relationship with the client and moves the clinician into the role of a trustworthy source of information (Kamphuis and Finn, 2019).

The process of collecting a client's AQs is valuable because we gather useful information about the client's current understanding of their existing problems, including their fears and pathogenic beliefs (see Box 5.2 for the concept of pathogenic beliefs and the Control-Mastery Theory). Clients sometimes directly communicate their pathogenic beliefs through their AQs (e.g., "Am I crazy?"). Other times their pathogenic beliefs are seen in AQs that describe the client inaccurately or with a lack of compassion. For example, a client with depression asks, "Why am I so lazy?" This type of AQ may reveal client's inaccurate understanding of their problem, in this case, as a flaw in their capacity for volition. It also reflects their lack of self-compassion, as the word "lazy" has a negative connotation in Euro-American culture. Other AQs, reveal a pathogenic belief when their goals seem contradictory or impossible, exemplified by a client asking, "How can I learn to rely solely on myself and not others?" This question suggests that the client believes relying on others is wrong, and they express the impossible desire of becoming a person without a need to be dependent.

Box 5.2 Pathogenic Beliefs and Control-Mastery Theory

Control-Mastery Theory is an integrative theory originated by Joseph Weiss (1924–2004) and further developed and researched by Hal Sampson (1925–2015) and the many theoreticians associated with the San Francisco Psychotherapy Research Group. Within this theory, psychopathology is seen as arising from pathogenic beliefs, developed as a result of "shock" traumas (one-time traumatic events) or repeated traumatic interactions in childhood with attachment figures or important others. Trauma is mainly considered to be "any experience or ongoing life circumstance which leads an individual to believe that an important goal, be it an instinctual wish or an ego striving, must be given up in order to avoid the interrelated dangers of damaging one's love objects or being damaged by them" (Bush & Gassner, 1988, p. 232). Pathogenic beliefs are conscious or unconscious irrational explanations of how one's behavior caused the trauma to occur, and how one must behave in order to avoid the danger of being retraumatized. For example, a child with unresponsive parents might feel responsible for the parents appearing drained of the energy necessary to respond to their needs. The child might develop the belief that, as a general rule, expressing their needs will drain others' energy and they will become reluctant to express their needs to avoid being abandoned. Once established, pathogenic beliefs are extremely hard to disconfirm. They are used as a guide in people's daily activities and significantly constrict their ability to develop and function successfully in the world. Examples of pathogenic beliefs may be "I am personally responsible for almost everything," "I am fundamentally a bad person," "I will hurt others with my accomplishments," "I have little value in the world," "I am helpless to intervene with life to change my fate," "The only way to stay in connection with others is to be passive and dependent," and "The world is a very unsafe place and I need to be worried much of the time." The reader will notice the overlap here between Control-Mastery Theory and self-verification theory, mentioned in Chapter 1.

In Control-Mastery Theory, clients are seen as active participants in therapy, working unconsciously to disconfirm their pathogenic beliefs by testing them in relation to the therapist. The fundamental work of the therapist is to help the client in this endeavor, by maintaining a therapeutic stance and not responding as the pathogenic belief predicts: "If patients experience the therapist as passing their tests (i.e., disconfirming their pathogenic beliefs), they will feel safer with the therapist, less anxious, and generally more productive in the therapy session" (Silberschatz, 2017, p. 2). There are two ways that clients may test the therapist. One is that clients unconsciously turn *passive into active*. This means that they treat the therapist the same way they have been treated and unconsciously hope that the therapist will not be traumatized but will instead be able to maintain a therapeutic stance (Bush & Gassner, 1988). For example, clients might become verbally abusive, contemptuous, or dismissive toward the clinician, as a way to test the belief that one deserves to be treated this way and must submissively accept it, or that in relationships you can be either an abuser or a victim, as they learned through childhood experiences. In these instances, the experience of a therapist who contains them without becoming abusive and eventually helps the client reflect upon what was moving them to behave this way can help disconfirm the client's pathogenic belief.

Another way to test the therapist is through *transference repetitions*. This refers to times when clients relate to the therapist repeating those behaviors which characterized their relationship with their parents and led to them being traumatized. In this way, clients are unconsciously testing whether the therapist, like their parents, will respond in a manner that the client found traumatic as a child (Bush & Gassner, 1988). For example, a child might have repeatedly experienced harsh punishment from their parents when they were acting independently and not following their rules. They may have developed the pathogenic belief that disobeying authority figures will lead to punishment and rejection. As an adult, to test this belief in therapy, they might push the therapist to make suggestions and then repeatedly "disobey" to see if the therapist will react in the same way as the parents did, but unconsciously wish to receive acceptance for their expression of independence.

While collecting questions that suggest pathogenic beliefs, and in the subsequent conversations, we value understanding the client's experiences that contributed to such beliefs, and we help them reconsider those experiences to revise their views. This helps clients become aware of the inaccuracy of their narrative and they begin to think about things differently, resulting in new behavioral options. Even when the client's AQs do not directly suggest a possible pathogenic belief, such beliefs may become evident through the way they describe themselves and the emotions that they express.

For example, Charlotte was a 35-year-old woman working at a bank, and began the first session asking, "Am I depressed?" The clinician inquired about what made her think she is depressed, and it was evident that Charlotte was afraid of the possibility of a positive answer to her question, as she was self-blaming about her sad mood, and lack of energy and interests. She stated, "I don't want to become a useless person who is just a burden to others." Listening to her comments and her self-blame, the clinician hypothesized that for Charlotte, having depression might mean she is fundamentally wrong. Therefore, the clinician explored her thinking (e.g., "Do you have any thoughts about where the idea that if you have depression you are useless comes from?"). In response, Charlotte talked about her mother who suffered from depression and was criticized by the family for having problems. Charlotte's mother was unable to recover from her depression or from being the outcast of the family. Understanding Charlotte's pathogenic belief about her potential depression helped the assessor bring into focus an important therapeutic goal. Throughout the TA, the clinician was mindful about how to help Charlotte draw a distinction between being depressed and being useless or wrong, so that if the test results indicated depression, it would lead to a productive therapy and not just confirm her pathogenic belief. Early detection of possible pathogenic beliefs connected to the client's questions may help the clinician avoid the risk that the TA becomes a traumatic experience.

Finally, the client's AQs indicate where their stories are open to change, and therefore they can later be used as "open doors" (Finn, 2007, p. 10) to discuss difficult information and begin shifting the client's narrative. Through their AQs, the client conveys, "This is what is important to me and what I want to know," and we respond, "I respect your goals and will work with you to figure out the answers." Over the course of the TA the AQs are ostensive cues and prime the client to open their ET so that they can assimilate new understandings of themselves (Kamphuis & Finn, 2019).

The Structure of the Initial Session

In this section, we present the general structure of the initial session. This is not a rigid schema, as different clients might need several of these steps, and only some of the steps are part of all first sessions of a TA (e.g., identifying AQs and gathering relevant data). It is also recognized that certain workplaces have specific expectations about the initial contact between a client and assessor, and clinicians are encouraged to use these ideas flexibly to meet those requirements.

Help the Client Feel Welcomed and Accepted

Most clients meeting with a professional for the first time enter that session with some anxiety and a sense of vulnerability. To help them feel at ease, we provide a warm welcome that aligns with the clinician's personality and individual style. This often includes statements such as, "Welcome. It's a pleasure to meet you," and small talk about finding the office. In these initial moments, we introduce the session from a collaborative perspective, by explaining that our priority will be to discuss the client's goals for the TA and the steps in the process, answering any question the client might have. We also inform the client that we will work together to develop a list of questions that they would like to find answers to.

Introduce the "Task"

The explicit task for the session might be presented to the client this way: "What questions do you have about yourself, your relationships, or about things connected to your life? Are there things that you would like to better understand because it would have a positive impact on your life?"

Help the Client Identify and Frame the AQs

In response to our request about formulating AQs, clients react in different ways. Some clients, following the initial phone contact and after reading the information sheet, have already formulated one or more questions that they immediately share with us. Some have written them down, while others have just started to think about possible AQs and elaborate in response to our invitation. When this is the case, we write down their questions **in their own words** and start collecting background information to understand the context from which they arise.

When clients present their questions, a complication might be that sometimes we do not judge them to be good openings for the subsequent TA, and we help clients refine them to be both good reflections of their concerns and helpful instruments for our work. This sometimes happens when clients have questions that have been asked by their partners. Questions such as, "Why am I such a narcissistic husband, as my wife says?" or "What's wrong with me that I am not as interested in sex with my partner?" In such situations, we ask the client how much these questions reflect their concerns or their partner's questions. Once the assessor clarifies this, the clients are encouraged to consider if they are interested in such questions or not, and whether they want to rephrase them to better reflect their point of view (e.g., "How can I help my wife to see that I care for her?," "What is missing in my relationship and what will help me become more open to sex with my partner?"). Other times we simply redirect the conversation back to what the client believes to be most important.

In other instances, clients seem initially incapable of formulating questions about their struggles and need our support. They might start telling us about their problems, but do not have much curiosity about themselves. For example, this might happen with under-regulated clients who feel anxious and overwhelmed. With these clients, it is useful to use a combination of accurate mirroring and finding language in their descriptions where there might be an implicit question that the clinician can suggest. For example, a client may talk about how their last intimate relationships failed, and we ask, " ... and do you have any questions about intimate relationships?" We may also tentatively suggest a question that we imagine captures the client's concern, such as, "So, would you be interested in understanding why you are having a difficult time making your intimate relationships work?" If the client agrees with our observation, we further stimulate collaboration by asking, "How would you formulate the question in your own words?" and then write down the client's AQ.

Even with clients who are able to formulate questions at the beginning of the session, it is important to listen for other potential issues they might want to address and put into questions. For example, some clients may talk about challenges they have faced in friendships without explicitly identifying a question. After letting them share a bit, we ask whether the client has a question about that topic, in this case friendships. In this way, we end up with questions about different parts of the client's life (e.g., different relationships, work or school, emotional life, sense of self.)

This type of collaborative exploration of the client's life often leads to different questions that allow us to view the problem from various angles. For example, Henry initially asked a "how" question (e.g., "How can I get rid of my anxiety when I am around others?"). The assessor explored his experiences of anxiety, and Henry's trust and curiosity grew, which led to a "why" question (e.g., "Why do I feel so anxious when I meet new people?"). Clients who are able to identify a mix of how and why questions have an optimal set of AQs. "Why" questions help us identify important experiences and contextual elements that have contributed to the client's problems, while "how" questions typically include the solution or path forward. At the end of Henry's TA, the assessor used the test data and exploration of early experiences to identify the answer to why he has social anxiety, and then used their knowledge of anxiety to answer how he can have less anxiety when he is around others.

Collecting Background and Contextual Information

After identifying an AQ, we ask questions to collect relevant information about the issue targeted by that question. This is a question-centered inquiry that differs from traditional clinical and background interviews or anamnesis (i.e., gathering the patient's developmental/clinical history according to the clinician's agenda). We inquire about the problem signaled by the client as significant (through the AQ), with the goal of reaching a detailed and contextualized understanding of that issue. We aim to have a clear understanding of how the problem looks in their daily life. To meet this goal, one technique we use is circular questioning (Selvini et al., 1980; Tomm, 1988). This approach was initially used by family therapists but can be beneficial with individual clients, as "the questioning is aimed at creating or maximizing difference and then drawing connections in order to provide information that frames problems in new ways" (Brown, 1997, p. 109). As this concept and its use has evolved, more recent theorists have suggested that this approach would better be labeled "additional perspectives questions," highlighting that the questions help clients gain a different perspective on their difficulties (Hornstrup et al., 2015, p. 10). We find that the use of circular questioning during the first session results in AQs that are more specific and contextualized. Tomm (1988) identified different types of circular questions and we use these to explore the AQs and related to context:

1   How the problem might have changed across time (e.g., "When did the problem begin?" "Was is it harder or easier to deal with when you were younger?").
2   How it impacts relationships with different people (e.g., "How does the problem look or change with strangers versus familiar people, with authority figures versus peers, with your mother or your father?").
3   How it presents in different contexts (e.g., "Is the problem worse or better at work or at home?" "When is the problem absent?").
4   How it connects information about behaviors and feelings (e.g., "What happens when you start crying and people around you try to cheer you up?" or "How do you feel before and after cutting yourself?").

Often, when clients engage in the circular questioning process, they start building insight into their struggles. This is most likely to happen with clients who perceive their problems as overgeneralized (e.g., "I am an angry person") and disconnected from contextual factors. Through our questions, they start seeing how their problems differ based on context, and they leave the first session having already learned something. In this way, along with building a secure connection with the client, circular questioning is a primary intervention during this session.

There are two additional questions that we might pose to the client to collect important information: (1) "If you had to answer your question today, what would you say?" and (2) "What would be the most difficult thing to hear at the end of the assessment?" The first question helps us understand what the client is already aware of (Level 1 Information). The second question may reveal Level 3 Information, that is not part of their conscious understanding of the problem, and may need to be carefully integrated eventually. The client's answer to the second question may also give us an idea of what would be most difficult to discuss, if verified by the test results (e.g., "I am afraid that you'll tell me that I am depressed and I need to take medications"). We do not always ask these questions, as we do not have a set list of questions. However, these questions might be helpful for understanding clients who have a strong, and perhaps fixed, narrative about their problems, the likes of which would lead them to rejecting certain test results. With these clients, a clear understanding of their story allows us to take it into account and validate the reasons why their narrative developed the way it did, before trying to gradually shift it (should it be inaccurate) during the course of the TA.

What is most important during the first session is that we use our curiosity to collect enough information about the client's problems to get a vivid picture of them, and build our understanding of the client's self-knowledge. Equally important, while inquiring about the client's AQs, we are doing parallel work of building an alliance through the processes described above.

Respect the Client's Right to Privacy

In contrast to a traditional clinical interview, during this session we ask face-valid questions that are directly tied to the client's AQs and related areas of their life. This further conveys to the client that their agenda for the TA holds central importance for us. For example, if a client has an AQ about depression, and we sense there may have been some adverse childhood experiences, we do not ask about such topics unless they are explicitly connected to what the client is discussing. On the rare occasions when we need to ask a question that is not related to the client's concerns, we ask permission and explain why our question is connected. For example, with a client who is describing dissociative symptoms that seem connected to their AQs, we ask permission to inquire about the possible traumatic origin of such symptoms. We may say, "Given what I know about psychology, the kind of experiences you are describing may be related to traumatic or emotionally overwhelming events in your past. Is it okay if I ask you some questions about that?"

Importantly, we allow clients to declare certain topics off limits, and we are realistic about how that may affect our ability to answer the client's questions. When a client is unwilling to talk about a certain topic during the first session, we might discuss the possibility of asking about that subject later in the TA, if it becomes evident that it is necessary information to answer an AQ. For example, we may say, "We do not need to talk about this now, and I'll work to answer your question with the other information that we'll discuss about you. However, if after I review test data and consider our conversations it becomes evident that it's not possible to fully answer your question without talking about those experiences, is it okay if I broach that topic again?"

Respecting the client's right to withhold information about themselves until they feel safe to disclose it is a central aspect of how we work during a TA and particularly during the first session. This strategy reduces the power imbalance between clinician and client and demonstrates the respect we have for our client's healthy epistemic vigilance. We may say something like, "It really makes a lot of sense to me why you wouldn't want to discuss that part of your life, as we just met and for all you know I may be a charlatan. I hope you come to see over time that I can be helpful to you." When we meet this kind of resistance we do not take it personally, but we consider it important information about how best to work with the client, and that it may take time to build trust so they feel comfortable sharing sensitive information. We also feel a sense of security knowing that if the undiscussed topic is significant in the client's life, it is likely to enter future conversations, and hopefully when it does, trust will have been built.

Assessors trained in the traditional information-gathering model of assessment may wonder how we obtain information that is typically part of a clinical interview (e.g., educational, medical, and mental health history). We find that over the course of the TA, these topics naturally enter the conversation during the Extended Inquiries (EIs) or other discussions. However, when those topics are discussed in a natural way, rather than as a requirement the clinician has to meet during a session, clients often feel more comfortable sharing about these areas of their life. In this way, our goal of keeping the client's agenda paramount is maintained. Clinicians working in settings in which documentation standards require certain information be collected during the first session will need to be flexible about this part of the model.

Obtain Permission to Contact Other Professionals

We ask the client about obtaining past records and contacting others they have worked with (e.g., medical doctor, therapist, spiritual guide). We explain why such records or contact will be helpful and clarify what information the client will allow us to obtain and share. If possible, we invite the client to help with this process and have them collect information (e.g., a past psychological report, school records). This empowers the client to take ownership in the TA, and helps them feel more secure by giving them control over the information that is obtained.

Review the RP's Questions

As discussed in Chapter 4, we usually collect the RP's questions prior to the first TA session and discuss with the RP to what extent they already shared or are going to share their questions with the client. However, even if the RP states that the client knows about their questions, it is important that we discuss them during the first session. In so doing, we remain transparent with the client and have an opportunity to obtain their opinion of the RP's concerns.

When RPs have posed questions that we can share with clients, we typically review them at the end of the first session. By prioritizing the client's concerns before discussing the RPs questions, we reaffirm that this process is for the client. While reviewing the RP's questions, we may discover that a client is confused about them, and we empower the client by suggesting they discuss the questions with the RP. When this happens, we inform the RP that we suggested the client reconnect about their questions. Toward the end of the first session, we also take time to discuss what type of contact we will have with the RP during the TA (e.g., how and when we will inform the RP about test results) and obtain a signed release of information.

Restate the Client's AQs

We restate the AQs before ending the session, to ensure we captured the client's language, and that we are addressing their salient issues. In this moment, we are finalizing the agreement on the client's goals for the TA, and we invite clients to modify the questions if they need editing. We also ask if they want to pose further questions on issues that were not discussed during the session.

When our efforts to build a secure relationship with the client have been successful, clients with epistemic hypervigilance (EH) may now share one or several new questions they previously withheld. When this occurs, we consider if the client feels shame about these areas of their life, and that shame contributed to them being cautious about discussing these topics. When a client shares new questions at the end of the session, we take a few minutes to inquire about them and then move toward ending the session. However, if the client poses several new questions about topics that were not previously discussed, we may schedule a second session to explore these AQs before beginning testing. Importantly, when clients reveal these types of questions at the end, we validate their honesty and attend to any shame that arises using the interventions described.

Completing the Assessment Contract

We begin closing the session once we have finished discussing the client's AQs and related topics. Assessors will need to manage their time well (reserve 15–20 minutes), as there are still important things to cover in this last part of the session.

A primary point of discussion during this last portion of the session is establishing how the TA will occur and the cost. Depending on the usual practice or cultural expectations of clinician and client, this could include discussing the timing of the TA, and the number of hours and sessions, or time span in terms of months. We may also discuss common procedures, such as the number and type of tests, our preference to conduct the Summary/Discussion Session at the RP's office, and that a letter will summarize answers to their AQs. This is also a time to discuss how the assessor will have contact with the RP, and in settings where the client pays out of pocket, the cost of the TA. At this point, we typically have a good idea about what will occur to answer the questions posed, but we also build some flexibility in the contract in case we later realize that the process will be longer than expected. For example, after a few sessions we may realize we need to administer more tests than initially expected or may come to learn that the client will need a formal report in addition to a TA letter. At this point in the first session, in settings where this can occur, some clients may ask about negotiating the cost. Therefore, it is important that we have that discussion with a clear idea of the amount of work required (see also Chapter 12 on billing for a TA). Again, we may be flexible on this negotiable aspect of our practice but should not alter our cost if this will result in us later feeling resentful or exploited. If appropriate, we can also discuss the possibility of reducing the cost by limiting the length of the TA. When this occurs, we explain the limitations of reducing the scope (e.g., we might not be able to answer all the client's AQs), so that they can make an informed choice on how to proceed.

After we agree on a plan, we schedule the next session which is typically a testing session (see Chapter 6).

Allow the Client to Ask Questions

During the final part of this session, we invite clients to ask questions about us and the process. This is another way to reduce the power imbalance between us and the client and to build collaboration. The client might have questions or doubts about us that are important to discuss before proceeding. For example, clients with a lot of shame might be worried about what we think of their problems and may ask us what we are thinking about them, but this question was shared only because we invited the client to do so. We might say, "So, we are almost done with this session. Today I asked you a lot of questions and I'm wondering if you have any questions about this process or about me that you would like to ask." A client with a lot of shame may respond, "I am wondering if you think that I am crazy." Such comments provide another opportunity to make a shame intervention.

In other situations, clients might question if we have enough personal or professional experience to understand and help with their problems. With these clients, we discuss our education, training, or experiences that have contributed to our expertise. For example, if a client asks, "Have you ever been that depressed? Do you think you can really understand what that means?" We may respond, "I have never been that depressed myself, but I have worked with depressed clients who have taught me a lot about what it is like to be so low. However, most importantly, I have learned from them that each person has his or her own way of experiencing depression. I really want to know everything I can about your way of feeling this way."

If a client asks a question that we feel is inappropriate to answer (e.g., "Do you masturbate as much as I do?"), we ask how knowing that information would be helpful to them. We might discover that the client is concerned about what we think about a certain topic (e.g., "I am wondering if you think I am a pervert because I masturbate so much."). In such situations, we provide an answer to the client's concern while maintaining our professional and therapeutic stance. We might say, "I don't think you are a pervert. I think that in ways we still have yet to understand, masturbating has been helpful to you not just because it feels good."

Last, it is also important to discuss any questions or doubts that the client has about the TA process. Sometimes clients who are overwhelmed or confused during the first call and at the beginning of the first session, become more regulated as the relationship builds. Now at the end of the session, they are in a position to better understand and incorporate information about the process and we share whatever would be helpful.

Metaprocessing

Before ending the session, we invite the client to reflect upon the experience they had with us in the session. We ask questions such as, "So what was it like to talk about these things today?," or "How are you feeling as you leave today?" This type of metaprocessing aligns with interventions that are part of Accelerated Experiential Dynamic Psychotherapy (AEDP; Fosha et al., 2009: Fosha, 2000; see Box 5.3). The clinician invites the client to reflect on the conversation that occurred and what it was like to connect, and as Fosha states:

> "The explicit sharing and processing of the experience of the relationship results in a moment of deep connection. It is the creation of instant attachment and affirms that the client and the therapist are in this together. The client doesn't walk out alone [after the end of the session]." (retrieved from aedp.eu)

Box 5.3   Metaprocessing

Accelerated Experiential Dynamic Psychotherapy (AEDP) therapists propose that therapists can metaprocess in two ways, referred to as "capital-M" metaprocessing and "small-m" metaprocessing (Fosha, 2000). Capital-M metaprocessing is when the client experienced a change for the better during psychotherapy and the therapist asks the client to reflect upon the experience. Small m metaprocessing involves reflecting on a smaller shift. For example, the client says something, the clinician makes a remark, and tears come to the client's eyes because they feel understood. The clinician may then ask, "When I said that, it seemed to have moved you. What's that like for you?" This is small-m metaprocessing, and occurs with both positive and negative emotions. As another example, the clinician may say something and the client turns away or averts their eyes. These behaviors may indicate a significant moment, or a meaningful change, and it is best to stop and process what occurred. The clinician is not expected to have preconceived ideas about what the client's behavior means. Rather it is a moment for the clinician to more fully understand the client's experiences in a precise way (https://www.psychotherapy.net).

In TA, we may metaprocess the client's reactions multiple times, not just at the end of the first session. It might happen, for example, after mirroring the client's emotions and seeing a visible reaction (e.g., client's eyes tearing up), or when we discuss a test result that is important in building a new narrative and we want to make space to process the client's reaction to hearing it. Another example is when the client falls into shame, and we intervene in a way that has a positive effect. In each of these cases, it is important to stop and ask questions like, "What was it like for you to hear me say that?" and then discuss the experience with the client.

Metaprocessing is a way to increase the sharing of emotions and experiences between clinician and client. It fosters the process of emotional attunement and collaboration and strengthens the intimacy of the therapeutic relationship, while promoting client mentalization.

In TA we metaprocess at the end of the session to make the implicit experience of meeting and engaging in a conversation with us explicit. This increases the client's awareness of the experience and consolidates the work done. In other sessions, we also metaprocess at the end, especially when a significant therapeutic experience has been part of the meeting. For example, after a meaningful EI discussion or a powerful Assessment Intervention Session (AIS), reflecting on the experience is often beneficial to the client.

Post-Session Tasks

After the client leaves, we take some time to reflect on our experience of the client and the session. We note initial impressions, hypotheses, emotional reactions, or anxieties that the client might have provoked in us. This is useful information for the next session and informs our growing conceptualization of the client. We also reflect on how well the session went and ideally the client left feeling calm, curious, and hopeful about the process (Finn, 2007). We review and type up the client's AQs, and often, "an informal 'factor analysis' of the questions posed by the client can be fertile soil for hypotheses of what might be driving the client's core issues" (Kamphuis & De Saeger, 2012, p. 136). That analysis also should inform our decision making regarding which tests to begin with, as further discussed in the next chapter.

Working with the Referring Professional (RP)

The involvement of an RP in a TA may create some challenges in collecting the client's AQs. Sometimes we note that the client's AQs contain psychological jargon that does not align with how clients typically talk about themselves (e.g., "Why am I a masochist?"). Other times clients are more interested in talking about other topics that are not covered by the RP's questions. This is most likely when the client is working with a therapist who is not familiar with TA and with the concept of AQs. Some RPs take on too much of a role in shaping the client's AQs, resulting in language that is confusing or misaligned with how the client thinks. In these situations, we discuss the questions with the client and edit them, so they are focused on relevant issues. We then inform the RP that our work with the client led to a modification of the AQs. We also reassure the RP that the issues that are not covered by the client's AQs but are significant to the RP, will be included in the focus of the TA.

Common Mistakes and Challenges in the First Session

Difficulties in Balancing the Tasks of Building a Therapeutic Relationship and Collecting the Client's AQs

Our experience in learning and teaching TA is that it is difficult, especially for beginners, to balance the tasks of building a therapeutic relationship with the client, and structuring the session so AQs can be formulated. At times, clinicians slip into a therapist role, and lose the focus on collecting AQs. For example, a client may start talking about their problems, and rather than formulating an AQ we work therapeutically with the client, providing support and validation. In these situations, we may spend too much time in this role and fail to identify AQs and important contextual elements.

At the other end of the continuum, it is a mistake to be over-focused on the task of collecting AQs and be predominantly in the assessor role. Assessors may conduct something akin to a traditional clinical interview without collaboratively engaging the client. When in the assessor role, our focus is often on our questions and our written notes, and we may miss the client's nonverbal communication suggesting they need support (e.g., signals of shame or defenses against shame). When this occurs, assessors are not adequately attending to the goal of building a secure and trusting relationship with the client. A similar but slightly different type of mistake would be collecting a list of AQs but failing to collect relevant background information. This is problematic as clinicians will not fully understand how the questions are related to the client's life, which in turn impacts our case conceptualization (see Chapter 7).

Those learning TA are encouraged to be mindful about both the assessor and therapist roles and work towards an optimal balance to ensure the goals of this session are met.

Clients Who Are Not Participating Fully

Some clients may express skepticism or ambivalence about the process with statements such as "I don't know if I want to do this" or "I'm anxious about the things you will find out." These clients may display dismissive or withdrawn behaviors in response to the clinician's questions and comments. In these instances, we do not take the client's ambivalence personally but encourage them to express their skepticism and thinking. Sometimes when clients have doubts about the process, it is a test to see if we are asking for blind trust, contrary to healthy vigilance which allows them to choose the right people to trust. Such skepticism could also be connected to the client's dilemma of change, where part of them wants the answer to their questions and another is afraid of what the answers could be. With such clients, we ask about their reservations, exploring and mirroring the possible dilemma and normalizing their uncertainty. We also encourage the client to continue and as the sessions unfold, consider whether the process is helpful. In so doing, we show respect for the client's perspective and reinforce the collaborative nature of TA. We might also address the client's reservations by clarifying certain aspects of the contract, if appropriate. For example, suppose a client is afraid of feeling overwhelmed when they are at home after talking about vulnerable topics. In that case, we tell the client about our availability between sessions to provide support or discuss self-soothing and emotion regulation techniques.

Dealing with Client's Relational Tests

As described in Box 5.2, clients might test us to disconfirm their pathogenic beliefs, and it is not always easy to detect these tests and respond therapeutically. To illustrate these ideas, we provide a few examples of relational tests that might occur during a first TA session, and some ideas on how to respond.

Clients Who Treat Us in Ways That Are Similar to How They Have Been Treated

Some clients might act in disrespectful, abusive, or intrusive ways, to disconfirm a pathogenic belief connected to past experiences of being treated similarly by important others. According to the Control-Mastery Theory, individuals who experienced traumatic abusive, disrespectful, or intrusive behaviors in their childhood may develop the belief that people should accept being treated this way, as they had no choice but to do so (Weiss, 1993; see Box 5.2). These clients might unconsciously test us, hoping that we will respond in appropriate ways, therefore disconfirming their pathogenic belief. To be therapeutic with these clients, we benevolently set limits, without becoming abusive ourselves.

For example, Devon, a 32-year-old client, asked for a TA because of his insomnia and compulsive use of the internet at night, which he defined as an "internet addiction." The first session was scheduled before lunchtime and Devon entered the office, sat on the couch, and said that he needed to eat a little snack. The clinician allowed this and while they were talking about his AQs Devon began eating unshelled peanuts, spilling broken shells on the couch. The clinician handed him a trash can, and Devon used it a few times, but then returned to spilling on the couch. The clinician grew increasingly angry and offended by Devon's behaviors, and decided to gently but firmly ask Devon, "Can you please use the trash can for the shells? I'd really appreciate that." Devon responded affirmatively, and almost looked happy while cleaning up the couch. After this exchange, Devon was more focused and involved in identifying AQs, and opened up about himself. He disclosed that his father—with whom he was still living—had become very anxious and would enter his room without warning to check on Devon's "internet addiction." The clinician asked Devon how he felt about his father's lack of respect for his boundaries. Devon replied that he had not thought much about it as he has been used to it for a long time, but it felt controlling. The clinician retrospectively thought that perhaps Devon's initial behavior was a test to see if the clinician would respond to someone being disrespectful about personal boundaries in a more adaptive way.

Clients Who Repeat Behaviors That Caused Traumatizing Reactions from Important Others

Some clients unconsciously repeat behaviors they believe caused reactions from their parents or other important figures in their life, which were traumatic. They unconsciously hope that we will not react in traumatizing ways, so that their belief of being the cause of these behaviors will be disproved. For example, during the first session of her TA, Lisa, a 45-year-old woman, often answered the clinician's questions with vague and non-elaborated sentences and laughter. The clinician was confused about these behaviors since they starkly contrasted with Lisa's interest in finding an answer to her AQ, "Why am I so alone, and why am I not able to keep dating the same person and build a stable relationship?" Lisa had described how her partners repeatedly cheated on her, were abusive and in one case became physically violent. She repeatedly blamed herself for being "stupid," as she did not realize when her partners were cheating and stated that they probably had the right to treat her badly, because she was a bad girlfriend. In her story, her negative self-view was supported by the fact that she did not have a successful career and was an overly dependent and anxious person. Her conclusion was that she deserved being alone. With her vague statements and her frequent laughter, the clinician suspected that Lisa was trying to test whether he would find her annoying and scold her or treat her harshly. On this basis, the clinician decided to react mainly to the serious comments and answers that Lisa was providing. The assessor ignored the behaviors she was unconsciously exhibiting to test whether he would attack her. This strategy seemed successful, as Lisa became increasingly more focused and less vague, and there were moments of authentic connection with the clinician.

Clients Who Test Our Capacity to Be Trustworthy and Competent

Some clients might question our capacity to fulfill the TA contract and may ask if we will really be able to answer their AQs. In these cases, we might feel anxious, as every individual is a "complicated puzzle" that we will never be able to fully "solve." Moreover, if we think about the task of responding to the client's AQs as a solo enterprise, we might wonder if our psychological tests will provide the information needed to answer to complex questions. In these cases, it is important to remember that what we need is enough understanding of the client to answer their questions, and that we will not do this alone, but in collaboration with the client. Ideally, we also make sure that if we need support, we can access a trustworthy supervisor or consultant, who might help when we feel uncertain about a certain client or aspects of the TA process.

To address our client's concerns about our abilities, we restate the TA process, and emphasize that we will work hard to answer these questions, and the results will come through us working collaboratively together. We might say, "I will contribute with my expertise in testing and psychology and you with your knowledge of yourself. Through our collaboration, I am confident that we will find answers to these questions."

As a concluding remark, we note that some clients might have cultural expectations or personal inclinations that guide them to work with a competent clinician who will answer their questions from an expert (one-up) position, similar to the traditional physician-patient model of relationships. With these clients, over emphasizing the collaborative nature of TA might be counterproductive, as it would push the client to explore relational patterns that are too unfamiliar (Aschieri, 2016). With these clients, we feel secure in addressing their concerns about our capacity to help them reach their goals and may say, "This model has proved to be effective in helping with different kinds of problems, and I have used it successfully to answer many different client's questions, so I am confident I'll be able to do the same with yours."

From Easy-to-Answer Questions to Questions That Are Impossible to Fully Answer

When we collect the client's AQs, we often privately wonder how useful they are as instruments for our subsequent work and how difficult it will be to identify answers to them. This is an important evaluation that we do not share with our clients, but we use our reflections to decide if we need to work with the client to refine further their questions, instead of simply accepting them.

Questions We Know We Can Answer

We might have AQs that we can immediately answer, often because the answer depends on what our test results will tell us. For example, a client may ask whether they are depressed or have another mental health issue that one or more tests can assess. In these cases, we accept the question the client posed and proceed by asking for background information and then to the testing to find the answer.

In addition, sometimes we are confident we can answer the AQ and *we already know the answer* because the client gave us enough information about the issue to respond based on our professional knowledge. In these cases, if we understand that the answer is near the client's conscious narration about the self, we might start discussing what we think. An example might be a client wondering about depression, and in the first session they list all the symptom-related criteria for this diagnosis. We might recognize that talking about depression does not make them anxious and judge that they are looking for an expert opinion to explain their problems. We may say, "Based on what you shared, I can see how depression is part of what's going on and let's also see what the test results indicate." On the contrary, if we judge the client might have a difficult time hearing out thoughts, we wait to "consult" the tests. For example, we would wait to respond to a client who says everyone is convinced his physical symptoms are psychosomatic, and he wonders if that is true despite negative medical test results. The client might say that his physical symptoms tend to worsen when he is stressed, and we might recognize that somatizing is part of what is occurring. With this client, it might be best to devote time to building a relationship that will allow us to support the client in hearing difficult test results and postpone the answer until later in the TA. The test results will then be an alternative, more convincing source of information. In addition, other test results may validate the part of the client that does not feel that underlying distress is a good explanation for their symptoms.

Often, clients who engage in a TA are looking for help on broad issues rather than simply finding a diagnosis. Given this, we usually collect questions that require both good testing and complex clinical skills to be answered, as these are questions that a predetermined set of test results cannot address. For example, a client may ask, "Why is it difficult for me to feel really close to my partners? And how can I learn to become a better partner for my girlfriend?" The accuracy of the answer will rely on the degree to which the entire TA is successful. To answer such questions, the assessor will need to administer tests that help identify the client's relational style and how that may impact intimate relationships specifically. However, the clinician's work of building a trusting relationship with the client fosters the client's openness, which is necessary to provide useful, detailed information that is a fulfilling answer to their AQs.

Questions That Are Too Broad

At times we encounter AQs that are too broad, making them difficult to answer. For example, if a client asks, "Am I a good person?" it will be hard to find a satisfying answer. The concept of being a "good person" is vague, personally defined and includes multiple aspects of an individual. In this situation, we ask the client what it means for them to be "a good person," and help them narrow the question, by asking questions such as, "Are there specific parts of being a good person that you are worried about?" Such discussions often lead to a more refined version of the initial question such as, "Why do I have a hard time being available when my wife and children ask for my attention?"

Questions That Are Impossible to Answer

Some questions are impossible to answer, or it is not possible to articulate a full answer. We often see two types of questions in this category. The first are questions about future scenarios that do not solely depend on the client's behaviors or choices. For example, if a client asks, "Will I ever be able to find the right partner?" we know that we will not be able to find a definitive answer, as finding the right partner depends not only on the client but also on an undefined number of factors. When working with such a question, we might explore why the person doubts that they will be able to find the right partner and discover for example, that they have had a series of disappointing relationship experiences due to being too trusting. With this client, we might end up with a question such as, "Why do I often disregard signs that tell me another person is not trustworthy? How can I learn to see those signs and use that information when selecting my future partners?"

The second type of impossible questions to fully answer is focused on other people in the client's life who are not participating in the TA. An example would be, "Why is my partner always angry at me?" If the partner is not part of the process, we can speculate with the client about some of the reasons the partner is angry. However, this is limited by the client's awareness of the issue, and we will not have necessary information that would contribute to a complete explanation. In this situation, we might explore whether we should empower the client to ask the partner why they are angry or how they can respond in a more effective or self-protective way to their anger. This might result in an AQ such as, "How can I feel more confident about asking my partner about their feelings and how can I best manage when they are angry?"

When to Stop Inquiring About the AQs and Begin Testing

In TA, we usually have one, 90 minute session to collect the client's AQs and relevant background information. Even with this amount of time, we might feel anxious about gathering enough information. At the end of the first session, we consider the choice of scheduling a second session to continue the discussion or moving to the testing phase. In deciding how to proceed, there are a few issues to consider. First, it is useful to explore the client's psychological functioning and life experiences until some test results are necessary to understand them better. For example, at a certain point we realize that the client cannot provide more information that will enhance our understanding, and the conversation becomes redundant. This is a clear sign that moving to the testing is the best choice. A second consideration is related to the fact that we might be out of time during the first session, despite feeling that further discussion would be helpful. If we deem a second session is unnecessary, we feel secure in proceeding knowing that we will get more information through the testing and the EIs (see Chapter 6). Even though we can only develop a limited understanding of a client in a 90-minute first session, we trust that our understanding of the client will deepen during the other steps of the TA.

However, there are instances when we decide to conduct a second session to continue working on the AQs. This might occur when clients are disorganized and overwhelmed, and the first session is focused on regulating their emotions and we cannot collect AQs. There may also be clients who tell us at the end of the first session something particularly important (e.g., a traumatic experience) that we cannot explore because of time constraints, but we recognize that it needs to be explored before we move to testing. Finally, some clients are apprehensive about the TA and need time to build trust in the assessor and their curiosity about themselves. In these cases, the best choice is to recommend a second session to continue working on AQs. When this occurs, we renegotiate the contract with the client, as another session will also make the process longer and more expensive.

Clinical Case: Initial Session with Emma

We return to Hale's account of the TA with Emma.

It took some time before Emma and I could have our initial meeting. Emma delayed setting the meeting time and twice rescheduled after the meeting had been set. Her explanation was that she was too busy. I wondered if this behavior hinted at ambivalence she had about the assessment or whether it reflected her difficulty being organized in her daily life. When we finally met, the first session began with me welcoming her and noting it had been a while since we had talked on the phone. She agreed and said she had been busy but had been thinking of questions. I structured the session by explaining our main goals, which were getting her questions and understanding the background, context, and details around them. Emma was pleasant but initially uncomfortable in the room. Her arms were crossed in a defensive posture, she nervously looked around the room, and she talked rapidly. I tried to make Emma feel appreciated and valued and to create a warm feeling in the room by being welcoming, happy to see her, and interested in what she had to say. She initially talked with some pressure so I let her talk, hoping it would calm her some. It also gave me a chance to observe her way of being and to get know about her life.

During this initial part of the session, Emma talked extensively about all the psychological and spiritual work she had done on herself. I did not interrupt because it seemed important to her to convey this information. She went on to share that during college she developed problems with alcohol but had been able to stop drinking after about 10 years with the help of Alcoholics Anonymous and self-development. Emma reported she had been sober for more than 15 years. It seemed as if she was working hard to convince me that she had reached a place of great self-understanding and self-control.

Emma had an unusual conversational style, going off on long detours that often were tangential and self-justifying. A few times I tried to clarify her point, but this did not seem to help organize her. This led me to wonder if her attachment system became under-regulated in emotionally arousing contexts, such as the first session with an unknown clinician. She also had subtle, unusual eye movements and facial mannerisms, as if she could not see well. Noticing my reaction to her, I also considered what effect her communication style might have on others. As she talked, she seemed to become more comfortable and uncrossed her arms. When she seemed more comfortable, I tried to bring the conversation around to the goal of getting her questions. Here is some dialog beginning about 20 minutes into the session.

Hale: Well, it sounds like you know a lot about yourself. *[Hale responds with an empathic and attuned comment to Emma's efforts to show the psychological and spiritual work she already had done, so that she could feel seen and understood.]* I remember you mentioned some possible questions in our phone conversation a few weeks ago. And I wanted to follow up with that and develop together the questions that would be helpful to have answered by the assessment. I hear a number of possible ones in what you just told me. *[Hale gently introduces the task of collecting assessment questions that capture Emma's current concerns and frame it as a collaborative enterprise. He also makes an explicit connection to the content of the phone conversation, so that Emma feels that he is able to hold her in mind since the beginning of their relationship.]*

Emma: Yes, but the biggest one is, is there a possibility that when I was really, really young, did I have like some sort of brain injury that led me to have these tendencies or to have a partial learning disability? Because I think I am borderline learning disabled. I do not think I am full-on, but I think that is the question. *[Hale noted to himself that this question, along with the nature of the behaviors and the discussion, suggested she might indeed have some underlying neuropsychological issues.]*

Hale: Do you have a learning disability? *[Hale writes the question down]*

Emma: Yes, am I learning disabled. Yeah.

Hale: So, knowing that would be helpful?

Emma: Absolutely! Yes, I really want to know. Am I in a situation where I'm learning disabled or am I ADHD? I really want to know that too because I was hyperactive as a kid, and a while back I went to an ADHD seminar and there were some things that I struggled with. My memory is not one of them but all the other things where I get distracted easily or I have trouble keeping track of where things are, which is some of that ADHD, and where I move so fast that I think, "Oh wait, what was I doing?" So, I kind of explored that with this woman who was kind of consulting, but she was not a full-on counselor. I felt uncomfortable in the neighborhood where they met. It was late at night, like you would get out at like 8:30 and it was off of Sayles Drive and 14th Avenue, you know it just did not feel very safe, so I stopped going and …

Hale: So, some troubles keeping track of things and remembering what you are doing, that kind of thing. *[Since Emma seems to be again going off track, Hale intervenes to keep the focus, because under-regulated clients need the clinician to take an active approach in containing and structuring their somewhat disorganized discourse ("sit forward"). This signals Hale's active presence and support, which may work in the direction of reassuring Emma.]*

Emma: Yes. And organizational skills. *[Emma re-focuses herself, showing that Hale's previous intervention was helpful.]*

Hale: And organization, ok. And you wondered if you were hyperactive as a child?

Emma: Yes, and I think I was. I think I was very hyperactive. I mean it was hard for me to sit still. I was not a low-energy kid.

Hale: So, we might put your concerns into a question like "Do I have a learning disability or attention deficit hyperactivity disorder?" Would this be a good way to word it? *[Hale proposes the formulation of an Assessment Question, as Emma needs help to organize her thoughts. But he also makes sure she agrees with the wording because he wants to continue fostering the collaboration with Emma]*

Emma: Yes! Exactly!

Hale: Tell me what makes you suspect a learning disability. *[Hale starts gathering background information.]*

Emma: Well, I had trouble keeping up with other kids in school. I didn't get things as easily. They would be off on something else, and I was not ready. My teacher would get frustrated with me. I remember one teacher who thought I was doing it on purpose, and I felt bad about that.

Hale: That must have been confusing. You didn't do anything wrong, but she accused you of not trying! She really misunderstood you. *[Hale directly combating Emma's shame.]*

Emma: It hit me hard. I didn't want to go to school after that. I was afraid of that teacher.

Hale: Oh, I can imagine. That was really hurtful. *[Hale attuning to Emma's experience.]*

Emma: It did hurt me. I went into a shell. But my next teacher the next year, she was really nice.

Hale: Good! That must have been a relief. Were some things harder than others? *[Hale continuing to deepen understanding of Emma's experiences with school.]*

Emma: Well, everything was hard. But I especially had trouble with math.

Hale: When did you first notice that others were going faster than you?

Emma: I always felt like that.

Hale: Did you get any help from anyone?

Emma: Not really. In those days, they didn't know much about LD. Now at my school we really pay attention at the slightest thing. But my kids are not really doing much academic work yet.

Hale: Boy, it sure is unfortunate that in years past people with an LD didn't get any help, or even any recognition of the problem. *[Again, Hale addressing shame.]*

After gathering some additional background information on learning, attentional and hyperactivity issues, I asked about other questions. A long and somewhat disorganized discussion of relationships issues ensued, during which I interrupted Emma several times to redirect the focus. At one point, she expressed concern that she was talking too much.

Hale: No, I really appreciate your openness. I am certainly getting a clearer picture of what is going on. But I might interrupt you some when I feel the need to clarify something or to keep us focused on understanding you better. *[Hale responds both counteracting Emma's shame expressed in her self-criticism and clarifying his responsibility in structuring the dialogue to best serve Emma's needs.]* It seems like the fundamental question here is, "Why have I not been able to have a successful long-term relationship?"

Emma: That is pretty spot on, yes. I mean, here we are. Because it's not like I don't want one. But I am also afraid that I will get into one and then it will end. I am so tired of ending relationships. I do not like it. And I mean it is embarrassing that I have had this many partners in a lifetime already. It is kind of strange. It is really strange to me.

Hale: It is a great question. It seems like that is exactly what you are looking for answers on, so you can finally get to the bottom of it and move ahead the way you want.

Emma: I do, I want to get to the bottom of it. *(Emma smiles)*

Hale: So, "Why have I not been able to have a successful long-term relationship?"

Emma: Yes, I think that is a good question.

Hale: Well, let's organize the testing we do and our focus around trying to answer these questions. It's going to take you and me working together to do the best job here. I am an expert in testing, and you are an expert on yourself *[Hale underlines again the foundations of their collaboration.]*

Emma: So, are there two things we can explore? Because I really want to know if I am LD or if I am ADHD.

Hale: Yes, definitely. And if there is another question too, we can handle that. One question we have now is in the academic area. The other is in the relationship area. Is there another question that would be important?

Emma: Yes, one of them is … how do I propose this? Why have I never been able to maintain a long-term position in a field that I am passionate about?

Hale: Meaning a job?

Emma: Yes, meaning a job, yeah. *[Hale writes down the question in Emma's words.]*

Hale: Ok. Good work. We are going to have to wind up here, so the questions that we have are three. One is, "Do I have a learning disability or ADHD?"

Emma: Yes, and once we find that out, "What can we do about it, and how can I compensate in my life?" *[Hale adds this new piece to the first question.]*

Hale: Alright and then another one is … .

Emma: And also, can you backtrack first?

Hale: Sure.

Emma: Also, "Do I have a head injury?" Because I have heard iffy things that ADHD people sometimes have head injuries, closed head injuries that cause them to act a certain way. Or they get overloaded, I get overwhelmed sometimes, and I have to kind of shut out the world.

Hale: That question would be in the neuropsychological area, and I am not an expert in that area, but I think if we delve into the question we have, we can at least develop some directions for you to go with that, if it is necessary, maybe a referral for that. Does that seem ok? *[Hale states the limits of the work he can do with Emma, so that they can agree on a clear contract and set the stage to building a trusting relationship, while avoiding the risk of Emma developing inaccurate expectations that might lead to later disappointments.]*

Emma: Yes. Ok, thank you.

Hale: Alright so there is that one, and then we have … I think we boiled this down to, "Why have I not been successful in long-term relationships?" *[Hale keeps on framing the collection of questions as a collaborative endeavor, asking Emma's input on how to formulate the questions.]*

Emma: Right.

Hale: And then one we will talk more about next time, "Why have I never been able to maintain a long-term position in a career that I am passionate about?"

Emma: Yes.

Hale: Does that seem to cover things?

Emma: And I think a really big question for me is, "Why am I so afraid to commit?" And not necessarily in a relationship but in general in the world. Like it is really hard for me to commit to something. I might be busy. I take care of my mom. I do this. I do that. I can't do that. I have a real fear of commitment to anything. *[Notice that as the session goes on, Emma gets increasingly vulnerable and open with Hale.]*

Hale: So, "Why am I so afraid to commit?"

Emma: Yes.

Hale: So, since we are approaching the end of our meeting, next time we will talk more about that one too. Hmm, "Why am I so afraid to commit?" Does that seem like ... ? I see you are smiling .... *[Hale keeps watch for Emma's nonverbal communication as important aspects of the first session.]*

Emma: I am smiling because I am like, this was a lot easier for me to do than I thought it would be. But I am like, "Wow this is a lot. It is a lot!" I am surprised how easy it was to share with you, but it is pretty intense stuff, and this was my first time I have ever met you, and I am surprised that I am able to just let it go. I mean just share stuff, and I am happy. I am glad I could do it. I am glad I was not too mentally, emotionally exhausted today to do that. I am surprised.

Hale: Well, you did share a lot. You talked about a lot of very important things. A lot of really important history I think, and I really appreciate you being able to do that and willing to do that. And I hope that it will all help this collaboration between us. *[Hale mirrors Emma's sense of openness and hope.]*

Emma: I think so. And I would rather not have you delve into it each week like, "Tell me what is going on. Why are you so ...? You know, you are kind of quiet today." I would rather it just be like I am going to lay it out on the table. This is the truth. Because I mean, I don't have time to waste. *[Emma's commitment to continue to be open seems a good response to Hale's mirroring her efforts and a positive sign that Hale was able to build a trusting relationship during the session.]*

Hale: I appreciate you letting me know what's helpful and if you feel like I'm asking too many questions, let me know.

Emma: Great. Thanks

Hale: Well, we certainly accomplished our goal for today, to get the questions and then to get as much important background on the table as we could. Now we should probably spend a little time talking about our next meeting.

Along the way, I learned that Tessa was seven years older than Emma and that they had always been and were still close. Tessa had been a caregiver and protector of her since childhood. Their father had been a successful, hard-working businessman and her mother worked in the home. Emma said that she and her father were similar in their desire to achieve academically, and while he could be very nurturing and loving, sometimes she felt that her "learning disabilities" might have disappointed him. Emma portrayed her childhood as normal but then proceeded to talk about her struggles with compulsions that developed around age 12, such as needing to do a certain number of sit-ups and exercise during the night even when on a sleepover with friends. She acknowledged these behaviors created difficulty in her friendships.

Both of her parents were college-educated, and she seemed to idealize them both, particularly her father. She reported he had been very protective of her for as long as she could remember. She stressed that his death had been extremely difficult for her and ultimately precipitated her going into therapy with Jeanne. She had recently found out (from Tessa) that on his deathbed her father had asked Tessa to make sure Emma was taken care of, and she was both surprised and confused by this. She earned her college degree in early education and after graduation was employed as a teacher. Currently, however, Emma was employed half-time as a teacher's aide, a job to which she was devoted but about which she was anxious, particularly working with other teaching aids. Emma also described how she had had numerous romantic relationships and was struggling with one currently.

We had developed four questions that were central and meaningful to her:

1   Do I have a learning disability or attention deficit hyperactivity disorder? And if so, what can I do about it?
2   Why haven't I been able to have a successful long-term relationship?
3   Why have I never been able to maintain a long-term position in a career I am passionate about, like teaching?
4   Why am I so afraid to commit to anything?

Reflections of the Initial Session with Emma

I felt good about the session. While it had started with Emma being anxious and disorganized, by the end she seemed to have a sense of trust, collaboration, and hope. I noted that several of her AQs were similar and reflected Emma's difficulty claiming her own life. I liked her and her gentle and sincere spirit, and I felt intrigued to know more. However, I was puzzled by her rambling and tangential thinking and whether it was disorganization, defensiveness, anxiety, or something else. Also, I was concerned that there might be some underlying neurological issues that I might not know enough about to understand Emma's "brain damage," that she had mentioned. I knew her funds were limited and wanted to make the best of them for her. In any event, I understood that the roots of her troubles seemed in her birth or early in life. I looked forward to our next meeting to learn more.

Second Session

The second session was scheduled for the following week, and Emma arrived on time. Given that in our hour and a half first session we had not clarified her last two questions, we started the second session completing that before we began testing. I also wanted to ask additional questions about her first questions; first, because I had some, but also because having some follow-up questions would let Emma know I had been thinking about her and our work. Additionally, I hoped this beginning would continue the spirit of collaboration and trust from the first session.

Hale: So how was the last session for you?
Emma: It was good. I apologize for unloading so much. I don't know why I did that—I had just met you. But I feel good to have gotten things on the table—just a little embarrassed to have gone on and on.

Hale: You had a lot of important things to say. I appreciated your openness. It seems like a good start to our work together. *[Hale directly and actively responds in a positive manner to counteract Emma's shame.]* Does anything stand out for you?

Emma: Well, I thought we got things on the table. And it felt good to put all that together into questions that I hope we can answer.

Hale: I am glad. So, what I thought we would do today is start by making sure the questions we developed still seem right, and then for me to get some additional background information, and then to flesh out the questions you brought up at the very end of the last session. With that we will know the tests to use to answer the questions. And then we can use the rest of our time getting started with some testing. *[Hale structures the session at the beginning, to help Emma and him stay on track.]* Does that sound okay? *[Hale also tries to keep the collaboration going.]*

Emma: That sounds good.

Hale: So, the questions that I have that we came up with last time. *[Hale shows Emma a typed list to reinforce the central focus of her questions.]* The first one was, "Do I have a learning disability or attention deficit hyperactivity disorder. And if so, what can I do about it? Why have I not been able to have a successful long-term relationship?"

Emma: I still want to know, yes.

Hale: "Why have I not been able to maintain a long-term position in a career I am passionate about, like teaching?"

Emma: Yes.

Hale: And, "Why am I so afraid to commit to anything?"

Emma: Yes, I still stand strongly by that. And I would like to add, "Why am I so afraid to fail or succeed?" I am going to include that.

Hale: You want to add that one? *[Hale writes down the new question.]*

Emma: Yes, because you know, if you fail at something, it does not mean that you are really a failure, it is just that you have to process the information in order to try and eventually get to succeed. And sometimes succeeding creates pressure on a person. If you are extremely successful, there is a lot of pressure on you, "Well, you did this, now do this, do this, do this, do this." Why am I afraid of that?

Hale: So, have you had that experience with succeeding when you felt that pressure that you are talking about? *[Hale asks for examples to bring Emma's experience to life and find contextual aspects.]*

Emma: Yes, when I graduated from college and then got a teaching job, I was not emotionally mature enough to handle everything that came my way, and now I believe my alcoholism, even though it was not blatant, definitely created developmental delays. Like it creates a way to have failure to launch properly, so it makes us more immature than we really should be at that age. I did not care. I was just like, "I will be fine at this. I know how to do this. I understand teaching really well, and I know how to handle kids." But then all of a sudden, I had this extremely unruly classroom that I did not know what to do with.

Hale: Sounds like you were thrown into the deep end! *[Hale mentalizes Emma's experience.]*

Emma: Yes, thrown to the wolves, and the job didn't work out. And I have always blamed myself. I have always said, "If you were not so careless, stupid, nonchalant, if you did not procrastinate so much, if you were not so involved with your boyfriend, if you were serious about your career." You know so I have really beaten myself down to a pulp about what a rotten teacher I was. And I have worked very hard to not be that way. But it has always been a skeleton in my closet for years.

Hale: Thinking bad about yourself, being self-critical? *[Hale tentatively names this tendency to see if Emma is aware of it.]*

Emma: Yes. I have worked really hard at not being like that anymore, but it is something that creeps in sometimes. I am not good enough. I do not visit my mom enough. I do not know how to communicate with people well enough. I should take over a classroom at my school, but I do not. I am afraid to commit to it because there is a lot of pressure at that school, and I don't know if I can handle it. Knowing my mom is eventually going to die you know, and I just, there is a lot of pressure. *[Here Hale considered suggesting a question about her self-criticism as a way of drilling down under her 'fear of failing or succeeding' question. But he decided to wait, thinking her original question might better capture her focus and that in any event, self-criticism would be addressed through her wording.]*

Hale: So, any thoughts about where that pressure comes from? Where did that start?

Emma: *(long pause)* I don't really know. I really don't. I really wish I had a handle on it.

Hale: Any guesses?

Emma: *(short pause)* The fear of disappointing people—that is where it roots from. If I commit to something, what if I disappoint them? What if I am not up to par for them? What if they are like, "Oh clearly you are not right for this. You are really horrible at this. I don't even know why you went into this field."

What followed was a disorganized but open and vulnerable discussion of Emma's curiosity about the history of her problems, the context of the problems, and her current theories. She discussed seeing a psychiatrist as a child and taking Mellaril for an extended period, which did help stop her compulsive routines; her experience of alcoholism starting in college and continuing for about 10 years; and the context of numerous job failures. Much of this story was filled with confusion, blaming herself, and unspoken shame.

I asked along the way what would be the worst answer we might find to her question, "Why am I so afraid to fail or succeed?" She thought briefly and replied, "That I am not as smart as I think I am." She then told me that her college entrance exam scores were "really bad," but she thought it was maybe due to "terrible test anxiety." I listened, provided support, and validated her experience. As the conversation wrapped up, I gave her a copy of the questions (see Table 5.1) and kept a copy on my desk in case we wanted to refer to them during the testing. With this, we started testing.

Table 5.1 Emma's Assessment Questions

1 Do I have a learning disability or attention deficit hyperactivity disorder?
2 Why haven't I been able to have a successful long-term relationship?
3 Why have I never been able to maintain a long-term position in a career I am passionate about, like teaching?
4 Why am I so afraid to commit to anything?
5 Why am I so afraid to fail or succeed?

Reflections on the Beginning of the Second Session with Emma

After the beginning of the second session, I felt confident that Emma was fully engaged in the assessment. She had given extensive context to her initial questions and had added and explained another thoughtful question. She was increasingly open with me, acknowledging how self-critical she was and revealing her core fear of not being smart. I also noted her ambivalence about getting some questions answered. Finally, it felt like we had cemented good rapport and deeper trust. I felt the time we had taken at the beginning of the second session was well-spent. We then agreed to start testing and moved to the testing table in my office.

Note

1 The content of this section is derived from a workshop given by Stephen Finn entitled, "*Am I to Blame or Are You? Working with Shame and Coping Mechanisms Against Shame in Psychotherapy and Psychological Assessment*," in Milan, Italy, November 28-December 1, 2018.

References

Ackerman, S., & Hilsenroth, M. (2001). A review of therapist characteristics and techniques negatively impacting the therapeutic alliance. *Psychotherapy, 38*, 171/185.

Aschieri, F. (2016). Shame as a cultural artifact: A call for reflexivity and self-awareness in personality assessment. *Journal of Personality Assessment, 98*(6), 567–575. doi: 10.1080/00223891.2016.1146289.

Aschieri, F., Fantini, F., & Smith, J. D. (2016). Collaborative/Therapeutic Assessment: Procedures to enhance client outcomes. In S. Maltzmann (Ed.), *Oxford handbook of treatment processes and outcomes in counseling psychology* (pp. 241–269). Oxford University Press. doi: 10.1093/oxfordhb/ 9780199739134.013.23.

Bakermans-Kranenburg, M. J., & van IJzendoorn, M. H. (2009). The first 10,000 Adult Attachment Interviews: Distributions of adult attachment representations in clinical and non-clinical groups. *Attachment & human development, 11*(3), 223–263. doi: 10.1080/14616730902 814762.

Beebe, B., Knoblauch, S., & Rustin, J. (2005). *Forms of intersubjectivity in infant research and adult treatment*. Other Press, Llc.

Brown, J. (1997). Circular questioning: An introductory guide. *Australian and New Zealand Journal of Family Therapy, 18*, 109–114.

Bush, M., & Gassner, S. M. (1988). A description and clinical research Application of the Control-Mastery Theory. *Clinical Social Work Journal, 16*(3), 231–242.

Dearing, R. L., & Tagney, J. P. (Eds.) (2011). *Shame in the therapy hour*. American Psychological Association.

Finn, S. E. (2007). *In our clients' shoes: Theory and techniques of Therapeutic Assessment.* Erlbaum.

Finn, S. E. (2012). Implications of recent research in neurobiology for psychological assessment. *Journal of Personality Assessment, 94*(5), 440–449.

Finn, S. E. (2018) *"Am I to Blame or Are You? Working with Shame and Coping Mechanisms Against Shame in Psychotherapy and Psychological Assessment,"* workshop organized by the European Center for Therapeutic Assessment, Milan, Italy.

Fischer, C. (1985/94). *Individualizing psychological assessment.* Brooks/Cole.

Fonagy, P., Luyten, P., Allison, E., & Campbell, C. (2017a). What we have changed our minds about: Part 1. Borderline personality as a limitation of resilience. *Borderline Personality and Emotional Dysregulation, 4*(11), doi: 10.1186=s40479-017-0061-9.

Fonagy, P., Luyten, P., Allison, E., & Campbell, C. (2017b). What we have changed our minds about: Part 2. Borderline personality, epistemic trust, and the developmental significance of social communication. *Borderline Personality and Emotional Dysregulation, 4*(9), doi: 10.1186/s40479-017-0062-8.

Fosha, D. (2000). Meta-therapeutic processes and the effects of transformation: affirmation and the healing affects. *Journal of Psychotherapy Integration, 10*, 71–97.

Fosha, D., Siegel, D. J., & Solomon, M. (2009). *The healing power of emotion: Affective neuroscience, development, and clinical practice.* Norton.

George, C., & West, M. L. (2012). *The Adult Attachment Projective Picture System: Attachment theory and assessment in adults.* Guilford Press.

Hornstrup, C., Tomm, K., & Johansen, T. (2015). *Interventive interviewing revisited and expanded.* https://wagner.nyu.edu/files/leadership/Expanding_Questioning.pdf.

Kamphuis, J. H., & De Saeger, H. (2012). Using Therapeutic Assessment to explore emotional constriction: A creative professional in crisis. In S. E. Finn, C. T. Fischer, & L. Handler (Eds.), *Collaborative/Therapeutic Assessment: A casebook and guide* (pp. 133–155). John Wiley & Sons, Inc.

Kamphuis, J. H., & Finn, S. E. (2019). Therapeutic Assessment in personality disorders: Toward the restoration of epistemic trust. *Journal of Personality Assessment, 101*(6), 662–674.

Knox, S., & Hill, C. E. (2003). Therapist self-disclosure: Research based suggestions for practitioners. *Journal of Clinical Psychology, 59*(5), 529–539.

Linehan, M. M. (1993). *Cognitive-behavioral treatment of borderline personality disorder.* Guilford Press.

Miller, W. R., & Rollnick, S. (2002). *Motivational interviewing: Preparing people for change* (2nd ed.). Guilford.

Riem, M. M. E., van Hoof, M. J., Garrett, A. S., van der Wee, N. J. A., van IJzendoorn, M. H., & Vermeiren, R. R. J. M. (2019). General psychopathology factor and unresolved-disorganized attachment uniquely correlated to white matter integrity using diffusion tensor imaging. *Behavioural Brain Research, 359*, 1–8. doi: 10.1016/j.bbr.2018.10.14.

Rogers, C. R. (1980). *A way of being.* Houghton Mifflin.

Safran, J. D., & Muran, J. C. (2000). *Negotiating the therapeutic alliance: A relational treatment guide.* Guilford.

Schore, A. N. (1998). Early shame experiences and infant brain development. In P. Gilbert & B. Andrews (Eds.), *Shame: Interpersonal behavior, psychopathology, and culture* (pp. 57–77). Oxford University Press.

Selvini, M. P., Boscolo, L., Cecchin, G., & Prata, G. (1980). Hypothesizing-Circularity-Neutrality: Three guidelines for the conductor of the session. *Family Process, 19*(1), 3–12.

Silberschatz, G. Control-Mastery Theory. (2017). In *Reference Module in Neuroscience and Biobehavioral Psychology*, Elsevier, 2017. ISBN 9780128093245

Siegel, D. J. (1999). *The developing mind: Toward a neurobiology of interpersonal experience.* Guilford Press.

Silberschatz, G. (2017). Control-Mastery Theory. *Reference Module in Neuroscience and Biobehavioral Psychology*, Elsevier, 1–8. doi: 10.1016/B978-0-12-809324-5.05280-9.

Sullivan, H. S. (1953). *The interpersonal theory of psychiatry*. W. W. Norton.

Tomm, K. (1988). Interventive interviewing: Part III. Intending to ask lineal, circular, strategic, or reflexive questions? *Family Process, 27*, 1–15.

Tronick, E. Z., Bruschweiler-Stern, N., Harrison, A. M., Lyons-Ruth, K., Morgan, A. C., Nahum, J. P., Sander, L., & Stern, D. N. (1998). Dyadically expanded states of consciousness and the process of therapeutic change. *Infant Mental Health Journal, 19*, 290–299.

Watzlawick, P., Weakland, J. H., & Fisch, R. (1974). *Change: Principles of problem formation and problem resolution*. W. W. Norton.

Weiss, J. (1993). *How psychotherapy works: Process and technique*. Guilford Press. https://www.psychotherapy.net/interview/AEDP-Diana-Fosha (n.d.). Retrieved from https://www.psychotherapy.net. (n.d.).

6 Administering Psychological Testing and Conducting the Extended Inquiry

The second step of a Therapeutic Assessment (TA) overlaps with traditional assessments, given that we focus on the administration, scoring, and interpretation of standardized tests. However, the use of these instruments is embedded in the collaborative framework of TA, so each choice we make, or technique we use, enhances this client-centered approach. We divide this step into two parts: (1) Administering psychological testing, and (2) the Extended Inquiry (EI).

Administering Psychological Testing

After the first session, during which we collected the client's Assessment Questions (AQs) and built a therapeutic relationship, we have some sessions during which we administer one or more psychological tests to the client. We select standardized measures with strong psychometrics, which are administered according to standard procedures. The test results from these measures provide nomothetic data that help us understand the client; how they compare to others and along certain dimensions (e.g., openness to experience). We often combine these measures with non-standardized tests that are useful sources of idiographic information about the client's struggles.

The psychological tests we administer help us understand our clients' strengths and difficulties, and identify diagnostic classifications and suggestions for subsequent treatment, exactly as occurs in the traditional information-gathering model of assessment. However, as described in Chapter 1, in TA, psychological tests are considered more than just sources of nomothetic data. They are "empathy magnifiers," as they help us identify our client's current symptoms, stories, defenses, coping strategies, and dilemmas of change (Finn, 2007). We review test results as they are obtained, and our case conceptualization grows alongside our capacity to mentalize the client, which fosters their epistemic trust (ET; Kamphuis & Finn, 2019). As further elaborated below, the exploration that occurs during the EI is often a meaningful discussion, during which clients build insight into themselves and their difficulties. We also consider test results in accordance with psychological theories that consider psychopathology as the best adaptation that an individual employed, often unconsciously, because their environment lacked important elements for healthier growth. (These ideas are further elaborated in Chapter 7).

DOI: 10.4324/9780429202797-8

Test Selection

Broadly, we align with the current emphasis in the assessment field that a multimethod approach is best (Hopwood & Bornstein, 2014). Our test batteries are varied, with a mix of cognitive, performance-based, and self-report measures. Consistent with the client-centered nature of TA, we administer tests that will help us answer the client's, and the referring professional's (RP), questions. For example, if a client's primary goal is to determine whether they have a learning disability, we administer intelligence and achievement tests. If we suspect that a client's self-reported "memory problems" (which are the focus of an AQ) are periods of dissociation, we will ask the client to complete memory testing and a standardized checklist of dissociative symptoms. We do not use a predetermined test battery with every client but flexibly choose among the   instruments we have available, with consideration of which will help us answer the client's AQs.

When choosing among psychological tests, it is helpful to consider the type of information they provide. Self-report measures, especially broad personality inventories, "produce information that is related to clients' self-presentations and their conscious views of themselves at the time of testing" (Finn, 2007, p. 66). Self-report tests such as the Minnesota Multiphasic Personality Inventory-3rd Edition (MMPI-3; Ben-Porath & Tellegen, 2020), provide valuable information about what clients know about themselves and their current struggles. We expect these test results to contain information congruent with clients' existing self-views (Level 1 Information), and when told about the results, they likely will say, "That is definitely me" (Finn, 2007).

Performance-based and storytelling tests provide information about clients based on their responses to prompts (e.g., "Tell me a story based on this picture" or "What could this be?"). These tests often reveal the client's implicit characteristics or schemas (Finn, 2012; Martin & Frackowiak, 2017). Their emotionally evocative and ambiguous properties often increase a client's level of emotional arousal, thus providing in-the-moment data about how they function in such situations. We find that these tests provide us with some Level 1 Information, but more often Level 2 and 3 Information (i.e., information that somewhat or significantly differs from the client's current self-view; Finn, 2007). These test results are extremely important, given our goal of helping clients assimilate and accommodate Level 2 and 3 Information. However, we also need to understand the client's current narrative. That information allows to deeply understand the client, which is part of the relational process that prepares them to incorporate new information.

As described in Chapter 1, the combination of these two kinds of tests, and particularly when they both measure similar constructs, help us understand clients' traits that they are not aware of and dissociated affect-states (e.g., shame that is core to the client's identity, but is not recognized because of character defenses). We highly value performance-based test results, as they help us understand what is contributing to the client's difficulties, and help us construct a more holistic case conceptualization. We may also compare self-report results with observer rating scales to detect aspects of the client's functioning that are outside their conscious self-view. We believe these different types of test results are crucial to understanding the client, and we also recognize that there is no "perfect" set of standardized tests and the test selection process is idiosyncratic.

How to Sequence the Order of Tests Administered

In TA we recommend beginning the testing sessions with measures that clearly address the client's major goals, which are identified in their AQs. We strengthen the collaborative relationship with clients and build their sense of security by starting with tests that are face valid. For example, for a client whose primary question is, "Do I have a learning disorder?" we begin with intelligence and achievement testing. By making such a choice, we communicate to the client that we take their goals seriously and ally with the part of them that is curious about these issues. As another example, if a client asks, "How have my experiences with my family impacted how I deal with relationships today?" we may begin with a measure focused on early memories. For clients who have both types of questions, and it is unclear which is most important to them, we ask, "Would you rather we start by exploring your question about relationships or your question about a possible learning disorder?"

Scheduling Testing Sessions

When possible, we schedule testing sessions with time in between, and we rarely administer the full battery in one day. One and a half to two-hour testing sessions once or twice a week give the client time to reflect upon and incorporate what they learned after each test and EI[1]. Furthermore, the EI can be an intense emotional experience for clients, and they might need time after to process the experience. By scheduling the testing in shorter appointments across days, we protect clients from becoming overwhelmed by taking in too much information at once.

Beginning the Testing Sessions

The number of testing sessions conducted is connected to the number of AQs developed and the tests needed to identify answers. Some clients may have only 3-4 testing sessions, while others require 6-8 appointments based on the need for more tests or tests that take longer to administer. Here and in the next section, we explain how to execute these sessions. The structure, approach, and skill set employed are the same for each testing session.

After greeting the client and allowing them to get settled, we check in to see how they have been doing since our last session. We start every TA session this way, not solely out of politeness, but what the client shares helps establish a context for what occurs during the remainder of the session. This is illustrated in the following excerpt of the second session with Adriana, a 30-year-old woman who was having difficulties completing tasks at work:

Clinician: How have things been going Adriana?
Adriana: Okay, I guess, but I was fired from my job yesterday. (Gets teary eyed).
Clinician: Oh, I'm sorry. How are you feeling?
Adriana: It is not a complete surprise. In fact, I was sort of expecting it, but I was hoping they might hold off until you and I could figure out why I've been doing such a horrible job.
Clinician: Yes, I remember that was your major question for our work … (pause). Does getting fired change your feelings about us exploring that question?

Adriana: Well, at first it made me not even want to come today. I figured there was no use, but then I realized this assessment is now even more important. Before I look for another job, I want to know what went wrong with this one.

Clinician: Of course. That makes a lot of sense. Sounds like a rough couple of days. Do you still feel up to doing some testing today like we planned?

Adriana: Uh huh, but you should know that I didn't get much sleep last night.

Clinician: Thanks for telling me. How is that affecting you now?

Adriana: Well, being tired always makes me more emotional. If I'm sad, I cry easily, and if I'm angry, I can't control my anger. Maybe we can do something today that won't be too difficult. Is that possible?

Clinician: I think so. Let's talk a little more before we decide how to spend our time today.

Although Adriana may have spontaneously told the assessor about being fired, the assessor's inquiry provided a good opening for her news. Importantly, what Adriana shared about her recent experiences helped both her and the assessor decide how to proceed with the session. When a client is facing challenging life circumstances, it may be advisable to not administer testing and switch to what we refer to as a mid-TA therapy session. This is not a planned step but occurs naturally during one of the testing sessions when clients are experiencing some difficulty that is occupying their attention. An assessor may say, "It sounds like what has been going on is pretty stressful for you. I recommend that instead of doing testing today, let's just talk about what's been happening." The clinician stays primarily in a therapist role when this occurs. However, if the client shares something that is connected to the test data collected to date, the clinician may share some of those results, if they might help to the client. Such sessions are an opportunity to deepen the relationship with the client and are beneficial in lowering epistemic hypervigilance (EH).

Following the first session, we type up the client's AQs and print them so they can be reviewed. After the check-in at the beginning of the first testing session, we share that document and ask the client to review their questions. Typically, clients read and approve their AQs, and then we begin testing. If they have edits, we update the document to reflect the changes. In this early part of the session, we also ask clients if they have any more thoughts about the first session. This question, as well as reviewing the AQs, may lead to new revelations. For example, Anna, a 40-year-old woman who identifies as lesbian, had AQs focused on herself and her marriage. Anna initially was against the possibility of involving her wife for a couple's TA, because she believed that the issues in her marriage resulted from her personal problems. She also clarified during the first session that her wife was not interested in participating. What follows is the beginning of her second session.

Clinician: Here are the questions you identified last week. Let me know what you think and if they need any editing. (Hands Anna the written questions).

Anna: (Reads questions). These look good.

Clinician: Did you have any thoughts or reactions after our meeting last week?

Anna: Yes, I felt pretty low afterwards and wasn't sure I really wanted to go ahead with this.

Clinician: You mean go ahead with our work here?

Anna:	Uh huh. Maybe I'm better off not knowing the answers to those questions.
Clinician:	Do you think that about all the questions, or about certain ones in particular?
Anna:	I guess mainly the ones about my marriage. I didn't realize until after we talked how unhappy I've been.
Clinician:	And is that when you started to feel low? When you were thinking about that?
Anna:	Yes. I guess I've been getting along by not paying too much attention to the problems with my wife.
Clinician:	That can be a good coping strategy until we're ready to face things more directly. But if you've been doing that, I can see how you might feel overwhelmed by the questions we came up with. Maybe we could talk more about the pros and cons of examining your marriage at this time in your life?

This excerpt illustrates a common scenario in TAs. After enthusiastically developing questions in the first session, Anna later got in touch with the part of herself that did not want to change or learn new things about her situation. During this second session, the assessor prioritized exploring her ambivalence to strengthen the alliance and make a joint decision about whether, and how, to move forward. The assessor mitigated a possible mistake of moving too quickly in the exploration of Anna's marriage when she was not ready to do so. This was also an important moment for Anna, as she started to realize she had been avoiding thinking about her situation, and the assessor supported her in this new understanding.

Introducing Tests to Clients

After the initial check-in, we introduce the test we intend to administer. To build the client's cooperation, we explain the test, why it was chosen, and how it will help answer their AQs. The explanation is brief, and we do not share information that might invalidate a standard administration. One simple approach is to introduce each test connected to the AQ it most closely addresses. For example, "This test is called the Beck Depression Inventory, and will help us answer your question about whether you are clinically depressed." After that test is administered and explored, we may say, "Next, I'd like us to do the Rorschach inkblot test. This is another test that will help us understand any depression you may be experiencing." We pay special attention to tests with low face validity as related to the client's concern. For example, we might say, "This is a true-false test called the MMPI-3. You will see that it has some items related to your problems and some items that are unrelated. However, I'm having you take it because it provides useful information about your personality and relationship style. That information could be helpful when we explore why you keep dating men who are aggressive."

Emotional Support During Test Administration

Some clients have strong emotional reactions during standardized testing, and when this occurs, we usually suspend data gathering at an appropriate point and "make room" for their feelings. To illustrate, 72-year-old Sandra recently had a stroke and participated in testing that included neuropsychological measures. The following discussion occurred during the EI after she was administered the California Verbal Learning Test 2nd Edition (CVLT-II; Delis et al., 2000).

Sandra: Oh, that was horrible! (Starts to cry).

Clinician: I'm sorry. (Hands the client a box of Kleenex and waits.) Are you upset because it was so difficult to remember the list of words?

Sandra: Yes. (Stops crying). I know I could have remembered all of those before the stroke. I feel impaired and stupid. (Covers her eyes). *[Sandra's words and gestures signal to the clinician that she is feeling shame].*

Clinician: How sad and frustrating. It reminds me of when I broke my knee and had to give up skiing. Every time I would see a ski commercial, I would start crying. *[The clinician, after making an empathic comment, uses self-disclosure as a shame intervention].*

Sandra: You did? And did you ever get over it?

Clinician: In some ways maybe, but I still get sad sometimes. Are you thinking you should be over your feelings about your stroke?

Sandra: I guess so. Sometimes I think I'm being a big baby about it. After all, a lot of people have it worse. I can still talk and get around. *[Sandra again expresses shame about grieving the loss of certain abilities.]* But frankly, I never planned on this part of getting old.

Clinician: I don't know if anyone does. And it certainly makes sense to me that you're sad about the abilities you've lost. *[The clinician makes an intervention actively counteracting shame].*

Sandra: Really? You're such a nice young man. Well, I guess we should get back to seeing what this old dame can still do. (Smiles).

In this scenario, the client resumed testing after experiencing the clinician's emotional support. However, sometimes clients need more attention, and it becomes necessary to suspend the testing to talk, and then continue testing during the next appointment. Supporting clients emotionally as they develop new insights is essential to an assessment being beneficial and not traumatic. In Sandra's case, her feelings of shame about her loss of abilities became evident, and the assessor learned that she could use him as a source of support. If we are too focused on "getting data" from the standardized testing, we may inadvertently inhibit important emotional processing, limiting the therapeutic value of our work. This is particularly true in TAs when the client is self-referred, as there may be no other professional to help the client process feelings stirred up by the assessment sessions.

The Extended Inquiry (EI)

Definition and Rationale

After the administration of a test, we conduct the Extended Inquiry (EI). The EI is an exploratory discussion focused on the client's experience of that test, or specific test responses, or both (Aschieri et al., 2016). This conversation often produces meaningful idiographic information, in contrast to the nomothetic data we get from test profiles and scores. During the EI we collect important information that helps us build a more complete case formulation. Further, the EI builds our collaboration, as we are genuinely curious about the client's experiences. As further described in the following sections, psychological tests are standardized versions of situations a client experiences in the world. A successful EI helps the client and assessor better understand how the client acts, feels, and thinks in everyday life.

The EI serves three primary goals:

1 To learn new information about the client that helps us individualize their test results. We accomplish this goal by engaging the client in clarifying and expanding on the meaning of certain behaviors and responses.
2 To test our initial hypotheses about the meaning of some test results or test responses right after the administration. In this sense, a successful EI helps us further expand, confirm, or disconfirm our hypotheses about the client's difficulties.
3 To help clients reflect on their test behaviors and responses. When this occurs, often a meaningful conversation takes place helps clients revise their stories about themselves and their difficulties. We meet this goal by using information from a test as a catalyst for client self-reflection. Importantly, this is not a feedback process, but a moment of collaborative exploration.

We encourage the client to take the lead on the EI, and we have our own hypotheses and ideas about the clinical meaning of certain responses and behaviors. Inevitably, our thinking will shape the conversation. For example, Yua was a 55-year-old woman who struggled with depression for several years, and the assessor hypothesized that her sadness was connected to the losses she experienced as a child. She was administered the Adult Attachment Projective (AAP; George & West, 2012) to understand, in part, how she was still being affected by her grief. One stimulus from the AAP is a drawing of a child and a woman looking out a window, while outside two paramedics carry a stretcher to an ambulance. Yua became sad and shut down when telling a story to this drawing. The assessor supported her, and then explored her experience and story. The assessor held a hypothesis based on their knowledge of how early loss impacts children, Yua's behaviors, and the assessor's understanding of the test. This hypothesis impacted the questions the assessor asked during the EI with Yua.

In summary, conducting an EI after a test administration helps us to shape and refine our hypotheses about the client, and clients are also affected as we work together to understand their test responses and experiences. When clients reflect on their responses and behaviors, they build insight and a new understanding about themselves and their problems emerges. Simultaneously, our capacity to mentalize the client grows through the combination of test data, the client's narrative, and our experience with them, which helps the client develop ET (Kamphuis & Finn, 2019).

When to Conduct the EI

It is possible to conduct an EI after any test following the standardized administration. Waiting to do the EI until after the test is completed allows us to follow the standard administration procedures so we can obtain valid tests scores. For example, we do not discuss the Rorschach (Exner, 2002; Meyer et al., 2011) with a client until both the Response phase and the Inquiry or Clarification phase have been completed, and we do not inquire about Wechsler Adult Intelligence Scale 4th Edition (WAIS-IV; Wechsler, 2008) subtests until all the subtests are administered.

Our preference is to conduct the EI immediately following the test administration, which has the value of engaging the clients while the experience is vivid and in their awareness. However, some clients take longer than expected on a test, and it is counterproductive to begin an EI if there is an inadequate amount of time. In such situations, we dedicate the following session to the EI on the test just administered.

We also intentionally postpone the EI to the next session in two situations. First, some clients become tired or overwhelmed by the testing process. When this occurs, we still briefly solicit their opinions about the test, but then shift to helping them with their emotions and closing the session. Second, at times assessors do not have expertise on a test or need to review the data before conducting the EI. In these situations, it is best to first score and interpret the test. Importantly, when we postpone the EI to the following session, we make sure our notes capture important moments, so that we can recall that information in the next session.

After every test, we ask at least a few questions about the client's experience. For example, "What did you think of that test?" The client's first impression of a test might provide useful information to contextualize their performance (e.g., if the client found it hard and anxiety provoking or fun). We also ask this question to see if the client had an emotional reaction to the testing that requires our support. This may lead to an EI focused on what the client found significant about the test-taking experience, although at other times our exploration may be simple. For example, a client may complete a brief self-report measure, and when we ask what it was like, the client responds, "That's about what I expected." Even when brief, the step of inquiring about their experience invites collaboration and helps the client understand that following each test, their opinion and experiences will be discussed. In this way, we continue to build our collaborative relationship with the client.

In the next section, we identify specific scenarios that assessors look for to inform their thinking about the EI and to identify areas to explore.

1   During the administration of each test, we gather observational data about the client which may inform the EI discussion (see Table 6.1 for client behaviors that draw our interest). We pay attention to "the psychological and interpersonal processes that occurred during the administration of the tests" (Aschieri et al., 2016, p. 6). When we directly administer tests such as cognitive measures or the Rorschach, it is standard practice to note behavioral observations, and most clinicians are familiar with this practice. However, we also consider such data for tests we do not directly administer. For example, Noah completed a self-report test on a computer in the assessor's waiting room. When the assessor scored it, he saw that it took Noah twice as long to complete as the average client. Later in the office, Noah completed a brief self-report measure on anxiety, and Noah quickly marked a choice for some items and for others he stared off in thought before marking a decision. During the EI, the assessor explored each of these behavioral observations with Noah to see what could be learned.

As a different example, throughout the administration of the Thurston Cradock Test of Shame (TCTS; Thurston & Cradock O'Leary, 2009), Louis' leg was shaking in an

Table 6.1 Client Behaviors During Testing that May Be Areas to Focus on During the EI

- Difficulty formulating a response. A client stutters or becomes silent.
- An increase in the rate of speech with accompanying excitement.
- Blushing.
- Sighing.
- Client's eyes well with tears.
- Signs of anxiety, such as shaky legs or hands.
- Client shows irritation or expresses frustration with the test
- Signs of shame, such as avoiding eye contact or dismissing the task.

---

anxious style, while he seemed to "white knuckle" through the test. Our curiosity is stimulated by such behaviors, and we explore our observations with the client during the EI. We hold a hypothesis that such behaviors may reveal something important about how the client experiences similar tasks in the world, in this case, situations eliciting the client's shame. The assessor broadly explored Louis' experience of the TCTS, and he said, "That seemed pretty easy for me." The assessor responded, "I noticed you seemed quite fidgety during this test. Can you tell me about that?" Louis and the assessor explored both his comment that it was easy and the observed behavior to see what could be learned.

2   When the client's performance on the test changes during different parts of the test (e.g., the client almost falls asleep during a verbal subtest on an intelligence test and is much more energized and focused during a subtest measuring visual memory). For some tests, we know that certain parts have a specific meaning, and we develop hypotheses about the client's life challenges that we want to explore when we see behavior changes in response to these differences. For example, research on the Rorschach suggests that the colored cards are more emotionally arousing than the achromatic cards (Ishibashi et al., 2016). While administering the Rorschach, we might observe that a client becomes quieter and gives fewer responses to the colored cards when compared to the first seven cards. When we see such changes in behavior, we hypothesize that the client's withdrawal from the task is connected to difficulties in emotionally arousing contexts. Given our view that test-taking experiences provide data about how the client moves through the world, we explore this hypothesis with them to see if it fits. After an initial exploration of the testing experience, we may say, "It seemed like for those last few cards your voice became quieter and you seemed less engaged. Did you notice anything happening during those cards?" The client responded, "I did. I really didn't like those last ones. Too much color and too much going on. Like there is a lot of drama." The assessor continues the exploration to see what can be learned about the client when they are in situations where there are high emotions.

3   When the client provides responses or uses imagery that are unexpected. For example, we get curious about idiosyncratic responses to Card V of the Rorschach, where the popular response is a bat or a butterfly, or even popular responses that are described in uncommon ways (e.g., "Such a boring bat that no one will ever notice, nor will anyone care about his destiny").

4   When something interests or surprises us about the client's test performance or the test responses, and what we observed appears connected to their AQs. For example, a client asking, "Why am I not able to defend myself with partners who

hurt me?" might see "A volcano without lava," on Card IV of the Rorschach. During the Inquiry phase they added, "Here's where the lava should be but there's no lava." This response might stand out to us, as typically volcanos would be coded as Aggressive Content (AGC), but in this response the aggressive element seems removed. We might hypothesize that this image captures the client's ambivalence about their aggressive impulses. If the client had very low scores on scales measuring aggression on the self-report measures, this hypothesis might be confirmed. We may wonder if their anger is split-off, and this is part of the answer to their question about partnerships. Therefore, during the EI, we might talk to the client about this response.

Conducting the EI with Different Types of Tests

Performance-based and Storytelling Tests

We almost always conduct an EI on performance-based and storytelling tests, since these instruments often provide us with images and metaphors capturing relevant personality features that are often out of the client's conscious awareness. Therefore, discussing such images and metaphors during an EI might help both us and the client better understand their meaning and any implications for the client's personality functioning and difficulties. Table 6.2 lists some questions we may use during an EI with these types of tests.

When we inquire about Rorschach responses, we ask the client to review the responses with us and identify any that have personal significance. We might say, "We often look back at responses, because some responses may be metaphors of some aspect of a person's life or characteristics." We elaborate further and may say, "We can also try to put 'I am' before each response. Would you like to see if anything stands out for you?" At times we also use storytelling techniques with Rorschach responses, such as asking, "If this monster could talk, what would he say?" or "Could you tell me a story about that smashed cat?" Such questions help the client use the Rorschach imagery to express and further elaborate personal meanings. When the client responds or tells a story, we see if they can identify a connection between themselves and what the monster said, or how the smashed cat felt.

When we use storytelling tests (e.g., Thematic Apperception Test (TAT), Murray, 1943), we ask the client if they see a relationship between the situations described in their stories and their life. For example, "Do any of these stories feel familiar or seem connected to your life?" We may also ask what they think about how certain

Table 6.2 Potential Questions to Ask a Client Following Administration of a Performance-based or Storytelling Test

- Did you find any cards especially challenging? Especially easy/enjoyable?
- Did you notice any responses/stories that felt familiar?
- Are there characters or stories that you relate to? Does anything seem connected to your life?
- Is there anything about your stories that seem connected to your questions?
- Sometimes Rorschach responses or a client's story can be a metaphor for parts of a person or a person's life. Do any stand out to you in that way?
- What was this test like for you compared to that other (true/false; cognitive) test you took?

characters handled the problem in the story, and whether they see a relationship with the way they handle similar situations.

TA assessors often use other performance-based tests, such as the Wartegg Drawing Completion Test (WDCT; Wartegg, 1953), administered, scored, and interpreted according to psychometrically validated systems, such as the Crisi Wartegg System (CWS; Crisi & Palm, 2018). The WDCT was administered to a 40-year-old Italian man, Antonio, who took part in a TA and lamented that he and his wife stopped having sex some years ago. He developed an AQ about how to deal with this issue. Antonio was convinced that the couple's problem with sexual intimacy was because his wife had been sexually abused as a child. Antonio completed the Wartegg, and the clinician observed that he drew common contents in all the boxes, except in Box 7, the box theoretically related to intimacy and vulnerability. In this box, Antonio drew "slimy worms and nasty spiders." This drawing and response made the assessor wonder if Antonio had difficulties with intimacy. During the EI, the assessor explored all of Antonio's drawings, and when discussing the worms and spiders, asked him what he thought about his drawing. Antonio said, "The insects are not nice images ... they make me feel uneasy." The assessor then asked Antonio if he had a hypothesis about what that drawing might say about him, and he answered, "Hmm ... these animals, maybe they are related to some animal instinct[2]?" This was surprising to the assessor who explained that this box is related to intimacy, and maybe what being sexual is like for a person. The EI continued with Antonio being more open about his discomfort with sex. This was connected to his own traumatic early history, and part of what was contributing to the problems targeted by his AQ.

Self-report Tests

We often select critical items from self-report measures to review, although we may choose any responses. Our criteria for deciding which items to discuss are connected to how relevant they are to the client's AQs, or if they suggest significant issues that are worth exploring. For example, we might ask a client to share with us what they were thinking for their response of "true" to the Minnesota Multiphasic Personality Inventory-2-Restructured Form (MMPI-2-RF; Ben-Porath & Tellegen, 2008) critical item, "Sometimes I can read other people's minds." For some clients, this might suggest a psychotic process, but that remains unclear without further exploration. In response to our question, a client might say, "Yes, I'm a very sensitive person and I often understand what people think or feel before they say it." Such discussion builds our collaborative relationship and understanding of the client and also helps us avoid erroneous interpretations.

Cognitive Tests

As cognitive tests include a wide variety of tasks connected to different cognitive abilities, the EIs with such tests will look different for each. However, the EI with such tests primarily focuses on two dimensions:

1   The client's way of performing on a specific task when mistakes or unexpected responses or behaviors occur. Asking the client about these could help the

clinician understand the client's cognitive processes that lead to a certain result. For example, while completing the Block Design subtest on the WAIS-IV, a client studied the picture and flipped each cube so that it was red on top. He then proceeded to correctly copy the figure. This type of behavior (organizing the boxes first) is atypical, and the assessor wondered if the client needed to organize himself or his environment before engaging in cognitive challenges. The assessor explored this hypothesis with the client during the EI.

2   The impact of the client's emotional state on a cognitive task, as emotions can play a powerful role in influencing cognitive performance. We may ask the client how they felt before, during, and after completing a test or subtest. Such an inquiry may help the clinician and client develop insights into the role of emotions in the client's struggles or successes. At the end of this chapter you will read the EI conducted with Emma after the WAIS-IV, which exemplifies this idea.

Next, we provide some broad guidelines for conducting the EI and how best to scaffold clients, before turning to specific types of EIs based on client responses and behaviors.

How to Conduct an EI

Conducting an EI does **NOT** mean that we give feedback to a client about a test result. We also do **NOT** move quickly to telling the client what we think the meaning is of a certain behavior or test response. Rather, we begin a dialogue with the client, where we are guided by our curiosity, and engage the client to clarify or expand the meaning of certain behaviors or responses. We give the minimum necessary support to the client so that they can start forming ideas about what these behaviors or responses might mean about them. As the EI can have a strong emotional impact on clients, we are ready to support clients when needed. If the client cries, feels ashamed, dissociates, or is overwhelmed by emotions, we stay in our therapist role. We do not simply continue to ask questions, and rather, we pause our inquiry and provide support.

During the EI, we always start by exploring the client's experience and then link the emerging understandings that may be connected to the client's life. We also consider how what we are discussing is related to the client's AQs or vice versa (see Figure 6.1). This is connected to Fischer's belief that "throughout the assessment process, it is life

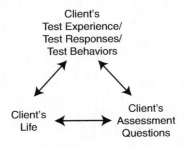

Figure 6.1 Connecting Elements in the Extended Inquiry.

events that are primary data. In contrast to traditional practice, test scores are secondary, derived data" (Fischer, 1979, p. 117).

The concept of scaffolding is central to the EI. The term is an elaboration of
Vygotsky's conceptualization of the zone of proximal development (Vygotsky, 1934/
1987). When we scaffold, we provide in-the-moment support to our clients through
verbal and nonverbal means to help them think about their behaviors and responses.
When successful, clients gain new knowledge about how they act, think, and feel. This
is a collaborative process that helps clients author, in "first person," the new story that
we are creating together about them and their difficulties (Aschieri et al., 2016). A
synonym for scaffolding is taking "half-steps," where we allow the conversation to
unfold step by step. In contrast, we do not take "full-steps" and quickly label what is
occurring or make connections that we understand, but the client cannot see.

The following guidelines help clinicians scaffold correctly.

1   We move from broader questions about the client's experience of a test to
    questions that target a specific response or set of responses, or a specific behavior.
    We first ask questions such as, "What was that test like for you?" or "Did you
    notice anything while doing that test?" We listen and follow up on what the client
    says. Some clients quickly draw conclusions and can see themselves reflected in
    their responses. For example, after completing the TAT, Rob was asked what he
    thought of the test and he responded, "Well, it looks like everyone in my stories
    just avoids conflict and eats when they have a problem." The assessor had noted
    that Rob solved most stories with avoidance and eating, but by allowing Rob to
    take the lead, he empowered him. Furthermore, by asking Rob first, the assessor
    avoided the risk of making an early interpretation that was potentially not in
    Rob's awareness and might either overwhelm him or trigger a defensive reaction.
    In contrast to Rob's understanding of his stories, it is also possible that a client
    may not recognize anything relevant in their responses or behaviors. In that
    situation, we may scaffold them towards areas of exploration. We might say
    "Let's look at the story you told for this card" or "Let's consider this subtest in
    particular" and "Did you notice anything about what you said or the way you
    completed it?"

2   We primarily use open-ended questions rather than close-ended questions, which
    may result in a "yes" or "no" response from the client. For example, during an EI
    on the Rorschach, we may ask, "What do you think about the way you responded
    to the colored cards?" instead of "Did you notice that you gave responses with less
    detail for the colored cards?"

3   We allow clients to first notice and interpret things before we offer our thoughts.
    However, we also guide the client towards specific moments or responses that may
    be opportunities for learning, but which will be more significant if authored by the
    client. We believe this tactic leads to our having a stronger impact on the client's
    self-narrative.

4   When we have a hypothesis about the meaning of certain behaviors or responses,
    we are patient when we guide the client towards those areas we are considering.
    We first ask the client questions to see if they see what we see. If we sense that
    what we think is not within reach of the client's awareness, we restrain ourselves
    from saying it and wait for other occasions in later sessions to help the
    information emerge. One simple way of knowing how much a client may explore

is illustrated by this example. After completing a storytelling test, one client may say, "Wow. Did you see how much each of those stories is like me?" In contrast, a different client may say, "That was ok. I'm not sure any of this really relates to me." With the first client, we would move more quickly towards meaningful areas of exploration, while the second client may need more scaffolding. Importantly, during this phase of a TA we are just beginning to understand the client, so we do not pressure ourselves or the client to find answers to their AQs. We have trust in the process and believe that through testing and conversations during the EI and AIS, the answers will emerge.

5   When inquiring about a behavior or response, we hand the client, or put in front of them, the related testing material (e.g., Rorschach card or specific storytelling cards). We read back to them their response or story, allowing the combination of visual and auditory information help the client reconnect with what they were thinking and experiencing when they first responded. In this way, we are creating an "experience-near-moment" that is close to the client's first encounter with the test.

6   We end the session by metaprocessing the experience and discussion with the client. We may ask broad questions such as, "What was it like to explore this test and your stories with me?" With other clients, we may be more specific, "We talked about some harder feelings today that were connected to your stories. I'm wondering what that was like for you?" If the client clearly has some new insights, we specifically ask about that with a request such as, "Tell me one or two things you learned today that you will keep thinking about." As described in Chapter 5, metaprocessing with these types of questions fosters emotional attunement and collaboration, and increases the client's awareness, consolidating the work that has been done.

EI of a Testing Experience, of a Sequence of Responses, or of a Single Response

Next, we provide some examples of how to conduct an EI targeting the client's experience of a test, a sequence of responses, or the content of a single response given to a test.

EI of a Testing Experience

As explained, the EI of a testing experience focuses on the client's meaningful reactions to the experience of completing a test. In the following example, we will describe the EI with Angie, a 26-year-old woman who was having difficulties with her job in a publishing house. One of her AQs was, "Why has it been so hard for me to accomplish job tasks I had no problem completing in the past?" The EI described below occurred after the administration of the Rorschach.

Clinician: So, what was that like for you?
Angie: Very interesting. I was just noticing that I didn't like the colored ones at all, especially those last three.
Clinician: Really, what was your experience?
Angie: I don't know why, but the black and white ones were better for me. I

found them easier and I ... didn't I see more things on them compared to the colored ones?

Clinician: (Looks back over the record sheet). Yes, in fact you did. Do you have any ideas why the colored cards were harder for you?

Angie: I think it has to do with feelings.

Clinician: Yes, it might indeed have to do with feelings ... tell me more about the way you experienced those cards. (Places the three colored cards on the table in front of Angie). *[The clinician expresses support for Angie's insight, which is consistent with his knowledge of the Rorschach. The combination of open-ended questions and showing Angie the testing material scaffolds her toward expanding her description and understanding of her experience].*

Angie: These have more emotion to them. (Pauses). They make a stronger impact, all these colors ... made it harder to see things.

Clinician: Harder in what way?

Angie: Everything was more confused. The impact of the colors made it harder to see the shapes. It was harder to say what I saw. I think I wanted to move on quickly. The other cards were more fun. I could see many things.

Clinician: Well, that's very interesting, Angie, because the research on this test suggests that these colored cards may indeed stir up more emotions in people. It is interesting to hear the impact they had on you. It seems that all these emotions made you feel confused. *[The clinician uses the link to research to support Angie's insight and mirrors the way she described her experience using her language].*

Angie: Yes, I don't like feeling confused and having no answers. (Smiles).

Clinician: So, do you see this as a more general characteristic of yours?

Angie: Sure, I need to be calm and relaxed to stay focused.

Clinician: Do you have an example of how emotions may make you feel confused in your everyday life? *[Here the clinician takes a half-step, guiding Angie towards how what is being discussed might appear in her life, but does not take the full step of directly connecting it to her work problems.]*

Angie: Mmm ... I guess at work with my new boss. He arrived in the last year when my old boss retired. He is a good man, but he can be very pushy about deadlines, and he often shouts or gets angry for nothing.

Clinician: Really? And when he does that what happens to you?

Angie: Well, I start feeling agitated and confused. I don't understand why he acts this way. The old boss was so much calmer and easy-going, and the work was done with no problems. When the new boss is pushy or critical, I feel so bad. I don't know what to say and just try hard not to cry. I try to get back to my desk as soon as possible. But then sometimes I don't really remember what he wanted me to do.

Clinician: Wow, that must be really hard for you. It seems really unnecessary for him to treat you this way.

Angie: Yeah, thank you for saying that. I really feel the same.

Clinician: Angie, I wonder if all this helps us understand something about your question, "Why has it been so hard for me to accomplish job tasks I had no problem completing in the past? What do you think?

Angie: I guess you're right ... it's the emotional impact of this new situation. I really have a hard time tolerating it.

In this example, instead of giving Angie feedback about the meaning of her test behavior (producing significantly fewer responses to the Rorschach colored cards), the clinician used questions and emotional support to help her reflect upon her test experience and how it connected to her life and her AQ. In this way, the test behavior became an occasion for Angie to reach a deeper understanding about herself and the problem she was experiencing.

EI on a Sequence of Responses

We find that sometimes a sequence of responses is meaningful in understanding a client's way of functioning and worth exploring. An example is the EI conducted with Bao, a 30-year-old man employed in marketing, who struggled both with being a consistent worker and forming relationships. The EI occurred after completion of the WAIS-IV and started with the clinician's broad inquiry about Bao's experience. Since Bao did not have any significant reactions or thoughts about the test, the clinician guided the conversation to his performance on the Digit Span subtest.

Clinician: I was wondering what you noticed about the way you handled that task when I was saying numbers and you had to repeat them. Do you have any thoughts about that one?

Bao: Not really. How did I do? *[Since Bao does not have thoughts, the clinician provides some information.]*

Clinician: Well, I was curious about one thing. (Shows score sheet). Do you see how you frequently missed shorter ones, and then got the longer ones correct?

Bao: Yes. Is that unusual?

Clinician: Yes, in fact, it is. Most people find the shorter ones easier and then reach a point where they can't do the longer ones. Do you have any sense of what was going on in your mind when you missed the easier ones?

Bao: Well, I would lose my concentration for a minute and then bomb one. At first I started to get upset, but then I told myself, "Just calm down and focus on the next one." I guess it worked some, but I kept getting distracted again.

Clinician: Any ideas about what was distracting you?

Bao: I'm not really sure. Unless ... well I guess sometimes I was worrying about how I was doing.

Clinician: Hmm ... that's interesting. It's good that you found a way to refocus yourself, Bao. But I wonder if what you are describing is connected to your question, "Why do others get mad at me and say I'm always inconsistent?" Do you think that question relates to what happened here?

Bao: I don't know. (Looks puzzled). Are you saying I was inconsistent on this test?

Clinician: Well, usually when people start getting them wrong, it's because they've reached a point where they can't go further. That wasn't true for you, and I kept feeling surprised because I couldn't predict what you would do next. I guess some people might describe that by saying that you were inconsistent. It wasn't a problem for me here, but I wonder if in other situations people might find your unpredictability frustrating.

Bao: I get it. It's because they can't predict me that they get upset. Yes, that could be pretty annoying.

Clinician: And in this case, it looks like you were inconsistent simply because you kept worrying about your performance. Might that apply to other situations in your life?

As demonstrated, the clinician first gave Bao a chance to react to his performance before offering an observation of their own. The assessor also refrained from offering interpretations, instead asking questions, and offering information that helped Bao put words to his experience.

EI of the Content of a Single Response

Sometimes, we get curious about a single response that the client gives to a test, and we decide to inquire about it. The following is an example of an EI conducted about an MMPI-3 item. Liam was a 23-year-old adult who requested a TA to understand what might help him complete his major in economics, as he had been unable to complete a required exam. During the first session, he described how he was overwhelmed with anxiety while studying. As a result, he avoided classes and stayed home, where he would study alone with his books and his peers' notes. This, however, increased his anxiety, leading him to avoid class even more. He started to feel stupid and powerless, and was unable to focus or motivate himself to study. From the onset of the TA, the symptoms Liam reported pointed to an anxious-depressive clinical picture. His low self-esteem, lack of motivation, and helplessness were accompanied by fatigue and problems with sleeping, eating, and his sex life. Despite this, his MMPI-3 did not suggest a depressive picture. There were moderate elevations on scales measuring physical complaints (RC1 = 72), unusual experiences or beliefs (RC8 = 68), and a low score on the Cynicism Scale (CYN = 39), suggesting a naïve approach to life.

During the EI following the administration of the MMPI-3, the assessor focused on the item "I have had very peculiar and strange experiences."

Clinician: So, one item you endorsed as true on the MMPI was, "I have had very peculiar and strange experiences." Can you tell me more about that?

Liam: Well, I don't know if they qualify as strange ... but, when I was a kid, my mom took me to an exorcist.

Clinician: Well, that's certainly something strange. Why did that happen?

Liam: My family was very involved in local politics, so my parents were well known and respected by everybody in the community. When I was 6 or 7, I can't remember exactly. I started to behave in crazy ways with my friends, so my mother took me to see an exorcist.

Clinician: What do you mean by "behave in crazy ways?"

Liam: For example, once my father threw a party in the yard and my friends and I started throwing pebbles in the goldfish pond. We wanted to see who could hit the fish. Also, at school I was disrupting class and didn't care if I got punished. Then, when my parents asked why I was doing these things,

I was so stupid. I never answered their questions … so my mother thought there was something bad in me and took me to an exorcist.

Clinician: Wow … so, your mother did not have other explanations for your behaviors, such as what might be normal for that age, or how you might be expressing something psychological in nature, such as depression or something else.

Liam: Not at all! (Laughs).

Clinician: And what does she think today about your problems with school?

Liam: She keeps telling me it's my lack of commitment. That is the reason I don't make it to classes. This time, I think she might be right.

In this example, the clinician discovered several important pieces of data to enrich his understanding of Liam. First, Liam's parents had a limited ability to think about his behaviors being connected to mental health issues. Second, his parents had a hard time with behaviors that deviated from their view of a respectable family, such as Liam's aggressive impulses, regardless of whether they were normal for his age or an expression of some underlying emotion. In this context, Liam might have developed a negative view of himself, with his behaviors viewed as "bad." Third, Liam may have learned early in life that the origin of people's struggles are rooted in their lack of moral development (being somehow "evil," or lacking the capacity to take on responsibilities and fulfill commitments). The clinician's hypotheses based on the information collected during this EI were still far from Liam's awareness, so the clinician refrained from pushing Liam to find a connection between this information and his AQs about school.

Often, the responses given by clients to storytelling tests illuminate important aspects of the client's way of functioning, and are single responses we target during EIs. For example, Greg was a 50-year-old man who requested a TA to understand why he cheated on his wife for over a year. When the affair was discovered, he decided to search for help before considering beginning couple's therapy. His key question was, "Why did I get to the point of betraying my wife?" His profile on the Millon Clinical Multiaxial Inventory 4th Edition (MCMI-IV; Millon et al., 2015) contained elevations on scales consistent with his self-presentation as a strong and assertive man, prone to anger at the workplace and in his intimate relationships. The Narcissistic Scale (BR = 77) and Sadistic Scale (BR = 75) were the highest elevations, and none of the Clinical Scales were elevated. This was surprising to the assessor, given that Greg's life was in upheaval and his marriage was on the cusp of a divorce. The assessor wondered if sadness was a split-off affect for Greg, and if he had learned as a child that it was best to dismiss so-called "softer" feelings and rely more on himself than others. The stories he told for the TAT added to the assessor's growing conceptualization, with more data suggesting that Greg managed distress with dismissing defenses. This is the first part of the EI discussion following the TAT.

Clinician: I am wondering if you have any thoughts or impressions about these pictures and the stories you told.

Greg: Not really. They didn't impress me much.

Clinician: I am curious about one of the stories. The one you told in response to this card. [The clinician handed Greg card 3GF, depicting a character *leaning on a door frame in a posture often interpreted as desperate or hopeless].* You told this story: "I think it's a woman. She seems sad. She probably just left her bedroom. She is wearing a dress, and she's tired after doing some housework. It's not a happy moment. It suggests loneliness and maybe she's thinking. She's trying to figure something out and solve some problem. In a minute, she will get busy with something else. Back to work. It doesn't seem to be the best moment. (What happened before?) She was doing some housework and she stopped. Nothing bad happened. She's thinking about something that didn't go as she expected. She won't stay there long because that position is not comfortable."

Greg: Right, she doesn't seem happy, but it's not a big deal.

Clinician: And how does she deal with her unhappy feelings?

Greg: She thinks a little bit about her problem and then she straightens up and keeps on cleaning or something else. She doesn't want to waste time with being unhappy. It's not worth it.

Clinician: Why is it not worth it?

Greg: Because it doesn't bring you any good to be unhappy. It's a waste of time. I can't stand people who complain about their lives, especially when they say things like, "Life is shit." I can't stand it.

Clinician: I see. And have you always thought like that?

Greg: I think I became convinced of that after my brother committed suicide when I was 12 years old. Since then, I have thought that any complaint about life is a waste of time.

Clinician: Wow, I didn't know that you had such an experience. Can I ask you a few questions about that?

The assessor obtained valuable information during this EI, as the process opened up a crucial part of Greg's history. Talking about those experiences helped both the clinician and Greg make more sense of why Greg had been dealing with the "unhappy" feelings he was holding about his marriage by acting out, instead of finding other ways of managing them, such as talking with his wife or seeking couple's therapy.

Caveats

When we decide to do an EI, we are aware of the possibility that reviewing specific behaviors or responses with clients might affect subsequent retesting. In some EIs, we may disclose aspects of the test materials that we typically keep confidential. For example, when we discuss the MMPI-3 Critical Items, the client is now aware of their importance, or if we reflect upon a client's strategy when completing the Rey Complex Figure Test (RCFT; Meyers & Meyers, 1995), the client will learn something about how that test works. Given these possibilities, it is important to be cautious about how the EI is conducted in certain settings or with certain clients. For example, many clients with chronic cognitive issues participate in neuropsychological assessments every few years. Other clients may be frequently retested to ensure they qualify for certain services (e.g., educational accommodations). In these situations, we are cautious and may limit the post-administration discussion to how the client experienced the test.

Common Mistakes when Conducting an EI

Conducting a successful EI can be difficult in different ways, and we discuss some of the common mistakes that can negatively affect the process and its effectiveness.

Taking Full-steps Instead of Half-steps

As explained, we consider the EI a process where we support clients through half-steps (i.e., scaffolding) in expanding their understanding of their behaviors or responses, and connecting this understanding to what occurs in their everyday lives. During the discussion, we ask questions about certain behaviors, what contributed to their decision-making, and what they experienced emotionally. We form hypotheses about the answers to the AQs, and sometimes we take a full-step and push the client with suggestive questions or premature conceptualizations. This mistake risks introducing information that is not in the client's level of awareness (Level 3 Information) and may activate their defenses. We consider full-steps a mistake because we are mis-attuned to the ideal pace the client needs to modify their self-understanding. Full-steps often happen when we assume too much of an expert role and have abandoned our goal of helping clients use their expertise to author their new narrative.

A client's reaction to what we share often tells us when we have taken a full-step. Some signs that we have made this mistake include clients who start stuttering, seem confused, assume a more rigid body posture, disagree with us, or previously talkative clients become silent. Such non-verbal behaviors suggest the client is experiencing some hard emotion, such as anxiety or shame.

We illustrate this mistake by revisiting the TAT with Greg, but in this case, the assessor makes a misstep.

Clinician:	I am curious about the story you told for this card. *[The clinician handed Greg card 3 GF, depicting a character leaning on a door frame in a posture interpreted as desperate or hopeless].* You told this story: "I think it's a woman. She seems sad. She probably just left her bedroom. She is wearing a dress, and she's tired after doing some housework. It's not a happy moment. It suggests loneliness and maybe she's thinking. She's trying to figure something out and solve some problem. In a minute, she will get busy with something else. Back to work. It doesn't seem to be the best moment. (What happened before?) She was doing some housework and she stopped. Nothing bad happened. She's thinking about something that didn't go as she expected. She won't stay there long because that position is not comfortable."
Greg:	Right, she doesn't seem happy, but it's not a big deal.
Clinician:	Well, you know, most people see a desperate person here. *[This would be a full-step as Greg has not demonstrated that he is open to being in touch with feelings such as desperation].*
Greg:	Really? (Silence. Looks at the card). I don't see that. It would be too much to be desperate here. She is probably just a little frustrated by something that happened earlier.
Clinician:	Why do you think that most people see a desperate person here, and you don't? *[Again, the clinician is trying to make Greg see what the clinician sees, but is moving too fast].*

Greg:	(Frowning and looking uneasy). I have no idea.
Clinician:	Could it be because you do not like sad feelings and try to see things differently? *[The clinician is offering a premature interpretation that is too far away from how Greg perceives himself].*
Greg:	(Places the card in front of him and crosses his arms). I don't think so. I do not see things differently than other people. I just saw what I said. *[Greg's comment and body language tell the clinician they have mistakenly taken full-steps].*

Inquiring on Responses by Defaulting to Traditional Practices

It is a mistake to conduct the EI process using "fixed" ways of inquiry. An example would be to believe that exploration of Card IV of the Rorschach must happen with every client because it is the "father card." Sometimes, there are interesting test responses or behaviors that we ask about, even if we are uncertain about their relationship to the client's AQs. However, fixed or "rote" ways of querying that do not consider the client's individual assessment goals are in contrast with our view of TA as a client-centered process where we collaborate with clients to answer their AQs.

Giving Feedback on the Test Instead of Exploring the Test Process or Content

As we have explained, the EI is a guided exploration of the client's experience of the test and not feedback. Providing feedback to a client is a unilateral process, where we tell the client what we understand about their tests and how we think their test results answer their AQs. Sometimes clinicians make the mistake of taking on the expert role and telling clients what they think, instead of exploring the client's point of view and helping them reach their own insights. During an EI, we share a piece of information about the client's test results or propose a way we interpret their responses or behavior. However, we are tentative, and see if our interpretation makes sense to the client. If they disagree or seem uncertain about what we say, we drop that topic, knowing that with more time we might help the client understand what we are considering. The tentative information we share should support the client's explorations and insights and not be an effort to convince the client of something that is potentially Level 3 Information. Therefore, we are clear about when and why we share our thinking and interpretations, even if it is a single test result. Importantly, we avoid sharing solely because of our anxiety about answering the client's questions.

To summarize, the EI is an exploration that we conduct with clients on their test-taking experience and test responses. That exploration helps us individualize their test interpretations, and we can test our hypotheses about the meaning of some test results. During an EI, we also scaffold clients in reflecting upon their test behaviors and responses, which can sometimes lead clients to reach insights about themselves. To avoid the risk of making full-steps, those just learning TA may find it useful to focus their EI mainly on the *exploration* of the client's responses and experience. However, expert TA practitioners may also find occasions during the EI to perform small spontaneous *interventions* that are similar to what happens during an AIS through processes and techniques that we will describe in Chapter 8. Those learning TA will benefit from reading Chapters 6 and 8 in conjunction, as the ideas presented in each overlap. Readers will also find an example of a small intervention during the EI with Emma at the end of this chapter.

Discussing Test Results Prior to the Summary/Discussion Session

Traditionally in the TA model, the Summary/Discussion Session (Chapter 9) was the only time when test results were discussed with the client. However, the model is flexible and there are clinicians practicing TA who prefer to give feedback about one or more tests midway through the process, often shortly after the test was administered. This practice is not a substitute for the Summary/Discussion Session, where we conduct a detailed discussion of the answers to the client's AQs. Rather, it is a half-step that may help the process of collaboratively building the client's new narrative, which is then completed in the Summary/Discussion Session. Mid-assessment feedback is also not a substitute for the EI that we conduct on the same test. If feedback is given, it occurs after completing the EI, so that opportunity is not lost.

There are various reasons it might be beneficial to provide feedback about a single test after it is completed. This practice can be helpful with clients who initially asked for therapy and want to talk about themselves and their difficulties. Discussing test results is a way of engaging the client in a different type of activity than testing, and the conversation will create shared knowledge that will be useful for future conversations. Other times, clients are anxious about testing and what might be revealed. Providing feedback helps reduce their worries and strengthens the alliance with the clinician. In particular, feedback on self-report measures is helpful to build trust, and we expect that those results will be Level 1 Information that verifies what clients knows about themselves. Seeing themselves reflected in the test results often builds clients' interest and motivation, and even self-report profiles with no elevations are an opportunity to talk about clients' resources and strengths. Finally, discussing a test in this phase of TA might be a way to prepare the client for the AIS, as shared language could be further explored and refined during that session, allowing the assessor to help the client try out new solutions for their problems (see Chapter 8).

However, there are also reasons why sharing feedback early in the process is not the best choice. First, if the test results are discrepant from the client's self-understanding (Level 2 or 3 Information), it may be best to discuss that data when the client is more ready to hear it, which is likely to be in the final phase of TA. Similarly, assessors are encouraged to wait to share test data when a result is likely to confirm a client's pathogenic belief. For example, a male client may ask, "Why do people I care for accuse me of being selfish? Is that the way I am?" This client might have self-report test results that confirm his tendency to behave in egocentric ways. However, providing this feedback would confirm the client's negative belief about himself, without integrating it into a more compassionate narrative that explains why he behaves this way. With such clients, we are likely to get important information from performance-based or storytelling tests that will help create a more complete narrative. We wait until the Summary/Discussion Session to share test results, as that will be a more positive experience for the client. Second, sometimes we are unsure about the meaning of a single test finding and to provide accurate feedback, we require additional information from other tests or through conversation. For example, a client who is quite sad, distressed, and overwhelmed during the first session might produce a self-report profile with low scores on the internalizing scales (e.g., anxiety, depression, demoralization). These results would stand in sharp contrast to our experience of the client, and thus both additional conversation and test data would help us better understand this seemingly contradictory information. Third, we make sure that providing feedback to a client after a test administration is not a way for the clinician to avoid other more challenging interactions. As described, the EI requires us to be patient, contain what we know, and guide clients at their pace towards discovering the meaning of their behaviors and responses. This is not always easy, especially when we feel pressured to find answers to AQs or help our clients quickly. However, because we prioritize helping clients reach their own insights during a TA, we do not give feedback about a test just because it is easier in situations when an EI is appropriate.

Working with Referring Professionals: Maintaining Contact During the Testing Phase

Assessors have consistent contact with the referring professional (RP) during the testing phase, to meet a few goals. First, by sharing what is occurring with the client, we help the RP stay involved in the process and understand how the TA is proceeding. We provide updates about what is being revealed in the test data and conversations, and we gather information about the effect of the TA on the client. Second, sharing information about the client's reactions to the testing and certain test results helps the RP begin to integrate important information. Ultimately, that information is further organized and summarized in the Summary/Discussion Session. Third, during these conversations we also ask RPs to share their perspective of the client and their work to date. In this way, we build our collaborative relationship with the RP and have an opportunity demonstrate our respect for their expertise and work.

Consistent connection with the RP is of particular importance if the test results suggest that their case conceptualization is misaligned with what the data is revealing. We conduct conversations with RPs in a way that is similar to how we talk with clients. We present the information from the testing and EIs tentatively, asking the RP to provide their insights on their meanings while carefully attending to their interpretations. In this way, the assessor respects the RP's knowledge of the client, and further builds the relationship. This is important so that the RP can also adequately integrate the new information emerging about their client, and use that to provide the best care.

Finally, when the RP and the client continue with therapy sessions during the TA, the assessor benefits from hearing the RP's feedback about how the assessment is unfolding. Learning how the TA is affecting the client's symptoms and their relationship with the RP is often very useful for better attuning to the client's needs and pacing the upcoming sessions.

Often RPs share information that validates that our work is helping the client. However, at times clients feel more comfortable revealing to their therapist, rather than us, that some aspect of the testing was difficult. We use such information to adjust our work to best meet the client's needs. Other times RPs provide information about the client that we were not aware of, and that data helps us better understand what we are seeing in the test results.

Clinical Case: Testing Sessions and Extended Inquiries with Emma

We again return to Hale's account of the TA with Emma.

After deciding upon the final AQs and collecting relevant background, Emma and I moved to the testing table in my office to begin testing. To answer Emma's question about a possible learning disorder and ADHD, I planned to assess her cognitive ability and academic performance as well as use self and other behavior surveys to get a picture of her behavior as an adult and as a child. I chose the following tests:

Tests to Help Determine ADHD or a Learning Disorder
Wechsler Adult Intelligence Scale—Fourth Edition (WAIS-IV)
Woodcock-Johnson Test of Achievement-III (WJA-III; Woodcock, et al., 2001)
Conners Adult ADHD Rating Scale (CAARS; Conners et al., 1999)
Behavior Assessment System for Children, Second Edition (BASC-2; Reynolds et al., 2004)
Conners-3 Parent form (Conners, 2008)

A battery of self-report and performance-based personality tests was needed to answer Emma's questions about her fears, struggles with a career, and not being able to find a long-term relationship. I chose the following:

Personality Tests
Minnesota Multiphasic Personality Inventory 2nd Edition (MMPI-2; Butcher et al., 2001)
Rorschach Performance Assessment System (R-PAS)
Wartegg Drawing Completion Test, Crisi Wartegg System (WDCT/CWS)
Adult Attachment Projective Picture System (AAP)

During the course of testing, I added the Early Memories Procedure (EMP; Bruhn, 1992a, b), because I thought it might be helpful to get a glimpse into meaningful events in Emma's early life that would shed light on the roots of her struggles. My goal was to tailor the testing to address Emma's AQs with flexibility as understanding evolved.

We started with the WAIS-IV but only did a few tests each session. The WJA-III went faster but still took parts of three sessions. We filled in the time with personality tests and behavior surveys (for Emma and Tessa). Emma put strong effort into all the cognitive tests but seemed stressed by them. As a result, I decided to spread them over multiple sessions. At the end of each session, she expressed how exhausted she was. Her behavior during these tests carried meaningful information in demonstrating how tension and anxiety affected her. Emma's strong emotional reaction to the Block Design subtest that prompted the first EI (described below) reflected her tension. At the same time, she generally had a positive attitude, and the other tests were not as stressful, but the pace of meetings was still slow.

The testing itself took eight sessions, each about 90–105 minutes. However, Emma's claims of being very busy caused those meetings to be spaced out, with varying periods of time between meetings. Overall, the testing itself took about four months. It was as if Emma was titrating her emotional experience, which I respected and I did not push to meet more frequently. I also suspected that doing the assessment over a longer period of time facilitated growth and change. During sessions, Emma often shared about her overwhelming responsibilities with work (including struggles with her fellow teachers-aids), with her mother (with whom she visited weekly), and with her on-and-off boyfriend (who was a constant challenge). However, Emma was cooperative and worked hard each session and, by not pushing to meet more frequently or to do more work on testing within each session, I tried to be sensitive and responsive to her limits.

EI with Cognitive Testing

The first opportunity for an EI came quickly. Emma and I started the WAIS-IV right after we had formalized her AQs. I explained to Emma that this battery of subtests would help us answer her question about learning disabilities and ADHD. We had begun with Block Design (BD), the first subtest on the WAIS-IV, when an unexpected but promising opening for an EI appeared. Emma was able to get the first several items on the subtest correct and seemed quite proud of herself, but when the items got more difficult, she missed one and suddenly broke into tears. We stopped testing, and I gently asked her what happened. She berated herself for being "stupid." It was surprising how quickly she melted down, from being excited about testing to sobbing. She told me that she felt "really bad" when she struggled on tests and added that working with puzzles like the blocks was particularly difficult for her. I acknowledged that being tested seemed quite stressful for her. When asked when she first noticed this, she responded that it seemed it had always been that way. Intelligence had been very important to her father, and ever since she was a child, she worried about letting him down. She went on to say that her brain sometimes didn't seem to work right. She had difficulty staying focused on tasks, and anxiety took over. We noted that she had said earlier that her worst fear for our assessment was that it would show she was not as smart as she thought she was. I asked if she had tried anything to decrease her anxiety about testing. She said she had tried deep breathing and meditation, but with little effect, and claimed she just wasn't very smart.

It took about 10 minutes for Emma to recompose herself. I then asked if she felt like going to the next test, and she did. We proceeded to the next subtest, Similarities. She gave good responses to many of these items, and I could clearly see her confidence return. At the end of that subtest, when I inquired, she said she felt fine. I asked her to rate on a scale of 1 to 10 how confident she felt, with 1 being "not at all confident" and 10 being "very confident." She rated herself at a 9. I asked if she thought she could maintain that confident feeling, and she was sure she could. I asked her to focus on that feeling and not let anything disturb it. Then I said, "This might seem strange, but I want us to go back to the previous test and try something." I again reiterated that she should hold on to the confident feeling. We went back to Block Design and tried the item after the one she had become upset with—and she got it correct! She also got the next two items correct before meeting the cutoff to discontinue the subtest.

Emma was amazed and elated that she had done better. We saw that her anxiety interfered with her performance and seemed to impair her ability on the test. It was a powerful moment for Emma to understand that her anxiety had such a debilitating effect. I reminded her that she had told me that test anxiety had limited her score on the college entrance exam. She nodded her head in agreement, seeing more evidence of the importance of her anxiety—and perhaps more importantly, she had had the actual experience of calm confidence improving her performance. We concluded that if Emma could learn not to get upset, her performance would likely be better on tests—and perhaps in other areas of her life as well. I also was aware that although we had focused on anxiety, underlying shame seemed to be generating the anxiety Emma had about her performance. I noted this to myself and was curious to explore where the shame had come from.

At this point, Emma and I were near the end of our scheduled time, and we agreed to stop until our next meeting. I think we both left the session excited to be solidly in the work. I want to be clear here that I omitted Block Design from her test results because it was not done by standard administration, and I substituted another similar test for it. It is important in TA to follow standardized administration procedures in order to get good nomothetic data. I also want to point out that this EI expanded into an unplanned mini-AIS, as EIs sometimes do. I thought the intervention at this point was very useful in starting to shift Emma's story about herself.

EI with the Wartegg

During the seventh session, I administered the WDCT using the Crisi Wartegg System (see Figure 6.2). In the following session, after consulting with Alessandro Crisi, the developer of the system, I once again saw an opportunity to develop a deeper understanding with Emma by looking at her drawings together. For the Wartegg Box 5, she had drawn a bicycle pump moving toward the bottom left of the box, which would be scored Opposite Direction (OD; see Figure 7.1 for part of the WDCT profile). The hypothesized meaning of this score is that the test-taker's aggressive energy is blocked and that they tend to turn their anger against themselves. I hoped that Emma and I could explore that idea and see if it was relevant. There were other drawings she had done that were pregnant with meaning as well, but with Emma, the bicycle pump was most promising in my mind.

Hale: If it's ok with you, I want to go back to the test we ended with last time and talk about that some more.

Emma: Sure! It sure was an interesting test. I don't know how you get anything out of that one!

Hale: Well, there is a complicated scoring system that I will use later, but the part I would like to talk about is what you can make of your drawings. (Hale hands Emma the stimulus page). Looking at these drawings, do you see anything that might say something about you?

Emma: (looks over the drawings) I really liked my butterflies.

In concert with how the EI is conducted, I followed her lead and we talked about her drawing of two butterflies in Box 6, which I also considered meaningful. I asked what moved her to draw them. She explained that she just liked butterflies; they are "pretty and light and fun." I explained to her that research showed that each of the boxes pulled for an expression of a certain aspect of a person's personality, and what a person drew in a box told us about how they were functioning in that area.

Emma perked up, became very curious, and asked what Box 6 said about her. I explained that it generally says something about how one sees and deals with reality and how organized and practical they are. I asked if knowing that brought any thoughts to her mind. She explained she was just trying to make the box pretty and light and fun. We considered what that might say about her, and she offered that she tries to be highly organized but isn't. I questioned if she often makes efforts to make things pretty and light. Emma said she always tried to look at the positive in everything, and we understood that being positive was a big part of her approach to life. I confirmed, "So you work hard to make the world positive and

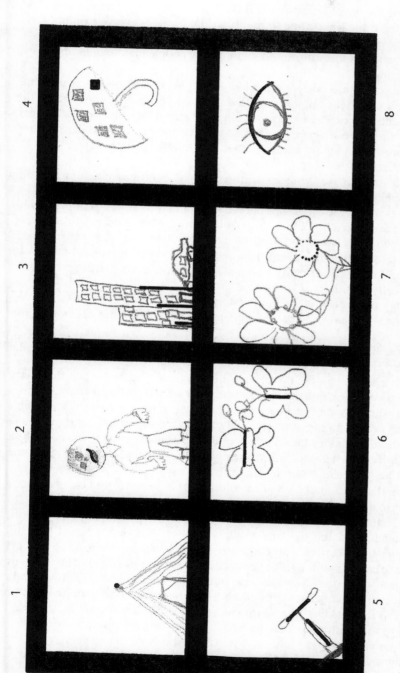

Figure 6.2 Emma's Wartegg Drawing Completion Test—Crisi Wartegg System (CWS). *Note:* Emma's drawing descriptions: Box 1 = *A tent. A circus tent or a regular tent. Just a tent, nothing specifc.* Box 2 = *A gentleman with a moustache. It's a little hard to show the mouth.* Box 3 = *Two skyscrapers and a car in front of the building.* Box 4 = *An umbrella (What is the mark?) Part of the pattern.* Box 5 = *A bicycle pump. You put your feet here and pump. Like an old-fashioned bicycle pump.* Box 6 = *A couple of butterflies.* Box 7 = *Number seven is a couple of flowers.* Box 8 = *An eye. A human eye.* The WDCT form is reprinted here with permission of Hogrefe (9/27/21). Please note that this test form is only a sample. Any kind of reproduction is strictly forbidden. A valid test result can only be obtained by a professionally qualified test administrator and using the original test materials. The test material can only be ordered at the Hogrefe Publishing Group *www.hogrefe. com;* For any questions please contact rights@hogrefe.com.

happy," and Emma agreed. We concluded that she put pretty butterflies "on life," and this became an important metaphor that we referred to later. Next, I asked about Box 5.

Hale:　How about this box? (Pointing to Box 5) What are your feelings about it?

Emma:　Again, I just drew what came to me. It struck me like a bicycle pump. Does this Box have a specific meaning, too?

Hale:　Often this one gives us information about how people handle their aggressive energy or anger.

Emma:　Well, a bicycle pump doesn't seem like a very aggressive object, which kind of tells you that I am not someone that is filled with a lot of anger. Or I'm not someone who expresses so much anger or puts a lot of energy into anger.

Hale:　You don't put it out there. We talked about turning anger inward before, and I think what you are saying is that you hold onto it, you feel it.

Emma:　Yes, I feel it.

Hale:　You just keep it to yourself rather than being outwardly angry or adversarial. *[Hale is carefully scaffolding.]*

Emma:　And I'm aware of the difference between keeping it to myself and processing it and holding a grudge. I'm not really big on keeping grudges. I think they are ugly, and they create resentment, and resentment creates cancer, and I don't believe in that. It is like I have seen too many people that hang on to their anger, and they are really walking around with a red face all of the time. I don't really like that.

Hale:　So, you try not to feel it for long? *[Another half-step]*

Emma:　Yes, I guess. *[Emma accepts the comment, suggesting Hale did not go too fast.]*

Hale:　With some degree of success. *[Hale mirrors the positive aspects of Emma's approach.]*

Emma:　Yes, I think so. But maybe not always. I mean there are times when I'm pretty mad. I'll never forget one time I really did truly see red. I was so angry. It was a situation where a man was being sort of made fun of in a grocery store. This older man needed an explanation of how the coupons worked. He didn't quite understand the deal on his coupons, and he asked the woman checking him out to clarify that. The woman was really sweet with him. But there was some jerk two people behind him in line who was saying, "Oh, seriously this guy doesn't understand math. What an idiot, what a moron," and carrying on. I don't normally do this, but I walked over from where I had been to move to another counter because he annoyed me so much. I was tempted to tell him off, so I walked away and went to another counter. But then I heard him still sabotaging this old man who obviously didn't have the retention to get it. I really have compassion for older people. My parents were older. Then I finally walked into where they were checking out, and I said, "Excuse me, if you don't stop criticizing this person, I'm going to file an elder abuse complaint. You better stop it right now! I'm not going to put up with this, and he shouldn't have to put up with you. You need to just be quiet right now."

Hale:　Oh my, so you really let him have it! *[Hale validates Emma's anger.]*

Emma:　I literally saw red. My God, I've never seen red before, and it kind of freaked me out. But I didn't care. I was going to tell him off. I was really mad because he was enjoying making fun of this man. He was just such a mean-spirited person. I let him know, "Don't do that! It's not OK with me. I see elder abuse right now, and you're not going to do that to him." I really lit into him. Then he got quiet and walked away, and then everybody around me was thinking, "Who is this crazy woman?" *[Notice Emma projecting her own shame about her anger.]* I finally said to the woman at the counter who was helping him, "I apologize for my outburst, but I am not going to tolerate people being mistreated. This man obviously has problems with elderly people, and I can't stand it." She said, "OK, that's cool." I said, "You were very nice to him, and I really appreciate that. But I'm very protective of people and that really bothered me." *[Emma felt the need to explain herself due to her shame about anger.]*

Hale: Wow! I can see you were really mad! You even seemed mad talking about it.
Emma: So, I'm very capable of anger … I am like all-nothing.
Hale: Yes, your first reaction was to get in another line and get away from it. But then you came back and really blasted that mean man!
Emma: Right, I tried to get away because I could feel seeing red coming on, because he just kept doing it. He was taunting this man, and it just felt like he was a bully. I said, "You better stop bullying right now! This is not OK with me." I felt like at that moment it was justified because he was a jerk, and the old man was just trying to understand how the numbers worked and how he got his discount.
Hale: That was kind of you to stand up for the old man. *[This is a shame intervention, with Hale reframing the behavior that Emma was clearly ashamed of.]*
Emma: Yeah, but it was a weird little outburst.
Hale: It seems like this box really speaks to us in a way, doesn't it? First, you try to walk away, avoid the feelings, but when it gets too much, you see red. It takes a whole lot to burn your fuse down.
Emma: Yes, I guess so.
Hale: I wonder what it would be like for you to harness your anger and use it, express it in a more modulated way? Not all-nothing. To feel it and express it appropriately and not carry it all yourself.
Emma: Hmmm. Interesting.
Hale: And I wonder if all this might tell us anything about some of your Assessment Questions, such as why it's been hard for you to have a long-term relationship or stick with a long-term work position?
Emma: That's really interesting

She then changed the topic and proceeded to ask me about Boxes 3 and 4, and we briefly discussed how she related to the pull of those boxes. She was excited to learn that Box 3 suggested that her energy was blocked, as indicated by drawing cars parked right up against the three lines making upward movement impossible. She commented that it was absolutely true, she was always exhausted. We then both marveled at her drawing of an umbrella in Box 4, the box related to authority and father. She exclaimed, "That is perfect. My father was so protective of me just like an umbrella." She was delighted with this test.

At the end of the eighth and final testing session in which we did the AAP, I explained that in the next session we would do another test that I hoped would help us get a better understanding of the answers to her questions about her fears, career, and relationships. Emma expressed gratitude that we were finally getting near the end of testing, but she also said she was amazed at such interesting tests.

Reflections on Emma's Testing Session and Extended Inquiries

While the testing had taken much longer than usual, Emma seemed different. Her presence in the room had gradually exhibited more life, more confidence, and more fun. She also seemed more hopeful. I thought the decision not to push the testing had paid off. It had created the space for Emma to integrate in her own time and had increased the possibility of a successful AIS. The two EIs had served well in moving Emma toward a new understanding. The Block Design EI had offered Emma some hope that things could change, she could do better on tests by managing her emotions better, and it was good that it happened at the very beginning of testing. The Wartegg EI had led to a deeper and more accurate understanding of a test score (OD in Wartegg Box 5, see Figure 7.1) than we might have had without the EI. We learned that Emma's anger was not completely split-off, but was unintegrated. Her anger that came out in the grocery store triggered her shame, which likely inhibited future expressions of anger and kept her stuck. Seeing this dynamic offered hope that we might be able to foster a more accurate and compassionate understanding of her anger in the AIS.

Notes

1 It is understood that in some work settings this type of schedule is not possible, given the length of appointments and how clients are scheduled. While some tests require more than an hour to administer, in general, what we describe can be accomplished across multiple sessions that are briefer in duration. For example, during one session a test is administered, and during the next session, the EI on that test is conducted. Other clients may travel a long distance for appointments and in those situations, we may need to administer numerous tests in one appointment. Clinicians are encouraged to adapt their way of doing TA to the demands of their setting.
2 Antonio used the Italian expression "qualcosa di animalesco," which can refer to sexual activities and other human behaviors that are more connected to instincts than reasoning.

References

Aschieri, F., Fantini, F., & Smith, J. D. (2016). Collaborative/Therapeutic Assessment: Procedures to enhance client outcomes. In S. Maltzmann (Ed.), *Oxford handbook of treatment processes and outcomes in counseling psychology* (pp. 241–269). Oxford University Press. doi: 10.1093/oxfordhb/ 9780199739134.013.23

Ben-Porath, Y. S., & Tellegen, A. (2008). *MMPI-2: Restructured Form (MMPI-2-RF) manual for administration*. University of Minnesota Press.

Ben-Porath, Y. S., & Tellegen, A. (2020). *Minnesota Multiphasic Personality Inventory-3 (MMPI-3): Manual for administration, scoring, and interpretation*. University of Minnesota Press.

Bruhn, A. R. (1992a). The Early Memories Procedure: A projective test of autobiographical memory (Part I). *Journal of Personality Assessment, 58*, 1–15.

Bruhn, A. R. (1992b). The Early Memories Procedure: A projective test of autobiographical memory (Part II). *Journal of Personality Assessment, 58*, 326–346.

Butcher, J. N., Graham, J. R., Ben-Porath, Y. S., Tellegen, A., Dahlstrom, W. G., & Kaemmer, B. (2001). *Minnesota Multiphasic Personality Inventory-2: Manual for administration, scoring, and interpretation, revised edition.* University of Minnesota Press.

Conners, C. K. (2008). *Conners 3rd edition manual.* Multi-Health Systems.

Conners, C. K., Erhardt, D., & Sparrow, E. P. (1999). *Conners' adult ADHD rating scales (CAARS): Technical manual.* Multi-Health Systems Inc.

Crisi, A. & Palm, J. A. (2018). *The Crisi Wartegg System (CWS). Manual for administration, scoring, and interpretation.* Routledge.

Delis, D. C., Kramer, J. H., Kaplan, E., & Ober, B. A. (2000). *California Verbal Learning Test* (2nd ed.). Psychological Corporation.

Exner, J. E. (2002). *The Rorschach: A comprehensive system.* Wiley.

Finn, S. E. (2007). *In our clients' shoes: Theory and techniques of Therapeutic Assessment.* Lawrence Erlbaum Associates.

Finn, S. E. (2012). Implications of recent research in neurobiology for psychological assessment. *Journal of Personality Assessment, 94*(5), 440–449.

Fischer, C. T. (1979). Individualized assessment and phenomenological psychology. *Journal of Personality Assessment, 43,* 115–122.

George, C., & West, M. L. (2012). *The Adult Attachment Projective Picture System: Attachment theory and assessment in adults.* Guilford Press.

Hopwood, C. J., & Bornstein, R. F. (Eds.). (2014). *Multimethod clinical assessment.* Guilford Press.

Ishibashi, M., Uchiumi, C., Jung, M., Aizawa, N., Makita, K., Nakamura, Y., & Saito, D. N. (2016). Differences in brain hemodynamics in response to achromatic and chromatic cards of the Rorschach: A fMRI Study. *Rorschachiana, 37*(1), 41–57. doi: 10.1027/1192-5604/a000076

Kamphuis, J. H., & Finn, S. E. (2019). Therapeutic Assessment in personality disorders: Toward the restoration of epistemic trust. *Journal of Personality Assessment, 101*(6), 662–674.

Martin, H., & Frackowiak, M. (2017). The value of projective/performance-based techniques in Therapeutic Assessment. *SIS Journal of Projective Psychology and Mental Health, 24*(2), 91–95.

Meyer, G. J., Viglione, D. J., Mihura, J. L., Erard, R. E., & Erdberg, P. (2011). *Rorschach Performance Assessment System: Administration, coding, interpretation, and technical manual.* Rorschach Performance Assessment System.

Meyers, J. E., & Meyers, K. R. (1995). *Rey Complex Figure Test and Recognition Trial: Professional manual.* Psychological Assessment Resources, Inc.

Millon, T., Grossman, S., & Millon, C. (2015). *MCMI-IV: Millon Clinical Multiaxial Inventory-IV—manual.* NCS Pearson.

Murray, H. A. (1943). *Thematic Apperception Test.* Harvard University Press.

Reynolds, C. R., Kamphaus, R. W., Pearson (Firm), Psychological Corporation., & American Guidance Service. (2004). *BASC-2: Behavior Assessment System for Children.* NCS Pearson.

Thurston, N. S., & Cradock O'Leary, J. (2009). *Thurston Cradock Test of Shame (TCTS).* Western Psychological Services.

Vygotsky, L. S. (1987). Thinking and speech. In R. W. Rieber & A. S. Carton (Eds.), *The collected works of L.S. Vygotsky Volume 1: Problems of general psychology* (pp. 39–285). Plenum Press. (Original work published 1934.)

Wartegg, E. (1953): *Schichtdiagnostik-Der Zeichentest* (WZT) [Differential diagnostics-The Drawing test.] Verlag für Psychologie.

Wechsler, D. (2008). *Wechsler Adult Intelligence Scale–Fourth edition (WAIS-IV).* Pearson.

Woodcock, R. W., McGrew, K. S., & Mather, N. (2001). *Woodcock-Johnson III.* Riverside Publishing.

7 Case Conceptualization

Case Conceptualization as part of a Therapeutic Assessment (TA)

Our view of case conceptualizations aligns with common definitions of this concept and yet differs in some unique ways. At its foundation, "a case conceptualization is a method for understanding and explaining a client's concerns and for guiding the treatment process" (Sperry & Sperry, 2012, p. 3). Clinicians' theoretical orientation informs the conceptualization, and we consider various ways of understanding a client's symptomology, personality, contextual elements, and their lived experience. TA assessors' conceptualization is informed by various schools of psychology such as psychodynamic, systemic, and cognitive-behavioral theories of psychopathology and therapy. We encourage assessors to lean on their psychological knowledge to best understand their client. Our review below will not focus on these orientations as much as specific elements of case conceptualization when conducting a TA. So, in addition to the traditional ways of thinking about a client, we consider the case conceptualization as including the emerging new narrative about the client's psychological functioning, struggles, and resources, that is co-authored by clinician and client during the TA. These narratives help assessors summarize and make sense of the client's difficulties, and when discussed with the client in the Summary/Discussion Session, help them understand themselves in a more coherent, less shaming, and compassionate way.

Assessors build the case conceptualization through both an individual endeavor and a process of meaning-making co-constructed with the client (Fischer, 1985/1994), because they are involved as collaborators throughout a TA. A good case conceptualization depends on two variables. The first is the assessor's capacity to integrate and synthesize information from the assessment so that the formulation is useful when answering the client's Assessment Questions (AQs). The second variable is the assessor's ability to collaboratively engage the client in the narrative-building process. For example, the client's contribution during Extended Inquiries (EIs; see Chapter 6), helps the assessor develop a more nuanced conceptualization.

We begin to build the case conceptualization during the initial contact with the client, and it is continuously modified and enriched. We listen carefully to what clients say during the first phone call, and develop tentative hypotheses about their problems and underlying issues. Next, we use the client's AQs and the initial interview data to expand the conceptualization, and during each subsequent step of a TA, the assessor uses data from behavioral observations, discussions, and test results to refine the conceptualization and make choices about the next steps. The assessor should have a well-formulated and coherent case conceptualization by the time the testing phase is

DOI: 10.4324/9780429202797-9

complete. That conceptualization is used to design and implement both the Assessment Intervention Session (AIS) and the Summary/Discussion Session (see Chapters 8 and 9).

Main Features of a TA Case Conceptualization

We describe some primary ways we think about clients and test results below. These ideas align with our TA values and are useful when it comes to considering what will help a client change.

A Contextualized Case Conceptualization

When clients complete a psychological test, they are responding in a controlled condition that parallels how they behave in various situations. For example, self-report tests are akin to structured, familiar, and non-interpersonal situations in which clients act in certain ways, while performance-based tests may capture how they behave in unstructured, interpersonal, and emotionally arousing conditions (Meyer, 1997). Our case conceptualizations always include the specification of "what happens *in which context,*" Finn (1996) described a useful model for integrating and contextualizing test results from different types of tests. He focused on the Rorschach Comprehensive System (Exner, 2003) and the Minnesota Multiphasic Personality Inventory Second Edition (MMPI-2; Butcher et al., 2001), but this model can be extended to data from other self-report and performance-based tests. We will continue to refer to the MMPI-2 and Rorschach to illustrate these ideas, but assessors can consider other similar tests if those measures are unfamiliar. Finn's model (1996) is useful when creating a case conceptualization, in that it explains how to consider discrepant data collected from different types of measures. Furthermore, this model allows assessors to formulate hypotheses about how clients understand their difficulties and why their difficulties may be present in different parts of their lives. In Finn's model, the congruence or discrepancy between performance-based and self-report test results are categorized in five configurations or cells (Table 7.1). We consider which cell best captures the client when reviewing test data, and this contributes to our developing case conceptualization.

"Cell A" clients have a high degree of distress and/or disturbance on both the MMPI-2 and Rorschach and are likely to have problems in both structured and

Table 7.1 Integration of Data from Self-report and Performance-based Tests

	High Degree of Distress/Disturbance on Self-report Tests	Low Degree of Distress/Disturbance on Self-report Tests
High Degree of Distress/Disturbance on Performance-based Tests	Cell A	Cell B
Low Degree of Distress/Disturbance on Performance-based Tests	Cell C-1 Cell C-2	Cell D

[a]Cell C-1: Performance-based test results suggest adequate client engagement.
[b]Cell C-2: Performance-based test results are constricted.

unstructured situations. This type of client frequently accesses mental health services and seeks help due to anxiety, depression, or problems with emotional dysregulation. Clients in this cell are aware of their problems, given that they endorsed test items capturing their difficulties on the MMPI-2. Thus, when we review their test results with them from either the MMPI-2 or the Rorschach, those results are likely to be Level 1 Information.

"Cell B" clients have low or limited distress/disturbance on the MMPI-2 (e.g., a flat profile) and more severe signs of distress/disturbance on the Rorschach. These clients are less likely to access mental health services than Cell A clients, although their ways of managing emotions may lead to maladaptive behaviors (e.g., drug/alcohol issues) or relationship problems. The discrepancy between the tests is connected to underlying psychopathology that most likely emerges in emotionally arousing, interpersonal, or unstructured life situations. These clients function better in familiar and well-defined situations, and often report fewer difficulties than Cell A clients. Because Cell B clients do not endorse significant difficulties on self-report tests, we hypothesize that they are less aware of their underlying problems, and the Rorschach results specifically may be Level 2 or 3 Information.

There are two types of "Cell C" clients, and while both have elevated scales on the MMPI-2 their Rorschach scores are in the average range, which suggests healthy psychological functioning. For some of these clients (Cell C-1), they are over-reporting psychopathology on the self-report measure. This may be a "cry for help" and, if so, we validate these clients by letting them know we see and appreciate their distress. Other C-1 clients may see themselves as mentally ill for various reasons but have considerable strengths they do not recognize. Sometimes their negative self-view results from a narrative that developed throughout childhood, during which their family members cast them in the role of the "sick" family member. Other times, C-1 clients may be using a disturbed self-view to protect themselves, as one client did, explaining that the only way he could get a break from his family was to tell them he was depressed.

The second type of "Cell C" pattern (C-2) occurs when a client has a low level of engagement with the Rorschach. Such clients' Rorschach responses were simple, with minimal elaboration, resulting in less language and fewer codes. Some signs of these "constricted" Rorschachs include a high percentage of Pure Form (Form%), little use of chromatic color (i.e., low Weighted Sum of Color determinants), and/or few human movement (M) responses. We often realize we have a C-2 client during the Extended Inquiry (EI) on the Rorshach, when their comments indicate that the test was hard or tedious for them. The C-2 pattern typically indicates that these clients "shut down" in emotionally arousing, interpersonal situations.

Last, "Cell D" clients are characterized by low levels of disturbance on both the MMPI-2 and the Rorschach. Such clients function well in both structured and unstructured situations and do not commonly access psychological services due to emotional or social concerns. When they are referred for a TA, it may be because they are being considered for career advancement, or they may be part of a family system doing a TA.

In recent years, neuroscience research has supported the distinction between the different levels of personality functioning mapped by self-report and performance-based tests, captured in the different cells described here. In various publications, Schore (1994,

2002, 2003, 2009) has described how right-brain and subcortical system connections are responsible for the right hemisphere being dominant in the reception, expression, and communication of emotion, as well as in the control of spontaneously evoked emotional reactions. Such reactions tend to be evoked by performance-based measures. Based on this research (see also Buchheim et al., 2006; 2008), Finn (2012) described important implications for the use of different types of tests in psychological assessment. He posited that performance-based tests, "because of their visual, emotionally arousing stimulus properties and the emotionally arousing aspects of their administration procedures, tap into material that is more reflective of right-hemisphere and subcortical functioning" (p. 9). On the contrary, self-report tests "utilize more left-hemisphere cortical functions because of their verbal format and non-emotionally arousing administration" (ibid.). For these reasons, Finn concluded that performance-based tests "allow us to access parts of the brain that are difficult to reach with other methods … and are extremely useful in measuring different aspects of emotional and interpersonal functioning that are not well captured by other assessment procedures (p. 12)." These ideas align with the 5-cell model described earlier. Thus, by considering what each test adds, we develop a more contextualized case conceptualization.

A Compassionate and Non-shaming Case Conceptualization

We create a case conceptualization that helps clients understand themselves while also, ideally, decreasing their shame. Some clients begin their TA by locating the source of their struggles inside themselves. This is particularly true for clients suffering with anxiety or depression, who hold self-blaming narratives about themselves and their difficulties. With these clients, the assessor tries to move the source of their problems outside of the client[1] by highlighting the contribution of certain contextual factors. For example, a client with a self-blaming story about their partnership may think that they are "weak" because they are overly passive with their partner. The client's test results suggest that their relationship difficulties are connected to traumatic experiences with neglectful parents and previous partners. These traumatic experiences left the client believing that they were unlovable and not worthy of standing up for their needs. Often such clients are unaware of all that influences their behaviors and self-perceptions. With such a client, we form a case conceptualization in which the etiology of their difficulty is externalized, and there is a more realistic view of how such behaviors came to be. If the client comes to see the impact of their past experiences as the test results suggest, the assessor could say during the Summary/Discussion Session, "Given what I have learned about you, I understand why it is so difficult for you to confront your partner about some of their behaviors, because in past relationships that would have led to negative consequences." When we collaborate with the client to develop such a narrative, we reduce their shame and build their self-compassion.

In contrast, clients with externalizing psychopathology who struggle with acting out behaviors, dysregulated anger, or substance abuse tend to locate the source of their problems outside themselves. A compassionate case conceptualization for these clients takes into consideration how their behaviors are connected to internal psychological factors, while not losing focus on protecting their self-worth, as internal causes may contribute to inappropriate guilt or shame. The assessor helps this type of client understand how the problematic behavior developed so that they could adapt and survive in an adverse environment. For example, a male client had multiple extramarital affairs and felt deep shame because he could not stop these behaviors nor leave his partner. The assessor helped the client connect his acting-out tendencies with early memories in which he was repeatedly placed in dangerous situations without adequate support from his caregivers. The client eventually recognized he needed to develop a greater connection with his emotions and also build other coping mechanisms. This case conceptualization helped the assessor to hold compassion for the client's difficulties.

An Intersubjective and Developmentally Framed Case Conceptualization

Various theories and research influence two beliefs we hold about the origin of our clients' difficulties, and these perspectives inform our conceptualization. First, psychological adjustment and maladjustment depend on the interplay of biological and environmental factors (for example, see the diathesis-stress model; Ingram & Luxton, 2005). Second, the client's identity is shaped through relational processes and contextual elements (for example, see intersubjective psychoanalysis; Stolorow et al., 1994; Bromberg, 2011; or the Bioecological Model, Bronfenbrenner, 1995). Assessors consider both of these ideas when building the case conceptualization, and when this information is shared with clients, it may help them understand how their life experiences influenced the development of their problems. For example, we often explain how the interaction between biological vulnerabilities and life stressors may contribute to psychopathology. By doing this, we create a less shameful narrative by recognizing contextual factors that may have affected the client, and highlight that they had limited control over these variable. Furthermore, by focusing on the role of the client's relational experiences, we create a therapeutic conceptualization that promotes the client's self-understanding and self-acceptance. Also, the intersubjective perspective recognizes that in the present, clients act differently in different interpersonal contexts. When clients realize that their behavior is continuously shaped in response to others' behaviors, they typically feel less shame and have more hope for building relationships with people who are responsive and positive.

Theories and Research that have Proven Useful for Building Case Conceptualizations in TA

In this section, we briefly mention other theories and research that have proven useful when building a case conceptualization during a TA. This list is not exhaustive, and most good case conceptualizations combine the contribution of different theories and knowledge.

Attachment

As described in Chapters 1 and 5, attachment is a biologically based system that promotes the survival of the individual and species by ensuring that parents, tribe members, and partners have an investment in protecting and caring for important others (Bowlby, 1958). Research on human attachment has shown that early experiences have a profound influence on personality development, sexual and social relationships, the ability to regulate emotions, and mental health. In TA, a case conceptualization based on attachment theory can help clients develop self-compassion as they come to understand how their symptoms and behaviors were effective ways to cope with intolerable fear, psychological pain, and loneliness. We often find that the identification of attachment defenses plays a central role in the case conceptualization (see Box 2 in Chapter 1).

For example, Samira, a 34-year-old female, began a TA asking why she dated men who lied, cheated, and were verbally abusive. Results of the Adult Attachment Projective Picture System (AAP; George & West, 2012) indicated that she had a preoccupied attachment status and relied on cognitive disconnection to protect herself from feeling lonely, worthless and empty. Behaviorally, this presented as accelerated speech, circumstantial thinking, and shallow affect. During the Early Memories Procedure (EMP; Bruhn, 1992a, b), Samira reported painful memories from her childhood in which she struggled to be seen and attended to by her parents, who had ongoing conflicts before they divorced. The case conceptualization for Samira emphasized how she had been affected by early experiences of loneliness and worthlessness in her family of origin. The assessor shared the results from the AAP and used the case conceptualization when answering Samira's AQ about partnerships. With the assessor's support, Samira was able to make the connection between her early experiences of feeling lonely, and her difficulty setting limits and leaving untrustworthy partners. Her subsequent psychotherapy helped her make sense of those reoccurring, frightening feelings and assisted her in building a more positive view of herself.

Epistemic Trust

Epistemic trust (ET), epistemic hypervigilance (EH), and epistemic hypovigilance are useful concepts when helping clients make sense of their current interpersonal difficulties in that they consider an individual's previous relationship experiences (Kamphuis & Finn, 2019). As described in Chapter 1, early adverse relational experiences, may contribute to adult clients having difficulties determining who to trust. Such clients may have EH and an inability to learn from social experiences, while other clients may be overly trusting (i.e., hypovigilant). Some clients vacillate between the two, as is the case with Catherine below. Importantly, when the client's capacity for ET is integrated into the case conceptualization, it helps both the client and assessor build compassion. Many clients with high EH behave in ways that are overly rigid, frustrating, or even off-putting to assessors. Our difficult countertransference can be mitigated, however, by recalling that these behaviors have helped the client stay psychologically safe. As described, ideally over the course of a TA the client's capacity for ET grows, and this contributes to their ability to learn from the assessment and their social world.

Catherine began a TA in response to distress caused by the psychiatric hospitalization of her 17-year-old son, Marc. Catherine felt guilty about having requested her son's hospitalization, as she did not feel she could manage his behaviors. Marc had become prone to angry outbursts and developed an interest in Satanism, which combined with social withdrawal, school refusal, and an insistence that he would only talk to "spirits." At the beginning of the TA, Catherine wondered if something in their family history could shed light on what led her son to have such problems. During several sessions, she recalled memories of being a lonely mother who was abandoned by Marc's father. It became clear to the assessor that Catherine was struggling to select trustworthy people for help, and she leaned on people who eventually let her down. Her sister abandoned her and an early therapist mistakenly diagnosed Marc with mild anxiety, and then years later he was diagnosed with a severe hyperactivity disorder. At the same time, her group therapist focused solely on "breathing" exercises and accused her of unconsciously provoking his symptoms. Catherine' Rorschach revealed conflicting signs of distrust and fear of manipulation with strong dependency needs. The assessor conceptualized Catherine's experiences with untrustworthy others as involving large swings between epistemic hypovigilance and hypervigilance. Catherine often felt obliged to accept help from others without first gauging their level of trustworthiness (hypovigilance). This was largely due to early traumatic experiences, which hindered the development of her "trust meter." When the people she had trusted eventually disappointed her, she became highly skeptical of others and felt more desperate. Additionally, her son did not receive the help he needed, and his problems continued to worsen. In the case conceptualization, the assessor highlighted Catherine's efforts in raising her child, not only on her own, but despite several untrustworthy relationships. When the assessor shared these thoughts during the Summary/Discussion Session, Catherine cried in relief and said she felt deeply understood.

Trauma

Overwhelming and life-threatening experiences accompanied by insufficient interpersonal support can have major deleterious effects on aspects of human functioning (van der Kolk, 2014). Trauma experienced early in life may affect the development of many behavioral and affective systems. Unresolved trauma specifically may be a significant factor in clients' problems in living, and yet many clients are unaware of this (Porges, 2001). During a TA, we often identify clients' trauma and sequelae symptoms through the testing, and then provide psychoeducation about how adverse life experiences can lead to automatic ways of thinking, feeling, and acting. This is an important intervention for some clients, as it reduces shame and builds hope, and it helps them both recognize the impact of their trauma and understand the benefits of trauma-informed treatment.

For example, Charlie was a 27-year-old client who initiated a TA with his parents, and as were all concerned about his reckless behaviors. At birth, Charlie's parents learned that he suffered from a congenital kidney malfunction. He underwent repeated surgeries during childhood, and his parents blamed each other for his illness. As an adult, Charlie tried to become an entrepreneur in several fields but consistently failed. His failures frustrated his parents, because he relied on their financial support for his poorly-developed business initiatives. In response to their anger, Charlie increased his use of drugs and alcohol, which increased the risk of potentially fatal complications from his kidney disease. Charlie's test results showed signs of medical and relational trauma. The case conceptualization highlighted the role of Charlie's traumatic experiences in his reckless behaviors, and helped him and his family make sense of his failures to launch.

Split-off Affect States and Shame

Emotions are an important source of information about our immediate environment. Attachment theory suggests that children learn to recognize and regulate their emotions through their relationship with their primary caregivers (Bowlby, 1958). Many clients were raised in situations in which the family dynamics led them to avoid certain emotions. For example, in some families, achievement, accomplishment, and seriousness are valued over leisure, fun, and silliness. Children raised in these types of home environments may have difficulties expressing joy and playfulness. Many of our clients' emotional and relational difficulties are related to split-off, or poorly integrated, affective states that resulted from family environments in which certain emotions were rejected by caregivers. These clients become unaware of these feelings or have difficulty identifying them because of these formative experiences. As a result, they are missing important information about organizing interpersonal schemas. For example, by not feeling fear, some individuals may put themselves in danger. Other individuals who are not in touch with their anger may have difficulty protecting themselves (see also Chapter 1 regarding split-off affect states).

Shame has a fundamental role in an individual's emotional and social development. Shame is a painful emotional experience that helps humans adapt to living in groups, by controlling (inhibiting) impulses and behaviors that the group or attachment figures find threatening (Dickerson et al., 2004). Shame may develop in response to the way the environment responds to the individual displaying primary emotions, such as fear and joy. If a child's attachment figures respond with withdrawal or rejection to one or more emotions expressed by the child, the child learns to associate the internal signals of these emotions with pain, and thus avoids situations that may elicit them (Fosha, 2001). As adults, these individuals may be conditioned to not feel these emotions through the emergence of shame. Shame tells us that experiencing certain affective states would lead to rejection/withdrawal from others. Certain affects have become dissociated or split-off, and shame is triggered whenever changes in the environment activate them (see Chapter 1 for more explanation on the role of shame in split-off affect states, and Chapter 5, Box 5 for more elaboration on shame). Psychological testing is very effective for identifying split-off affective states, which do not disappear, but continue to exert an influence on the person.

For example, Ethan was a 50-year-old restaurant manager who had been married to Sarah for ten years. Ethan sought out a TA to understand why he was having an affair, and he could not decide whether to stay with his wife or begin a new life with his mistress. The assessor's case conceptualization detailed an independent man whose life experiences taught him to avoid vulnerability and dependency on others. During their 10 years of marriage, Ethan and his wife faced multiple challenges, such as their daughter's severe medical needs, as well as Sarah's long-standing depression. Due to the nature of these stressors, Ethan's self-taught avoidance of vulnerability and dependency resulted in his use of distracting behaviors. As challenges mounted at home, he dedicated more time to work and built an exciting parallel romantic life as this felt safer than expressing his feelings and seeking solutions with his wife. During the Summary/Discussion Session, Ethan came to realize how difficult it was for him to be vulnerable and ask for what he needed. He subsequently ended the affair, and began individual and couples therapy.

These are just some theories that we consider when building a case conceptualization during a TA. We strongly encourage clinicians to educate themselves about different orientations, as this practice can be helpful in viewing clients through different lenses. The capacity to build a strong conceptualization is a skill that professionals need to continuously hone. Equally important is the capacity to build a relationship with the client and then effectively communicate the case conceptualization to them. That communication is a collaborative endeavor, in which we work with the client to build a new and developing narrative. As assessors, we choose images, metaphors, and words that are meaningful to the client and/or were co-constructed with the client during the TA. As described in Chapters 2 and 8, we consider the Levels of Information model when reviewing our data, recognizing that some information may be too discrepant for the client to integrate (Level 3 Information). Often it is the mix of collaboration, test results, and psychoeducation that helps clients build and accept a new narrative. In Chapters 8 and 9, we describe how to help clients assimilate Level 3 Information during an Assessment Intervention Session (AIS), and how to communicate our case conceptualization during the Summary/Discussion Session.

Potential Mistakes When Building a Case Conceptualization

There are a few mistakes assessors may encounter when they build a case conceptualization that effectively integrates assessment data into a new narrative about that client's struggles that answers AQs and is therapeutic.

Sometimes, case conceptualizations are not contextualized and adequately linked to the history or the interpersonal world of the client, and instead emphasize intrinsic characteristics of the client. These case conceptualizations fail to be therapeutic, as they likely communicate to the client that they are "responsible" for their presenting problems. In addition, such intrinsic features are often perceived by clients as permanent and non-changeable; viewing the client in this fashion may enhance shame and a negative self-view. The standard classifications for personality disorders are helpful tools for diagnosis and communication with other professionals, but a more compassionate conceptualization sees the client in terms of their development and adaptation to present and past situations.

Another difficulty in building case conceptualizations is related to how much assessors can integrate clients' characteristics such as gender, gender identity, sexual orientation, ethnicity, religion, immigrant status, economic background, and physical challenges, as well as the relationship between these variables and the client's life context. We strive to consider all these elements and invite clients to consider the role of their intersecting identities. As described, consideration of context is extremely important in a TA, and so we think about our client's communities and the systems in which they live. For example, a good case conceptualization considers how low-resource communities can exacerbate a client's difficulties, or how cultural differences in the perception of mental health services may appear in assessment results. We are careful not to over-pathologize, and endeavor to give due consideration to those diversity and environmental elements that are influencing the client. When these factors are well considered, we have a conceptualization that is "culturally tailored and ecologically relevant" (Clauss-Ehlers et al., 2019, p. 239). Case conceptualizations that fail to consider these issues risk being stereotypical, erroneous, or incomplete, and may send potentially damaging messages to the clients (see Chapter 1 for examples).

Working with the Referring Professional

When a referring professional (RP) is involved in a TA, the assessor develops a case conceptualization that is helpful for answering both the client's and the RP's questions. Assessors build a more complete and useful conceptualization through discussions with the RP, as it allows the RP's perspective on the client to inform the assessment. When the RP and assessor share a common language and have similar orientations, then the integration of each professional's ideas is often easy. When such shared elements are not present, the assessor collaborates with the RP to find common ground through which to conceptualize the client.

If the RP's questions are connected to a treatment impasse, the conceptualization may include consideration of how the RP's actions or reactions to the client contributed to those difficulties. It is not helpful for clients to have different professionals disagree over elements of treatment, and this is part of the reason we emphasize relationship building with the RP. Additionally, we may make erroneous assumptions about the RP, sometimes based on what clients tell us. Given these factors, we present information to the RP tentatively, and with respect and humility.

Clinical Case: Emma's Testing Results

Cognitive Tests

Wechsler Adult Intelligence Scale, Fourth Edition (WAIS-IV)

The results of the WAIS-IV (Wechsler, 2008; See Table 7.2) showed that Emma's overall ability fell in the average range of intelligence (FSIQ = 97). Her Crystalized Intelligence fell in the high average range and was both a personal strength and a normative strength. However, using the Keith five-factor model, a discrepancy emerged between her highest factor score, Crystalized Intelligence (Gc = 116), which was over a standard deviation above average, and her lowest factor score Visual Processing (Gv = 87), nearly a standard deviation below average. This discrepancy was nearly two standard deviations (29 standard score points). This suggested that the difference between Emma's verbal and visual intelligence was highly significant and probably affected her life a great deal. Having that large a difference must have been confusing to her and to others. She might have disappointed herself, teachers, and parents who expected her to be equally capable in all areas. It also could have created uncertainty and doubt about her true ability.

Woodcock-Johnson Test of Achievement, Third Edition (WJA-III)

Emma's cluster scores on the WJA-III (Woodcock et al., 2001) ranged from top scores of 115 on Story-Recall Delayed and 113 on Spelling to her lowest score of 88 on Broad Math. The high scores on verbally mediated achievement tests were commensurate with her Crystalized Intelligence, while her lowest score on Broad Math was

Table 7.2 Emma's Scores on the Wechsler Adult Intelligence Scale—Fourth Edition (WAIS-IV)

	Factor	Score
Keith 5 Factor Model	Gc (Crystalized Intelligence)	116 (personal and normative strength)
	Gsm (Short-term Memory)	100
	Gv (Visual Processing)	87 (personal weakness)
	Gf (Fluid Reasoning)	102
	Gs (Processing Speed)	94
	Factor	**Composite Score**
Wechsler Index Model	Verbal Comprehension	110
	Perceptual Reasoning	90
	Working Memory	92
	Processing Speed	94
	Full Scale IQ**	97
	Scale	Scaled Score
Verbal Comprehension Index	Similarities	10
	Vocabulary	13
	Information	13
	Comprehension	10
Perceptual Reasoning	Block Design	X6 (omitted)
	Matrix Reasoning	10
	Visual Puzzles	9
	Figure Weights	11
	Picture Completion	9
Working Memory	Digit Span	10
	Arithmetic	7
	Letter-Number Sequencing	10
Processing Speed	Symbol Search	7
	Coding	11
	Cancellation	7

Note
** The Full Scale IQ is not a meaningful measure of Emma's overall intellectual ability because of the large discrepancy among Index scores.

commensurate with her low average visual abilities. Other cluster scores were relatively close to her FSIQ score. This discrepancy on achievement testing aligns with those on ability testing, and may have reinforced Emma's high levels of self-doubt, as well as her efforts to hide what she saw as her deficiencies Table 7.3.

Behavior Measures

Conners Adult ADHD Rating Scale (CAARS)

Emma's self-ratings on the CAARS (Conners et al., 1999) showed below-average scores, indicating no problem areas related to ADHD. Her highest score was on Inattention/Memory Problems, but it was only slightly above average (T = 52). Other scales were below average, and some were very low: Hyperactivity/Restlessness (T = 41), Impulsivity/ Emotional Lability (T = 39), Problems with Self-Concept (T = 44). DSM-IV Inattentive Symptoms (T = 44), DSM-IV Hyperactive-Impulsive Symptoms (T = 33), DSM-IV ADHD Symptoms Total (T = 37), and ADHD Index (T = 43).

Table 7.3 Emma's Scores on the Woodcock Johnson Test of Achievement—Third Edition

Cluster	Standard Score
Oral Language	95
Broad Reading	99
Broad Math	88
Calculation	92
Math Reasoning	93
Academic Skills	104
Academic Fluency	102
Spelling	113
Story-Recall Delayed	115
Understanding Directions	92

These low scores suggested that it was improbable that Emma's attentional lapses were due to ADHD. The scores also surprised me in that in the initial session, Emma seemed convinced she had ADHD but did not report significant difficulties on the self-report measure.

Retrospective Observer Ratings

Behavior Assessment System for Children, Second Edition (BASC-2) and Conners-3

Because a pre-requisite for adult ADHD diagnosis is that a client exhibited ADHD symptomatology as a child, I asked Emma's sister Tessa to complete a broad-spectrum measure of problem areas for children (BASC-2; Reynolds et al., 2004), and the Conners-3 Parent Form (a measure focused on ADHD symptomatology; Conners, 2008), as she remembered Emma at 6-7 years of age (Tessa would have been 13–14 years old at the time). I knew Tessa had been a caretaker of Emma and believed she likely would offer valuable insight into Emma's functioning at that time.

The results of the BASC-2 Parent Rating showed good validity and numerous elevations suggesting maladjustment: Hyperactivity (T = 70), Anxiety (T = 88), Depression (T = 71), Somaticizing (T = 81), Internalizing Problems (T = 87), Withdrawal (T = 71), and Attention Problems (T = 66). Activities of Daily Living, Functional Communication, and Adaptive Skills also fell into the area of concern.

Results from Tessa's ratings on the Conners-3 showed a very high elevation on Inattention (T = 90), and lower but still significant elevations on Hyperactivity (T = 77) and Learning Problems (T = 69), while Defiance/Aggression (T = 50) and Family Problems (T = 56) fell in the average range. Conduct Disorder (T = 42) was below average.

Considered together, these scores suggested that Emma displayed some significant behavioral problems at an early age, including some characteristics of ADHD. This, in combination with the CAARS scores, raised two possibilities: (1) Emma had ADHD as a child, but had outgrown it; or (2) Emma's ADHD-like behaviors as a child were related to broader emotional problems (e.g., depression and anxiety) that had continued into adulthood and were no longer expressed as impulsivity and hyperactivity. I knew that depression in children could mimic ADHD, so I leaned towards the second possibility.

Self-report Measures

Minnesota Multiphasic Personality Inventory-2 (MMPI-2)

Emma worked hard to complete the MMPI-2, working attentively for nearly two hours. When I scored the protocol, I was surprised to see no elevations in Emma's profile. All the clinical scales fell in the normal range (Welsh code: 65/3917482:0# KL-/F:). The validity scales suggested Emma had been unusually consistent in her answers (VRIN, T = 38) but had made an effort to downplay problems (K, T = 65) and present herself at her best (L, T = 63). Her highest clinical elevation was on Scale 6 (Paranoia, PA, T = 56) and the highest Restructured Clinical Scale was Ideas of Persecution (RC6, T = 58). None of the content scales were even above average, with the highest, a T-Score of 45 on the Anxiety scale (ANX). Emma's profile showed one slight elevation (T = 64) on the supplementary scale Overcontrolled-Hostility (O-H). This did not surprise me, as it was consistent with my impression that Emma tried to avoid anger. Thus, Emma had presented herself on the MMPI-2 as having no significant emotional problems, and the high scores on both L and K suggested she tried to downplay her difficulties. All of this let me know that if I suggested to Emma that she had emotional or psychological problems, it would likely be Level 3 Information for her. In keeping with TA theory about "defended" test protocols (Finn, 2007), I also wondered if Emma feared being judged by me or her sister, and if I needed to do even more work on building alliance and establishing trust.

Performance-based Measures

Early Memories Procedure (EMP)

Puzzled by Emma's flat MMPI-2 profile, I wondered if she would be more forthcoming on an open-ended measure that was not focused on difficulties in functioning. I asked her to complete the EMP, hoping it might shed some light on challenges in her early life. However, consistent with her approach to the MMPI-2, Emma reported only good memories, including pride in her grandparents sitting in kindergarten with her, excitement about a new puppy, and pride when she rode her bike unassisted for the first time. Emma's approach to the EMP was consistent with her report that she tended to "focus on the positive," and also suggested that she was not ready to think about any parental or familial influences on her current problems. I had the impression from previous discussions and from the EI on Box 4 of the Wartegg Drawing Completion Test (WDCT; See below) that Emma tended to idealize her parents and her childhood, and her responses to the EMP gave added support to this hypothesis.

Looking back, I realize the EMP would have been an excellent opportunity for an EI. In reviewing Emma's stories, I might have observed, "most people write at least some negative memories, but I did not see any in your stories. They were all happy memories." Then I could have taken half-steps to gain better insight for both of us into themes that eventually emerged later in the TA. In retrospect, I think I did not attempt this type of exploration because I sensed Emma was not yet at the point where it would succeed.

Rorschach Performance Assessment System (R-PAS)

Emma's R-PAS (Meyer et al., 2011) offered the first glimpse beneath Emma's see-mingly normal presentation (see Table 7.4). Her Complexity score was well above average (SS = 120) and indicated that she was burdened by more stressors and de-mands than she could manage, which put her at risk of being overwhelmed and having difficulty coping. Also, Emma's R-PAS scores suggested significant difficulty thinking and managing herself in the world (TP-Comp, SS = 121, EII-3, SS = 121). The ele-vation on these indicators was based largely on difficulty in perceptual accuracy (FQ-%, SS = 131), especially in understanding others (M- = 129), despite seeing common responses others tend to see (P, SS = 99). In short, Emma's view of the world and of others could be highly inaccurate, and I wondered if she distorted certain situations in order to avoid negative emotions and memories, and/or to maintain her self-professed "positivity." One other notable score was her elevation on space reversal (SR, SS = 121), suggesting she was oppositional, strove for independence or was harboring anger that she might not be aware of.

Table 7.4 Emma's Scores on the Rorschach Performance Assessment System (R-PAS)

Domain	Variable	Standard Score
Administration Behaviors and Observations	Pr	89
	Pu	96
	CT (Card Turning)	87
Engagement and Cognitive Processing (Page 1[*])	Complexity	120[***]
	R (Responses)	109
	F% (Simplicity)	106
	Blend	87
	Sy	96
	MC	102
	MC – PPD	107
	M	110
	M/MC	111
	(CF+C)/SumC	96
Engagement and Cognitive Processing (Page 2[**])	W%	85
	Dd%	111
	SI (Space Integration)	80
	IntCont	118
	Vg%	92
	V	94
	FD	111
	R8910%	111
	WSumC	86
	C	95
	Mp/(Ma+Mp)	105
Perception and Thinking Problems (Page 1)	EII-3	121
	TP-Comp (Thought & Perception Com...)	121
	WSumCog	79
	SevCog	94
	FQ-%	131
	WD-%	118
	FQo%	92

(*Continued*)

Table 7.4 (Continued)

Domain	Variable	Standard Score
Perception and Thinking Problems (Page 2)	P	99
	FQu%	91
Stress and Distress (Page 1)	YTVC'	75
	m	92
	Y	87
	MOR	87
	SC-Comp (Suicide Concern Comp.)	90
Stress and Distress (Page 2)	PPD	94
	CBlend	95
	C'	94
	V	94
	CritCont% (Critical Contents)	72
Self and Other Representation (Page 1)	ODL%	94
	SR (Space Reversal)	121
	MAP/MAHP	–
	PHR/GPHR	119
	M-	129
	AGC	76
	H	118
	COP	108
	MAH	108
Self and Other Representation (Page 2)	SumH	116
	NPH/SumH	96
	V-Comp (Vigilance Composite)	108
	r (Reflections)	95
	p/(a+p)	100
	AGM	93
	T	109
	PER	108
	An	86

Notes
* Page 1 = R-PAS Summary Scores and Profiles – Page 1.
** Page 2 = R-PAS Summary Scores and Profiles – Page 2.
*** With a Complexity score greater than 115, complexity adjusted scores are recommended and reported here.

The findings also suggested that Emma tended to rely on her cognitive skills and even intellectualize rather than lean on emotional experience and spontaneity. In other words, Emma seemed to be a person who preferred to live in her head rather than to dwell in emotions (M/MC, SS = 111; IntCont = 118). In keeping with this hypothesis, other indicators suggested that Emma tended to constrict her emotions (WSumC, SS = 86), perhaps in part because she tended to get caught up in emotional situations (R8910%, SS = 111). One indicator suggested her coping mechanisms to manage the stress in her life appeared to be adequate, but not abundant (MC-PPD, SS = 94), and there was evidence that there were more negative psychological forces working on her than was true of most others (PPD, SS = 112). When I thought of Emma's AQ about why she had not succeeded in work or in personal relationships, I hypothesized that much of her psychological energy was being consumed keeping negative emotions at bay. And while Emma's scores indicated a healthy affinity for others (H, SS = 118; COP = 108; MAH = 108), and below-average aggressive impulses and preoccupations (AGC, SS = 76; AGM = 93), they also suggested she had had significant negative experiences with others (PHR/GPHR, SS = 119) and was hypervigilant (V-Comp, SS = 108; Dd% = 111). I wondered what past relational experiences had created such a lasting negative effect on her.

Wartegg Drawing Completion Test (WDCT), Crisi Wartegg System (CWS)

Emma's WDCT (Wartegg, 1953) drawings in themselves are revealing (see Figure 6.2), particularly in Boxes 3, 5, and 6. Wartegg Box 3 pulls for metaphors of available energy. As discussed in Chapter 6, people with full available energy typically draw something that extends to the upper right corner, like stairs. Emma did not, and instead drew a "parked car" to block any movement up and to the right. This response suggested that Emma's energy for achieving life goals was blocked. Box 5 elicits images related to how a person manages their aggressive energy. If an individual draws something that is directed to the upper right of the box, it indicates that they can effectively feel and act on their aggressiveness and anger. Emma drew a bicycle pump, with the direction of movement going down and to the left. This suggested that she did not express her anger outwardly, but rather turned it toward herself. Refer to the EI with Emma in Chapter 6 to better understand how we used her drawing in this box to help her see her tendency to not express anger appropriately. Box 6 pulls for metaphors of how a person relates to the world. If an individual draws a rectangle or box with the stimulus lines connected, it suggests they are connected to the realities of life. Emma drew two butterflies. This unusual drawing suggested that she did not perceive or relate effectively with the world and that she metaphorically imposed "pretty butterflies" on reality. This reminded me of her Rorschach scores that suggested Emma could distort reality in order to ward off painful affect states and maintain her positive view of others.

The CWS (Crisi & Palm, 2018) scoring (see Figure 7.1) was consistent with the Rorschach in suggesting that Emma had a strong tendency to repress her aggressive energy, ruminate, and direct frustration toward herself (OD in Box 5; Box 5 = D). Furthermore, the scores suggested that Emma's vital energy was blocked (Box 3 EC% = .5; Box 3 = D), and that this impaired her ability to plan and organize. In fact, on CWS scores related to functional intelligence, Emma scored low (Box 3 = D; IST = 7; M = 0), and there were signs she had limited ability to achieve life goals (Box 3 = D). All these indicators seemed related to the clear signs of depression in Emma's protocol (Global Assessment = PTL; EC+% = 38; Negative IIT-2), and in fact, there were signs on the CWS that depression inhibited Emma's ability to use her intelligence.

Furthermore, the CWS scores revealed that Emma struggled with emotion management (Ratio A/F = 2.5/3.5). The test predicted that in adaptive, structured life situations, Emma would likely be overcontrolled (Ratio A/F in Adaptive Area = 1.0/3.0), but that in emotionally arousing situations she might lose control (Ratio A/F in Affective Area = 4.0/4.0). The WDCT also suggested that Emma tried to manage her poorly integrated emotions by staying rigidly controlled and hypervigilant towards her environment (Box 8 = AC with PAT eye content). While the CWS indicated that Emma felt insecure and dependent on others, it also showed that she over-compensated for this by staying distant and by being overly independent (2 NC, one in

SCORING

* TEST OF SEQUENCE NOT PERFORMED *

Boxes	I	II	III	IV	V	VI	VII	VIII
Order of sequence	1	2	8	4	3	7	5	6

Test Completion Time **10** Minutes   # Completed boxes **8**

Box	E.C.	A.Q.	F.Q.	Content PR.	Content SE.	FR.	SPECIAL SCORES			Movement M/m	g	d	I.R.
1	0,0	0,5	1,0	OBJ			AS CB						
2	1,0	1,0	1,0	H		P	AS CB						
3	0,0	0,5	1,0	ARC	OBJ	P	AS CB						
4	0,0	0,5	1,0	OBJ		O	AP AS						
5	0,0	0,5	1,0	OBJ			AS CB	OD					
6	0,0	1,0	1,0	A		(O)	II						
7	1,0	1,0	1,0	BOT		(P)	AS CB						
8	1,0	0,0	1,0	PAT			AS						

ANALYSIS OF SEQUENCE 1

	I	II	III	IV	V	VI	VII	VIII
Order of Sequence	1	2	8	4	3	7	5	6
Evocative Character	0,0	1,0	1,0	0,0	0,0	1,0	0,0	0,0
Affective Quality	0,5	1,0	0,0	0,5	0,5	1,0	0,5	1,0
Code	NC	C	AC	NC	D	PC	D	AD
Form Quality	1,0	1,0	1,0	1,0	1,0	1,0	1,0	1,0
A/F Ratio	0,5 : 1,0	1,0 : 1,0	0,0 : 1,0	0,5 : 1,0	0,5 : 1,0	1,0 : 1,0	0,5 : 1,0	1,0 : 1,0
Impulse Responses								

ANALYSIS OF SEQUENCE 2

Adaptive area
(1 - 8)

1   2
NC   C

Adaptive area
(3 -6)

8   4
AC   NC

Affective area
(5 - 7)

5   6
D   AD

Affective area
(2 - 4)

3   7
D   PC

INDICES

EC+%	38	AQ+%	63	FQ+%	100	A/F	2,5/4,0	P%	31	P+%	100

0%	19	0+%	100	IIT- 1	1,500	IM.	0,63	A.I.	0,88	IIT- 2	2,0:6,0

IIT 1 ADJ **1,500**   IIT 2 ADJ **,4:7,6**

AC = 1	AD = 1
NC = 2	D = 2

W.I.P. : Quadrant **D**   Area **γ** Gamma

UNRESOLVED

M/m = 0/0

Figure 7.1 Emma's Wartegg Drawing Completion Test Profile.

Box 1 and one in Box 8). Some evidence for this may be in the way she depended on her sister in some ways (e.g., companionship, advice), but at the same time insisted on her autonomy (e.g., being frustrated with her sister for suggesting she might need public assistance). The same dynamic might be seen in her relationship with her boyfriend, and maybe even with me, by asking me to call her sister to arrange the payment for the TA and by slowing down the assessment process with long gaps between meetings.

Emma's performance in WDCT Box 6 demonstrated distorted and avoidant representations of reality (Inadequate Integration, AD, last in the Order of Sequence, and the only box with FQ = .5). Additionally, the test results suggested that Emma did not pick up on environmental cues as well as others do (EC+% = 38; EC+% in Adaptive Area = 25), and thus had some difficulty seeing a consensual reality. However, CWS results did not suggest a formal thought disorder (FQ+% = 94, P+% = 100, O+% = 88), again consistent with the Rorschach.

Finally, the CWS results indicated that Emma had difficulty with authority (Box 4 = NC with AP), and difficulties understanding others (EC+% in Adaptive Area = 25). However, there were also indications of good potential for relationships (H% = 13, AQ+% = 63).

Adult Attachment Projective (AAP)

Given Emma's question about relationships, I administered the AAP to gain a better understanding of her relational tendencies and perhaps glean some insight into their origins. To my surprise, Emma achieved an overall secure (i.e., flexibly integrated) attachment status on the AAP. (See Table 7.5). Perhaps her early years with her mother had nurtured elements of secure attachment, or her protective father and sister had given her a secure foothold. Another possibility was that Emma's general "positivity" created a response set that helped her tell AAP stories with synchrony, agency, and connectedness. A closer examination in consultation with two experts on the AAP (Melissa Lehman and Carol George) revealed a more nuanced interpretation. They noticed that Emma's stories to the first four scorable pictures showed her potential to integrate and buffer from attachment distress, which is the basis of secure attachment. However, Emma's stories to the last three pictures showed quite a different behavior. As the pictures increasingly stimulated her attachment system, as they are designed to do, it seemed that Emma had defended against overstimulation that threatened her internal sense of safety and had retreated into dismissive attachment strategies to protect herself from distress. So, it seemed that Emma's potential to integrate challenging attachment affective states only went so far before she reverted to defensive strategies to protect herself. It was as if a siege of affect broke through the first walls of protection (integration and buffering), causing Emma to retreat behind stronger walls (dismissing strategies) where there was no connection, but there was at least safety.

Emma's stories bore out this pattern and suggested a unique dynamic of variable attachment strategies depending on the level of attachment distress. Some support for this hypothesis came from how Emma related to the distress her boyfriend caused her by not working but living in Emma's house because his only other option was to live with his parents. Additionally, she did not report markedly high levels of distress in response to her mother's decline. Rather, her focus seemed to center around her responsibility as a good daughter who needed to take care of her mother.

Table 7.5 Coding Summary Sheet for Emma's Adult Attachment Projective Picture System (AAP)

| Subject ID | Emma | | | | | Classification *F – SECURE* | | | | | |
| | Dyadic | | | | | Alone | | | | | |
	PE	Synchrony	Ds	E	Seg		Agency	PE	Connected	Ds	E	Seg
Departure (3)	0	2–2 people		E		Window (2)	1 CTA–girl ask GM for cookie; sit down and have snack together →2 HOS–GM comfort	0	3–HOS/GM	Ds	E	
Bed (5)	0	2–Mother/boy	Ds	E		Bench (4)	2–young lady ISB →1 CTA–try to swim	0	3–ISB	Ds	E	
Ambulance (6)	0	1–GM/boy/person		E	R	Cemetery (7)	1 CTA–person take job out of state	0	*not coded Father*	Ds	E	R
						Corner (8)	1 CTA–boy rejection; hang out w/friends and play game	0	*not coded*	Ds	E	R SStr 1

Note: Coding abbreviations. PE: Personal Experience; Ds: Deactivation Marker; E: Cognitive Disconnection Marker; Seg: Segregated System; R: Resolved Segregated System; SStr: Segregated System Trauma Marker; GM: Grandmother; HOS: Haven of Safety; ISB: Internalized Secure Base.

Conceptualization

Emma's test results were characterized by multiple discrepancies: Verbal versus visual ability, reported versus actual functioning, secure versus dismissing attachment strategies, and finally, an overarching discrepancy between her current functioning and her test results. In general, these various discrepancies suggested Emma was a complex person, with many unintegrated aspects of self that might be confusing to herself and others.

The large discrepancy between Emma's verbal comprehension ability and perceptual reasoning skills was substantial. While this discrepancy was not considered a formal learning disorder under current nosology, it likely had a big effect on Emma's life. A discrepancy this large often creates confusion for the individual, as well as for their teachers and caretakers. Teachers and others expect a person with good verbal skills to be equally capable in other areas of cognitive function, and they sometimes erroneously conclude that the person is not trying, is lazy, or has some unknown character flaw. This feedback can be confusing to the person who is trying hard. Furthermore, while that person feels accomplished and confident in some areas, in other areas they are perplexed, frustrated, and defeated. Emma likely had this experience, which contributed to early confusion in an area (i.e., intelligence) that she perceived as vitally important to impress her successful father. Given Emma's comments throughout testing, she resolved this confusion and need to please her father by seeing herself as on the high end of intelligence, while harboring hidden uneasiness about her real abilities. This uneasiness made it likely that if put in work situations where she felt she was not living up to her own or others' expectations, Emma would become distressed or might find an excuse to leave.

At the time, in the state where the assessment was conducted, the discrepancy model was used to identify learning disabilities. The guidelines for diagnosing a learning disability specified that an FSIQ of 97 required an achievement score in at least one major area that falls at or below 78. Emma's lowest cluster achievement score on Broad Math (88), was significantly higher than the cutoff for a learning disability. Interestingly, Emma's achievement scores mirrored the difference between verbal and visual abilities, suggesting that her achievement in both areas was commensurate with her ability. Thus, Emma's scores did not support a diagnosable learning disability, even though the verbal/visual discrepancy itself likely had a significant impact on Emma's learning and experience in the world. As happened with the Block Design subtest of the WAIS-IV, if Emma felt she was failing at a non-verbal task, she could become extremely anxious and ashamed and begin to disintegrate. My successful intervention (of "holding onto confidence") suggested that with appropriate encouragement, Emma could overcome such distress and function better. But I was aware that type of support was not readily available in most achievement situations.

Beyond the cognitive issues, the discrepancy between self-report measures and performance-based measures showed a large gap between Emma's self-evaluation and the reality in which she lived. Basically, her self-concept was being a healthy person without significant emotional problems; she could maintain this position in structured, non-stress situations. However, the performance-based tests suggested Emma's functioning could break down when faced with challenging, emotionally arousing situations, and that her perceptions of the world could then become highly inaccurate. This mis-match between Emma's self-view and her emotional functioning created even more confusion for her, which only furthered her crippling self-doubt and fear about her true abilities and emotional stability. Her father's and her sister's strong protection likely deepened that self-doubt by inadvertently reinforcing Emma's belief that she was not capable. This interaction then could create an interpersonal dynamic in which others would unconsciously fill in for Emma (as I had by calling her sister at the beginning of the assessment). As a result, she was protected from feeling overwhelmed but was also kept in a developmentally immature place.

The test findings that suggested Emma's blocked energy and distortions of reality (i.e., perceptual inaccuracy, misunderstanding people, and difficulty seeing others accurately) were rooted in her efforts to make her world the safe place she needed it to be. However, by "imposing butterflies" on reality, Emma ignored difficult parts of her world and avoided the hidden confusion and pain she seemed to have carried since childhood. Emma openly acknowledged that she avoided negative emotions, which she couched as an achievement of her spiritual growth. However, Emma was not aware of the cost of this strategy nor its roots in her history. Taken together, the MMPI-2, WDCT, and Rorschach scores suggested that Emma split-off certain emotions that presumably were overwhelming or not tolerated in her family as a child. The split was most apparent in her experience of anger: First trying to ignore anger, but when that failed, becoming uncontrollably angry.

Because we had already made in-roads in understanding how Emma handled anger, this topic seemed like a good entry point to dig deeper beneath the surface to the still hidden parts of her experience and personality dynamics. There were also healthy parts of Emma, including potential for better functional success and good relationships. The question now became how to help her better understand the key findings and reach greater success in work and relationships.

I wondered if Emma had signaled her readiness for this next step in her AAP Cemetery story. She had described a man at his father's grave, struggling with whether to take an out-of-state job or to stay where he would be able to continue visiting his father's grave frequently. I saw this story as a possible metaphor for Emma's dilemma of change. Would she continue to be loyal to her family, idealize them, and stick with old patterns and roles (as the child who needed to be cared for)? Or would she bravely cut strings to the past and her role as her father's "girl," differentiate psychologically, and move to a different state of being where she was more independent and capable of handling emotions?

Emma demonstrated several strengths during the testing and our work together. She was interested in self-growth and wanted to feel more stable, as was clear from her AQs. She had a mixed, but largely positive view of interpersonal relationships, which was apparent in her ability to make and keep friends. And this fit with my experience that she could readily make use of my support during the assessment (e.g., during the Bock Design EI). Last, Emma showed a capacity for perseverance and challenging herself, demonstrated in seeking the TA. This was evident in her commitment to her job, which kept her active and engaged, although it had its problems and was frequently overwhelming.

As I sat with my growing understanding of Emma based on her test results and our interactions, I felt more confident that I could continue to challenge her in the next steps of the assessment, and that this would ultimately be to her benefit. I knew I would need to balance any challenges with clear emotional support, but I was confident of Emma's and my ability to work together to bring her closer to her goals.

Note

1 TA adopts and expands the concept of the externalization of the symptom, a technique originally developed by White (1995) in his family therapy work with children suffering with encopresis. In this example, externalization helps the child move from *being encopretic* to being a child coping with a problem. In so doing, children were able to see their identities as different from their symptoms (i.e., the symptoms were externalized), so that they could attempt more active and deliberate approaches to problem solving.

References

Bowlby, J. (1958). The nature of the child's tie to his mother. *The International Journal of Psychoanalysis, 39*, 350–373.

Bromberg, P. M. (2011). *The shadow of the tsunami and the growth of the relational mind.* Routledge/Taylor & Francis Group.

Bronfenbrenner, U. (1995). The bioecological model from a life course perspective: Reflections of a participant observer. In P. Moen, G. H. Elder, & K. Luscher (Eds.). *Examining lives in context: Perspectives on the ecology of human development* (pp. 599–618). American Psychological Association.

Bruhn, A. R. (1992a). The Early Memories Procedure: A projective test of autobiographical memory (Part I). *Journal of Personality Assessment, 58*, 1–15.

Bruhn, A. R. (1992b). The Early Memories Procedure: A projective test of autobiographical memory (Part II). *Journal of Personality Assessment, 58*, 326–346.

Buchheim, A., Erk, S., George, C., Kächele, H., Ruchsow, M., Spitzer, M., Kircher, T., & Walter, H. (2006). Measuring attachment representation in an FMRI environment: A pilot study. *Psychopathology, 39*, 144–152. doi: 10.1159/000091800

Bucheim, A., Erk, S., George, C., Kächele, H., Kircher, T., Martius, P., et al. (2008). Neural correlates of attachment dysregulation in borderline personality disorder using functional magnetic resonance imaging. *Psychiatry Research: Neuroimaging, 163*, 223–235.

Butcher, J. N., Graham, J. R., Ben-Porath, Y. S., Tellegen, A., Dahlstrom, W. G., & Kaemmer, B. (2001). *Minnesota Multiphasic Personality Inventory-2: Manual for administration, scoring, and interpretation, revised edition.* University of Minnesota Press.

Clauss-Ehlers, C. S., Chiriboga, D. A., Hunter, S. J., Roysircar, G., & Tummala-Narra, P. (2019). APA Multicultural Guidelines executive summary: Ecological approach to context, identity, and intersectionality. *American Psychologist, 74*(2), 232–244.

Conners, C. K. (2008). *Conners 3rd edition manual.* Multi-Health Systems.

Conners, C. K., Erhardt, D., & Sparrow, E. P. (1999). *Conners' adult ADHD rating scales (CAARS): Technical manual.* Multi-Health Systems Inc.

Crisi, A., & Palm, J. A. (2018). *The Crisi Wartegg System (CWS). Manual for administration, scoring, and interpretation.* Routledge.

Dickerson, S. S., Gruenewald, T. L., & Kemeny, M. E. (2004). When the Social Self Is Threatened: Shame, Physiology, and Health. *Journal of Personality, 72*, 1191–1216.

Exner, J. E. (2003). *Basic foundations and principles of interpretation. The Rorschach: A comprehensive system* (4th ed.). John Wiley & Sons Inc.

Finn, S. E. (1996). Assessment feedback integrating MMPI–2 and Rorschach findings. *Journal of Personality Assessment, 67*(3), 543–557.

Finn, S. E. (2007). *In our clients' shoes: Theory and techniques of Therapeutic Assessment.* Lawrence Erlbaum Associates.

Finn, S. E. (2012). Implications of recent research in neurobiology for psychological assessment. *Journal of Personality Assessment, 94*(5), 440–449.

Fischer, C. (1985/94). *Individualizing psychological assessment.* Brooks/Cole.

Fosha, D. (2001). The dyadic regulation of affect. *Journal of Clinical Psychology, 57*, 227–242.

George, C., & West, M. L. (2012). *The Adult Attachment Projective Picture System: Attachment theory and assessment in adults.* Guilford Press.

Ingram, R. E., & Luxton, D. D. (2005). Vulnerability-Stress Models. In B. L. Hankin & J. R. Z. Abela (Eds.), *Development of psychopathology: A vulnerability-stress perspective* (pp. 32–46). Sage Publications, Inc.

Kamphuis, J. H., & Finn, S. E. (2019). Therapeutic Assessment in personality disorders: Toward the restoration of epistemic trust. *Journal of Personality Assessment, 101*(6), 662–674.

Meyer, G. J. (1997). On the integration of personality assessment methods: The Rorschach and MMPI-2. *Journal of Personality Assessment, 68,* 297–330.

Meyer, G. J., Viglione, D. J., Mihura, J. L., Erard, R. E., & Erdberg, P. (2011). *Rorschach Performance Assessment System: Administration, coding, interpretation, and technical manual.* Rorschach Performance Assessment System.

Porges, S. (2001). The polyvagal theory: Phylogenetic substrates of a social nervous system. *International journal of psychophysiology. 42,* 123–146. doi: 10.1016/S0167-8760(01)00162-3

Reynolds, C. R., Kamphaus, R. W., Pearson (Firm), Psychological Corporation., & American Guidance Service. (2004). *BASC-2: Behavior assessment system for children.* NCS Pearson.

Schore, A. N. (1994). *Affect regulation and the origin of the self: The neurobiology of emotional development.* Erlbaum.

Schore, A. N. (2002). Dysregulation of the right brain: a fundamental mechanism of traumatic attachment and the psychopathogenesis of posttraumatic stress disorder. *Australian and New Zealand Journal of Psychiatry, 36,* 9–30.

Schore, A. N. (2003). *Affect regulation and the repair of the self.* W.W. Norton.

Schore, A. N. (2009). Relational Trauma and the Developing Right Brain. *Annals of the New York Academy of Sciences, 1159,* 189–203.

Sperry, L. & Sperry, J. (2012). *Case conceptualization: Mastering the competency with ease and confidence.* Routledge.

Stolorow, R. D., Atwood, G. E., & Brandchaft, B. (Eds.). (1994). *The intersubjective perspective.* Jason Aronson.

van der Kolk, B. A. (2014). *The body keeps the score: Brain, mind, and body in the healing of trauma.* Penguin.

Wartegg, E. (1953). *Schichtdiagnostik-Der Zeichentest* (WZT) [Differential diagnostics-The Drawing test.] Verlag für Psychologie.

Wechsler, D. (2008). *Wechsler Adult Intelligence Scale–Fourth edition (WAIS-IV).* Pearson.

White, M. (1995). *Re-authoring lives: Interviews and essays.* Dulwich Centre Publications.

Woodcock, R. W., McGrew, K. S., & Mather, N. (2001). *Woodcock-Johnson III.* Riverside Publishing.

8 Assessment Intervention Session

The Assessment Intervention Session: Definition and Rationale

The Assessment Intervention Session (AIS) occurs after the completion of testing and before the Summary/Discussion Session. To orient the reader to what is considered one of the more complex parts of a Therapeutic Assessment (TA), an analogy is first provided.

Imagine that you have decided to pursue competitive bicycling and set a goal of participating in a triathlon. You approach a bike coach seeking guidance about improving your biking skills. She instructs you to bike on a regular basis and take notes about what you observe as you adjust to different challenges such as changes in elevation and road surfaces. Imagine also that a kind of paper and pencil bike test existed, and the coach said, "This paper and pencil test is designed to help us understand you as a biker. Take the test and I will score the test and review the results with you so we can learn about your biking abilities."

Such tactics might help you improve your biking skills, but it would be far more beneficial to combine them with also taking a bike ride with your coach. She could observe your physical posture, cadence, and how you approach changes along the road. As the coach noticed areas where you could improve, she would offer suggestions. Self-observation of your biking skills could provide information that would not be collected in a joint ride with the coach. However, the direct observations of the coach may have a fundamental impact on the improvement of your biking skills, as your understanding of your biking would be improved by the coach noticing things you did not catch yourself, and you could make adjustments in the moment and see how they turned out. In turn, this process would allow you to develop muscle memory and a lived experience of the best strategies to improve your biking.

When we complete psychological testing, feedback is provided to build client insight and understanding, so that clients can use that information to better understand themselves and their difficulties. For example, for clients with Assessment Questions (AQs) about difficulties in intimate relationships, we might explain how their fears of abandonment are managed by using controlling behaviors with those they care for, and how addressing their anxiety and resulting behaviors could improve their relationships. Such feedback might contain information that is discrepant from the client's existing story about themselves, and yet that new information might be the most essential for them to understand to have a more accurate and useful story. When such feedback is highly discrepant from the client's existing story, it is difficult for

DOI: 10.4324/9780429202797-10

them to assimilate, and thus they might reject it, or at best, just partially grasp it, but not integrate it in a new way of thinking, feeling, and acting.

Unlike the bicycle coach, we cannot follow our clients around waiting for their difficulties to emerge so that we can draw their attention to what is occurring. However, during the AIS we attempt to bring those problem behaviors into the room, focusing on aspects the client is not aware of, so that insight is lived and not just cognitively grasped. By using our psychological tests and therapy techniques, we elicit clients' problematic behaviors and use our principles of collaboration, curiosity, and respect to explore the experience with our clients and facilitate learning. We hope clients leave the AIS understanding important parts of their difficulties through a lived experience, while we provided them support and guided them towards more adaptive responses.

We conduct the AIS after the testing is completed and we have developed an initial case conceptualization as described in Chapter 7. The AIS is a key step in the model, in that it prepares the clients for the Summary/Discussion Session, helping them become more open to hearing information that is new and potentially disturbing (i.e., lowers clients' epistemic hypervigilance [EH]; Kamphuis & Finn, 2019).

The AIS was the last of the steps developed in the TA model and understanding the model's evolution helps us appreciate the goals and approach to this session. When TA was being developed, there were occasions when despite clinicians' best efforts, clients were unable to assimilate new information during the Summary/Discussion Session (Finn, 2007). This experience prompted Finn (1996) to develop the "Levels of Information" model, which is an empirically supported strategy for organizing test findings. Finn's heuristic is based on self-verification theory (Swann, 1997, see Chapter 1), which posits that people are more willing to take in information that confirms their pre-existing self-views or schemas (even when this information is negative), and less willing to accept feedback that contradicts these views. In this model, Level 1 information is familiar to the client and congruent with their existing self-image. Level 2 information differs somewhat from their current self-image but does not produce undue anxiety and mobilize the client's defenses when properly presented. Level 3 Information significantly differs from the client's current self-view and if presented without proper preparation, will raise the client's anxiety and could result in a rejection of the findings or, worse, a disintegration experience. In many cases, clients are not ready to integrate Level 3 Information at the end of a TA, and it requires a strong therapeutic alliance and a good deal of time to prepare the client for those new learnings. Recognizing that Level 3 Information was often the most important for clients to understand, Finn began experimenting with ways of preparing clients to assimilate that information before the Summary/Discussion Session and developed the AIS. The experiential nature of the AIS also took into consideration that clients would be able to better integrate new ways of thinking and being through "bottom up" learning rather than a "top down" explanation (Finn, 2015).

In summary, the primary goal of the AIS is "to bring into the room those problems-in-living of the client that are the focus of the assessment, where they may be observed, explored, and addressed with various therapeutic interventions" (Finn, 2007, p. 14). The problem behavior targeted during the AIS is connected to the client's AQs, which serve as ostensive cues, priming the client to integrate new information. As the client's problem behavior has been evoked, we collaboratively discuss what is being observed and we have another opportunity for them to develop a more compassionate and realistic narrative about this part of themselves. We are particularly attuned to the client's emotional state during the AIS and assist them by being both a secure auxiliary attachment figure and helping them tap into their own resources. We also help some clients try out new adaptive solutions to manage the problem behavior. Trust in the self and others grows from such experiences. Last, we help clients identify how they can employ the adaptive behaviors we have practiced in session outside of the office. Provided our client's social world contains beneficent and benign (i.e., not malignant) individuals, employing these more adaptive behaviors allows them to further learn from their environment, which is an important component of change (Fonagy et al., 2015; Jurist, 2018).

What follows are sections designed to help clinicians prepare for and execute the AIS. We describe two fictional clients who will be used throughout this chapter and the chapter ends with the presentation of Emma's AIS. It is our experience that those new to TA will best develop their understanding and skill set for the AIS by grounding themselves in the basic theories and steps that are presented in this chapter, and reading the numerous examples found in the literature (see table in appendix).

Planning the AIS

Narrowing the Case Conceptualization and Choosing the Target Problem Behavior for the AIS

The most crucial step prior to implementing the AIS is to develop a case conceptualization of the client as described in Chapter 7. As stated, at this point all the standardized testing, Extended Inquiries (EIs), and interviewing are completed. Assessors review the data they have obtained, as well the client's life experiences, developmental level, countertransference experiences, and the conversations that occurred to date. To narrow the focus of our conceptualization for the AIS, we review the client's AQs, our current formulation of the answers to the AQs, and importantly, which part of the answers the clients seem close to understanding. Often, we are targeting Level 2–3 test results during the AIS. As discussed in previous chapters, from the onset of the TA, assessors build hypotheses about what emerging information is more or less discrepant from the client's self-narrative. As we identify the target behavior for the AIS, we consider the discrepancies between what the client says about themselves and their problems, and what emerges from the testing and the EIs. We also examine the discrepancies between the results of self-report and performance-based measures, or between observer ratings and clinician's direct observations, and the client's self-ratings. It is in the identification of these discrepancies that assessors can formulate a strong hypothesis about what results the client is already aware of, and which diverge from their narrative. In this way, our case conceptualization, the client's AQs, conversations with the client, and their test results help us identify what problem behavior to target in the AIS.

In this chapter, we will use the term *problem behavior* to refer to behaviors, affect states, clients' implicit schemas, or other psychological variables that become the target of the AIS and which we try to elicit *in vivo* in the session. What we target is always connected to one or more of the client's AQs and often builds on the conversations that have already occurred. For example, in Emma's case at the end of the chapter, some of the discussions regarding her tendencies to avoid conflict prior to the

AIS helped the assessor choose the problem behavior. Therefore, that problem behavior was "low hanging fruit," which would help Emma, if she integrated that new information into a more complete understanding of herself and her difficulties.

Tailoring the AIS to Client Type

Finn (2015) identified two client types that are helpful to consider when planning the AIS. While many clients have aspects of both types, identifying which client type they match best with is one consideration when identifying the problem behavior to target and how best to work with it in the session. Clinicians should not think too dichotomously about these types of clients, as some under-regulated clients may benefit from the strategies we describe for over-regulated clients and vice versa. To illustrate these ideas and those that follow, fictional clients of each type are described (Marco and Priya).

Under-regulated Clients

Under-regulated clients struggle with emotional dysregulation and inadequate coping mechanisms (Finn, 2015; Tarocchi et al., 2013). They are often anxious, tend to be talkative and active in sessions, and have questions related to their emotional world. For many such clients, the AIS can be a valuable moment where the assessor helps them understand how their emotional world gets dysregulated and also helps them identify coping skills that may be useful during moments of emotional overwhelm. Some of these clients have lost sight of their healthy abilities to cope, and we help them get back in touch with those skills. For others, they may have not had an opportunity to learn more adaptive ways of coping, and the focus is on teaching them a healthier response to distress.

Given many under-regulated clients have a history of trauma, it is important that the assessor understand how to work with emotional dysregulation and not create a situation that is overwhelming for the client. It is beyond the scope of this chapter to cover all the ways clinicians can help clients with heightened emotional states, and we have found that most professionals have techniques they favor. For example, behavioral techniques such as progressive muscle relaxation or deep breathing may be useful and familiar to most professionals. Those who work with clients experiencing trauma symptoms are likely to be familiar with grounding techniques, such as paying attention to elements of the environment or physical objects. Additionally, many of the skills that are part of Dialectical Behavior Therapy (DBT; Linehan, 2014) are helpful. Specifically, skills such as the STOP (stop, take a step back, observe, proceed mindfully) and self-soothing skills can help clients decrease and manage distress.

During the AIS with under-regulated clients, it is likely that we will need to help them manage emotions and teach them methods to do that as well. Those skills are practiced in session so that the client can experience them and then we identify ways for them to practice these skills outside of the office. There are fewer examples of these types of clients in the literature than the over-regulated clients. However, Finn & Kamphuis (2006) demonstrate the use of grounding techniques with a client who became anxious after creating stories for TAT cards. Additionally, in Tarocchi et al. (2013) a client with complex post-traumatic stress disorder successfully completed a

TA and developed a more compassionate understanding of herself and how to work towards her goals.

To illustrate how to work with an under-regulated client, we present the case of Marco. Thirty-year-old Marco was referred for a TA by his individual therapist. He identified as a cisgender, gay, Mexican, and grew up in a large metro area in the United States. His parents immigrated from Mexico before Marco was born, and he and his two siblings were raised by them in an intact marriage. Marco was a bright and socially connected child, who was well loved by peers and teachers. His father was an emotional man, prone to anger outbursts, which Marco recalled as scary and unpredictable. His mother was warm and nurturing but at times ineffectual in helping Marco make sense of his negative emotions. Marco came out to his family after his first year of college. His coming out created the conflict Marco expected, as his parents struggled to accept his sexual orientation, and he cycled between feeling resentful and inadequate. He began seeing a therapist at his college student counseling center because he was having difficulties with school work, and he had a recent breakup following a tumultuous relationship with an older man.

Marco's test results suggested anxiety, depression, and emotional overwhelm. A preoccupied attachment status was identified by the Adult Attachment Projective Picture System (AAP; George & West, 2012) and borderline traits were prominent throughout the other test profiles. While PTSD symptoms were not suggested, there were test results suggesting unresolved relational trauma, and anger was a primary split-off affect state. Throughout the TA, Marco was engaged, but also quite emotional and required support and containment from the assessor. Two of Marco's questions were: "Why do I have so many mood swings?" and "How can I create and sustain a healthy relationship with a partner?"

Marco was conceptualized as having deep feelings of insecurity and shame about himself. He struggled to regulate his emotions, in part because his fears of rejection and abandonment were frequent and strong, which left him constantly feeling anxious and distressed. Marco also had split-off anger and difficulties with conflict, which contributed to the problems he experienced with his previous boyfriend and were part of the answer to his AQ about how to create a healthy relationship with a partner.

Over-regulated Clients

In contrast to the under-regulated client, over-regulated clients may appear emotionally constricted or even stoic (Finn, 2015). Such clients may have a dismissive attachment status and they are often quite self-reliant, having learned that it was best to repress and deny softer, relational feelings (George & West, 2012). These clients often have split-off affects such as sadness, anger, and joy, and they have coping mechanisms that leave them having little access to their emotions or, conversely, they numb themselves in other ways (e.g., drug and alcohol use).

When working with over-regulated clients, we frequently chose a target that helps them see the costs of their coping style or gets them in touch with a split-off affect (Fosha, 2000; McCullough et al., 2003; Finn, 2015). For such individuals, underlying grief or anger about experiences with caregivers are common, and experiencing those feelings may be the target as they are usually not aware of the impact that these affect states have on their presenting problems. However, such clients may have also lost touch with their joyful and playful sides, and the AIS may target those affects too, as might occur if we engage a client in art therapy or play therapy technique.

Over-regulated clients often have dismissive defenses that are linked to problematic behaviors, and thus during the AIS we might help them see this link and understand how these defenses can be costly. For example, such clients often have an independent problem-solving (logic) approach and may find it difficult to receive support from others, because they have a hard time feeling vulnerable and have strong rejection fears. During the AIS, we might help them get in touch with their vulnerable side and understand the origin of their fears of being rejected. We may also see if they can become more aware of the costs of being so independent. If this is successful and they get curious about new ways of behaving, we scaffold them towards using others for a more relational problem-solving approach. These clients tend to be more emotionally "hardy" given their defenses, but like the under-regulated client, they too can become overwhelmed if asked to do things differently (Finn, 2015).

Priya was in her 40s when she self-referred for a TA, and is an example of an over-regulated client. She identified as a heterosexual, Asian-Indian. She was raised by her parents who were born in the United States but spent most of their life in New Delhi. Priya was an accomplished orthopedist, following in her parents' footsteps, as they both worked in the medical field. She had no siblings and described her childhood home as quiet and serious, with both parents working long hours. Priya had a small group of friends from school that she saw on occasion, but she lived a busy adult lifestyle, working many hours. When she was in her 20s, she felt pressure to be married and have children but that was no longer the case, although she often felt lonely and disconnected. Priya's one experience with therapy occurred during her residency, and she saw a counselor two times to help with stress. She referred herself for testing as she noticed difficulties with focus and inattention at work. Additionally, she wondered if she was being impacted by the decline in her parents' health and being passed up for a leadership role in her department. Her AQs centered around her ambivalence about relationships and her work strivings: "Are there things getting in the way of me having an intimate relationship?" and "How can I reach my work goals without so much stress?"

On self-report measures, Priya appeared to be functioning well, with few signs of anxiety, depression, or other mental health issues. Rather, those measures suggested she tended to value logic, rationality, and self-reliance. However, on the performance-based measures, there were more signs of anxiety, depression, unresolved grief, and anger. These affect states seemed to be related to her early experiences with her parents who neglected her emotional needs and left her alone to deal with them. A dismissive attachment status was indicated by the AAP. Priya possessed strong defense mechanisms that helped her keep distressing feelings out of conscious awareness, and she was intellectually curious about her test results and serious throughout each session. She would frequently dismiss the assessor's emotionally validating comments such as, "That sounds difficult," replying, "I don't let things bother me."

In Priya's case conceptualization, two elements stood out as potential targets for the AIS. First, the split-off affects of sadness or anger could be evoked, so that Priya could see how these emotions were disallowed. It was hypothesized that some of those affects were contributing to the stress she experienced, as anxiety might be an emotional signal that core, dissociated emotions are about to surface (McCullough et al., 2003). Furthermore, these split-off emotions could be part of her difficulty opening up in intimate relationships. Her tendency to focus on achievement and individual problem-solving strategies, instead of looking for support from others when she felt distressed, could also be targeted in an AIS, to help her understand how those defenses impeded her ability to create more intimate relationships.

Relationship Considerations

To assist in planning the AIS, we turn our attention to the relationship we have created with the client. We consider the quality of the relationship and the client's ability to use us as a source of support. At times, the connection is strong, and we have had emotionally difficult discussions and feel secure in bringing difficult affects and learnings into the room. One could see how with a client like Marco this might be the case, as often such clients become distressed during sessions and elicit support from others, including the assessor. At other times, developing trust in the assessor and using them as a support has not come easily for a client. With Priya this could occur, given her "stoic" tendencies and history of relationship disconnection. When the relationship is more tenuous, we may choose a problem behavior and approach that has less emotional intensity. At this point in the TA, there likely is only so much a clinician can do to further build the relationship, although we often look for what we refer to as mid-TA therapy session to further connect with the client (see Chapter 6).

Client's Current Life Circumstances and Contextual Elements

We also consider the client's current life circumstances and contextual elements in preparing for the AIS. Is the client in a particularly stressful life period? Does the client have friends? Such factors are important for two reasons. First, we want clients to take their new learnings out into the world and share or implement them with others. Second, given the AIS can be emotionally powerful, we want to consider what type of supports clients have and what else is going on in their lives, so as to not overwhelm them.

For example, during Marco's TA he shared that he was considering a new relationship with a man named Jake. Marco was very interested in Jake but recognized he might be slipping into a caretaker role with him, given that Jake had experienced multiple traumatic events during his childhood and was often in distress. Marco found himself acquiescing when he did not agree with Jake, and they smoked marijuana and got high together before a class, which was something Marco did not want to do. The assessor considered Marco's difficulties with conflict as a potential problem behavior to target during the AIS, but recognized that if Marco began to assert himself, that could challenge his relationship with Jake. This is not to say that the assessor would abandon the plan to target anger, but consideration was given to what might occur in Marco's social world if he started behaving in new ways. When assessors are aware of these potential consequences, they are prepared to discuss with clients the pros and cons of getting in touch with certain feelings, such as anger in Marco's case. Consideration of these advantages and disadvantages is fundamental to understanding a client's dilemma of change. In Marco's case, the dilemma might be between remaining passive and acquiescent in relationships, avoiding the risk of raising conflict and being abandoned, versus owning his anger and being assertive, which might not only lead to healthier relationships in the long term but also increase the risk of being rejected by a partner.

In considering Priya's circumstances, during discussions prior to the AIS she described how within the next three months she planned to relocate to another city. Throughout the assessment, it was clear that the upcoming move was stressful, despite her excitement about a fresh start. In planning the AIS, the assessor considered these parts of Priya's life, recognizing that if the targeted problem behavior was her underlying sadness about her experiences with her parents, and Priya began to grieve those experiences deeply, that might be too much given her current circumstances. Given this, the assessor chose to target something with less potential overwhelm for Priya. The assessor decided that the underlying grief captured in the testing would still be reviewed with Priya during the Summary/Discussion Session, and related suggestions would be provided, but the assessor would take into consideration the timing of any future interventions.

To facilitate choosing the goals and the strategy of the AIS, assessors can consider the aforementioned concepts to address the questions listed in Table 8.1, and select the best course of action.

Table 8.1 Key Questions for the Assessor to Consider when Planning the AIS

Question	Strategies to Consider
To what extent have the client and assessor already discussed important assessment results (Level 2–3 information)?	When the assessor and client have had more discussions about important assessment results during Extended Inquiries (EIs), then the AIS can focus on "building more adaptive behaviors." If there have been fewer conversations about the assessment results and there is still undiscussed Level 2–3 information, then the focus of the AIS will likely be about the client learning new things connected to the answers to their AQs.
Which type of client am I working with?	With under-regulated clients, we may focus more on decreasing emotional dysregulation and inadequate coping mechanisms. With over-regulated clients, we are more likely to work toward the integration and regulation of split-off affects.
How strong is the relationship with the client?	When the relationship is strong, the assessor can consider targets that may produce intense emotions.
To what extent are the client's life circumstances and social connections supportive and safe?	When a client's life is relatively stable and they have good supports, then the intensity of the AIS can be greater and there is less need for the assessor to provide extra support after the session. Conversely, instability in the client's life and fewer social supports may indicate that the assessor should plan a less intense AIS and to provide additional support as makes clinical sense.

Alternative Plans

At times we enter an AIS with more than one plan and approach for targeting the client's problem or we may have more than one problem behavior we are considering. Often the decision to do so is guided by the fact that the relationship is tenuous, or the client has been a more difficult client to engage and understand. Even with our best case conceptualization, we may plan an AIS that targets a problem behavior that is too difficult for the client. We may also realize that the client is not able to engage in a task the way we anticipated, and thus shifting to another task is best. When this occurs, we still learn valuable information about the client that will help guide the Summary/Discussion Session and our suggestions. For example, we may hypothesize that an over-regulated client will respond to storytelling stimuli eliciting sadness, by telling stories where such affect is minimally described and is managed with rationalizations or other dismissing strategies. However, during the AIS, we might discover that the client's stories contain sad characters but the dismissing defenses do not show up as expected. In such a situation, we stay curious and explore this unexpected outcome collaboratively with the client, as that new information will help us further develop our case conceptualization. In another circumstance, we may try and help an under-regulated client employ Dialectical Behavioral Therapy (DBT) skills to manage distress and discover that they are unable to do so effectively and are disparaging of the approach. We now know that if we are to recommend DBT for this client, it may be difficult for them to engage in that treatment and it may take some time for them to use DBT skills.

Common AIS strategies for Evoking the Problem Behavior

Clinicians are encouraged to think creatively when it comes to what will evoke the problem behavior. In the Appendix is a table that contains all published case studies that include examples of an AIS with an adult client. Reviewing these as well as Fischer's (1985/1994) chapter on Assessing Process (see also Box 8.1 on the Development of AIS) will help assessors both build an understanding of AIS strategies and identify techniques that may work with a given client. Those new to TA will also appreciate reviewing how the AIS is conducted in the child, adolescent, and couples TA models, and could review David & Bertucci (2015), Tharinger et al. (2008), and various chapters in Finn et al. (2012). We present three broad types of psychological tests that are commonly used to demonstrate how clinicians select and implement testing materials when conducting the AIS.

Box 8.1   Development of the AIS

Fischer's (1985/1994) *Individualizing Psychological Assessment* was influential in the development of the AIS, and her book includes a chapter titled Assessing Process. She highlighted how the term "process" is about taking steps forward, like advancing and progressing. She recognized that when clients are engaged in testing, we have access to how they approach challenges in life. Thus, "the process though which a person approaches, goes through, influences and is changed by situations, is most accessible when the person is directly observed coping with challenges then discusses what it was like" (p. 85). She emphasized the importance of approaching the exploration of test results and the client's experience of the test with openness, and cautioned us to not interpret too quickly, but remain curious and focus on what has been elicited. Fischer (1985/1994, p. 87) identified questions assessors can ask themselves in preparation for such conversations:

- How could this event have come into being?
- Where does this experiaction[1] bring the client?
- How and when does it work for him or her? When not?
- What is the short-term outcome? Long-term?
- Is the person winding up at places that were not intended? Where else is the person going? And coming way from? And avoiding?

In addition, she identified how clients can "develop options" and "alternatives" (Fischer, 1985/1994), which we describe as more adaptive behaviors and solutions. Here, her goal was to help clients see what is "personally viable" (p. 99) when it comes to changes in behavior, holding what fits given who they are and their goals. She highlighted the importance of practicing new behaviors in session using psychological tests and identifying what might help clients employ these behaviors in their lives. For example, she helped a 24-year-old client shift from light, barely visible marks, to quick and heavy ones on the Bender Visual Motor Gestalt Test, to help her gain a sense of agency and control. This was followed by a role play in which the client practiced being more assertive.

Finn's collaborative relationship with Fischer contributed to the development of the AIS, in which he refined Fischer's approach, by attempting to elicit expected moments of experience rather than having them occur naturally, as is the case in the Extended Inquiry (EI; Finn, 2015).

Storytelling and Performance-based Tests

As discussed in chapter 6, performance-based measures and storytelling tests are often beneficial for identifying implicit schemas clients have about themselves and others (Finn, 2012). During the AIS, such tests can elicit "reactions that are otherwise hidden from the client (and consequently from self-report data) but which fuel problematic behavior" (Martin & Frackowiak, 2017, p. 94). These attributes make these tests quite effective for evoking the problem behavior targeted in an AIS. To illustrate these ideas, we will use the Thematic Apperception Test (TAT; Murray, 1943). However, many TA assessors use cards from other storytelling tests as well (e.g., Roberts Apperception Test-2nd Edition; Roberts & Gruber, 2005). The various cards that comprise the TAT allow us to tap into different emotions and relationship patterns that are not evident (i.e., implicit schemas) to the client. For example, and as elaborated in the case study at the end, Card 4 depicts a man and a woman, and the man appears to be pulling away from the woman, while for Card 9GF a young woman looks from behind a tree at another woman running on a beach. For each of these cards, clients often create stories that contain conflict between the characters, and the absence of such a story may be indicative of conflict avoidance, as was the case with Emma. Other times, TAT cards are useful for tapping into difficult emotions such as sadness, with Card 3GF often used during the AIS. In this card, a woman stands in a doorway, her hand on her head, which is down. This card may pull for clients' experience with despair, sadness, and grief, and how they might manage such feelings.

When using storytelling tests, we typically begin by providing the standard instructions of having the client create a story with a beginning, middle, and end, and they should include what the characters are thinking and feeling. However, we often use more prompts and direction and may even ask specific questions such as, "Why is that character doing that?" with the hope of eliciting the target problem behavior. Recall that the goal of the AIS is not to necessarily obtain new test results that can be used for nomothetic comparisons. Rather, we use the test to evoke a specific problem behavior. Given that goal, we often deviate from standard test administration instructions. We also typically choose several cards that pull for the problem behavior and may administer all of them before returning to explore certain stories. By choosing multiple cards we increase the likelihood of bringing the problem behavior into the room with the type of contextual elements we are looking for. Additionally, by having several stories we often have multiple representations of the problem behavior, and thus the pattern that emerges can also be an area of exploration.

For illustration, imagine that Priya created the following story for TAT card 3GF:

Priya: This woman had a difficult day, and she is feeling a lot of stress and sadness. She is leaning against the door, barely able to support herself. She is really struggling and feels unsteady.

Assessor: What do you think was happening right before this?

Priya: Right before this she had a difficult conversation with someone and learned some hard news, which is why she is so distraught right now.

Assessor: What might happen next?

If Priya created this story, we would expect her to answer the assessor's question with an outcome that is dismissing of the woman's experience or to employ an independent problem-solving approach. These tendencies are the problem behavior we targeted, and we hope that Priya can see reasons why she has struggled with relationships. Priya finishes her story adding, "So it was a difficult day, but it wasn't a big deal, and she is confident she will use this experience to motivate her at work." We see in this part of the story that Priya neutralizes the emotional experience and distracts herself though work and a focus on accomplishment, which are common behaviors for those with a dismissing attachment status (George & West, 2012).

When the AIS goes as planned, the problem behavior we are targeting shows up in similar ways in the stories told by the client to the multiple storytelling cards administered. If this happened with Priya, the assessor could ask her if she noticed a pattern in her stories and then discuss it with her. Importantly, we scaffold the client towards a bottom-up learning experience when we discuss the stories. We start broadly (e.g., "Do you see any similarities between your stories?") and work toward the goal (e.g., "Do you see any similarities in the way the characters in your stories deal with difficult problems that make them feel distressed?"). Once Priya and the assessor observe and name the pattern in her stories (e.g., independent problem-solving, or Priya's language, such as "being a rock when facing problems"), the assessor would ask her if the pattern fits with her everyday life. The assessor may say, "So, your characters seem to address their problems like a rock, sturdy and independent. This woman even solved the problem of her distress by using it to motivate her for work. What do you think about this strategy?" and "Does this relate to you in any way?"

If Priya recognizes her way of dealing with difficult emotions, this would be an opportunity to discuss how this defense helped her reach important goals in her life, such as being a successful professional. The assessor would validate the utility and importance of Priya's defense. This type of positive support is particularly beneficial to clients like Priya who do not have close, supportive relationships.

The assessor might then ask Priya if she sees any costs to "facing problems like a rock." This would be a point to reference her related AQ about what might be getting in the way of an intimate relationship. If Priya agrees that her dismissive problem-solving approach could be responsible for her difficulty in relationships, and she expresses interest in other ways of handling distressing problems, the assessor could work with her to see what occurs if she tries other approaches. The assessor might have Priya finish the story with an alternative way for the woman to deal with her distress that involves others. For example, the assessor could say, "Let's keep in mind how being independent and sturdy like a rock might get in the way of having intimate relationships. If that was the case for this woman in the story (handing her the TAT card), I'm wondering if you can think of any other ways she might help herself feel differently?" We would be open to Priya's response and see what arises, but we may need to scaffold her further with a prompt such as, "Can you tell the story and have someone come in and see her in distress? What happens then?" A half-step further would be, "Can you tell the story so that the woman finds someone (non-specific person) to talk to about what's going on?" Given Priya's question about intimate relationships, we may also half-step her in that direction. "Can you tell the story so that the woman approaches her partner (a specific person) looking for support?" The goal would be to help Priya become more aware of her tendencies in such situations and help her consider other strategies besides being sturdy. We do not push our clients to explore and try out alternatives that might be distressing, until the client agrees that the experience could be helpful to reaching their goals as captured in their AQs.

As described previously, with under-regulated clients we aim to bring into the session enough affect to work with, and we are careful not to completely dysregulate the client. However, we need the client to get somewhat flooded by emotion, as happens in their life, so that we can focus on practicing and teaching useful coping skills. Once the emotion is evoked, we help the client identify what the character is feeling and then depending on the client's story, see if the client can see the relationship between the story and aspects of their personal experiences, as demonstrated with Priya.

When conducting an AIS with an under-regulated client like Marco, TAT card 3GF might elicit the same story as was initially told by Priya, about a woman who had a difficult day and is feeling a lot of stress and sadness because she learned some hard news. However, Marco's story might unfold in a different way, such as, "She goes into her room and throws herself on her bed and feels completely out of control until she falls asleep." We might discuss with Marco his stories with characters who are distressed and dysregulated, and see if he identifies how these experiences are related to his life. If he became emotional, we would empathize with how hard it is to deal with strong feelings of insecurity. We might then see if Marco understands the connection between the amount of shame and insecurity he is harboring and his AQ "Why do I have so many mood swings?" After supporting Marco with his emotions and connecting to his AQ, we see if he is curious about how to better approach moments of emotional overwhelm. We might say, "So Marco, let's get back to the story of this woman (handing him card 3GF). You identified how she feels quite distraught and out of control. Before she falls asleep, can you take the story from there and have the character do something that helps her feel more in control?" We listen for whether Marco can find an adaptive solution such as, "She calls a good friend who will come over, listen to her and then they'll watch a movie together." We would then inquire how the character is feeling, expecting a change for the better, and explore with Marco if this occurs in his world, and if not, why that might be and how it might start happening. If Marco is unable to identify an adaptive solution, we try to scaffold him towards identifying an adaptive one, first in the story and then taking it out into "his" real world.

Sometimes when we use storytelling cards during the AIS, clients create healthy stories that are the opposite of what we predicted, and when this occurs, we are capturing something important. Through a discussion of their story, we may discover that the TA has already had an impact on them, and they are now demonstrating that growth through a healthier narrative. Other times, we discover that certain contexts help the client produce a more adaptive story, and thus in their life, a more adaptive behavioral choice. Returning to our example of Marco and his response, "She calls a good friend who will come over, listen to her and then they'll watch a movie together." We may inquire about how this response mirrors his life and is beneficial. Marco may say, "It was easy for me to create a story where the client asked for help, because I have a friend like that, and the two characters were equal. It would be much different if the second character were older." However, he may also say, "I think having you here providing encouragement really helped me think of a more positive ending for this story. Normally I would never dream of calling a friend if I felt that way." Whatever context is identified is where we focus to see how that might be incorporated more routinely in the client's life.

At other times, we discover that with scaffolding, clients create healthy stories conveying a wish they hold or difficult emotions they have been unable to process. For example, in Turret (2015) an adult client is scaffolded to a TAT story that captured her deep longing to be fully accepted by another. This led to her crying and expressing the sadness she was holding, and the assessor provided her support and validation in a corrective experience.

When clients are unable to create a story with a positive outcome, it may be appropriate for the assessor to tell the client a story, which is like Gardner's Mutual Story Telling technique (Gardner, 1969). This is a useful intervention when the clinician hypothesizes the client is longing for a more adaptive story resolution and yet despite their best efforts, they are unable to do so.

Returning to Priya's story for TAT card 3GF, if she was unable to reply to our scaffolding question "Can you tell the story so that the woman finds someone to talk to about what's going on?" we may ask instead, "Can I take on the story from here?" We find that most clients welcome this opportunity, and we expect an affirmative reply. The assessor says, "So, this woman is really distraught, and she finds her partner and says to him, 'I'm having a really hard day and could use some help.' The partner says, 'Of course. Let me put away what I'm doing and let's talk about it. I love you and always want to support you when you are in pain.'" In this story, the assessor is hypothesizing that Priya is longing for unconditional love and acceptance from a partner, which at this point may be Level 2 Information. The assessor also hypothesized that she is really longing for the same thing from her parents, and by not having received such validation, has unresolved grief about those experiences. However, such information may be Level 3 Information and thus building Priya's insight about that may be too lofty a goal to achieve during the AIS. Telling a client a story typically creates a moment of vulnerability for both assessor and client and so when we implement this strategy, we consider both the relationship and what it might be like for the client to be witness to the assessor's vulnerability. However, often when the assessor's story "hands back" to the client exactly what they have been longing for, tears and gratitude follow, and the client recognizes what is contributing to their difficulties.

In addition to storytelling tests, other performance-based measures can be used in a similar fashion. Rorschach cards can be used to elicit emotions and Handler used black and white photocopies of the cards to help a client recognize what might occur if the emotion (color) is removed (Finn, 2017). The Picture Frustration Study (PFS; Rosenzweig, 1978) is often helpful in exploring clients' way of dealing with anger and assertiveness. Client drawings are also a possibility, and we often use the client's House, Tree, Person, or Kinetic Family Drawings to explore themselves and their relationships. Handler's fantasy animal drawing (Handler & Hilsenroth, 1994) can be a powerful tool for exploring the client's sense of self and similarly, the Draw a Person in the Rain Test (Lichtenberg, 2014) may allow the client's ways of managing stress to enter the room.

Cognitive Tests

Cognitive tests or subtests are also useful to evoke certain problem behaviors. A client's scores on such tests and their experience of the test are often helpful when the target problem behavior are issues such as low frustration tolerance, poor problem-solving, or the role of negative affect on performance. Additionally, such tests can help clients develop a more realistic view of themselves when negative self-evaluations arise in the face of responsibilities and achievements. When working with cognitive measures, the steps named remain the same, but part of our conceptualization should include information about the client's cognitive abilities based on the tests administered. We do not want to try an AIS with a cognitive measure without such information, because our hypotheses about the client's cognitive abilities may be inaccurate. We turn to our conceptualization and the client's AQs and identify our target problem behavior, and then consider various cognitive tests that may be able to elicit the problem in living. For example, for a client whose test results reveal that their performance was impacted by the interpersonal nature of the problem, the Drawing and Symbols subtests of the Test of Nonverbal Intelligence 4th Edition (TONI-4; Brown et al., 2010) could be used during the AIS. These subtests could help such a client see how their cognitive performance differs when responding to everyday life, real objects versus abstract drawings.

As a different example, a client may perceive themselves as unintelligent, but the assessor may come to realize that performance anxiety is a contributing factor to this self-view, and when not facing certain external pressures, they are able to think at a higher level. For such a client, administering timed subtests with comparable non-timed subtests to help them understand this difference could be beneficial during the AIS. As a third example, for a client who has an AQ about learning issues and possible accommodations, we can use subtests related to their difficulty (e.g., reading subtests for dyslexia) and work with the subtest and their test-taking approach until they are able to perform their best. Lastly, throughout Fischer's (1985/1994) book, there are many examples of the use of the Bender Gestalt Visual Motor Test, and she demonstrates how a client's approach to drawing often mirrors how they approach other life tasks.

At times, we follow the administration directions carefully so that we can score the test and help the clients learn something about themselves. For example, a client who tends to be self-disparaging may believe that their performance on a cognitive subtest was below average, and when presented with test scores suggesting the opposite, may come to realize how they are impacted by their negative self-talk. Other times we are less concerned about the client's scores and thus can alter the administration in some way. For example, Finn helped a client see how his anger contributed to aggressive behaviors with co-workers, by having him complete Block Design from the WAIS-IV (Fischer & Finn, 2014). For the first nine-block pattern the client was only given seven blocks, making for an impossible task that resulted in an anger outburst. With Finn's aid, the client was able to see how his verbal aggression manifested when frustrated and the impact it had on co-workers.

The other problem behavior that often can be successfully evoked with cognitive tests is the impact of a client's emotional state on their cognitive abilities. For these clients, we typically have test data showing that they are experiencing some type of emotional disturbance that is impacting their cognitive functioning, but overall, there are no signs of neurocognitive deficits. Such clients often have questions related to their inability to attend to work tasks or they may wonder if they have a learning disorder or ADHD. One such example of this type of AIS includes use of Digit Span while the assessor used scaling questions and emotion regulation techniques with the client (Finn, 2003). As the client was able to decrease feelings of agitation, his performance improved on Digit Span, helping him see the connection between being emotionally flooded and his difficulties concentrating.

One of the more detailed cases in the literature of using a cognitive test during an AIS is Sapozhnikova & Smith 2017 article, in which they used the Rey–Osterrieth Complex Figure Test (RCFT; Meyers & Meyers, 1995). A client with average scores on other cognitive measures performed poorly on the first administration of the RCFT. The test was re-administered during the AIS, and by receiving support and some simple guidance from the clinician, the client was able to tap into his own problem-solving abilities to approach the test in a better fashion, allowing him to produce a better copy of the figure. This helped the client shift his understanding of himself and his cognitive deficits from a fixed view that he was incapable of certain tasks, to one that was more compassionate with acceptance of his limitations, and he recognized that his cognitive issues could be further ameliorated.

Additional Strategies

Interventions from a wide variety of theoretical orientations and approaches could be used to evoke the problem behavior and a few other ideas are presented. At times we consider how a client's use of language is beneficial or a potential obstacle for meeting our target. For example, a highly intellectualized client with well-developed verbal abilities may employ defenses that thwart achieving the AIS target. With such a client, it may be best to use tactics from art therapies that do not use words. A client with an unrealistic self-perception may benefit from engaging in a collaborative task of creating a self-collage using only pictures that allows them to capture something meaningful about how they see themselves. Finger painting could help an over-regulated client connect with playfulness or may help an under-regulated client identify how creativity and physical stimulation are relaxing. Last, the use of a personalized Sentence Completion Test is a surprisingly effective way to explore a client's life (See Smith & George, 2012 for an example). Often, such a form includes common sentence stems and then some edited to target areas of the client's life that might be problematic. For example, if the client's anger is split off, there may be a few sentences stems connected to anger.

The possibilities of what can evoke the problem behavior are endless, and clinicians are encouraged to use their creativity to answer the question: What will bring this client's problem behavior into the room?

Conducting the AIS

Scheduling 90–120 minutes for the AIS is often best and we have divided the session into five main steps:

1. Checking in and orienting the client to the session.
2. Using test materials to evoke and observe the problem behavior in the session.
3. Understanding the problem behavior.
4. Building more adaptive behaviors.
5. Exporting new behaviors to life outside the session.

While dividing the AIS into steps helps explain the process, it is also artificial, as ultimately, the various steps may be occurring simultaneously or minimally not in the stepwise fashion described. Flexibility and creativity are important abilities to tap into during this session, as even with well-crafted AIS plans the conversation often progresses in unexpected ways.

Checking in and Orienting the Client to the Session

The AIS can be one of the more emotionally challenging steps in a TA and it is important that we check in with the client to make sure that they are not entering the session with a recent personal difficulty (e.g., a fight with a partner). Once we are clear that the client is in a place to proceed, we continue, but for those clients who are in distress, we may alter the plan and provide support rather than conducting the AIS. This is an opportunity for a mid-TA therapy session as described in Chapter 6, and we simply schedule the AIS for the following appointment. However, assessors are encouraged to not abandon their AIS plan too quickly, as often clients enter a session having a recent difficulty that aligns with the AIS target. In such situations, we provide support and go ahead with the AIS provided the client is not too overwhelmed. We may say, "Actually what you are describing was something I was hoping to figure out with you today. Let's talk through this a bit more and then if you are up for it, we might proceed with what I had planned because it could help with the situation you are describing."

After checking in with the client we orient them to the session by explaining that we are going to do an activity designed to help answer one or more of their AQs. Depending on the related AQ(s) and the targeted problem behavior, we may be specific and read the client their related question(s). At other times we may be more general making a statement such as, "You have a few questions related to your relationships, and today we are going to see if we can figure out some of those answers." Clients are unaware that they are in a session that is different from earlier sessions and follow the clinician's lead.

Using the Test Materials to Evoke and Observe the Problem Behavior in the Session

Sometimes, after checking in with the client we turn directly to the activity we planned for the AIS. Other times, we start with some task or related test material that is a warmup for the client (e.g., choosing a storytelling card that does not pull for the problem behavior). This helps clients get centered and reacclimated to the process of completing a task with the assessor as a guide. We then work towards the goal of evoking the problem behavior using our test materials which have been organized with increasing specificity. For example, with Marco, in an alternative AIS we may target his split-off anger we have noted in the test results, instead of the impact of shame and fears of abandonment on his mood. The assessor hypothesized that Marco's difficulties with anger and conflict have contributed to him being unable to create the types of relationships he would like, and are connected to his question: "How can I create and sustain a healthy relationship with a partner?"

Using storytelling cards, we may start with one or two cards that are neutral or minimally do not pull for anger. Once Marco is engaged, we work towards the goal of bringing how he manages anger into the room. For example, card 13 of the Roberts-2 has a young person holding a chair above their head, in what appears to be a situation where they're going to smash it on the ground in frustration. This card pulls for anger and often is used in this type of AIS. However, this card has fewer relational elements related to anger than card 9 of the Roberts-2, in which a younger child is on the ground and an older child has hands raised ready to fight. Both cards pull for the same emotion, anger, with the latter having greater specificity as related to the relationships present. Thus, we may begin with card 13 and then administer cards with greater specificity as related to the problem behavior.

It often makes sense to try the various steps chosen to evoke the problem behavior and then return to the client's test responses that make the most sense to explore further. So, for Marco, we have him create stories for a few cards and then explore them, as occurred with Emma in the example later in this chapter. Similar to what happens during an EI, we begin our exploration with an open question, such as: "What do you notice about your stories?" How quickly the client's problem behavior is recognized and named by the client is variable, often depending on the client's level of psychological mindedness. Some clients quickly recognize what is occurring and label it themselves. For example, Marco could create a story for the boy with the chair in which, "He carefully places the chair back down in its proper place and then ensures the other chairs are all arranged correctly." In response to our question, Marco may remark, "The boy with the chair is so much like me. Whenever I get angry, I just want to tidy everything up." In such situations, the client has observed the problem behavior with minimal guidance from the assessor, and we explore with the client what they make of that observation. The assessor may respond, "I noticed the same thing. Why do you think the boy handles things that way?" At this point, we are observing with the client the problem behavior and trying to help them understand it. By asking about the boy's behavior, rather than Marco's own behavior, the assessor creates an opportunity for Marco to discover things about himself that he is not yet fully aware of. For example, he might say, "The boy is frightened and feels out of control. So, tidying up is a way to help himself calm down." Next, the assessor may ask if Marco does something similar.

Other clients do not recognize their problem behavior and need our assistance. As described, scaffolding is a primary skill when conducting TAs, and during the AIS we scaffold our clients to new insights. We start in broad and general ways, trying to half-step the client towards the new realization. For example, if Marco were unable to notice anything related after our initial question, we could ask more specifically, "What do you make of how these characters are dealing with their anger?" Here Marco may recognize himself and make a comment as he did above, in which case we observe and work with the problem behavior, but he may also respond, "Nothing really." If that occurs, we help Marco think about each story, repeating them back and seeing what he notices. We may need to guide Marco further, and the assessor may say, "In this story the person got angry and rather than express that anger, he made sure everything was tidy and in its proper place. Is that similar to how you deal with anger?" If Marco still cannot see how the story is connected to him, and he still is engaged, curious, and not ashamed, we could try making an interpretation, recognizing that Marco needs more of a top-down experience to understand what is occurring. The assessor says, "I want to teach you a bit about this card and what your story suggests. This card pulls for how people manage anger, and people who tell stories like you told often tend to stuff their anger and make sure everything is as it should be, to ensure there isn't further conflict. Does any of that fit for you?" Provided our target is not too lofty (i.e., Level 3 Information), such a statement should allow for a meaningful conversation about anger, how the client manages anger, and what they learned about anger as a child. We now can work with the problem behavior and help the client build further understandings and then, if appropriate, try out more adaptive behaviors.

When working towards the target, clinicians may find it useful to ask clients to rate different internal states (e.g., "fuzziness," anxiety, confusion, distractibility, sexual feelings, emotional overwhelm). This is mainly done when clients have questions about how and why they have certain experiences, such as "Why do I sometimes suddenly get confused and not know where I am?" or "What causes my anxiety?" At the beginning of the AIS, we establish their baseline, asking, "Right now, on a scale from one to 10, with 10 very clear and focused and one being confused and fuzzy, how would you rate yourself?" As the AIS progresses, and we use different ways of eliciting the problem behavior, we check in with questions such as, "Where are you now on that scale of one to 10?" A similar tactic can be used with over-regulated clients, although we may have them rate the problem-solving approach implemented using scaling techniques. "So, this story is about a man who got really angry, and he decided to keep that anger to himself. On a scale from one to 10, with 10 being the best way to deal with anger, what number would you give to this story?"

Understanding the Problem Behavior

Once the problem behavior has been evoked and observed by the client and the assessor, the client may need emotional assistance from the assessor depending on what has been discovered. Attending to any difficult emotions is an important first step. At this point, we use questions and curiosity to understand what is occurring for the client, by asking for example, "Tell me what you're feeling right now and how you know that?" Or "What is it like to recognize this for yourself?" Such questions are helpful so we understand the client's emotions and can provide the necessary support, and for the clients to metaprocess the experience and build insight (see Chapter 5, Box 7 for more on metaprocessing).

We also explore the context that contributes to the evoked problem behavior. In Marco's example, it is likely that he can express his anger more directly in some relationships than others and exploring the differences between those situations can be beneficial in identifying a more contextualized understanding of the problem. Most importantly, we recognize that these problems in living often were adaptive solutions to a client's experience at a previous point in their life. In many cases, we help clients understand that how they managed to split-off certain affective states was adaptive to reduce shame and adapt to their life contexts. Returning to Marco, the clinician may say, "Given how your parents had such a difficult time hearing your anger and could respond in aggressive ways, it really makes a lot of sense to me why you would keep anger to yourself and work on keeping everything tidy in your house." Such statements help clients build a more compassionate, contextualized and realistic narrative. Importantly, we confirm that the co-labored narrative is accurate for them through questions such as, "Does what I describe sound correct to you?"

Eventually, we hope to guide the client towards recognizing that there are consequences to these behaviors that may impede their goals. Remembering our technique of scaffolding, we may say to Marco, "Do you think what we figured out about how you keep anger to yourself is related to your question about the difficulty creating and sustaining relationships?" At this point, it is likely that Marco and the assessor have already begun to recognize how conflict avoidance has contributed to relationship problems. Our hope for Marco would be that he would respond with a statement such as, "I'm really starting to see how I stuff my anger and how that contributed to some of my relationships ending. I need to figure out better ways to deal with anger."

For some clients, having such insights is all that occurs during the AIS, and we ensure that they feel supported about their new understandings. We also build hope for change, with statements in response to Marco's above, such as, "I agree and when we meet to discuss the test results, I'm going to have some ideas for you to consider when it comes to building your comfort with anger." At times due to time constraints or because the client is not able to go further in the discussion, it makes sense to label and identify the problem behavior and encourage the client to be aware of what was figured out as they interact with others over the coming days. We then attend to the steps for closing the session, as described later in the chapter. However, for other clients, we could keep working to identify more adaptive steps.

Using Test Materials to Identify and Practice More Adaptive Steps

Understanding the problem behavior and using test materials to identify and practice more adaptive steps during the AIS allows many clients to frame their difficulties into a dilemma of change, as described in Chapter 1. For example, it may be helpful if Marco were to express his anger more routinely with important others, and his parents specifically, but we may also collectively realize that if he does so, he runs the risk of losing important others or suffering from retaliation. Similarly, if he begins to express anger with his potential new partner, that may be too difficult for Jake, given his trauma history. Thus, with Marco, we identify his dilemma as one of repressing his anger which is damaging to him or expressing it which could end a relationship. In this situation, we reduce Marco's shame by labeling the dilemma and validating how it must be difficult to have this conflict between wanting to express his anger more directly and not wanting to potentially end his new relationship with Jake.

Once the problem behavior is observed and understood, we can work to identify more adaptive steps using testing materials in non-standardized ways. We first defer to the client with questions such as, "I'm wondering if you have any thoughts about what else could be helpful to you in such a situation?" If they can identify some ideas, we help them develop those strategies. However, some clients will not have ideas, and then we may say to them, "Would you like to try an experiment to see what we can figure out about what else might be helpful in such situations?"

When working towards more adaptive strategies it is best to do so using the test materials that evoked the problem. We may ask Marco to tell the ending of his story to the Roberts-2 card again, but have the character use a different strategy for dealing with their anger besides tidying up. We would allow Marco to first identify strategies but then may guide him towards different ideas. For example, "Can you tell the story again, but this time have the person share their anger with someone they trust?" If Marco created a healthy story that involves a character being assertive, we may ask, "What do you think of this outcome for the character?" We would explore his reaction and then may ask, "What do you think of these two stories and their outcomes? Which do you think would be best?" We would then guide Marco in considering how he might implement similar behaviors in his world, as described in the next section.

For a different example, if we helped a client identify how emotional overwhelm contributed to them approaching a cognitive test in a scattered fashion, we would identify some ways for them to regulate themselves. Next, we would practice those emotion regulation skills and have them repeat the cognitive test to see if there is a difference. We would inquire about their experience of doing it this new way with questions such as, "How did that feel in comparison to the first time you completed the task?" Importantly, we work with the client until they experience some success.

Exporting New Behaviors to Life Outside the Session

After clients have realized new and more adaptive behaviors, we explore how these can be implemented in their life (Finn, 2007). For some clients, behaving in new ways in the office with a trusted assessor will be easier than various contexts in their world.

Given this, we engage the client in "thought experiments" where we consider various situations that may be more or less difficult to implement these new behaviors. We then problem solve, to help the client see what might allow them to behave in these new ways. Specificity is helpful in increasing the likelihood of success for the client, and we identify when they might try these new behaviors and in what situation. We frame implementing these new behaviors as an experiment, informing the client that if they are unable to complete them, we still have something to learn.

We continue the example of helping Marco express his anger more openly and we explore how to increase assertiveness in his life. Starting broadly is best, and we consider various contexts where he could be more assertive with others, be it with peers, family, or his partner. Given his AQ about relationships, we likely would guide him towards the idea of being more direct in his partnership by asking, "Is there any way that you could use what we identified to improve the relationship you have with Jake?" Provided Marco is interested in this idea and it does not produce too much anxiety for him, we may identify a specific situation where he could be more assertive, but then have him imagine what that would be like to build his awareness of how difficult that might be. Marco may say, "Actually, I think next time Jake asks me if I want to get high, I'm going to just say no." After validating this idea, we may ask questions such as, "How might Jake respond to that and what will that be like for you?" or "How easy or hard do you think that will be?" If a client identifies a situation that sounds very difficult, we might consider with them if a different situation might be better, so that the client can experience success. Or, in the case of Marco and Jake, we may help Marco explore alternatives that are more viable for him ("What about proposing to Jake that you smoke after class?"). We let them know that we will check in next session to see what occurred. Importantly, we tell the client that if there is a moment where they think about trying the new behaviors but are unable to do so, that is understandable and still an opportunity to learn.

Working with a Client's Emotional Reaction

The AIS can be one of the more intense emotional experiences that is part of a TA, and clinicians need to use their skills for working with clients' emotional reactions. Our experiences with the client and our conceptualization typically provide us with a good understanding of which emotions and reactions described in the next sections may arise. Most professionals have preferred methods for helping clients manage difficult emotions, but we provide some specific guidance for working with dismissing defenses, dissociation, shame, grief, and disintegration anxiety. We separate them to make the material digestible but recognize that these experiences overlap. Client emotional flooding and dysregulation are also possible during the AIS, and the previous section on working with under-regulated clients provides some guidance related to these situations.

Dismissing Defenses

We expect dismissing defenses to arise for our clients who are over-regulated, and by the time the AIS occurs, we have noted their tendencies to intellectualize and avoid emotions and connection. As described for Priya, our problem behavior for such clients is often a split-off affect such as sadness or fear that if recognized and felt by the client could produce shame and discomfort. As we scaffold clients towards those emotions, we watch carefully for their tendencies to dismiss and when we point out the emotion that is present, they often say things such as, "That's not a big deal," or "I don't care about that kind of thing." At other times, exposure to such feelings can lead to them becoming controlling, contemptuous, and even hostile. If pushed too far, these clients may refuse to participate in overt or covert ways.

A few strategies that are influenced by the work of Diana Fosha (2000) and other emotionally focused therapists are often beneficial. Scaffolding and working slowly with the client are important, as we understand that experiencing these feelings can feel overwhelming. We slow down with these clients by helping them recognize what they are noticing in their bodies, to help connect them with their emotions (e.g., "Describe to me what you are feeling right now. Where in your body do you feel that?"). We continue to slow them down by asking them to be specific and detailed, and we watch for moments where they try to move away from feelings using defenses such as intellectualization, rationalization, or avoidance. When those defenses arise, we gently direct them back to their emotional state and help them sit with their emotions. For clients who are highly dismissive, this may be a very brief experience of being in touch with their emotions.

Some clients with dismissive defenses begin to recognize how disconnected they are from their emotions, which often is our target problem. If this occurs, shame may enter their experience and we work with their shame as described in the next section. If that shame manifests in aggressive or angry behaviors, we validate the client's emotions but also encourage them to stay engaged to see if together we can learn anything about what is occurring for them.

These types of experiences with over-regulated clients are common during the AIS and are often connected to the specific AQs we targeted. For example, a client may have a question such as, "What gets in the way of me creating greater intimacy with my partner?" For that client, we first defer to them, with a statement such as, "Do you think what we are both experiencing right now with you trying to move away from your feelings, might be connected to your question about building intimacy in relationships?" Bringing the client's AQ back into the room serves as an ostensive cue, which primes their curiosity and interest which will help them remain engaged.

Some clients may be able to recognize themselves in what has already occurred and make statements such as, "I can see that you were trying to get me in touch with some emotion and that just made me angry." For others, we may need to help them see what is occurring, by being transparent about what occurred and our reaction. "I was having you get in touch with what is a more vulnerable feeling, sadness, and that seemed to produce anger in you and made me feel uneasy. I wonder if this occurs for you in relationships when partners share what they feel or ask you to share?"

Dissociation

At times clients will dissociate during emotionally intense aspects of a TA and the AIS specifically. Considering our conceptualization, we often know whether a client is prone to dissociation. When working with clients with significant trauma symptoms we do not want to produce a dissociation experience for them, and thus we are careful about our choices during the AIS and may choose a problem behavior and intervention that are less emotionally intense. Many such clients fall into the under-regulated category, and thus our AIS is focused on helping them not become over-whelmed and find adaptive ways to manage their emotions.

However, there are clients who prior to the AIS did not produce test results that suggested tendencies towards dissociation, and we did not observe such moments during previous sessions. The intensity of the AIS may lead to a moment of heretofore not evident dissociation, and clients may space out, stare, and seem disconnected from the conversation and environment. In such moments, we first work with the client to identify what is occurring for them and then assist them using grounding techniques, including helping them connect with their surroundings and body (e.g., "Describe to me the feeling of the couch against your back," Or "Can you name five things you see, feel and hear."). Additionally, strategies that engage the body such as holding ice, washing the face, or jumping, may be useful strategies.

Once the client is grounded, we work to build our mutual understanding of what occurred, and how this may be connected to whatever they experienced in the moments before they dissociated, while eventually helping them identify adaptive solutions. For example, a client who experienced some dissociation after being shown a storytelling card that pulls for anger would be encouraged to pay attention to what they notice when they are in such situations in their environment. We would also provide some psychoeducation about dissociation, ensuring that we normalize this is an experience many people have, and we teach the client some ways to stay grounded if this occurs outside of the office. This may include emphasizing that strategies used in the office can be implemented at home or we may problem solve how they can stay grounded by connecting with others. This may require helping them figure out who best to connect with, and clients often appreciate language they can use to explain the dissociation experience and what they need in the moment.

Shame

As described in Chapters 1 and 5, identifying and undoing problematic shame is paramount throughout a TA, and during the AIS we are particularly attuned to the likelihood of shame arising. We have found that three defenses identified by Morrison (1989) and further elaborated as part of the Thurston Cradock Test of Shame (TCTS; Thurston & Cradock O'Leary, 2009), are beneficial when it comes to recognizing client shame. First, some clients may exhibit deflation, which is characterized by nonverbal behaviors suggesting they are trying to hide themselves with downcast eyes, lowered head, slouched posture, or looking away from the assessor. Client language may include words such as "embarrassed" and they may become self-derogatory. At other times, clients may use aggression or anger to manage their shame. They may become frustrated and direct that anger at the assessor or the test materials present (e.g., "This stupid test is making me so angry!"). Lastly, some clients become contemptuous if not haughty. They may make disparaging and dismissive comments with eye-rolling or comments bolstering their sense of self.

When shame arises during an AIS, we establish eye contact with the client to ensure they hear us, and we may need to ask the client to look at us directly. We work to decrease their shame by identifying how their experience is a universal human one and quite understandable given their upbringing and life experiences. We often find that it is helpful to use the "mind reading" technique and we ask clients, "What do you think

I'm thinking right now?" Clients often respond with some uncertainty but also may wonder if we see them the way they see themselves. For example, upon experiencing shame when feeling sad, a client may say, "You are probably thinking I'm a big wuss for getting so sad." We then provide a corrective experience with a comment such as, "Actually I was thinking you are being really brave by expressing what you are feeling and it's understandable that you have some sadness given your life experiences."

We use these interventions first and, if appropriate and helpful, we may use self-disclosure. We hold a goal of not moving attention from the client to ourselves, and thus our self-disclosure is brief. Most importantly, we only do this when we can truly empathize with the client's experience given our own life experiences and issues that are resolved for us. We find that such interventions can be highly validating for the client and help undo some of their shame. Returning to the previous example, we may say, "I know what it's like to feel shame about feeling sad and how hard it can be to work through those feelings."

Importantly, when working with client's shame we are careful to not produce shame about shame. Often when clients feel shame about certain feelings or parts of themselves, others, including clinicians, will make comments such as, "You don't need to feel badly about that." While well-intended, affirming statements such as this do not shift shame and often produce shame about having shame. We find that clients who have heard such statements often feel inadequate or unintelligent, and will make comments such as, "I knew I didn't have to feel badly about myself, but I did. When family members tell me I don't need to feel bad I would recognize that as true, but then just felt stupid." We see joining around those feelings and recognizing that they are understandable given their life experiences as more effective interventions (Finn, 2016).

Grief

It is also possible that clients experience a grief reaction related to their learnings during a TA and the AIS specifically. This is most common when a client recognizes how their life may have been different if they had learned about this part of themselves earlier in life. For example with Priya, upon realizing how she has repressed her emotions, she may remember times when this occurred and the impact on relationships. She may say, "I can see for the first time why the man I dated in my 20s said I was too cold. I guess I was ...." What often follows for clients is a grief response that is the loss of what their life could have been in comparison to what it was. Priya continues, "Maybe if I had realized all of this when I was younger, we would have had a better and longer relationship." In this sentence, we can hear not only her grief, but also the shame she experiences about not having done things differently, and we would help her see both the grief and shame and help her build self-compassion. To do that, we might first acknowledge that grieving lost opportunities happens for many clients when they have a better understanding of their life circumstances. Then, we would build self-compassion by helping her realize that given her parents were less attuned than would have been ideal, how she has behaved in relationships is quite understandable. If she were able to continue, we might also help Priya build her inner soothing and supporting voice, and eventually connect this to the suggestions for continued therapy work. Importantly when a grief and shame reaction occur, we accept the client's experience, stay emotionally attached, and help them see we are with them in that emotion moving at their pace.

Disintegration Anxiety

As described in Chapter 1, we recognize that clients strongly maintain their sense of self and broader narratives because if they were to be challenged, they would have a disintegration experience. Disintegration can occur if a client faces irrefutable evidence that some core belief about the self is wrong. This concept was part of Kohut's work, and he identified disintegration anxiety as "diffuse anxiety because of the danger of the dissolution of the self." (1977, p. 104). During such an experience, a client may experience "fragmentation of and the estrangement from his body and mind in space, the breakup of the sense of his continuity in time" (p. 105). During such an experience, a client may feel confused, overwhelmed, uncertain, and conflicted. The experience can be quite destabilizing, and Kohut believed it to be the "deepest anxiety" a human can experience, but one that is difficult to define, because to "describe disintegration anxiety is the attempt to describe the indescribable." (Kohut, 1984, p. 16).

A disintegration experience can be powerful and given the associated pain, it is understandable that we all defend against such anxieties. When we compassionately work with our clients and recognize when they are not ready to hear certain information, we show respect for the power of a disintegration experience. Throughout a TA we do everything possible to avoid having the client fall into such a painful experience. However, if despite our best efforts during the AIS a client was to have such an experience, we would remain supportive and use many of the tactics described previously to assist them with their overwhelm, shame, and feelings of disorientation. It can be beneficial to explain to clients what is occurring, as having language for a known experience is likely to ease their mind some and help them recognize such feelings will pass. We ensure that part of the conversation includes identifying how the client can attend to self-care after the session, and importantly, connect with trusted others to build their sense of security. Scheduling an additional session soon after is recommended, so that the assessor can continue to assist the client through the experience.

In our experience, if we stay rooted in our TA values, understand the client's narrative, look to our test data to deeply understand our clients, and work with half-steps, the likelihood of a disintegration experience for a client remains low. One example of disintegration anxiety with lessons learned can be found in Chapter 13 of *In our Client's Shoes* (Finn, 2007).

Closing the AIS

The AIS ends with metaprocessing the session with the client (see also Chapter 5). We ask questions such as, "What was it like to have this conversation today?" It is also beneficial to have clients identify what they have learned during this session, with statements such as, "Tell me two or three things you are taking away from this conversation." If the client and clinician have identified a more adaptive solution, it is likely that the client has been given homework to implement in the time between the AIS and the Summary/Discussion Session. Reviewing the homework plan helps the client prepare for trying it out. For some clients, this is the point grief arises as they start to think about "what if" they had learned what they experienced during the AIS early in their life. When that occurs, we sit with the client and their grief, and help them mourn giving up on their old narrative. The AIS can be an emotionally challenging session for the client, and we commend the client for their good work. We let them know how we were touched by what occurred and coordinate the next step, which includes scheduling the Summary/Discussion Session. As described later in the chapter, we often connect with the referring professional (RP) after this session to share what occurred, and we check with the client to make sure they are comfortable with that. We may say, "I'm going to connect with your therapist so we can coordinate the Summary/Discussion Session, but I also think it would be helpful if I share some about what we figured out today. Are you ok with that?"

Post-session Reflection and Tasks

Once the session is over, it helps to reflect on what occurred. To that end, we review what we hypothesized would happen and compare that to what transpired and consider whether it unfolded as anticipated. If not, we think about what this tells us about the client and revise our conceptualization, but we also consider our own performance and whether we made some of the mistakes described in the next section. Even when an AIS does not occur as planned, it remains a helpful step and the utility of the session can be measured by three variables (Finn, 2015). First, the client gained some insight, and minimally Level 2 Information is now Level 1. Second, our hypotheses and conceptualization of the client are further clarified. Third, our understanding of what the client can, and more importantly cannot, assimilate is enhanced. We use our reflections to inform our preparation of the Summary/Discussion Session.

Next, it helps to attend to a few logistical tasks. Given the conversation that occurred as part of the AIS often contains useful moments and language that could be illustrative for the Summary/Discussion Session and TA letter, it helps to review the notes taken and add any reflections and summaries. Additionally, as it makes sense, we reach out to the RP after the AIS to let them know about the session. This is useful so that they are aware of what occurred and can potentially continue the conversation in their next session with the client. If the therapist has already seen the client by the time we connect with them, we ask about what the client shared and if there is any feedback that may be useful in planning the next steps.

Common Mistakes During the AIS

There are a few mistakes that can occur when implementing the AIS and recognizing these possibilities helps us prepare properly so they hopefully do not occur. First, at times assessors mis-pace the session as they are not patient enough. Ideally, the client recognizes what is occurring and labels the experience, with the assessor scaffolding them towards that realization. We may clearly see the problem behavior in the room, and our desire to help the client learn may contribute to us moving too quickly. Pacing the session by moving slowly and scaffolding the client with half-steps is our goal and helps prevent this mistake.

When the client begins making connections between what has been evoked and their lives, it may be a mistake to leave the test too quickly, especially if we are dealing with anxious, preoccupied clients who tend to move the conversation in different directions when they become dysregulated. For example, for a storytelling card, Marco may say, "The ending of that story is exactly like me and what happened last weekend. I was completely overwhelmed after a hard conversation with my parents and I just crashed." Knowing that information allows us to connect their story to their lived experience, and it may be quite tempting for the assessor to follow up with a statement such as, "Tell me more about what happened." However, such conversations can turn into a discussion of the client's life, and we do not want to prematurely leave the test and the client's stories behind. Rather, we first work with the client, the test, and their responses, before taking it out into their world. So, ideally, the client first gets in touch with the emotions evoked in the stories and identifies them, and then we talk about how these show up in their life.

We also find that at times, despite our careful conceptualization and planning, we have failed to recognize something important about the client. This may mean that information we thought was Level 1 or 2 was actual Level 3, or what we believed was "low hanging fruit" for the client, was something the client was not ready to learn (Finn, 2015). Similarly, we may fail to recognize that the relationship is less secure than we thought. Ideally, EIs with the client have prepared them for this moment, but at times our judgment of the relationship is incorrect, and amidst the intensity of the AIS, the client does not feel secure enough with us to make the insights targeted. When either of these occurs, it is best to slow the session down and further build a connection with the client. The assessor may abandon the initial plan and focus on whatever makes the most sense clinically to keep the client engaged and to not produce shame.

Sometimes, we may fail to recognize the dilemma of change the client has with regards to giving up old ways of doing things and adopting new ones. To that end, this may occur when we have not fully considered the costs of changing and behaving differently. For example, with Marco we may have failed to realize what could transpire with his parents or Jake if he is more assertive. Once we better understand the client's dilemma, a useful strategy in this situation is to recognize the dilemma with the client, apologize for our incorrect assumption, and increase our empathic understanding and convey that to the client.

Last, we find that the assessor's feelings about the client and AIS can lead to mistakes. When clinicians first start learning TA and they witness the changes that can occur during an AIS, they naturally get excited and hopeful about implementing this step with their clients. Often, they want all their clients to have a growth-enhancing experience. However, not all clients will, and that hope for the client can lead to clinicians failing to recognize how big a shift they are trying to create for the client. Relatedly, we may fail to recognize how our own needs to feel successful and impactful with the client are contributing to a conceptualization and plan that is faulty (Finn, 2015). There are also clinicians who are too tentative during the AIS, and such professionals may be defended against their own sadism and aggression. Others may have unresolved issues with the emotion they are trying to evoke. By taking stock of our feelings and wishes for the client and grounding ourselves in the test data, we may be able to recognize when these types of errors occur. More broadly, our own sense of security around these issues can be enhanced through personal psychotherapy or consultation. These potential mistakes are why clinicians learning TA often benefit from consultation to build not only their understanding of this part of the model but also to reflect on their personal reactions that contributed to them being overly or not ambitious enough with their AIS plan.

When an AIS is Unnecessary or Contraindicated

The AIS often is one of the most powerful parts of a TA and we believe it is a crucial step that should be included for most clients. However, two situations may suggest it is not necessary or needs to be modified in certain ways. First, as described, the AIS was developed to best prepare clients to enter the Summary/Discussion Session open to new learnings connected to their AQs. For some clients, the process of testing and test exploration through multiple EIs are adequate to prepare them for the Summary/Discussion Session. This is most likely to be true for clients with low levels of psychopathology, and those who can flex epistemic trust and epistemic vigilance. Some of these clients may have already had an "AIS-like" experience during an EI and have already learned important parts of themselves. For these clients, an AIS may be unnecessary.

Second, some clinicians question whether using psychological tests in a nonstandardized fashion is unethical and potentially problematic for clients who may be tested again in the future. As described in Chapter 1, some clients who are routinely tested may not be good candidates for a TA. However, we would posit that the benefit to clients outweighs the ethical risk of disclosing sensitive test data. Nevertheless, within the broad population of individuals receiving mental health services, there is a group that is more likely to participate in psychological testing at routine points in their life. In the United States, some individuals with severe mental illness complete testing every few years to qualify for certain social services. If we believe that future testing is likely to occur for our client, then we simply choose different approaches to the AIS, or alternative stimuli materials not taken from standardized tests, so as not to invalidate their future testing.

Conclusions

The AIS is one of the more complex parts of the TA model and yet it potentially can contribute to one of the most impactful experiences for the client. We see the AIS as a "bridge to new ways of being" (Martin & Jacklin, 2012, p. 172), that will have long-term benefits. We also build a deeper level of empathy and understanding of the client through this process, which enhances our planning and implementation of the Summary/Discussion Session and written feedback. Through studying this chapter, the identified AIS case examples, and professional consultation, we believe clinicians can begin to try out this step of TA, recognizing that it is another opportunity "to collaborate with the client while conducting an experiment whose outcome will always be valuable, even if it is different than originally anticipated" (Finn, 2015, p. 10).

Clinical Case: Assessment Intervention Session with Emma

Narrowing the Case Conceptualization and Choosing the Target Problem Behavior for the AIS

It was now time to plan the AIS, a session in which Emma and I both could experientially learn something to deepen our understanding to answer her Assessment Questions. I had some tentative understandings as reflected in the case conceptualization in Chapter 7, but they seemed incomplete. The big mystery was what circumstances had created Emma's split-off anger, deep insecurity, and anxiety. I suspected family issues were important, but there had been no real openings to explore this topic.

When I took stock, I considered that Level 1 Information included, that emotions impede Emma's success (like they did in the cognitive EI) and that she was highly self-critical. Level 2 areas I thought we needed to explore further included: how much access she had to underlying emotions such as shame and what impeded her aggressive energy and the discrepancy between her verbal and visual-spatial abilities. I speculated that Level 3 Information might involve the roots of split-off emotions (most likely family issues) and acknowledging how those early experiences and resulting underlying negative feelings hampered her. In particular, I was sure Emma was unaware of how her "positivizing" strategy led her to misperceive situations, herself, and others.

Thus, when thinking about what might be most useful for Emma, I considered that it might be acknowledging her underlying negative feelings that kept her insisting on butterflies. Avoidance of negative feelings seemed to keep her stuck in her life. This strategy had been with her for many years and would be difficult to give up, as it had served her well and allowed her to function (up to a point) even though she harbored huge amounts of underlying distress. This theme also seemed to define Emma's core dilemma of change: whether to abandon her insistence on butterflies and face feelings she feared might be unbearable, in order to function better at work and in relationships, or to continue to see the world unrealistically, in order not to risk disintegration.

I thought carefully about how to scaffold Emma in a way she could tolerate and grow from. Could she see that imposing butterflies on her life covered over issues that hampered her in ways identified by her questions? It seemed anger played an important role in her being stuck. From our EI with the Wartegg Drawing Completion Test (WDCT; Wartegg, 1953; Crisi & Palm, 2018), I sensed that Emma's unintegrated anger might be the "low hanging fruit" that could lead to deeper understanding. She appeared to have a dawning understanding that the way she handled her anger was problematic, but for some unseen reasons she still held tightly to rigid, self-protective patterns. We had not yet reached the tipping point that would allow Emma to shift to a new understanding. It would take a lot of courage for her to adjust major life coping strategies, especially at her age, but I had a sense she could do it, if she and I could engage her intelligence, relational potential, and supportive environment.

When I thought about what questions I would be addressing by targeting anger and negative emotions, it occurred to me that four of her five questions, those related to fear and failure, were in the crosshairs. Thus, I selected Emma's unintegrated anger as the target for the AIS.

Check in with Emma

Initially, I checked in with Emma and asked if she had any further thoughts about our previous session with the AAP. She disclosed that she was curious to hear more about the "big picture" of what I had discovered about the answers to her Assessment Questions and that she was willing to do more work together towards that goal.

Using Test Materials to Evoke and Observe the Problem Behavior

The Thematic Apperception Test (TAT) is a useful tool to get emotions and inter-personal issues into the room through the client's stories. By selecting cards with themes that are emotionally relevant to clients' dilemmas, we activate their right brain and limbic system, which can expose underlying emotions that their left brain cannot fully access. Thus, I felt that the TAT was a good instrument to use in Emma's AIS. I looked for TAT cards that would elicit emotions, especially anger. I selected Cards 1, 2, 4, 3, 7, 10, 18GF, 9GF, 13MF, and 16. I introduced the TAT by telling Emma that I thought this test would help us better understand her questions about fear and failure. I started with the standardized instructions and administered the cards until I thought I had enough material to effectively intervene. Emma's story to 9GF offered dynamics I thought could have some impact and provide a starting place for productive discussion. Card 9GF depicts a woman partly hiding behind a tree, looking down on another woman who is angrily storming along, not seeing the woman above. Emma told a very unusual story:

Emma:	Ok. This looks like a woman who was an artist, and she is looking at artwork and trying to replicate the painting at the art gallery. The art instructor said be sure you look at the value and the lines so you can replicate your painting. And she is a new artist—she can't wait to learn more and more. And she will continue with more art classes and get better and better with each painting.

After this and several other unrealistically positive stories, I decided to interrupt the TAT and asked Emma what she noticed about her stories. She said she thought she had told some good stories. I asked if any of the stories seemed to relate to her in any way. Emma thought a minute and couldn't think of any personal connection and said she liked the ones that had positive stories. I pulled out card 9GF and handed it to her. I asked what she noticed about her story to the card. She began to ramble, so I took half-steps to lead her towards a productive discussion.

Hale:	Well, I am a little curious that your story does not have any conflict in it.
Emma:	Harsh conflict you mean?
Hale:	Yes, any anger. Most people see anger in this card.
Emma:	Um … yes that is kind of strange. I don't know.
Hale:	What do you make of that?
Emma:	Um, maybe I don't prefer anger. Maybe when I look at a picture, I do not want to look at anger if I see it. But I honestly did not see anger. I was not deliberately like, "Oh, I am avoiding this angry woman."
Hale:	I see, but we're not talking about anything you are doing consciously. I am thinking of the time you told me about seeing red and defending the old man in the grocery line.

Emma: Yes! Hmm. I can see that.

Hale: What do you make of this story in light of that experience you had?

Emma: Well, I guess it means anger is not something that I really like to focus on. I mean I can feel anger like when I saw red, and I can feel resentful myself, but in my practice with my meditation group I really work on compassion. So, when I look at things now I am not, "Oh, he did this to me, and she did this to her, and she is just out to get him." I am like, "What is that person going through that might make them act in this way?"

Hale: Yes, that's admirable. The world would be a better place if everyone did that. But do I have it right? When you *are* feeling anger, you keep it inside and process it inside, like you tried to do in the grocery store.

Emma: Right. I don't bottle it; I just process it a different way.

Hale: You don't express it unless it gets to be too much, like in the grocery store.

Emma: It isn't that I bottle it and hide it and keep it repressed. I just say to myself I am so enraged right now that I might fly off the handle. Like yesterday I was really upset. *[A coworker had tried to make Emma look bad by telling their boss that Emma had done something wrong.]* And I thought, "Why in the hell am I even at work?!" So, what I did was I just called my sister, and I told her what happened, and I called my friend Marianne, and I said, "You know I am feeling this, and I don't know what to do. I feel like I am walking on eggshells." Then Marianne asked, "Do you need a hug?" and I said, "Yes, I need a hug." Then I just went back to my co-worker and went over-the-top Minnie Mouse cheerful, and I pretended like it did not happen. *[Hale took note of the Minnie Mouse reference as a key descriptor offered by Emma to represent her avoidance]*

Hale: So, you were Minnie Mouse.

Emma: I was Minnie Mouse. Inside it was like, "Don't you dare, don't you dare try and be bubbly and friendly with me!!" In my head. I am a great professional, and I was just very matter-of-fact with her.

Hale: What were you feeling?

Emma: "It's none of your business, woman, get out of my room!"

Hale: But what were you feeling?

Emma: I was very emotional! But I did not, I never let it show.

Hale: So, you have a lot that goes on inside that is pretty deep and pretty emotional, but you never let it show.

Emma: It is pretty emotional, but I don't reveal it. I was very upset at her.

Hale: As you are talking about this, I can see you were angry.

Emma: I was angry, very angry! But I didn't fly off the handle at her and see red.

Hale: So, you didn't express any anger at her.

Emma: Well, I describe it like this. I am a Scorpio, so Scorpios have really, really, really, long tails, so I have what I call a long fuse, and it takes a very, very, very long time to eventually get so mad that I am just like, "I have had enough. Get out of here. What is your problem? I do not want to talk to you anymore."

Hale: Was there a recent time when your fuse reached the end?

Emma: Well, with my ex-boyfriend. I just got home from work, he asked what is for dinner. I was pissed and thought, "I have been home ten minutes. You have pretty much been home half the day, and you are asking *me* what is for

	dinner?" All I said to him was, "I don't really know what is for dinner, but I need to go and pick up some groceries. So, how about when I return you find something for us to eat. How does that sound?" But inside I was angry!
Hale:	Whoa, even then you didn't fly off the handle, and you were really, really angry. But you didn't fly off the handle.

Understanding the Problem Behavior

Emma:	No. I have worked really hard on not screaming or revealing that ugly, angry thing. Because my mom used to be a rageaholic when she drank, and it was very scary to me, and I never want to appear scary to people.
Hale:	Oh ...
Emma:	I don't like being scary. She was very scary. At the witching hour, as my sister and I called it, about like five o'clock because my mom would never drink until about five. My dad would not come home from work because he avoided her because she was a nut, and she drank and would fly into rages. So, he would find excuses to work, not to come home from work right away.
Hale:	Oh ...
Emma:	And my mom would be infuriated if he didn't come home from work on time for dinner. So, all of a sudden you would hear cabinet doors slamming open and shut. You would hear her stomping around and storming throughout the house and just banging doors and just you know screaming at us, and then me and Tessa would go downstairs. My sister is six years older than me and there was a TV set downstairs, and we would just wait for my mom to just pass out.
Hale:	Wow, there is a powerful experience! I mean the way you tell that I could tell that was extremely frightening!
Emma:	Oh, it was scary! To this day there is some music that I still remember that I do not like. It is the *Thieving Magpie*—do you remember Clockwork Orange?
Hale:	Uh huh.
Emma:	I never saw that movie because it is about sadists, a group of sadistic people, and I do not like that, but my mom bought the soundtrack, and she used to play it all the time, and she would turn it up really, really super loud and stomp around the house.
Hale:	So that music has ....
Emma:	Oh yeah, it has a trigger. And even dinner time now sometimes brings an uneven, anxious feeling to me once in a while. Once in a while around five o clock, I don't feel so great. It is an old PTSD thing. But it isn't like I feel it every day, or I am like, "Oh my God, it is five o clock. I am terrified." It is just that I remember, I remember.
Hale:	Do you think it was traumatizing? *[Hale highlighted the idea of trauma]*
Emma:	Very traumatizing, yes.
Hale:	Very traumatizing.
Emma:	Yes. And one time I made my mom really mad. I did not put my toys away the way I should have, and so she threw them all away.
Hale:	Wow!

Emma: And then the next day she barely remembered. I went to her and asked, "Can I get my toys out of the trash?" And she said ok. So, I got all of my toys out of the trash, and brought them back into the house.

Hale: Wow!

Emma: Yes, so anger is ... I understand why people get angry, but I don't really think it is the most conducive emotion. I don't know if that sounds weird, but I think it is a very destructive emotion. I think there are reasons why people get angry, but I don't think it is the most, um ... problem-resolving emotion because usually when people get angry, they regret what they say.

Hale: So, now I can understand why these stories you told don't have any anger. You were traumatized by your mother's anger when you were a little girl.

Emma: Right ...

I felt that we had struck gold, uncovered a very important experience in Emma's early life that lay at the root of some of her questions. The energy in the room was electric. I could feel the power of these memories, and I tried to convey my understanding that they were indeed traumatizing to let Emma feel that I got it. I also wanted to connect her trauma and avoidance of anger to her current life and also explore the costs of her way of dealing with it.

Hale: I think we have discovered that your mother's rage had a big effect on you.

Emma: Maybe more than I thought.

Hale: Can you say more about how you are understanding that now?

Emma: Well, I can see it might affect the way I do anger.

Hale: That makes me wonder. You know it is good to control your anger.

Emma: Right.

Hale: But I wonder if there's not a cost too.

Emma: Well, sometimes if I really do feel angry, I just vent to a friend or like I write it ... anger feels like craziness.

Hale: And I agree it can be. And you certainly saw that with your mother.

Emma: It can be very crazy and that makes me nervous.

Hale: It can be crazy, but it also can be important. Now I wonder because of your experience early on, if you have been without good anger. You know what I mean? You look at a picture like this *(Hale refers back to the TAT card)* and your story is optimistic.

Emma: Yes, and it is so distant. *[Hale was thrilled that Emma herself could see a potential cost to splitting off her anger!]*

Hale: Yes, it is—just a painting. And I just wonder what effect that has had on your life.

Emma: Yes, maybe. Yes, I may have some pent-up anger that I need to figure out how to get the good anger out. Because frankly I was really mad at the parent who brought Santa Claus in and stirred up all of our kids at nap time last week. *(Emma was referring to an incident at school in which an over-involved parent had surprised the students with a visit by Santa Claus.)* I thought it was the most disrespectful thing. And I was furious, but

I could not say, "You rotten woman. How dare you?" in front of her kid and all of my kids. I had to say, "Ok guys, just wave to Santa today."

Hale: Maybe there is some middle ground. You wouldn't want to say, "You rotten thing" necessarily, but you wouldn't just want to say, "Oh, just wave to Santa" and be Minnie Mouse. *[Hale used a shared metaphor to get Emma fully on board.]* Maybe there is some middle ground in there.

Emma: Yes, but we tread pretty gently at work.

Hale: Good point. I understand at work you have to tread very gently, but maybe you could talk to that mother afterwards and say, "You know, that was problematic."

Emma: Yes. I addressed it with my director.

Hale: Not with her?

Emma: No

Hale: Well, I think this is an important area. Psychologists believe it is important developmentally for kids to develop a capacity to be appropriately adversarial.

Emma: Mhmm. Adversarial. I like that word. Conflict resolution?

Hale: Conflict might resolve it or not, but to able to engage in appropriate anger. And "appropriate" is the keyword. So, at your work at school, it is not appropriate to be angry at kids, right?

Emma: Right.

Hale: This could be something to think about: places in your life where you could be more adversarial in an appropriate way that might open up some space for you that has been closed off because of the trauma of your mother's raging.

Emma: Yes, there is a part of me that fears I could become a rageful person.

Hale: Of course! That is completely normal given your early experience. So, there is a lot of fear there.

Emma: I am aware of being addicted to emotions because people can be addicted to rage. People can be addicted to anger, and I am like, "I prefer not to be that way."

Hale: Having experienced what you have at such an early age, I can well understand that. It is not something you want to be addicted to.

Emma: No.

Hale: But maybe there is some middle ground?

Emma: That is pretty insightful. It never even occurred to me that I may be avoiding. It is weird, huh. *[At this point in the session, Hale rejoiced inside.]*

Hale: Well, the way you described it, it sounds like you have had a reason to avoid it. You have some trauma around it from when you were a little girl.

Emma: Yes.

Hale: I wonder if seeing anger as craziness had an impact also on your struggles with maintaining a long-term work position and a long-term relationship, like you asked about in your Assessment Questions?

Emma and I then discussed how avoiding anger might have played a role in her struggles with unruly classes or unhappy bosses, because she did not know how to set limits or assert herself in those situations and mostly felt helpless and insecure.

Building More Adaptive Behaviors

After this, I judged that Emma and I were ready to work on a different, more adaptive response to anger. I wanted to help her think about and try out a different story to Card 9GFG that incorporated at least a little confrontation. I hoped she would experience different feelings in the safety of my office.

Hale: This may sound a little strange ...

Emma: It's ok.

Hale: I would like you to tell me another story about this picture that is really angry and raging and just over the top. Ok? Can you do that? *[Hale hoped to get the feeling in the room]*

Emma: Sure. Ok. Um so this woman is a little younger than this woman, and she has been having an affair with her boyfriend. And she figured it out, and now she is spying on her. And she is just fuming. She is like, "What is it that my boyfriend sees in her that he doesn't see in me? How dare she think she can just go off and be this beautiful thing, and why does she think that she can just take my boyfriend away from me. I mean who in the hell does she think she is!"

Hale: What do you notice about that story?

Emma: Um, it is a common theme like in movies and stuff like that.

Hale: How about that the anger is still all inside her?

Emma: Oh, yes. She is not raging at her. She is like thinking, "How dare you? How could you do this to me? Why does my boyfriend want you over me? Why did my boyfriend cheat on me?"

Hale: Right. It's all just inside rumination, internal fuming. See if you can make it expressed.

Emma: Ok .... Um, "You better run as fast as you can because I am going to find out exactly what you have been up to, and all I know is that you have been hanging around my boyfriend, and I don't want you anywhere near him. Get the hell out of here! Right now!" *(with lots of emotion)*

Hale: What do you feel?

Emma: Just that she is expressing it to her, and now she is hearing it, and now she is running as fast as she can. She is like, "I get it, ok, sorry. Caught me red handed. I just left his house." She is taking off. *[Notice that Emma avoids Hale's question.]*

Hale: How do you feel?

Emma: Um, well that she can, she can express her feelings. She can say ... *[Emma avoids the question again, so Hale interrupts.]*

Hale: How does that make you feel right now?

Emma: Good. I mean ... *[Notice Emma's focus on the positive. Again, Hale interrupts.]*

Hale: Does it?

Emma: Yeah, I am not afraid of it or anything. *[Hale decides to probe again.]*

Hale: Does it feel awkward?

Emma: No, no, not really awkward, more like a release, like I have been thinking this for a long time, and I have been watching her, and I know that she is up to something, and I chewed her out, and now I am going to go back and talk to my boyfriend and tell him, "I am through with you. It is her or me. There is no other choice, so make a decision, and let me move on with my life." So, um relief. I mean it is just relief.

Hale: Relief.

Emma: Yeah, relief.

Exporting New Behaviors to Life Outside the Session

In order to keep her movement going, it was important to find some small step she could take during the week ahead to get some experience with it. I hoped she would be able to try expressing anger.

Hale: Maybe figuring out how to get appropriate anger back on track could be beneficial for you and would help answer your questions.

Emma: Sure.

Hale: For example, I was wondering how your relationships would look if you could express appropriate anger.

Emma: There is one person I got very angry at and that was my ex-fiancé. He made me angry because he made me scared. So, one time he was like sticking his finger in my face and talking to me like this, and I grabbed his finger and I said, "If you ever stick your finger in my face again, I will break your finger in half. Don't do that!"

Hale: Ah, now *that* was expressing anger! *[Hale thought this was hardly an example of the "middle ground," but he decided to mirror Emma's anger.]*

Emma: That was true appropriate anger, and I was like, "I mean it, I will."

Hale: How did that feel?

Emma: It was very empowering.

Hale: Was it?

Emma: Yes, it was very empowering.

Hale: I like that word—"empowering" *(writing it down)*

Emma: Yes, I need to be empowered.

Hale: That may be key here.

Emma: To get empowered.

Hale: Without becoming a rageaholic.

Emma: Right. There are some people I would like to tell, "I don't like the way you acted," or "I think that you are conniving." *[Hale saw these as examples of appropriate middle-ground expressions of anger and so felt Emma was truly integrating the concepts they were discussing. Hale decided to attempt the last step of the AIS—trying out the new solution in day-to-day life.]*

Hale: So, is there some small way you can do that this coming week? That you could just display a little of your power to people? Not internally, but face-to-face. I know your work would not be the place to do that.

Emma: Not at work. I don't feel safe there.

Hale: This would be just something that would be a small step where you could just put your toe in the water a little bit.

Emma: My ex-boyfriend has been trying to get me to get back with him again. And I am not saying I would never ever do that, but I need to see some change. I told him when he took me out to dinner one night that he had hurt me.

"This is why I asked you to leave the house. I felt like you disrespected me." So, I did use my empowerment.

Hale: Wow, you know when you say that, you seem empowered.
Emma: I am empowered, and I am in control of my life, and I'm not planning on getting back together with him any time soon. And it may never happen. But I'm in a place where I can talk with him and have communication with him.
Hale: So, you were empowered in telling him that. So maybe a little more of that?
Emma: Yes, I guess I could talk to him about it and tell him to go home. Yes.
Hale: You have a very different idea about what is going on and what is going to happen than he does. Here is an opportunity for you to be appropriately adversarial. *[Hale mirrors Emma, and then summarizes the new learning in the session.]* So, maybe a way to think about this then, is that anger is on a broad spectrum. You know at the extreme end is ragefulness and ...
Emma: Right, and seeing red.
Hale: At the other end is avoiding it. Pretending that it is not there. Being Minnie Mouse. In the middle is a lot of space. At your work, you need to be down at this end (motioning), but with your boyfriend you are more down this way. Does that feel right to you? [*Hale checks if he and Emma are on the same page.*]
Emma: Yes.
Hale: Uh huh, so maybe this week find more space for some of the feelings that you have about anger.
Emma: Ok.
Hale: If you have a chance, try it out and see how it feels.
Emma: I think I will.
Hale: And then you can tell me next time how it went and what you learned.
Emma: I will.

Given the length and intensity of the session, if Emma had signaled any type of negative emotions as a result of her new insights, I would have devoted time to meta-processing the experience of the AIS with her. However, I decided to close the session with her positive and energetic mood and told her that I was available by phone if necessary to further discuss the experience that we had together.

Post-session Reflections on the AIS with Emma

As you can see, this AIS required a lot of attuned, but tenacious work, and it ultimately uncovered a critical experience underlying Emma's fears that affected her life in many ways. Using the TAT as a launching pad to help Emma see her relationship with anger opened the door to a conversation that was rich and revealing and a therapeutic experience that led to meaningful insights and new ways of being for Emma. Notice how half-step scaffolding helped Emma discuss her early trauma and uncover its impact on her daily life. Guided by the test results, we worked to make sense of her life experiences in ways that she could see with new eyes. It was her openness and trust that had emerged from our hours of collaborative testing experiences that allowed a new, more accurate, and more self-compassionate understanding of her struggles. Importantly, I was aware that Emma and I had begun to look at how her early family dynamics had affected her and continued to influence her life. She now understood that her mother's rages had traumatized her, but she did not yet see that her father's avoidance implicated him in allowing that trauma to occur. I had a strong sense this was "Level 10" information for Emma, so while I was aware of it, I contained it with the plan to possibly share my thoughts with Jeanne, her psychotherapist.

Note

1 Fischer defined experiaction as "one's simultaneous affective/cognitive/actional engagement with the world." It is synonymous with comportment, or the way clients carry themselves.

References

Brown, L., Sherbenou, R. J., & Johnsen, S. K. (2010). *Test of Nonverbal Intelligence: TONI-4.* Pro-ed.

Crisi, A., & Palm, J. A. (2018). *The Crisi Wartegg System (CWS). Manual for administration, scoring, and interpretation.* Routledge.

David, R. M., & Bertucci, M. (2015). Tapping into the TA well: Examples of assessment intervention sessions in the literature. *The TA Connection, 3*(2), 11–15.

Finn, S. E. (1996). *Manual for using the MMPI-2 as a therapeutic intervention.* University of Minnesota Press.

Finn, S. E. (2003). Therapeutic Assessment of a man with "ADD." *Journal of Personality Assessment, 80*(2), 115–129.

Finn, S. E. (2007). *In our clients' shoes: Theory and techniques of Therapeutic Assessment.* Taylor and Francis.

Finn, S. E. (2012). Implications of recent research in neurobiology for psychological assessment. *Journal of Personality Assessment, 94*(5), 440–449.

Finn, S. E. (2015). The history of and recent thoughts about assessment intervention sessions in Therapeutic Assessment. *The TA Connection, 3*(2), 4–11.

Finn, S. E. (2016). Helping sexual minority clients heal from shame. *Japanese Journal of Psychotherapy, 42*(2), 5–60.

Finn, S. E. (September, 2017). *Let down your tap root: Leonard Handler's enduring contributions to Therapeutic Assessment.* Paper presented at the 2nd International Collaborative/Therapeutic Assessment Conference, Austin, TX.

Finn, S. E., Fischer, C. T., & Handler, L. (Eds.). (2012). *Collaborative/Therapeutic Assessment: A casebook and guide.* John Wiley & Sons

Finn, S. E., & Kamphuis, J. H. (2006). Therapeutic Assessment with the MMPI-2. In J. N. Butcher (Ed.), *MMPI-2: A practitioner's guide* (pp. 165–191). APA Books.

Fischer, C. (1985/1994). *Individualizing psychological assessment.* Lawrence Erlbaum & Associates.

Fischer, C. T., & Finn, S. E. (2014). Developing the life meaning of psychological test data: Collaborative and therapeutic approaches. In Archer, R. P., & Smith. S. R. (Eds.), *Personality assessment, 2nd edition* (pp. 401–431). Routledge.

Fonagy, P., Luyten, P., & Allison, E. (2015). Epistemic petrification and the restoration of epistemic trust: A new conceptualization of borderline personality disorder and its psychosocial treatment. *Journal of Personality Disorders, 29,* 575–609.

Fosha, D. (2000). *The transforming power of affect. A model for accelerated change.* Basic Books.

Gardner, R. A. (1969). Mutual storytelling as a technique in child psychotherapy and psychoanalysis. In J. H. Masserman (Ed.), *Science and Psychoanalysis* (pp. 123–125). Grune & Stratton,

George, C. & West, M. L. (2012). *The Adult Attachment Projective Picture System. Attachment theory and assessment in adults.* Guilford Press.

Handler, L., & Hilsenroth, M. J. (1994, April). *The use of a fantasy animal drawing and storytelling technique in assessment and psychotherapy.* Paper presented at the Annual Meeting of the Society for Personality Assessment.

Jurist, E. (2018). *Minding emotions: Cultivating mentalization ins psychotherapy.* The Guilford Press

Kamphuis, J. H., & Finn, S. E. (2019). Therapeutic Assessment in personality disorders: Toward the restoration of epistemic trust. *Journal of Personality Assessment, 101*(6), 662–674

Kohut, H. (1977). *The restoration of the self.* International Universities Press.

Kohut, H. (1984). *How does analysis cure?* The University of Chicago Press.

Lichtenberg, E. F. (2014). Draw a Person in the Rain Test. In L. Handler & A. D. Thomas (Eds.) *Drawings in assessment and psychotherapy: Research and application.* (pp. 164–183). Routledge.

Linehan, M. (2014). *DBT skills training manual, 2nd Edition.* Guilford Press.

Martin, H., & Frackowiak, M. (2017). The value of projective/performance-based techniques in Therapeutic Assessment. *SIS Journal of Projective Psychology and Mental Health, 24*(2), 91–95.

Martin, H., & Jacklin, E. (2012). Therapeutic Assessment involving multiple life issues: Coming to terms with problems of health, culture, and learning. In S. E. Finn, C. T. Fischer, & L. Handler (Eds.), *Collaborative/Therapeutic Assessment: A casebook and guide* (pp. 157–178). John Wiley & Sons, Inc.

McCullough, L., Kuhn, N., Andrews, S., Kaplan, A., Wolf, J., & Hurley, C. L. (2003). *Treating affect phobia: A manual for short-term dynamic psychotherapy.* Guilford Press.

Meyers, J. E., & Meyers, K. R. (1995). *Rey Complex Figure Test and recognition trial: Professional manual.* Psychological Assessment Resources, Inc.

Morrison, A. P. (1989) *Shame: The underside of narcissism.* Analytic Press.

Murray, H. A. (1943). *Thematic Apperception Test Manual.* Harvard University Press. Press.

Roberts, G. E., & Gruber, C. (2005). *The Roberts Apperception Test for Children-2nd Edition.* Western Psychological Services.

Rosenzweig S. (1978) *Aggressive behavior and the Rosenzweig Picture-Frustration Study.* Praeger.

Sapozhnikova, A., & Smith, B. L. (2017) Assessment Intervention using the Rey–Osterrieth Complex Figure Test: A clinical illustration. *Journal of Personality Assessment, 99*(5), 503–509.

Smith, J., & George, C. (2012). Therapeutic Assessment case Study: Treatment of a woman diagnosed with metastatic cancer and attachment trauma. *Journal of Personality Assessment, 94*(4), 331–344.

Swann, W. B. (1997). The trouble with change: Self-verification and allegiance to the self. *Psychological Science, 8,* 177–180.

Tarocchi, A., Aschieri, F., Fantini, F., & Smith, J. D. (2013). Therapeutic Assessment of complex trauma: A single-case time-series study. *Clinical Case Studies, 12*(3), 228–245.

Tharinger, D. J., Finn, S. E., Austin, C., Gentry, L., Bailey, E., Parton, V., & Fisher, M. (2008). Family sessions in psychological assessment with children: Goals, techniques, and clinical utility. *Journal of Personality Assessment, 90*(6), 547–558.

Thurston, N. S., & Cradock O'Leary, J. (2009). *Thurston Cradock Test of Shame (TCTS) manual.* Western Psychological Services.

Turret, J. (2015). Assessment Intervention: A doctoral student's perspective. *TA Connection, 3*(2), 15–17.

Wartegg, E. (1953). *Schichtdiagnostik-Der Zeichentest* (WZT) [Differential diagnostics-The Drawing test.] Verlag für Psychologie.

9 Summary/Discussion Session

This chapter provides guidelines for how to conduct the Summary/Discussion Session and share assessment results therapeutically. Two elements will help assessors ground themselves in how to prepare and execute this session. First, this session is called the Summary/Discussion Session because we "summarize and discuss" with the client. Those conducting psychological testing following the traditional information-gathering model, typically conduct a feedback session upon completion of an evaluation (Finn & Tonsager, 1997). Providing feedback is a unilateral process in which a hierarchy is established. The clinician is in a position of being the expert on the client, and is sometimes viewed as having oracular powers. Such an interpersonal stance is contrary to the values of Therapeutic Assessment (TA). As already stated, we believe that assessors are experts on psychological theories and testing and clients are experts on their lives. Thus, this session was titled the Summary/Discussion Session to reflect the broad goals of summarizing what has been discovered through testing and conversations, and collaboratively discussing that information with the client. Second, and as further detailed later in this chapter, the Summary/Discussion Session is designed with specific theories and research in mind. As such, it is an empirically supported framework for discussing assessment results with clients in a way that contributes to enhanced client care (Smith & Finn, 2014).

In understanding the Summary/Discussion Session, it is helpful to consider the evolution of sharing psychological test results with clients. Historically, assessors believed that sharing evaluation results with patients could be harmful to them. Thus, for many decades psychologists were instructed not to provide any feedback to clients and test reports were often marked "Confidential" (Klopfer & Kelley, 1946; Fischer, 1970). As consumer rights grew and a more collaborative medical and psychological services style became the norm in Western countries, this shifted. That change contributed to the addition of Principle 9.10 Explaining Assessment Results to the American Psychological Association (2017) ethics code addressing test feedback. Added in 1992 and updated in 2002, it states:

> Regardless of whether the scoring and interpretation are done by psychologists, by employees or assistants, or by automated or other outside services, psychologists take reasonable steps to ensure that explanations of results are given to the individual or designated representative unless the nature of the relationship prevents provision of an explanation of results (such as in some organizational consulting, preemployment or security screenings, and forensic evaluations), and this has been clearly explained to the person being assessed in advance.

DOI: 10.4324/9780429202797-11

Once clients began receiving feedback following an evaluation, research proved the clinical value of such discussions, and Finn & Tonsager (1992) among others demonstrated how a collaborative approach to discussing test results could decrease client symptomology, increase hope and self-esteem, and create an overall positive impression of the testing experience for the client (see Chapter 3). Over time, the more collaborative and relational approach to this capstone session of an evaluation has been endorsed more broadly by psychologists, and even those conducting testing following the traditional, information-gathering model are encouraged to consider the interpersonal stance of the clinician during the discussion of test results (Butcher, 1990; Groth-Marnat & Wright, 2016; Wright, 2011).

Goals and Principles of the Summary/Discussion Session

Understanding the goals and principles that guide the Summary/Discussion Session helps clinicians to prepare and conduct what is often the pinnacle session of a TA. During the Summary/Discussion Session, the primary goal is to answer the client's Assessment Questions (AQs). As described, the AQs are ostensive cues to the client which help them assimilate and accommodate what is being shared (Kamphuis & Finn, 2019). The Summary/Discussion Session is structured around the AQs to maximize client openness to new information and to respect the agreement we created in the beginning of the process. Together with the client, we collaboratively explore the answers to AQs using the test results, conversations that were part of the initial session and EIs, and by providing psychoeducation.

The way information is organized and presented during the Summary/Discussion Session advances the goal of helping the client develop a more useful and compassionate narrative (Finn, 2007). We weave the client's language and metaphors into the conversation, combining them with psychoeducation to construct a new story. We also rely on Swann's self-verification theory (see Chapter 1) to remain aware that humans primarily seek information from their environment to confirm their sense of self (Swann, 1997). Therefore, if a client's sense of self became threatened by the presentation of irrefutable information from a trusted other, they may defensively dismiss or become anxious about it, or at worst, experience psychological disintegration (Kohut, 1977, 1984; described in Chapters 1 and 8). To maximize the possibility of clients taking in new information about themselves during the Summary/Discussion Session, we follow Finn's ideas regarding the Levels of Information (1996, 2007) already described in previous chapters (see Chapters 2 and 8). Later in this chapter, we will clarify how the Levels of Information become a tool used to organize the data we present to clients.

Importantly, during the Summary/Discussion Session we continue to seek the client's input in order to refine and contextualize the new narrative being developed and to give them ownership of it. This action aligns with our belief that all knowledge is perspectival (Aschieri, 2012; Fischer, 1985/1994), and reality is created within the intersubjective experience that is occurring between clinician and client. When clients disagree with what the clinician is stating, we give them permission to express their stance and create a different and more nuanced understanding of the test results together (Aschieri, 2012; Aschieri et al., 2016). We also ask clients to share moments from their life that resonate with what we are presenting, and place equal value on their examples of times the problem occurs and times it does not. Engaging the client in this way helps them move from a black or white view of their difficulties, to one that is more realistic, contextualized, and recognizes the "grays."

During this session, we continue to convey our empathy and understanding of the client and focus on reducing shame. To accomplish this goal, we ask clients to share their reactions and stay attuned to what they express and share about their emotions.

The final goal of the Summary/Discussion Session is to acknowledge the end of the assessment process and build a bridge to the next steps for the client. We do this by weaving suggestions into the conversation, alongside our answers to the AQS, and by doing so, we help build hope for continued change. While we always provide clients written feedback (see Chapter 10) and schedule a Follow-up Session (see Chapter 11), we recognize the Summary/Discussion Session might be the last time we see a client, as not all clients will participate in the follow-up. Therefore, we make sure we thank the client for their good work and say goodbye.

Preparing for the Summary/Discussion Session

Logistical Preparations

Assessors need to address a few logistical matters to prepare for the Summary/Discussion Session. It is common to plan on a 120 minute session for most adult clients. However, some clients have more than one Summary/Discussion Session, and multiple sessions of shorter duration may be best for certain clients. This is likely to be true for clients who are under-regulated, still uncertain about the process, or have complex test data. We keep these factors in mind when we are planning our schedule and recognize that even if we allot 120 minutes, some clients may need a second Summary/Discussion Session. For those clients who continue in psychotherapy with the assessor, it may be the case that multiple, brief sessions are best, as that allows for a deeper exploration of test results or answers to AQs. However, for those clients who are moving onto the next steps in their therapy work, multiple sessions may only stall the next treatment.

We consider who, if anyone, should attend the session besides the client and the referring professional (RP), and below we describe how to work with RPs who are present. For some clients, it may be beneficial to have other professionals present, and the intervention may involve them. Chudzik (2016) wrote about the impact of sharing the results of a TA with an inmate's treatment team at a correctional facility, which contributed to a systemic shift in how the client was perceived. Other times, it may be helpful to have a family member such as a partner present. If others are invited to this session, this would be discussed beforehand with the client; some of those individuals would be involved in the TA at various points prior to the Summary/Discussion session, for example during the initial identification of AQs. In other situations, at some point in the TA, the client and assessor realize that sharing some of what is being discussed with others would be important. For example, a young adult who initially stated that they did not want their parents involved in the TA may come to see how relationships could be improved if their parents understood them better. In this type of situation, we conduct a Summary/Discussion Session with the client alone first, and then coordinate a second session. Together with the client and prior to the session, we consider the potential advantages and disadvantages of having others present.

Next, we print out copies of the AQs so that the client, and RP if present, can see them in writing. We also consider if there is test data or profiles that we want to share with the client, and print those. For some clients, it may be beneficial to show IQ scores and percentiles, and where a client's scores fall on the bell curve. At other times, figures such as Personality Assessment Inventory (PAI; Morey, 1991) scales help patients see how their scores compare to others. While we are not overly focused on numbers and scores during the Summary/Discussion Session, epistemic trust (ET) is built when the tests are presented as an authoritative source (Kamphuis & Finn, 2019). We also expect the self-report test profiles to contain mostly Level 1 Information that is self-verifying, builds ET, and prepares the client to be more open to Level 2, and possibly Level 3, Information.

Preparation with the Referring Professional

For clients who have been referred by their psychotherapist or other treatment providers, the preferred method of conducting the Summary/Discussion Session involves that professional. As described in Chapter 8, after the AIS it is often best to have contact with the RP to discuss what occurred during that session. In addition, that conversation is an opportunity to share assessment results, gather their perspective on our case conceptualization, and coordinate the Summary/Discussion Session.

Sharing and discussing the case conceptualization with the RP can be one of the more challenging moments of a TA that is consultation to ongoing therapy. As is customary in TA, RPs often pose questions for the assessment (see Chapters 4 and 5) and we use these questions as "open doors" through which we can discuss the new case conceptualization. The extent to which the conceptualization offered by the assessor can be heard and processed by the RP depends on several factors: The way the conceptualization is presented and the extent to which the assessor has included the RP in the assessment; the discrepancy between the RP's initial case conceptualization and the one developed during the TA; and the quality of the relationship between the assessor and RP (see also Chapter 7).

By having maintained contact with the RP during earlier sessions, the assessor may have had the opportunity to present some "building blocks" of the new case conceptualization, which hopefully helped to cultivate the RPs curiosity about it. By focusing on the RP's questions, the assessor continues to stoke this curiosity about the assessment findings. The initial conversations with the RP help the assessor understand which aspects of the conceptualization are new for the RP, and which may be harder for them to hear. When discussing our conceptualization with RPs, we employ the same values and principles used to present test findings to clients. That is, the assessor validates the RP's pre-existing case conceptualization by sharing Level 1 findings from the testing. Level 2 Information may need to be presented cautiously to help the RP understand the answers to their AQs. Working with the RP's Level 3 Information may involve discussing their potential contributions to the difficulties they experienced while treating the client (i.e., the therapist's "blind spots"). Assessors should be cautious about disclosing this information to RPs, because hypotheses about the RP's blind spots are often inferred and cannot be substantiated. For example, after the assessor and client recognize that mirroring emotional pain is beneficial, and the client reports that their relationship with the RP feels formal and dry, an assessor could conclude that the therapist may have difficulty being emotionally attuned to the client. We may hypothesize that the RP has a blind spot connected to being present with the client's pain, but again, this is only a hypothesis.

In these situations, assessors should carefully consider the need to address possible blind spots with the RP. We keep in mind that there is no certainty that the RP will use the shared information to improve the client's treatment, and there is a risk of damaging their relationship and increasing shame. At the same time, we have an ethical obligation to ensure a client is receiving the best treatment possible given their identified needs. Often we can engage the RP in reflecting on possible problems in their case conceptualizations, and scaffold them towards new ways of thinking about the client.

In addition to discussing the case, we also explain our plan for the session, and the RP's input helps with the choices being made (Finn, 2007). We find it beneficial to conduct the Summary/Discussion Session at the RP's office, when possible, as the client is likely to feel most at ease in that space. We inform the RP that we will step out of the session at the end, so they and the client can process what was discussed. In this way, we maintain our role as a consultant to both client and provider, and signal the end of our work, creating an opportunity for the two of them to continue the next steps.

When working with RPs who are unfamiliar with TA and this session, it is best to explain what will occur and provide some guidance, as can be seen in Emma's case at the end of this chapter. RPs may experience some anxiety about the session, as assessors are often placed in an exalted position given their expertise. We continue to build our collaborative connection with the RP to reduce that power difference. For example, we ask the RP to watch for moments when too much information is being conveyed, or times the client seems confused and we do not recognize it. We do this to ensure communication is clear (Finn, 2007). We also let the RP know they may want to take notes. Many TA assessors have developed a collaborative relationship with RPs, and when appropriate, the RP's notes are shared with the assessor as that information can be useful when writing the final document.

We also let the provider know that as test results are being shared, it can be helpful if they connect what is being shared with past discussions they have had with the client. An assessor may say, "So part of the answer to your question about why it's hard to motivate yourself is related to your depression." An astute RP may say, "This reminds me of what we talked about when you were really struggling at work after that hard weekend." While clients may make those connections independently, it can be beneficial for the provider to share their impressions. However, it is very important to let the RP know that if the client disagrees with a test interpretation, they should align with the client and not the assessor. By doing so, the client feels most supported, the therapeutic alliance with the therapist is strengthened, and a disintegration experience is avoided.

Clinical Preparation: Reviewing the Levels of Information

Ideally, during a client's TA, Level 2–3 Information becomes Level 1 Information through developing the AQs, exploring the tests during Extended Inquires (EIs), and through the Assessment Intervention Session (AIS), which often specifically targets this goal. In preparation for the Summary/Discussion Session, we consider what data falls into which Level and organize it into the appropriate Levels. Research suggests that when clients receive information about themselves that is mildly discrepant from their self-view (Level 2), it has a greater impact than information that is congruent (Level 1) or highly discrepant with their self-view (Level 3; Schroeder et al., 1993). Schroeder and colleagues showed that, in contrast to participants who received Level 1 and 3 Information, those who received Level 2 Information "felt that they had learned more about themselves, that the feedback was more self-confirming, that the session was more impactful, and that they had experienced more positive affect" (p. 3). This research aligns with Swann's views on self-verification (Swann, 1997) and guides the preparation of the Summary/Discussion Session. In order to have the greatest impact on clients during this session, information should ideally be presented in order, beginning with Level 1, moving to Level 2, and potentially Level 3 (Finn, 2007). We say potentially because for many clients the information presented during the Summary/Discussion Session will primarily be Level 1 and Level 2, with ideally the majority being Level 2 Information. Level 3 Information may still be too difficult for the client to integrate (Smith & Finn, 2014). However, it may also be, that information considered Level 3 at the beginning of the TA would be Level 1 or 2, and thus, more easily accepted (see Emma at the end of this chapter for an example).

Clinical Preparation: The Interpersonal Stance

Throughout the TA, we have been interacting with the client, and reviewing test data, and as our case conceptualization developed, so has our ability to empathize with the client. Now, as we prepare the Summary/Discussion Session, we consider our behavioral observations, test data, the client's self-descriptions, and their history as we attempt to be "in our client shoes" (Finn, 1996, 2007). Our test results are "empathy magnifiers" which guide us in identifying how the client is likely to experience discussing the answers to their AQs. For an under-regulated client whose test results suggest high levels of sensitivity, we consider times in our life when our sensitivities were heightened and try to be empathic to the client's needs. With this type of client, we consider a slower pace of discussion and ensure our language does not produce overwhelm or shame. In contrast, for a client who is well defended, highly articulate, and has hearty resources, it may be best to adopt a confident, professional demeanor, and use more formal language. In recognizing and adopting this empathic interpersonal stance, we attend to the most important part of preparing for the Summary/Discussion Session (Finn, 1996).

Clinical Preparation: Organization of Data

Preparation for the Summary/Discussion Session occurs throughout the TA and is influenced by the case conceptualization process described in Chapter 7. After each test is scored, it is helpful to gather interpretative notes in a working document that also contains the client's AQs. During the case conceptualization process and prior to the Summary/Discussion Session, the AQs are reviewed, and test results can be sorted underneath AQs to capture various parts of the client's psychology. For example, it is common for clients to have a question about mood or specific emotions. Because most tests results speak to the client's emotional life, test data related to emotions can be accumulated under the related question.

Three different methods are used when preparing a document to use during the Summary/Discussion Session. For most clinicians, at this point it is best to write a

Table 9.1 Primary Methods for Organizing Information for the Summary/Discussion Session

1 Order the AQs from Level 1 to Level 3 and answer each AQ weaving together test results, observations, conversations, and suggestions.
2 Briefly provide an overarching summary of the test results and then answer the AQs ordered from Level 1 to Level 3.
3 Give an in-depth review of the various tests, then answer the AQs ordered from Level 1 to Level 3.

detailed draft of what they are going to say to the client. This draft then also serves as a blueprint of the client's TA letter (see Chapter 10). Writing a draft will allow the assessor to identify useful language and have a kind of script to use when conducting the session. We take notes on this draft during the Summary/Discussion Session, adding clients' comments, examples, and reactions. This document then evolves into our final written communication to the client.

Our document, and thus discussion, will be structured in one of three ways, which are listed in Table 9.1. Method one is the most commonly used approach and works best for most clients.

Method two is useful when the test results and the AQs do not connect easily. For example, a client may have many questions about one area of their life (e.g., relationships). Yet, we now have broad test data not only related to relationships, but also their emotional life, thinking, and other parts of their psychology. Thus, it may be difficult to connect all of this varied data to the client's AQs. Given, however, that all test results are can equally help the client better understand the answers to their AQs about relationships, we want to discuss that information with the client as well. In such situations, method two may be preferable, so that the important test results are covered broadly before the AQs and discussed. Structuring the session this way may also allow clients to "use" the broad summary of their tests to find the answers to their questions. Many clients find it easy to engage in this "top-down" process of connecting general findings from tests to the answers to their AQs.

The third method, giving an in-depth review of the various test results before answering AQs, may be preferable when a client has been extremely interested in specific tests. Out of respect for their desire to hear about each test, we share a broad overview from each, or at least the tests they were most curious about. At other times, a specific test illustrates something important for a client. When this happens it is helpful to discuss the results and implications from that particular test. For example, an over-regulated client may benefit from being shown self-report test profiles that have low-scale elevations. Next, we may show them their Rorschach (Rorschach, 1942) profile with elevations suggesting distress, to help them see what is underneath their defenses. Here again, we are mindful about moving from Level 1 to Level 3 Information when making such choices.

As our working document is being created, we revisit the client's AQs and consider the order in which they should be answered. During the first session the AQs were identified in an order dictated by the client, and when we print them for the client to review in early sessions, we keep them in that order, demonstrating that the client's goals are paramount. Now, as we organize our data and answers to the AQs, we consider two factors. First, given the goal of moving from Level 1 to Level 2 and 3 Information, we may reorder the questions with consideration to the Level of

Information identified in each answer. We first discuss AQs that relate more to Level 1 Information and after that, address AQs that open the discussion to Levels 2 and 3. Second, some clients have multiple AQs with similar themes, or AQs which are answered the same way (e.g., multiple questions may be related to the client's relationships, mood or sense of self). While there may be nuances to each question that we do not want to miss, it may also be the case that some of these AQs can be grouped together and answered collectively.

In preparation for the Summary/Discussion Session, we also review interview data from the first session, EIs, AIS, and other conversations, identifying meaningful language relative to the client's AQs. Often, there were moments in those conversations that were particularly impactful, and we intentionally use language from those moments during this session. We also review qualitative test data for language or drawings that might serve as useful metaphors. Clients' stories for tests such as the Thematic Apperception Test (TAT; Murray, 1943), or their responses on a Sentence Completion Test, often contain language that illustrates the answer to an AQ. For example, if a client had an above-average number of aggressive content responses during the Rorschach, we likely discussed that during the EI following the test administration. Now, we review that data and notes from our discussion to see if their Rorschach responses or language from that conversation will help the client understand an answer to one of their AQs. For example, if during the Rorschach EI the discussion focussed on the client's response, "A volcano that is dormant, but ready to explode at any moment," using this same language and image during the Summary/Discussion Session would be best, as ET is enhanced by bringing in the client's experiences and shared language from previous sessions (Kamphuis & Finn, 2019).

For some clients, there might be an AQ that is extremely important to them and was the primary reason they participated in the TA. During the Summary/Discussion Session, if that AQ is not addressed first, the client may feel that their most important concern is not being prioritized, which may impact their ability to participate fully. If the answer to that AQ is Level 1 Information, structuring the session around addressing that question first makes sense. However, when the answer to that question is going to be potentially difficult for the client, discussing that AQ first would violate our goal of moving sequentially from congruent to new (and potentially overwhelming) information. Based on the premise that clients will be interested in hearing first about information that motivated the assessment, in such cases, we structure the Summary/Discussion Session to address that AQ first, and make sure to support the client through their emotional response.

To illustrate, Akio sought a TA because he was concerned his emotional difficulties were affecting his ability to be successful in college and asked, among other questions that were less important for him, "What is getting in the way of me achieving the way I would like in college? Is it depression? Anxiety? Something else?" Akio's test results suggested some mild anxiety and depression, but more noteworthy was an IQ at the low end of the average range, and the assessment results pointed to the fact that his cognitive functioning was the primary issue leading to academic difficulties. Akio's self-view before the assessment did not include this element. Two Summary/Discussion Sessions were scheduled with Akio, with the first focused on his prioritized AQ and including time for him to process the results and feel supported. During the second session, the conversation continued and his other AQs were discussed.

Steps for Conducting the Summary/Discussion Session

Check in, Orienting the Client to the Session, and Sharing an Appreciation

Like other TA sessions, we check in with the client to determine if there have been any issues or difficulties since the last meeting. Such a check in is appropriate, given that many clients will enter this session following the AIS, which may have been emotionally challenging. Assessors follow-up on the client's experience of the AIS and inquire about how it affected them. If it is the case that specific actions were identified as being helpful to take, we inquire about what transpired, recognizing that the client may not have been able to follow through.

During the check in, it is helpful to ask, "How are you feeling about meeting today?" Most clients enter the Summary/Discussion Session with understandable anxiety about what will be discussed and what they will learn about themselves. Even in cases when a lot has already been talked through over the course of the TA, and the client has developed some understanding or insight about their AQs, they often are still not holding a complete, coherent picture of their test results. Therefore, they might be nervous about what more they could learn. Additionally, when an RP is involved, the client might feel anxious as it is unusual to have two professionals in the room. We begin by normalizing those feelings and provide support so that the client feels comfortable with the process.

Next, we orient the client to the session by providing them an overview of what will occur. Depending on how we decided to organize the session we may say, "We're going to spend most of our time going through your questions and discussing answers to them using what we figured out together and the test data." However, for other clients, we may say, "I'm going to first review the results of your tests and then we will answer your specific questions." We also let them know that we will step out of the session towards the end, so the client and RP can process what was discussed.

As we are orienting the client to the session, we emphasize that we want to discuss (not just provide feedback about) the test results and provide answers to their questions. It is helpful to say, "As I review your test results and share my impressions of answers to your questions, if you hear things that feel true, please say so. If you hear things that do not sound like you, it is equally helpful if you share those thoughts." Such a statement continues our collaborative relationship with the client and gives them power over their narrative, which helps reduce EH (Kamphuis & Finn, 2019). We also acknowledge the fallibility of our tests with a statement such as "We have tests with good science, but they aren't 100% accurate and measuring parts of a person's psychology is complicated" or "Tests don't have the Truth with a capital T, they can also make mistakes sometimes."

The initial part of the Summary/Discussion Session closes with appreciating the client. Here, we are as specific as possible; during our preparation for this moment, we consider our experiences with the client and what touched or impressed us about them. We may make a statement such as, "I really appreciated how you stuck with the different tasks I asked you to do." However, other times we may make a more specific statement related to a test or something the client shared. When we share something we truly appreciate about the client, it leaves them feeling seen and validated, which helps set the stage for a collaborative discussion.

Reviewing the Test Results and Answering the AQs

Next, we move to a review of test findings and answering the client's AQs following the outline we chose, as described earlier in the chapter. At this point, if not earlier, we have given the client and RP a copy of the printed AQs. Although during the Summary/Discussion Session we need to take the role of expert more than we do in other phases, there are still various ways we continue to maintain a collaborative stance and encourage the client's participation. For example, with many clients we may answer their questions after first asking, "What have you have already figured out about your questions during our time together?" or "How would you answer your questions today, after our work together?" The client's responses to these type of questions often help us further refine our understanding of what they have already integrated and what areas may need more emphasis during the discussion. However, we may not ask this question to clients who are too anxious, eager to know what we have to say, or whom we think are still too confused about the answer to their AQs. This request might make them feel more nervous.

When sharing test results and our answers to clients' questions, we remain mindful about how much each of us is speaking, and we are careful to provide Level 2 Information in "half-steps." We read one of their AQs, begin sharing test data related to the answer, and then stop and invite input. We ask, "Does that seem like you? Are there times you've noticed more or less of that?" Our goal is to reinforce the client's expertise on their life and confirm that what we share matches their experience. If the client agrees, then assessors take another "half-step" and add more information to the answer of the AQ.

Given we have organized our data to follow the Levels of Information, it should be the case that early on, during the sharing of test results, clients' responses are affirmative, such as "That sounds exactly like me." During this part of the discussion, we contextualize what is being discussed by connecting test results to their life. Checking for ecological validity by asking the client to connect the data to their real-world experiences helps decrease epistemic hypervigilance (EH), which is partially how change occurs (Fonagy et al., 2017; Kamphuis & Finn, 2019).

For example, Shana had a question about improving relationships and her test results suggested that she manages feelings of vulnerability by becoming dominating and controlling. With Shana, the assessor explained how these test results connect to her relationship question. After making sure the results made sense to her, the assessor also inquired about how and when the feelings of vulnerability manifest in her life and trigger the dominating and controlling behavior: "So, this part of you that is a bit dominant and controlling seems to pop up in situations where you feel vulnerable and anxious. Can you think of specific examples of when that happens?" By inviting the client to share what they know about themselves, we contextualize our understanding of them, which further helps us refine our suggestions. We also help them recognize that these ways of being are not omnipresent but are more likely to emerge in certain situations. The client learns about those behaviors and the circumstances that elicit them, so they can be avoided or so that they can take steps to prepare themselves to best manage those situations (Finn, 2007). Building insight about these parts of the client often means introducing Level 2 Information. For example, Shana may respond, "I've always known I can be a bit dominating (Level 1 Information), but never realized it was because I was feeling vulnerable. I see now how it may become worse with coworkers when I'm worried about seeming competent or not (Level 2 Information)." By listening to the examples clients provide, we can also determine if they accurately understand what we have explained.

The process of sharing answers and discussing related test results while inviting the client's input continues as we move through each AQ. We use the relational skills and collaborative language that have been part of the previous sessions, and incorporate scaffolding and psychoeducation, as described later in this chapter. We simultaneously consider the client's emotional state and which topics need to be discussed and make decisions in the moment to organize our time. A client may become emotionally overwhelmed early on and require additional support, which may lead us to adjust our plan or consider whether adding an additional Summary/Discussion Session would be in the client's best interest. It can be a "delicate dance," but if we remain rooted in the TA values and hold in mind the principles and goals for the session, our conversation should result in the client feeling deeply validated and less ashamed, and having a more coherent narrative and a plan for the next steps.

Closing the Session

We close the session by attending to logistical tasks and metaprocessing with the client. We let them know when the letter will be completed and sent, and ask whether they would like it to be sent to other providers. We remind clients that if they are interested, we can schedule a Follow-up Session after they receive the letter, to further discuss it and any questions they have.

One important note relates to clients who have not been working with an individual therapist, but for whom we are recommending therapy. Ideally, for such clients, there have been discussions about whether the assessor can be the ongoing therapist if it is indicated. Often, if the assessor and client have already agreed to continue in therapy, then the Summary/Discussion Session becomes the first step towards therapy.

During the metaprocessing stage, we inquire about the client's experience during the Summary/Discussion Session and TA overall (See Chapter 5 for more on metaprocessing). We ask, "What was it like to hear this today?" and "What was this entire experience like for you?" We help them internalize what they have learned by asking, "What are the main things you are taking away from this process? From today's discussion?" Once those topics are covered, we check for questions. We specifically want to know their reaction to what was discussed and if they were surprised by anything. When a TA occurs with EIs and an AIS that are deep and meaningful, the Summary/Discussion Session pulls together all that has been learned, and typically there are no surprises for the client. However, if the client reacts negatively to something that was discussed, exploring that will be useful and will yield information that will likely be included in the final letter.

We next recommend that assessors share something that they learned from the client or some way that they were touched by them. Given we engaged with the client in a deep and human way, it is likely that our experience with them has led to our own moments of self-reflection, and we share these experiences with the client. For example, we might share information about ourselves (e.g., "Before closing, let me share with you that working with your growing confidence in expressing anger reminded me of the struggles I had in the past overcoming shame about being assertive and self-confident. You have helped me gain compassion for myself and I thank you for that."). At other times, we might share something about our professional practice (e.g., "Before closing, I would like you to know how deeply impactful your assessment was for me. During my training, I learned about the impact of abuse on children and adults, but your memories really made me realize the effect of such experiences. I will hold these understandings in mind in the future when working with other clients who have had similar experiences."). We ensure that our comments are concise so as not to draw the focus to us, and we say something we genuinely believe so that we do not sound insincere. We also understand that different cultures are more or less "effusive" and encourage assessors, as always, to adapt what they say to match what is best for the client.

Upon completion of the Summary/Discussion Session, we attend to a few tasks that will enhance our clinical care and learning. While we take notes during this session, it may be that important elements were not captured in writing. Taking time to review the notes taken and add impressions contributes to a final document that is more nuanced. It is also helpful to reflect on whether the goals for the Summary/Discussion Session were met; in doing so, we consider whether we shared the right amount, too much, or too little information. To facilitate this self-reflection process, Finn (1996) recommended considering three elements: (1) What did I learn about the tests administered that may enhance future test interpretations? (2) What did I learn about this client specifically or this type of client? (3) What did I learn about myself? We believe this process of reflection will build TA skills for future clients.

Specific Skills and Strategies to Employ during the Discussion

Scaffolding

We have described the importance of scaffolding clients towards new learning, and the three Levels of Information are built around this concept. We structure both our discussion and our answers to AQs in a way that scaffolds the client towards Level 3 Information. Scaffolding also occurs by engaging clients as "active interpreters of their own test results" (Aschieri et al., 2016, p. 13). What clients share in conversations, whether additional context or their disagreement about a test result, helps us decide if we are trying to get the client to make too big a leap (i.e., not providing enough scaffolding). In particular, when a client disagrees with a test result, we do not argue that we are right, nor do we discard the result too quickly if we are confident that it might be accurate. Instead, we ask the client if they think the result might describe something happening only in some context or if part of the result might be true. For example, 18-year-old Carlos disagreed with test findings that suggested uncertainty and confusion about his sense of self, and described times he felt grounded, confident, and proud. The assessor explored those moments during the Summary/Discussion Session, and engaged Carlos in trying to identify if he felt secure all the time or if there were moments in which he felt otherwise. By continuing the collaborative discussion, the assessor helped Carlos reflect on when and where he felt more or less secure. Through scaffolding, identifying context, and encouraging the client to continue to consider the test result, Carlos assimilated this additional information.

Psychoeducation

Psychoeducation is an important part of the Summary/Discussion Session and allows clinicians to tap into the wealth of information they have about psychological matters. By incorporating psychoeducation we help clients build a new understanding of their problems in a more organized fashion (Aschieri, et al., 2016). Clients' experiences and shame connected to certain emotions and behavior can be normalized. The goal is not to conduct a lecture on psychological matters, but to be concise and use new language that combines science and test results. We aim to avoid jargon, while being straightforward with the client. Two case examples that contain psychoeducation include Finn (2011) and Smith & George (2012). In each, there are useful illustrations of how to explain what an insecure or unresolved attachment status is and what the functional impact of it may be.

Working with Metaphors from the Testing

In our preparations, we review qualitative data to see if any of the client's responses, stories, or drawings, illustrate their difficulties and an answer to an AQ. By incorporating the client's own language (responses), we best explain what is indicated in the test results. In preparation, we ensure that we have that language in our working document so we are accurate in using the client's words. An example would be Nola, whose test results suggested that her negative self-view and feeling of hopelessness interfered with her ability to face emotionally challenging situation. One of her Rorschach responses which illustrated these features was, "A runner with a broken leg, the black color represents his pessimism about the future." During the Summary/Discussion Session, the assessor might use these words and images when presenting the results. For example, the assessor may say, "You may feel pessimistic about facing some situation, like you are running with a broken leg."

Another example of how to use storytelling data could be to say, "I think one of your TAT stories helps us see the answer to this question, so I'm going to read that to you first." After reading the story, we explore it and the connected AQ, and we ask the client to share what they observe in the story and how it may be connected to their question. We then offer our interpretation and summary.

The following example illustrates how a story, or in this case a client's memory, can capture a client's difficulties. Nick's Millon Clinical Multiaxial Inventory 4th Edition (MCMI-IV; Millon et al., 2015) consisted of a mild elevation on the Antisocial scale, and his Adult Attachment Projective (AAP; George & West, 2012) results suggested a Dismissive attachment status. Nick had a question related to his emotional life and how to cope with it differently, and one of his memories for the Early Memory Procedure (EMP; Bruhn, 1992), was:

> When I was in third grade we created posters that were a self-collage. I found images and mine was a little messy, but I didn't care that much. At the end of class, the teacher called me aside and said, "Look at this," and she grabbed another student's poster that was perfect and put it in front of mine and then she grabbed mine and was like, "What happened?" She was like, "This is really messy, and I don't know if you put your time and effort into it." And I was like ok. I was very disinterested, and I didn't care.

While preparing for the Summary/Discussion Session, the assessor considered this story, Nick's test data, and the observation that Nick often said, "I don't care," when discussing difficult emotions. The assessor read this memory to Nick when they discussed his question about managing emotions. Through scaffolding, Nick could identify how he managed his feelings in this memory (by dismissing them). Next, Nick and the assessor discussed how this dismissing behavior occurs for him with his partner, and also talked about ways he could increase acceptance of what he feels. The assessor helped Nick to see that he could shift from saying "I don't care" to "I care about that AND it's hard for me." In this example, the assessor's empathy and sensitivity in not shaming Nick allowed him to anchor his "I don't care" style to an experience in which he felt exposed and humiliated. Together, Nick and the assessor used this new information to identify ways he could behave more adaptively in his relationships.

Discussing Suggestions

As we proceed through the answers to the AQs, we share some of our suggestions with the client. We use the word "suggestions," and not "recommendations," and consider these ideas to be "possible next steps" for the client to consider. Doing so, lowers EH by building the client's agency (Kamphuis & Finn, 2019). Clients' interest about the next steps increases as they start to better understand themselves. Returning to Shana and her dominant style, after explaining that test data and exploring how it appears in her life, we say, "So during your therapy sessions, you could explore what it might be like to feel vulnerable without becoming dominant." We promote clients' psychological growth by connecting test results, the client's life, and suggestions together.

Towards the end of the session, we summarize the suggestions. The level of specificity we offer depends on what is being recommended and how much the client needs to hear about those next steps in that moment. Some clients are "mentally full" after the discussion that has occurred, so we check to find out whether it is helpful to review suggestions before proceeding. We always suggest a number of possible actions, including some that the client can carry out independently and are not connected to treatment (e.g., hiking, meditating, taking acting classes). If more or a different treatment is recommended, we always discuss both that suggestion and the rationale behind it.

In providing different types of suggestions, we try to order them according to how familiar or acceptable they seem to the client. If a client feels strongly about not needing psychotherapy, we first suggest other strategies that they could employ to reach their goals in life. We might then say, "And if none of these activities end up being helpful to you, you may want to reconsider psychotherapy as an alternative."

Working with New AQs or Revelations

TA assessors are prepared for the possibility that during the Summary/Discussion Session the client may reveal their most salient questions (Gomez & Guerrero, 2016; Smith, 2002, as cited in Finn, 2007). When this occurs, we believe the assessor has developed a trusting relationship with the client which has allowed them to lower their EH and reveal the part of themselves that feels ashamed. We accept the question and support the client's emotional response, while also providing an answer to the best of our ability. In a similar fashion, we find that at times during this session, clients reveal highly personal parts of themselves that relate to their shame. They may also do so with their therapist after we leave. If we are present to that moment, we are highly attuned to the client and provide support.

Common Mistakes in the Summary/Discussion Session

There are a few mistakes clinicians can make when conducting the Summary/Discussion Session. These are presented in the next section and broadly are connected to three areas that overlap. First, there can be problems with how findings and AQ answers are organized. Second, there can be mistakes related to a lack of attention to the assessor-client relationship or to the client's emotional reactions Last are mistakes related to the clinician's emotional response to test findings, AQ answers, and to the client.

Mistakes Connected to the Organization and Presentation of Tests Results

The most basic mistake clinicians can make when conducting the Summary/Discussion Session is talking too much and turning it into a feedback session. Those wishing to prevent this mistake may want to put reminders in their notes to ensure that they stop and ask for the client's input.

At times assessors under-report or over-report test results. The former is often connected to the clinician's emotions and is described in the section below. As for over-reporting, during our preparations we consider how much information to present and recognize that we often have more data than the client can assimilate. Many clinicians trained in the traditional model of assessment learned the importance of discussing all test results, and we are not suggesting that important findings are not shared. Rather, the opposite is true. However, for some clients, too much data will be emotionally overwhelming and not therapeutic; thus, rather than share everything, we focus on the salient points. When clinicians struggle with limiting the amount shared, it is often connected to what they have learned from trusted professors and supervisors, and how they have come to define a competent feedback session. Those struggling with not presenting everything may benefit from consultation to help them put into perspective how to align these ideas with past learning about how to conduct psychological testing.

A second mistake related to the information presented occurs when the assessor does not recognize various Levels of Information. While at times skilled assessors misjudge the Levels of Information, we believe that the previously described steps for how to recognize and organize test data should, in most cases, prevent this error from occurring. Assessors ensure their materials are organized so they follow their plan, and if we slip into Level 3 Information, we adjust and slow down the conversation.

Third, clinicians make the error of using clinical terms that are not well understood by lay people. We aim to discuss the test results in terms of action and behavior (Fischer, 1985/1994), and we help clients see how the results and answers connect to their lives, avoiding jargon. Those most familiar with a clinical, traditional approach to a feedback session may make the mistake of failing to recognize how they are overusing psychological terms. That being said, we may need to use psychological terms with some clients. At times clients will see their diagnosis and may have questions about it or how other providers might use it. For instance, a client referred to Dialectical Behavioral Therapy (DBT) may experience professionals discussing borderline personality disorder. For such clients, we define terms and diagnoses, help them understand controversies that exist in the field, and explain the fallibility of any diagnostic nomenclature.

Last, assessors sometimes make the mistake of not adequately checking that clients comprehend the test results and the answers to the AQs. We hold as a goal that clients leave the session with an accurate understanding of the test results, and at times we fail to adequately engage them in the discussion or ask for their impressions. Using our conceptualization of the client, we can largely gauge their capacity to understand what is presented. For example, if we have test data that indicates lower intelligence or a concrete thinking style, we consider that in our preparation and language choices. For such clients, we move carefully through the data, routinely check for their agreement on test results, and seek to confirm their comprehension of what was explained.

Mistakes Connected to not Adequately Attending to the Client's Emotions

As we proceed through the session we move carefully and patiently, which allows us to assess the client's emotional reactions to what is being discussed. We invite their input with questions such as, "How does that test result align with what you know about yourself?" Equally as important is to ask about their emotional reaction to what it is being shared and to attend to their nonverbal communication. In particular, we watch for moments when shame, anxiety, or sadness arise. We may then ask, "How does it feel to recognize this part of yourself and have me describe this to you?" However, we may also use top-down labeling to help the client recognize what is occurring emotionally, for example: "When I shared that you may still be affected by some of your childhood experiences, you appeared to get a little sad. Is that what you were experiencing?" Given that traditional approaches to evaluation have historically stressed a unilateral style of providing information to the client, it is understandable that clinicians may struggle to step out of the "assessor" role and into a "therapist" role. However, attending to the client's emotional response during the Summary/Discussion Session trumps the importance of covering data.

It is likely equally problematic to fail to process the client's emotional experience at the end of the session. Clinicians need to plan accordingly so there is sufficient time for metaprocessing and reflection. Clients typically enter this session with an elevated level of anxiety and can feel increasingly anxious and vulnerable as results are discussed. They then have the emotional challenge of finding closure in the assessment process and saying goodbye. Failing to provide the space and time for the client to process all those emotions at the end may result in clients leaving the Summary/Discussion Session feeling overwhelmed.

One of the more challenging issues that can occur during the Summary/Discussion Session is when a client rejects a finding, and clinicians find themselves fully engaged in the "delicate dance" with clients in such moments. On one hand, pushing an interpretation on a client who is not ready to hear it is never beneficial and is one of the biggest mistakes that can be made in a TA (Finn, 1996). In such moments, we may have failed to recognize how the client is trying to maintain equilibrium and prevent disintegration anxiety (i.e., the test result is Level 3 Information). If we sense that the client is becoming deeply troubled by what is being presented we attend to their emotions, we recognize that the data being shared may be too difficult for the client to assimilate at that moment, and we back off.

However, on the other hand, it is a different type of mistake to prematurely move away from a test interpretation that is rejected, particularly if the information arises from multiple tests. In that situation, we work with the client to see if any part of the finding might be "correct." To start, we attend to the client's emotional reaction, as a flat-out rejection may stir feelings of defensiveness. Next, we attempt to foster curiosity with the client, share the finding using different language, and provide an example. Sometimes this helps clarify the meaning of certain terms. For example, a young woman whose multiple test results showed signs of depression responded to the sharing of that data stating, "But I'm not depressed." The assessor explored her thinking, offering some descriptors of how the depression may manifest. Eventually, the client clarified that some time ago they had been severely depressed, but that was no longer the case. The assessor confirmed that the test results suggested similarly, but there were other results suggesting difficulty enjoying pleasurable activities (i.e., anhedonia). To this assertion, the client said, "Oh, that's definitely me."

A few other tactics can be beneficial when a client rejects a test finding. We may ask the client if any part of what was shared seems accurate (Finn, 1996). If they are able to find some element that resonates, we explore it in order to create a co-labored understanding of the test result and client. We also encourage clients to keep considering the idea and state that we will do likewise. To foreshadow, this connects to the client's letter, where we may again share this test data, but include language that captures the discussion that occurred during the Summary/Discussion Session. For example, we may say, "During our last session I shared with you some test results that suggested that you may have some tendencies towards being too self-focused, which results in you not noticing what others need in the moment. When we talked about this idea you did not think that was occurring but agreed to think about it. I'm including this idea here as part of the answer to this question and hope you'll keep considering this possibility."

Working with a rejected interpretation often requires us to carefully use our clinical skills. We consider both what has occurred with the client to date and what their emotional reaction has been. We watch for defenses that arise and respect that the client may try to protect themselves We also carefully consider the possibility that we made a mistake in the test scoring or interpretation. Simultaneously, we consider the importance of the test finding and the client's related AQ. Ultimately, in the moment we balance our ethical principles of nonmaleficence with integrity, in order to best serve our client.

Mistakes Connected to the Clinician's Emotions

As part of the preparation process, assessors consider how they are feeling about the Summary/Discussion Session, the client, and discussing the results with them. We are mindful of the potential mistake that our emotions may lead us to under report information. This error can be related to our experiences and feelings connected to certain test results. For instance, if we have experienced shame about our own anger, we may have a harder time addressing the topic with a client. It is also possible that we fear sharing certain test results because they may harm the client or make them angry. Clinicians who understand the course and prognosis for more severe psychological disorders such as bipolar disorder or schizophrenia may find that their worry for a young client leads them to fail to share essential information. We may also project our shame about those parts of their personality on the client, assuming receiving such feedback will harm them (Finn, 2005). At other times, we are uncomfortable with the power we have in the role of assessor and we may be equally uncomfortable with potentially being wrong. Finally, when we work with clients who have strong personalities characteristics such as dominance, sadism, or rigidity, we may feel uneasy about navigating the conversation.

The following points can help clinicians ensure that their emotions are not overwhelming. First, we need to establish ourselves as a secure, auxiliary attachment figure for our clients, and we need to act in ways that are in clients' best interest. This means we share test results with understandable language and with respect for the client's ability to discuss certain topics. By labeling their difficulty and opening a conversation about it, we help the client reduce shame related to that topic (Finn, 1996). Additionally, we can remove self-pressure by considering our findings as "tentative" and "meant as a concrete starting point for exploration" (Fischer & Finn, 2014, p. 401). Last, consultation with a trusted colleague is helpful when we feel uneasy about the Summary/Discussion Session because it lowers the likelihood of making the error of avoiding hard topics or not providing meaningful information (Finn, 1996). During consultation, we may ask our colleague to role-play parts of the conversation that could be difficult, so we can practice aloud.

Conclusion

The Summary/Discussions session is often the pinnacle of the client and assessor's experiences during a TA. The client's hard work is celebrated, a new narrative is created, the client is apt to feel hopeful, and a path forward is identified. Given current trends in conducting interactive feedback sessions as part of a traditional evaluation, we expect many clinicians to find some of these ideas familiar and useful. It benefits the client when assessors structure the data with consideration of the Levels of Information. Clients also benefit from the pacing and interpersonal stance of the clinician, as well as their careful consideration of the language used. Those wishing to learn more via case studies may appreciate Finn (2020), which contains useful information about working with a client who has a strong emotional reaction during the session. Equally helpful is Hinrichs (2016), which focuses on organizing Levels of Information, incorporating test responses from the Rorschach, and using non-pathologizing language. This study also mentions the "cup & saucer" analogy, which is commonly used by TA assessors during the Summary/Discussion Session to explain emotion regulation and early attachment experiences and is further elaborated in Finn (2003, 2007).

Clinical Case: Summary/Discussion Session with Emma and Jeanne

We now turn to Hale's case account.

Answering Jeanne's Assessment Questions

I had communicated with Jeanne by phone several times during the assessment to let her know where Emma and I were in the process and the results of some of the tests. I had also shared my thinking and sought her thoughts and reactions. After the AIS, I looked forward to talking about it and offering answers to her original questions ("What am I missing that is impeding therapy with Emma?" "Is there something organic underlying Emma's problems?"). The AIS had clearly laid out the underlying trauma and the likely root of many of Emma's struggles. Jeanne was shocked that Emma had not mentioned anything about her mother's rages in two years of therapy and wondered if she had played a role in this as her therapist. I pointed out to her that this was Emma's defense against the trauma, "Don't think about it, think about nice things, put butterflies all around." Jeanne knew about Emma's tendency to be positive about everything, so this made more sense to her. But I also was careful not to interfere with Jeanne's self-examination, as I had a sense that she too may have unconsciously avoided the underlying traumatic material. We marveled at how much was underneath the surface of Emma's presentation, and we were both sad and struck by how much pain she had been carrying through life. We recognized together that there were indeed a lot of important memories and emotions to explore, and that Emma's inability to discuss this material was impeding Emma's growth in therapy. We talked some about where therapy could go from here and agreed that fleshing out the early trauma and its effects would be a good starting place. I told Jeanne the discussion session would be a good place for all this to come out to Jeanne, since she would be present, and that the session could serve as a springboard to continued therapy. We also discussed Jeanne's second question about whether there was something organic underlying Emma's problems. I discussed with her the results of the cognitive testing and the discrepancies I found, which likely had and were still having an impact in Emma's ability to face some of her everyday life challenges. I also told her I had noticed some clearing of the symptoms of organic issues, but all was not resolved. I could not definitively say that there were not also organic issues (e.g., facial behaviors, rambling talk), but I hoped they would continue to clear.

Jeanne was grateful for the answers. I asked if she wanted any of it in writing, and she said that was unnecessary. We briefly discussed how to handle Tessa's wish to be included in the results and agreed that this was completely up to Emma. After this, we turned to the Summary/Discussion Session. This was the first time I would do such a session with Jeanne, and I wanted her to know what to expect and what role she might play to make it successful. I prepared her by letting her know that it generally works best for the therapist to be a witness to the discussion but also to ask questions that might facilitate her client's understanding. By being a witness to the discussion, she would have the results along with Emma, and could refer to them as helpful in their future work. This made good sense to her. I also pointed out that naturally it would be important to support Emma during the meeting. I added that it was usually helpful for the therapist to take their client's side if the client balked at any finding. She understood and agreed that she would join with Emma and hold any rejected feedback in mind to talk about with Emma later. We ended our discussion with Jeanne expressing appreciation for the wonders of Therapeutic Assessment.

Planning the Summary/Discussion Session with Emma

I felt good knowing that Emma and I had moved some Level 3 material to Level 2, and I was excited to talk with Emma and Jeanne about it. In planning for Emma's Summary/Discussion Session I reconsidered what information would confirm what she already knew (Level 1), what findings she could probably work with as part of her growth from the assessment (Level 2) and what information she would likely reject as not accurately pertaining to her (Level 3). I concluded:

Level 1 Information:

- She had done a lot of work on herself in wrestling with issues that had haunted her for a long time but that had proved difficult to overcome.
- She was very cautious in her life.
- Her caution began when she was a child and had frightening experiences that traumatized her as a little girl.
- She preferred to avoid confrontation.

Level 2 Information:

- She had made a number of adaptations in her early environment that she still used, even though they hindered her life as an adult. Specifically, not appropriately confronting others at work and in her private life, resulted in her feeling unsatisfied and insecure, and to withdraw.
- She sometimes did not see things clearly in her insistence on being positive.
- She did not have ADHD or LD and her early struggles in school might be related as well to her early traumas.

Level 3 Information:

- She might have another level of painful feelings that she was not aware of.
- Her father had also failed her by not protecting her from her mother's rages.
- She has a blend of secure and dismissing attachment tendencies.
- She likely did not have the superior intelligence she hoped for.

Planning the Summary/Discussion Session

Because the answer to a number of Emma's questions revolved around her early trauma, I decided to start with an overview of its effects and then move on to answer each specific question. I wanted to start the session with Level 1 Information but spend most of the time on Level 2. Of the Level 2 topics, the most important was helping her understand the adaptations she made to her early trauma that does not serve her well now. If things went well with Level 2 Information, I might continue with some of the Level 3 Information broached the last session with her, by seeing if she could integrate some understanding of the effects of her trauma on her relationships (i.e., her unusual attachment strategy). I saw this as important information to her questions about relationships, and I wanted to do my best to fully answer that question. If I triggered an adverse reaction, I would do my best to repair by downplaying the testing results as maybe not a fit for her. With all this information, I was a little concerned that Emma might not be able to stay focused and would become overwhelmed. If she did show any signs of this at any point, I would suggest that this was enough for now and schedule another session. I alerted Jeanne to that possibility, and she agreed we could meet another time.

Conducting the Summary/Discussion Session with Emma

It had only been a week since our last session when Jeanne, Emma, and I had the Summary/Discussion Session. Emma came into the office and said hello to Jeanne and quickly started talking.

Emma: I was thinking about the whole thing where I kind of suppressed my conflict. You know that issue with conflict?

Hale: Yes, what we were talking about last time.

Emma: I talked to one of my friends about the whole issue where he made me feel really weird when he belittled me about letting other people cheat me, trying to buy the house from us, and I finally confronted him.

Hale: This is Bob?

Emma: Yes, Bob. I told him, "I just have to tell you right now that I really felt like you were not supporting me when you said that. I miss the person that was there for me when my mom first moved into assisted living and my dad died, and you were so reassuring about how to handle things. But then later you were saying sarcastic and rude things to me like, 'Oh well you know you could just live in the library like some of my friends or whatever, if you don't have a place to live anymore.'"

Hale: So, you confronted him.

Emma: I confronted him. Yes. And he said, "I didn't really mean to come across that way, but I was so concerned that those people were going to flim-flam you and try and flip your house." And I said, "Well, I appreciate that." And he said, "I was trying to scare you into not letting that happen." And I thought, "That is a really weird approach. What are you trying to do, scare me straight?" He could have said it more gently than he did. I mean he was just so irritable and cranky that day and saying really off-the-cuff, strange remarks.

Hale: That was a mean comment. *[Hale aligning with Emma.]* Did you just think that, or were you able to say something?

Emma: I told him that, and he said, "I am really sorry that I hurt you."

Hale: Did he say that?

Emma: Yes, yes he said, "I didn't mean to do that to you. You know, I was irritable that day. My back had hurt, I had pulled my back out. There were a lot of things going on that day." You know I don't love conflict, and I don't love dealing with it, but I can.

Hale: So how did that feel?

Emma: Well, it felt really empowering.

Hale: Did it?

Emma: And it kind of renewed our friendship because for a while there I was avoiding having one with him. We usually get together for brunch or lunch or whatever, and I didn't really want to hang out with him. So, I have reconsidered, and we have renewed our friendship.

Hale: So, it really made a big difference?

Emma: Yes, yes it did.

Hale: Was it hard to bring it up with him?

Emma: Yes, it was a little hard.

Hale: How were you feeling?

Emma: A little anxious about it, but it went smoother than I thought. And we didn't spar, we didn't get in a fight, he didn't say, "Well, you are a big baby and you should deal with it." And he respected my feelings, and that was the most important thing.

Hale: So, it was a very different reaction than you might have gotten if you had stood up for yourself in your family growing up.

Emma: Yes, that's right.

Jeanne: That sounds really important. I think I have a lot to catch up on.

This was an auspicious start to the Summary/Discussion Session. I then thanked Jeanne for joining us and clarified for Emma that Jeanne and I had already talked about the test results. Emma also said she was very grateful to have Jeanne present in our meeting. Jeanne expressed her excitement to be there and acknowledged she knew what hard work had been going on. She said she would be taking some notes, and then Emma wondered if she should too. I reassured her it was not necessary because I would be preparing a letter recapping what we discussed. I wanted to start with being supportive to put Emma more at ease–and did so by expressing my sincere feelings about the work we did.

Hale: I hope you already know this, Emma, but I have to say to start out that I have really enjoyed working with you.

Emma: Thank you, you too, I know.

Hale: It has been quite a pleasure to get to know you and to do this very important work together. I so much appreciate all the effort and energy that you put into it because I know it has been grueling. *[As recommended, Hale starts the session by sharing an appreciation with Emma.]*

Emma: Thank you, yeah, well, I've enjoyed it too. I mean it was grueling, but I know that it's a journey that is worth it, and I think it'll help me be able to gauge how I want the rest of my life to go, and to tweak whatever I need to in my life that isn't working.

Hale: It is so clear that you have worked very hard on yourself through life, from reading and studying about psychology to working through AA to your spiritual growth. Your efforts are very admirable.

Emma: Thank you! I have worked hard.

Hale: I am glad to have had the chance to help with your questions that are still there in spite of all your work.

Emma: Me too. I think we really got some answers. Like you know I have been thinking about when we talked about me not liking the conflict thing last time. There I was telling a story like, "Well, it's women in a picture and the one woman is just posing and the other woman is just drawing a painting of her." Then it hit me, "Oh my god, Emma, that picture was full of anger and conflict." I guess I didn't want to see it because conflict scares me. *[Emma reveals that she has continued to integrate the work of the AIS. Notice how she takes credit for the new insight about conflict, instead of remembering Hale's role; this is exactly what we hope for when collaboration succeeds.]*

Hale: Well, let's talk more about that, but first let me review the questions we want to address today. And then we will spend our time getting to the best answers we can. "Why am I so afraid to commit to anything?" "Why am I so afraid to fail or succeed?" "Why haven't I been able to maintain a long-term position in a career I'm passionate about like teaching?" "Why haven't I been able to have a successful long-term relationship?" And, "Do I have a learning disability or have attention deficit hyperactivity disorder?"

Emma: Yeah, those are the questions.

Hale: So, keep in mind that I am looking to you to help make the best sense of the information we have from the testing and from our work together. It needs to fit you, so help me understand how it does or doesn't. *[Hale invites Emma to confirm or modify the assessment findings to make them fit for her.]*

Emma: Okay.

Hale: So, let's start with your first two questions, "Why am I so afraid to commit to anything?" And, "Why am I so afraid to fail or succeed?" The answers to these two questions are closely related, so I think we can put them together, if that is okay with you. *[Hale even invites Emma to collaborate on how the session is organized.]*

Emma: Sure, that makes sense. They are both about my fears.

Hale: One thing the testing told us is that you are very cautious, especially with your emotions.

Emma: That is very true.

Hale: I wonder if being cautious was one way to avoid conflict and avoid feelings you didn't want to feel.

Emma: Maybe so. Like in my story, I didn't want there to be conflict in the story because then I would just feel horrible, and I would just come to a dead end. I just wanted to make it nice, someone posing for the other woman to draw her. I totally did not see the anger.

Hale: We talked some about the effects your mother's rages had on you at an early age that was absolutely terrifying.

Emma: They were. When my mom was drinking, it was scary. I didn't dare confront her about anything. She was an out-of-control, raging ball of anger. She threw all my toys away one time and didn't even remember it until the next day when I asked her if could get them out of the trash. My sister and I would just go in the basement and watch TV and eat dinner downstairs and wait for her to pass out. You know alcohol can destroy families. I was very young, about 5 when she started drinking heavily, and she got sober when I was nine. That's a really pertinent age.

Hale: Yes, it is. So, when you get that frightened at such an early age it has a big impact on you.

Emma: From a normal mom to like this tyrant where it's like just hurry up and get drunk and leave.

Jeanne: I don't think that's something you and I have spent time on it in our work together. You know I think as we go along this may be an area that would be good to explore more. Help you to share some of what you're feeling. *(As mentioned earlier, Jeanne had been surprised to learn of Emma's mother's rages. Emma had avoided this topic. I was glad that Jeanne explicitly invited Emma to talk about her mother's rage in the therapy.)*

Emma: Yes.

Hale:	And on top of that, when she wasn't drinking, you told me she was a normal mom, so think about the confusion that a young child would have about that.
Emma:	She was a pretty good mom, not as attentive as she could have been, so my sister had to take care of me.
Hale:	So, it seems that your caution comes largely from powerful early experiences with a mother who was sometimes normal and sometimes rageful and terrifying.
Emma:	I can see that. It really hurt me.
Hale:	This early formative experience seems to go a long way to answer your questions about being afraid to succeed or to fail and afraid to commit to anything. It seems these early experiences left you with a lot of reasons to be cautious and uncertain.

We went on to discuss ways she had adapted to her frightening formative context. She talked about being a hypochondriac to get her father's attention, saying "I might have appendicitis, I might have this, I might have that, all to get him to come home, to get him to pay attention. And then I developed a lot of fear of going to bed at night, and I developed OCD at a young age. I started developing that when I was about 10 - and really severe OCD like I was up all night doing a lot of routines." We understood these behaviors as reactions to not feeling safe in the world. Emma offered that they were her attempts to create her own little world that made her feel safe.

Emma:	And sometimes I'd have panic attacks like we would go out to restaurants, and I couldn't eat anything, and my mom would say, "Well, we came here for the restaurant, so we are going to eat." And all of a sudden, my stomach hurt, and I couldn't eat anything. So, then I had to go to the bathroom. Yeah *(voice cracks, begins to tear up.)*
Jeanne:	What's coming up?
Emma:	Just that that was so awful that I felt so anxious that I had to leave the table to calm myself down and go to the bathroom. I mean I had no appetite. I was scared, and I didn't feel good. My mom was already sober by then, but I guess the damage was done.
Hale:	Well, you know that tells us just how much emotion you had to deal with, and it was too much for a young child. While your sister could make sure you were fed, she was not able to help you learn how to manage all those feelings. All you could do was find ways to psychologically survive. And you did.
Emma:	Yes, I had a lot of fear, but I managed. At least I thought I did.
Hale:	The testing shows us that one of the ways that you've learned to manage feelings is to pack them away, try to shut them off, shut them down, think about nice things, think about positive things, and as we expressed it, see butterflies. Keep your mind from going to those less safe places.
Emma:	You know that is very true. I have worked hard to manage my feelings, and I did what I could.
Hale:	I don't think you got a lot of help with your feelings growing up.
Emma:	No *(laughs)*. So sad. My god! Wow!

Hale: And that's a very important thing to do with kids, isn't it? You know that as a teacher.

I reminded her of our discussion after the Wartegg Drawing Completion Test (WDCT; Wartegg, 1953) about her blocked aggressive energy.

Hale: What you drew suggested that you tend to not put your aggressive energy out there, but rather hold it in and even turn it toward yourself. You beat yourself up rather than to appropriately express anger toward others. We talked about how important good anger and appropriate confrontation can be. I loved that you confronted Bob and am so happy it rejuvenated your friendship. How important that is!

Emma and I discussed how keeping all her aggressive energy inside while feeling it strongly ultimately did not serve her well. I agreed that shutting difficult feelings down when she was a child was a reasonable solution; she really had no other options. I suggested she couldn't go to her father because he wasn't available, and Emma agreed, which I hoped would open a door to discussing her father's role more in future therapy. And we agreed she wouldn't risk going to her mother. I then reminded her about the man belittling the older man in the grocery store. We had agreed that she only saw two options: Walking away to the other side of the grocery store to avoid it or seeing red and verbally blasting the man who was so mean. We discussed continuing to develop a wider repertoire of responses to her angry feelings. Jeanne agreed this would be an important area to work on.

We then segued into Emma's next question about not having been able to have a successful long-term relationship. I asked if she had any thoughts about what might have played a role in her not having a successful, long-term relationship. She said she was determined not to have an angry or mean relationship.

Emma: I mean that's why I'm probably not married. *(Reaches for a tissue.)* That's probably why I never got in a long-term relationship because inside it's like, "You're not going to mess with me. You're not going to hurt me. You're not going to abandon me. You're not going to do anything bad to me. You're not going to scream at me. You're not going to belittle me. You're not going to tell me I'm stupid, dumb, ugly, fat, or otherwise."

Hale: You were determined.

Emma: I was, and I'm very guarded. I know I am very guarded. I can see now that I really wasn't very open to one. But I thought I was.

Hale: So, you wanted a long-term relationship, and you worked at it, but something in you got in the way, something blocked your relationships from working out. I wonder how your experience with your friend Bob fits into the picture?

Emma: When he told me that if someone cheated me out of my house, I could just sleep with his homeless friends at the library, at first, I just stopped talking to him or seeing him, but a few weeks ago with your help, I told him I was hurt by what he said, and he apologized!

Hale: And it rekindled your relationship!

Emma made more connections and mentioned not confronting her boyfriend for not helping her with dinner when she was exhausted from work. We saw how holding her angry feelings inside might interfere with a loving relationship—and even set her up for bad relationships with people who might take advantage of her, if she didn't set limits. I asked her if she could think of any other instances when she held her anger inside. We discussed several times she had told me about not confronting people when she was seething inside. We agreed that under the surface there was a lot going on that others did not see. This discussion was successful in engaging Emma in honest and painful conversations about her questions. I then moved to talk about the results of the AAP.

Hale: I want to go back to your statement earlier about feeling sure you were open to a relationship. The results of the Adult Attachment Projective show you have the potential for healthy secure relationships, which is good news, but it also shows that when you are under relationship stress, your defenses rise to protect you and prevent you from being close, and you distance yourself from the other person in an effort to protect yourself from disappointment. That may be another way you adapted to your early environment in which you had a very caring father who had the ability to make you feel secure, but he was not always there, especially at those times you needed him most. Then you and Tessa were on your own to protect yourself from your mother who was inconsistent and at times rageful.

Emma: That is interesting information. But what does that mean to me now? I think my attachments to other people are pretty healthy. When I bond with other people, I think it's pretty healthy.

Hale: It certainly may be, but it might be good to pay attention to the tendencies when under relationship stress to not feel close, to distance yourself, to not expect that others will be nurturing, or to find ways to be dissatisfied with your partner, or maybe even subconsciously choosing someone who will ultimately disappoint you so you don't have to risk being hurt.

Emma: Wow! That is kind of spooky. Do you think I do that? *[Emma signals that what Hale has said is Level 3 Information.]*

Hale: It is just a possibility from that one test. I don't think tests say the truth with a capital T, sometimes they can be wrong, but maybe this might be something to keep in mind and watch in yourself. *[Hale attempts a repair by softening what he said.]*

Emma: Right, I will think about it… okay. *[Emma looks at ease again and signals that the repair has worked.]*

Hale: This leads us to the question "Do I have a learning disability or attention deficit hyperactivity disorder?"

I started the discussion with the ADHD rating scales that she and her sister had completed. I told Emma there were no elevations indicating ADHD that could not also be explained by her anxiety. She seemed somewhat surprised, but I had the sense this was Level 2 rather than Level 3 information for her. I said that on the forms Tessa had filled out as she remembered Emma at that age of 6 or 7, there was not an indication of ADHD, but there were significant elevations on the things we had been talking about: Anxiety, Somatization, Depression, and Internalizing

Problems. Emma was not surprised at those elevations, and we discussed that the hyperactivity she experienced might have been the result of other things, like her trauma.

Then I spoke about the Wechsler Adult Intelligence Scale-Fourth Edition (WAIS-IV; Wechsler, 2008) results. I reviewed with Emma from our previous discussions how all the subtests she took contributed to one of five factors: Verbal ability, visual-spatial ability, non-verbal reasoning, short-term memory, and speed of processing information. (I chose to present the Keith five-factor model for the WAIS-IV because it more clearly identified her strengths and weaknesses.) I explained to her that the most important part of the test is the relative elevations of the various types of intelligence. I also told her that scores can be affected by a number of factors other than intelligence, like anxiety, and referred back to how upset she became during the Block Design subtest and that, once she had time to calm herself, she did better on the test. She said she understood this.

I pointed out to her that the most notable result from the WAIS-IV was that her score on verbal abilities was considerably higher than the other four areas and that her visual-spatial score was the lowest. She confirmed that she always excelled in reading comprehension and language and was always in Advanced Placement classes in English and History. She said she had some trouble in math and wondered why her math was so much different from her "phenomenal verbal ability."

I offered that one possibility other than emotional interference could be that her early school years were tough times for her and perhaps this caused her to miss some early basics. In math, it is particularly difficult to catch up with those basics. She understood this and went on to say that her memory had also been excellent in school, so the math score being lower was confusing to her. I explained that performance on working memory and processing speed tasks was particularly susceptible to emotions. Emma summarized with, "So what you are saying then is that I have the potential to raise all my scores if I can just get in touch with my emotions." I clarified that I was saying that some of her scores might be higher if her emotions did not trip her up, but also that there likely were some true differences between her verbal ability and visual-spatial ability. I pointed out that having a big discrepancy between cognitive abilities can be confusing to a child. It can make a person feel uncertain about their real abilities—especially with children who feel competent in one area but don't feel competent in other areas. That brought up another factor contributing to uncertainty about herself, self-doubt.

Emma:　Well, you also mentioned that my potential is higher than what I give myself credit for. like I limit myself a lot. I don't understand how that works.

Hale:　I think it's true you haven't had all your energy available. And it seems like the early trauma that you had set in play a negative view of yourself that feeds on itself as time goes on. I think we saw several times through the testing that you let your emotions, doubts, the things that you keep inside get in the way of you functioning to your full potential

Emma:　*(laughing)* I'm not like laughing out of nervousness. I feel relieved that there's hope for me. I'm hearing you say that I have a lot of potential; I just don't realize it yet because my emotions have become such big obstacles, that I make a mountain out of a molehill.

Jeanne: It sounds like you end up feeling very overwhelmed and don't identify what you are feeling. I think if we work on that piece, you can learn to modulate your feelings, so you don't get to the place of feeling overwhelmed.

Emma had many questions about how her cognitive ability worked and what to do about it. We also discussed how her emotions tripped her up academically and in relationships. Emma came to the conclusion that she does indeed bottle things up, without even realizing it. We agreed that she doesn't have to do that anymore.

Emma: Both of you just clarified things and let me clarify too, but what does it really mean for my life, what does that mean for my future?
Hale: It means that there is a lot of hope for you and that you can have a better life than you have now—with more happiness at work and better close relationships.
Emma: Thanks. That helps a lot.
Jeanne: And this is something we can work on in our sessions together.

I knew that Emma probably wanted to talk more about her next steps, but we were out of time, and I also felt that she had taken in a lot of difficult information. I decided to close the session, even though we didn't have time for much meta-processing, as I knew Emma had Jeanne to support her.

Hale: So, we're actually out of time. I'm sorry, because I know there is so much more we can talk about. Emma, are you OK with ending?
Emma: Yes. I'm feeling a bit overwhelmed. I hope I can remember all this!
Hale: The next step for me is to write this down and get it to you. That will really help you, I think.

We then discussed the Follow-up Session in two or three months, in which we could see how things were going for her, clarify any questions about the assessment findings, or address additional questions she might have. I also let Emma know that if she had burning questions in the meantime, she could contact me directly, or have Jeanne contact me.

Hale: I look forward to seeing you then.
Emma: That sounds good. I look forward to that too. I feel good about some of this, and about some of it I feel a little sad.
Jeanne: Do you want to talk a little more with me now?
Emma: Yes, I would. But thank you, Hale. I really appreciate it. I enjoyed our journey and learning about myself. So, we will be in touch soon, in a couple or three months.

I left Emma and Jeanne to process the session more together.

Reflections on the Summary Discussion Session with Emma

I was pleased with how the Summary/Discussion Session went. I liked the exciting beginning with Emma reporting her success in confronting her friend. I thought

Jeanne had done a good job listening and contributing. And most of all I was pleased with Emma. She had been alert and asked good questions, and she seemed to non-defensively take in much of the information. I felt like we had consolidated our work together nicely. I realized I had stepped into Level 3 Information when I talked about the things she might notice in her relationships, but we had successfully repaired her unease, while planting a seed for future use in therapy. I was a little surprised at Emma's dwelling on the cognitive testing as she did and her efforts to interpret what I said as more favorable than what I had said. It made me realize just how important intelligence had been for her. I was glad to have touched on the spiral of concern about herself that made her hypersensitive to there being something wrong with her, which worked to fuel her self-doubt. I was not sure how to feel about not finding an opening to test the waters about her father's contribution to her struggles, having abandoned her when her mother was in rages. I talked with Jeanne later about this, and she wondered if that was necessary in order for Emma to thrive. I offered that it might be necessary to take him off the pedestal in order for Emma to ultimately have a good intimate relationship with a man. But all in all, I was happy and looked forward to the Follow-up Session.

References

American Psychological Association. (2017). *Ethical principles of psychologists and code of conduct* (2002, amended effective June 1, 2010, and January 1, 2017). www.apa.org/ethics/code.

Aschieri, F. (2012). Epistemological and ethical challenges in standardized testing and collaborative assessment. *Journal of Humanistic Psychology, 52*(3), 350–368.

Aschieri, F., Fantini, F., & Smith, J. D. (2016). Collaborative/Therapeutic Assessment: Procedures to enhance client outcomes. In S. F. Maltzman (Ed.), *Oxford handbook of treatment processes and outcomes in counseling psychology* (pp. 541–569). Oxford University Press.

Bruhn, A. R. (1992). The Early Memories Procedure: A projective test of autobiographical memory (Part I). *Journal of Personality Assessment, 58*, 1–15.

Butcher, J. N. (1990). *MMPI-2 in psychological treatment.* Oxford University Press.

Chudzik, L. (2016). Therapeutic Assessment of a violent criminal offender: Managing the cultural narrative of evil. *Journal of Personality Assessment, 98*(6), 585–589.

Finn, S. E. (1996). *Manual for using the MMPI-2 as a therapeutic intervention.* University of Minnesota Press.

Finn, S. E. (2003). Therapeutic Assessment of a man with "ADD." *Journal of Personality Assessment, 80*(2), 115–129.

Finn, S. E. (2005). How psychological assessment taught me compassion and firmness. *Journal of Personality Assessment, 84*(1), 27–30.

Finn, S. E. (2007). *In our clients' shoes: Theory and techniques of Therapeutic Assessment.* Taylor and Francis.

Finn, S. E. (2011). Use of the Adult Attachment Projective Picture System (AAP) in the middle of a long-term psychotherapy. *Journal of Personality Assessment, 93*(5), 427–433. doi: 10.1080/00223891.2011.595744

Finn, S. E. (2020). Communicating the assessment findings to Madeline G. In C. J. Hopwood & Mark H. Waugh (Eds.), *Personality assessment paradigms and methods. A collaborative reassessment of Madeline G* (pp. 183–223). Routledge.

Finn, S. E., & Tonsager, M. E. (1992). Therapeutic effects of providing MMPI-2 test feedback to college students awaiting therapy. *Psychological Assessment, 4*(3), 278–287.

Finn, S. E., & Tonsager, M. E. (1997). Information-gathering and therapeutic models of assessment: Complementary paradigms. *Psychological Assessment, 9*(4), 374–385.

Fischer, C. (1970). The testee as co-evaluator. *Journal of Counseling Psychology, 17*, 70–76.

Fischer, C. (1985/1994). *Individualizing psychological assessment.* Lawrence Erlbaum & Associates.

Fischer, C. T., & Finn, S. E. (2014). Developing the life meaning of psychological test data: Collaborative and therapeutic approaches. In Archer, R. P., & Smith. S. R. (Eds.), *Personality assessment, 2nd edition* (pp. 401–431). Routledge.

Fonagy, P., Luyten, P., Allison, E., & Campbell, C. (2017). What we have changed our minds about: What we have changed our minds about: Part 2. Borderline personality disorder, epistemic trust and the developmental significance of social communication. *Borderline Personality Disorder and Emotion Dysregulation, 4*(9). doi: 10.1186/s40479-017-0062-8.

George, C., & West, M. L. (2012). *The Adult Attachment Projective Picture System. Attachment theory and assessment in adults.* Guilford Press.

Gomez, E., & Guerrero, B. (2016). Getting to the heart of the matter. In B. Mercer, T. Fong & E. Rosenblatt (Eds.), *Assessing children in the urban community* (pp. 159–164). Routledge.

Groth-Marnat, G., & Wright, J. A. (2016). *Handbook of psychological assessment.* John Wiley & Sons, Inc.

Hinrichs, J. (2016). Inpatient Therapeutic Assessment with narcissistic personality disorder. *Journal of Personality Assessment, 98*(2), 111–123.

Kamphuis, J. H., & Finn, S. E. (2019). Therapeutic Assessment in personality disorder: Toward the restoration of epistemic trust. *Journal of Personality Assessment, 101*(6), 662–674.

Klopfer, B., & Kelley D. M. (1946). *The Rorschach technique.* World Book Company.

Kohut, H. (1977). *The Restoration of the self.* International Universities Press.

Kohut, H. (1984). *How does analysis cure?* The University of Chicago Press.

Millon, T., Grossman, S., & Millon, C. (2015). *MCMI-IV: Millon Clinical Multiaxial Inventory-IV—Manual.* NCS Pearson.

Morey, L. C. (1991). *Professional manual for the Personality Assessment Inventory.* Psychological Assessment Resources.

Murray, H. A. (1943). *Thematic Apperception Test Manual.* Harvard University Press. Press.

Rorschach, H. (1942). *Psychodiagnostics.* Grune and Stratton.

Schroeder, D. G., Hahn, E. D., Finn, S. E., & Swann, W. B. Jr. (1993, June). *Personality feedback has more impact when mildly discrepant from self views.* Paper presented at the fifth annual convention of the American Psychological Society.

Smith, T. P. (2002, September). Therapeutic Assessment with a client who couldn't reveal her questions. In S. E. Finn (Chair), *Recent advances in Therapeutic Assessment. Symposium presented at the XVII International Congress on the Rorschach and Projective Methods,* Rome, Italy.

Smith, J. D., & Finn, S. E. (2014). Therapeutic presentation of multimethod assessment results: Empirically supported guiding framework and case example. In C. J. Hopwood & R. F. Bornstein (Eds.), *Multimethod clinical assessment of personality and psychopathology* (pp. 403–425). Guilford Press.

Smith, J., & George, C. (2012). Therapeutic Assessment case study: Treatment of a woman diagnosed with metastatic cancer and attachment trauma. *Journal of Personality Assessment, 94*(4), 331–344.

Swann, W. B. (1997). The trouble with change: Self-verification and allegiance to the self. *Psychological Science, 8*, 177–180.

Wartegg, E. (1953). *Schichtdiagnostik-Der Zeichentest* (WZT) [Differential diagnostics-The Drawing test.] Verlag für Psychologie.

Wechsler, D. (2008). *Wechsler Adult Intelligence Scale–Fourth edition (WAIS-IV).* Pearson.

Wright, J. A. (2011). *Conducting psychological assessment. A guide for practitioners.* John Wiley & Sons, Inc.

10 Written Feedback

Traditional Reports in Psychological Assessment and how they Differ from TA Letters

Over the time that psychological testing has been conducted, the style and structure of the final written document have evolved. Early in the history of testing, reports did not have a standardized format and were written to help treating psychiatrists and other referral sources such as social workers make decisions related to the patient (Tallent, 1993). In this early era of testing, it was considered unethical for patients to read the final document, as it was believed that the information contained therein would be damaging to them (Klopfer & Kelley, 1946). Some psychologists challenged the ethics of this form of assessment and of not providing the client feedback in oral and written forms (Brown, 1972). These early critiques contributed to changes in the assessment process and the final report. Eventually, reports aligned with the medical model of documentation and were still largely written for other professionals. The report captured in professional language the answers to the referring professional's (RP) questions and documented the encounter as required by workplace policies, state rules and law, and insurance companies. Eventually, it was recognized that the client may read the report and, in the years before and after the APA adopted Principle 9.10 to its code of ethics (Explaining Assessment Results, American Psychological Association, 2017), psychologists were advised to write using language the client would understand.

In the current era, psychological reports written following the traditional information-gathering model of testing align with hypothesis testing and a deductive analysis of data (Wright, 2011). Testing is conducted for a few primary reasons (e.g., to identify treatment, academic or vocational recommendations; Wright et al., 2017). The reasons for referral inform the hypothesis (e.g., "Does this client have bipolar disorder?"), and as the clinician conducts the evaluation, other hypotheses are formed ("Does this client have bipolar disorder, borderline personality disorder, or both?"). The test results, interview data, and behavioral observations comprise the final report, with a summary that proves or disapproves the hypotheses, often resulting in a diagnosis or other legal or psycho-legal decisions (e.g., "This client is competent to stand trial"). Given these purposes, the primary readers of the report are often mental health professionals, school personnel, and those working in social services or legal contexts.

Various publications provide guidance on writing traditional reports, including guidelines for the topics and sections included (Bagby & Solomon-Krakus, 2020; Groth-Marnat & Wright, 2016; Schneider, et al., 2018; Wright, 2011; Zuckerman, 2019). Common elements

DOI: 10.4324/9780429202797-12

Table 10.1 Common Sections of Reports Conducted Following the Information-Gathering Model of Psychological Assessment

- Identifying Information.
- Referral Source and Question.
- Test Administered and Other Sources of Information.
- Presenting Problem and Symptoms.
- Psychosocial History.
- Mental Status and Behavioral Observations.
- Clinical Interview.
- Case Formulation or Summary.
- Diagnostic Impressions.
- Recommendations.
- Appendix with Test Results.

of a traditional report are presented in Table 10.1 and form the sections of such reports. Since feedback became an ethical requirement in 1992, there has been greater emphasis on reports that are tailored to the client (Groth-Marnat & Wright, 2016). Psychologists are now encouraged to write in terms of the client and not just document test results, and graduate programs are encouraged to train students "to write integrative assessment reports that are comprehensive, useful, and appropriate to the audience" (Wright et al., 2020, p. 5).

Having laid out the components of a traditional report, we turn to how written communication at the end of a TA differs. First, the primary purposes of the document are to capture the client's experience, answers to their Assessment Questions (AQs), and ideally, to further the client's growth. A traditional report may lead to change, but that is not the primary goal, as conclusions are drawn followed by prescriptions for change (e.g., "Given this client qualifies for a diagnosis of PTSD, trauma-informed treatment would be best"). Second, we consider the client the primary audience for the final written communication following a TA, and this is particularly true for the TA letter. If the client describes the document as helpful, that outweighs others' opinions. Third, the AQs form the body of a TA letter and are often included as part of a Therapeutic Psychological Report, given their importance to the client. Last, we get "in our client's shoes" when writing the final document, and use our empathy to make choices about language, style, length, and tone. These differences contribute to a personalized document that clients find highly valuable as it helps them remember the experience and implement new learnings (Kamphuis & Finn, 2019).

The Therapeutic Assessment (TA) Letter

The TA letter is often a polished version of the notes that guided the assessor during the Summary/Discussion Session. It holds the same relational tone of that session and includes the client's comments and reactions to the assessment findings discussed orally. It is similar to a personal letter and more than a summary of facts, in that it extends the collaborative interaction and "discusses both meaning and personal impact of the data and process" (Allyn, 2012, p. 175). By continuing the therapeutic goals of the assessment, it contributes to continued self-awareness and personal enhancement for the client (Fischer, 2011 cited in Allyn, 2012; Lance & Krishnamurthy, 2003).

We continue to hold the TA values in mind when writing to the client, and those inform the principles and goals of the final document. We write in terms of shared experiences, using the client's words and referring to context, and our collaboration with the client is evident. Specific examples and language from the Extended Inquiries (EIs), Assessment Intervention Session (AIS), and Summary/Discussion Session are included. We show respect to the client by deferring to their expertise on their lives, and we are humble about test results, recognizing we can only understand parts of a client's experience. Thus, we do not convey our findings and shared experiences as absolutes. Furthermore, we are not focused on tests or scores, but rather on what was figured out together. This does not mean nomothetic test results are not presented, but we use that data judiciously as a source of authority to make specific points. The documents are jargon-free and easy for the client to read, and ideally leave them feeling as if they had another conversation with the assessor. We offer specific suggestions, and we continue the narrative that we have been co-creating with the client, which leaves them feeling heard and held and helps them see a path forward. In this way, the document serves as a map, in that we "believe it can help the person get from one place to another in life" (Allyn, 2012 p. 179). Collectively, these principles and goals continue our mentalization of the client and contribute to further growth.

TA Letter Outline and Components

As described in the previous chapter, there are three methods for organizing the data for the Summary/Discussion Session and that structure is typically carried over in the TA letter (Table 10.2). Our focus will first be on the primary method of directly answering the client's AQs, and Table 10.3 has the subheadings that organize the letter with brief descriptions that are elaborated later in this chapter. While these three methods will work for most clients, what is best is dictated by the clinician's understanding of the client. Thus, we encourage assessors to use these ideas to organize data and then adjust to best serve their clients.

Table 10.2 Primary Methods for Organizing Information for the Summary/Discussion Session and the TA Letter

1 Order the AQs from Level 1 to Level 3 Information and answer each AQ by weaving together test results, observations, conversations, and suggestions.
2 Briefly provide an overarching summary of the test results and then answer the AQs in order from Level 1 to Level 3 Information.
3 Give an in-depth review of the various tests, then answer the AQs in order from Level 1 to Level 3 Information.

Table 10.3 Subheadings and Descriptions of Components of a TA Letter

Subheadings	Brief Description
Opportunities for Assessment	Following a salutation that sets the stage for the rest of the letter, the tests and other sources of data that informed the process are listed and described in paragraph form. The date of administration is included, and a brief description of the test brings the experience back to the client's mind.
Overview of Test Results and Answers to Assessment Questions (AQs)	A brief overview of the test results or a test-by-test summary may precede the client's AQs, followed by the answers. Other times this core part of the letter is solely the AQs and answers.
Suggestions	Ideas for viable next steps the client may consider to improve their life.
Closing	We close the letter and share what the assessor learned from the assessment and remind the client about the Follow-up Session.
Test Scores Appendix	Presentation of tests and test scores.

Salutation

The TA letter begins like other letters, with the date at the top and a salutation such as "Dear [client's first name]." An introductory paragraph follows and orients the client to the letter. It is common to begin with a statement such as, "This letter provides answers to your questions, with things we figured out together and some suggestions." For letters that follow one of the other two methods, we may write, "This letter first summarizes your test results, followed by answers to your questions and suggestions to consider." This first statement will vary depending on the structure of the letter but what is written provides the client a sense of what is to follow.

Following the opening sentence, we include a few sentences connected to our experience with the client. As described in Chapter 9, at the beginning of the Summary/Discussion Session we share an appreciation with the client and at the end, some way we were touched by our experience with them. In this first paragraph, we restate what was shared with as much elaboration as makes sense. We may write, "I want to again commend you for participating in all of the tests and discussions we had. I was touched by your ability to examine your life and appreciated your motivation to improve your relationships." The goal of this part of the introductory paragraph is to reaffirm that the client has done good work and that we were moved by our time with them. The introductory paragraph may end with a statement about our hope for the client, such as, "I hope you find what I've written here to be useful." This may also be a place to mention who else has received the letter. "As we agreed, I also sent a copy of this letter to your individual therapist."

Opportunities for Assessment

In this section, we name the various sources of data that informed the TA and letter. Typically, this includes the full name and acronym of each psychological test and the date of administration. Other sources of information, such as records reviewed and collateral information, are included. We recommend including descriptions of each test the first time it is mentioned in the letter that briefly reminds the client of each test and brings back the test-taking experience. Examples of these types of statements are found in Table 10.4.

The remainder of the letter usually follows the same structure that was used in the Summary/Discussion Session (Table 10.2). Hence, if the assessor decided to give the client an in-depth review of the various tests, and then answer the AQs ordered from Level 1 to Level 3, typically the feedback letter will have the same format. Occasionally the assessor may change the format of the letter if the earlier approach was not useful when giving oral feedback.

In this chapter, we highlight the sections of a TA Letter that follows a Summary/Discussion Session in which the assessor ordered the AQs from Level 1 to Level 3 and answered each AQ weaving together test results, observations, conversations, and suggestions.

Table 10.4 Examples of Sentences that Describe Tests as Part of the Opportunities for Assessment Section

Type of psychological test	Descriptive statement
Self-report measures such as the MMPI-3 or MCMI-IV.	You took two true/false tests (MMPI-3 & MCMI-IV) on the computer, and they helped us understand your personality and any difficulties you may be experiencing.
Performance-based measures such as the Rorschach or Wartegg Drawing Completion Test (WDCT).	I had you complete two different personality tests that help us understand parts of your personality that you may have less awareness of. For the Rorschach, you identified what you saw for different inkblots and during the Wartegg you drew pictures in eight boxes.
Storytelling tests such as the Thematic Apperception Test (TAT).	I had you create stories based on various pictures as part of the TAT, and that test helped us understand your emotional life, relational style, and how you typically solve problems.
Cognitive tests such as the Wechsler Scales.	We completed the WAIS-IV together to understand your cognitive abilities, and I had you complete various tasks, such as putting blocks together to copy a picture.
Continuous performance tests such as the Tests of Variables of Attention (TOVA).	The TOVA was that test you took on the computer, and you were asked to press a button for certain images. It helped us understand your ability to sustain your attention.
Self and collateral report measures such as the Conners' Adult ADHD Rating Scales (CAARS).	To gather data about ADHD symptoms, both you and your husband completed the CAARS on-line.

Core of the Letter

Method 1 for Organizing the Data: Answers to AQs

When we use the first method shown in Table 10.2 to organize the data, this section of the letter has a subheading such as "Answers to Your Questions" or "Questions for Assessment." Customary practice is to bold the AQ so that it stands out and orients the reader, as the AQs are ostensive cues that help the client engage epistemic trust (ET) to take in the information presented (Kamphuis & Finn, 2019). Strategies for writing answers are presented later in this chapter.

As described in the Summary/Discussion Session chapter, there is a sorting and reorganizing of AQs to maximize the client's assimilation of new information. The client's AQs were re-ordered and then discussed moving from Level 1 to Level 3 during the Summary/Discussion Session, and typically the letter has the same structure and sequence, unless we discovered that our ideas about levels of information were inaccurate. Similarly, questions that were grouped together given their common theme (e.g., questions about relationships) are grouped together in the letter. Depending on the number of questions, subheadings can help organize the information. For example, questions may be grouped under a subheading such as "Questions Related to your Emotional Life" or "Relationship Questions."

Method 2 and 3 for Organizing the Data: Summary of Results or Test-by-test Summary

For TA letters that are organized under method two or three (Table 10.2), in-between the Opportunities for Assessment and Answers to the AQs sections, we include another section. For method two, this may be entitled "Overview of Test Results," and we provide a broad overview of the tests results we shared during the Summary/Discussion Session. For method three, we have a section entitled "Test Results" or "Specific Test Results," and we review the relevant tests that we focused on during that discussion. As described in Chapter 9, using frameworks for integrating data that is part of a multimethod assessment process will aid in this section as well (e.g., Wright, 2011).

For methods two and three, we ensure the language used follows the same principles and goals. We also explain the section in a way that orients the client to that section. For method two we may write, "Just like I shared during our last meeting, I'm going to first summarize the test results before answering your questions." For method three we may write, "I want to start by sharing the results of the Rorschach. As you may recall, during our last meeting we reviewed those test results, because they really helped us understand what has been contributing to you feeling so stuck with anxiety."

Suggestions

This section of a TA letter is like the Recommendations sections of a traditional evaluation with some differences. Importantly, we use the term "Suggestions" and not "Recommendations" to raise client ET, as we respect the client's ability to make decisions about what ideas they will choose to implement following a TA (Kamphuis & Finn, 2019). Aligning with best practices, we make suggestions that are specific and comprehensive (Armengol et al., 2001; Brenner, 2003; Groth-Marnat & Wright, 2016) and that the client can viably use (Fischer, 1985/1994). We think broadly about what might be helpful to clients for living their best life and meeting their goals. We commonly include self-help suggestions related to books, podcasts, or movies that may be impactful. Additionally, we make suggestions for various aspects of a client's life such as occupational counseling, and academic accommodations.

We also typically have suggestions related to mental health treatment, and ideas for therapy are specific and based on what we have discovered through testing and conversations. Often, the lens of psychotherapy is sharpened following a TA. A client who was previously receiving therapy to address depression may now understand how part of their low mood is connected to unresolved grief (previously Level 2–3 Information), given what the tests revealed. This leads to a suggestion such as, "As I mentioned in the answer to your question about treating depression, some of what is occurring is unresolved loss. We talked how your dad worked three jobs, and as a child, you were left longing for a greater connection with him. That loss and others are worth exploring with your therapist to further grieve those experiences."

Assessors can either connect the next steps of treatment as part of an answer to an AQ or include those ideas the Suggestions section or both. In traditional reports, it is common to be general in therapy recommendations out of respect for the treating professionals. We also hold that respect but given our collaboration with RPs during the TA, we have already discussed ideas about treatment and thus can speak with greater specificity about the focus of therapy than might be the case in a traditional report.

It is also common to have suggestions related to other mental health interventions, and the test data helps clients take steps towards other forms of treatment that they previously declined. For example, when clients see high elevations on test scales measuring anxiety and depression, they may realize that their mental health issues require greater care. A referral for a psychiatric evaluation may be called for, but here again, the client's input helps with the wording of that suggestion. For instance, "As I shared with you, I think your anxiety could be further treated with medications. I appreciated what you said about how trying medications would not be an easy step for you given how handling problems on your own was really valued when you grew up. However, I share this suggestion again and hope you and your therapist will continue to discuss the possibility of a medication evaluation." Marital or family therapy may be other interventions suggested, and we make sure that we help the client understand how best to organize and implement such interventions. It is not beneficial to re-commend individual, couple, and family therapy, even when called for, without consideration of which should be prioritized and how to ensure the client is not overwhelmed with appointments. In most cases, these recommendations have been already discussed with the client during the Summary/Discussion Session, which makes it easier for assessors to emphasize the most relevant type of interventions.

Closing

We end the letter coming full circle with a closing paragraph that mirrors elements of the client's good work and, when we authentically feel it, we share something we have learned from the client. In general, we report what we already shared orally with the client during the Summary/Discussion Session (see Chapter 9). Importantly, we remind the client that a Follow-up Session has been scheduled or can be arranged, during which their reactions and questions to the letter can be discussed (see Chapter 11). We may write, "As I mentioned, I hope we meet for a Follow-up Session in the coming weeks to discuss this letter. That would also be an opportunity to further refine any of these ideas or explore new ones given what has occurred since we last met."

Finally, we ask the client to fill out the Assessment Questionnaire[1] (AQ; Finn at al., 2000) which we send along with the letter, and to return it to us or to bring it to the Follow-up Session. The AQ is an outcome measure that provides feedback about the client's experience of and satisfaction with the TA. We let the client know that completing this form would be helpful to us both in understanding their experience and also for honing our skills. The closing of the letter ends with our signature.

Appendix of Test Scores

An appendix with test scores is a useful way to capture test data that may be necessary to meet documentation standards or for other professionals to review. When we in-clude such an appendix, it is common to have an introductory statement such as, "The following test scores may be useful to other professional who work with you." Next, test scores are listed in a format like a traditional psychological report. While not harmful to include in any letter, some clients may not need such an appendix, as might be the case for a client who has only been working with an individual therapist who is not familiar with psychological testing.

Letter Style, Language, and Length

Our letter captures the conversations that occurred during the Summary/Discussion Session, and we integrate various parts of the TA: Test results, client's language and experience, our shared experience and psychoeducation. What follows is an example of an answer to an AQ with various elements labeled.

> Client's AQ: Why do I never get angry, and should I get angry more often?

> Of all your questions, it seemed this was the most important to you and where you learned the most *(shared experience)*. The short answer is that there are good reasons you don't experience anger, and it would be helpful to you if you could express those feelings more routinely *(psychoeducation)*. First, you may recall when we discussed the results of the self-report tests *(shared experience)*, they captured how difficult anger can be for you *(test results)*. I could see how that would be the case *(validation of the client's experience)*, given what you shared about what happened when you were angry with your parents, and how they would dismiss your feelings *(client report)*. It really seemed that everyone in your family struggled with anger and conflict *(validation of the client's experience)*, and as we discussed, you experienced a lot of shame when you got angry *(combination of test results and shared experience)*.

> However, I also witnessed what you're capable of when it comes to anger during that session when you created stories for the different pictures, and we kept experimenting with ways the characters could be more assertive *(the shared experience during the AIS with a storytelling test)*. Your final story for the last card was impressive! *(client validation)*. To remind you, for the last story you had a female character say to the other character, "It's not ok for you to shush me when I'm telling you I'm angry." When I asked you what it was like to say that, you said, "It felt good and it's really not that crazy of a thing to say." Exactly! *(shared experience with client validation)*. I think we both realized during that session that you can assert yourself and that it's not as scary as you thought it would be.

The answer continues with psychoeducation about how being more assertive could be difficult, but also beneficial to the client's relationships.

The style and language in the written document align with our goal of "getting in our client's shoes" to ensure what is communicated helps the client. We consider the formality of language and the overall warmth (Allyn, 2012). If the client is a highly educated professional with strong verbal abilities who can well integrate information, then the language and tone will be professional with complex concepts. In contrast, if the client is a young adult who has learning difficulties and is easily overwhelmed, then the language may be more simplistic. For most clients, we want to write a document that has a "professional but also personal and warm tone as culturally appropriate"

(Kamphuis & Finn, 2019, p. 2). This style of writing fosters ET as it allows us to demonstrate our expertise while valuing and respecting the client.

As related to style, it is helpful to consider the TA letter as capturing the conversation that occurred during the Summary/Discussion Session. The AQs are answered and the client is addressed directly and referred to in the second person, while the evaluator and moments of collaboration are in the first person. We may use contractions and punctuation marks–such as exclamation points–rarely seen in traditional reports. Our language is not test-focused; rather we describe the person and their behaviors and experience. We contextualize and convey the client's experience in terms of action, and the client's contribution is clear. In this way, the test results come to life and align with Fischer's (1998) axiom: "If we can't describe our findings in terms of the client's everyday life, then literally we don't yet know 'what in the world' we're talking about" (p. 1).

The length of the TA letter aligns with common practices for psychological assessment, and many letters are between eight and twelve pages. Given the focus on capturing the most salient points for the client and our understanding of the client's capacity to take in information, some letters may be shorter or longer. We ensure the important points are not lost in a lengthy letter, in which more information is presented than is useful for the client.

It is beyond this book to cover all elements of style to consider, but in its simplest form, we find that Fischer's (1985/1994) advice summarizes what we strive for:

> "Don't use jargon, don't write in technological terms, don't dehumanize the assessee, don't emphasize scores at the expense of describing the person, don't write in generalizations, don't hide behind tests, don't write from only within one theoretical framework.
>
> Do indicate the relevance of findings, do qualify general statements, do indicate context of reported behavior, do make concrete suggestions." (p. 148)

Creative Elements to Consider

There are a variety of ways assessors can be creative with their letters to help their clients. First, for some clients including language from their test responses can illustrate an important point. For example, in the Summary/Discussion Session chapter, we described how Nick's memory from the Early Memory Procedure (EMP, Bruhn, 1992) was discussed during that session to help him understand how he dismissed emotions. For Nick's letter, the EMP response was quoted in the answer of his related AQ to illustrate those points. A similar strategy can be used for items from a Sentence Completion Test (SCT) or Rorschach. Often, a client's response on the SCT conveys highly personalized and impactful language. Similarly, a Rorschach response may capture something metaphorical for the client and including it helps bring the memory of the discussion during the EI to mind.

For example, for Card V of the Rorschach, 20-year-old Sam had a response capturing their feelings of disconnection. They identified as non-binary, experienced rejection from family and peers, and were mistrustful. The following is part of the answer to their AQ: "What do I need to do to make friendships in the future?"

Sam, we talked about how the tests captured the high levels of social anxiety you have experienced and how challenging it has been for you to create the type of relationships you would like. You may recall our discussion after you completed the Rorschach, and we focussed on your response: *That's some alien, flying dark figure flying over the world to see if they want to land or not. It's not sure this world is safe for creatures like them and so they just keep flying and never land.* As we discussed, this captured your experience with family and peers, and how difficult it has been to find a "safe world." It is understandable why you are a bit leery and mistrustful around others, as you are protecting yourself from further rejection. During our last meeting, I shared how those experiences of being rejected have broken your "trust meter" and now it is difficult to know who to trust and how to develop a proper level of trust. I appreciated that we were able to build a trusting connection and believe that is a good example of what you are capable of when it comes to relationships. Learning how to further fix your trust meter is something that could be a focus in psychotherapy, so that you can connect with others and build friendships in a way that feels safe to you.

A second creative element is the use of pictures or figures in a letter. For instance, using a thermometer to capture various levels of anger is a common metaphor and including such a picture could illustrate the points made. Other clients may benefit from the inclusion of a simple figure that uses languages and shapes to show a client's difficulties and where they may intervene. For example, 21-year-old Hassan experienced moderate depressive symptoms, which he managed through avoidance and isolation, but these strategies only amplified his feelings of disconnection. Hassan and the assessor discussed this cycle and used the shared term "spiralling blues" to capture these experiences, which was connected to his question, "What will help me change the spiralling blues?" During the Summary/ Discussion Session this pattern was discussed with him, and it was suggested that he focus his therapy work on building skills to better understand and manage his feelings and relationships. Part of his letter follows and Figure 10.1 is the image included in the letter.

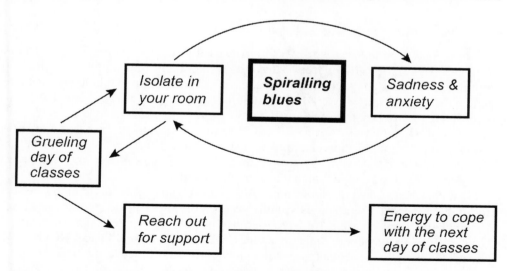

Figure 10.1 Example of a Figure Included in a TA Letter.

In therapy a focus on improving your skills related to understanding and managing your feelings is part of what will help with your depression and alter the "spiralling blues." It may take some time, but you can reverse the negative spiral of isolation, pessimistic thinking, and low mood that has contributed to this year's struggles. You want to go from the first cycle below to the second. These things all influence each other, so if you use tools to manage your mood, you'll become more connected to others, you'll have more happiness, and that will contribute to better days at school.

Third, at times we have clients edit or respond to a report, which is another strategy that validates and empowers the client (Finn, 1996, 2007; Fischer 1985/1994). In its simplest form, the letter is sent to the client with a space below the assessor's signature where the client is invited to write a response to what is written. A signature line could be included for them, and the client's comments are attached and shared with other future readers of the letter. However, it may also be possible to have the client review the letter and discuss their ideas and further collaborate on the final language that is included in the document. This method continues collaboration and ensures the client feels their input is integrated into the letter.

Last, in the Child TA model, it is common to write a fable to the child client to provide them written feedback (Tharinger et al., 2008). These stories involve characters the child has shown an interest in (e.g., Batman) and the narrative arc mirrors the child's experience ending with a realistic outcome. While a fable is likely to be too simplistic for an adult, some clients may benefit from an allegory. Using a client's story from a storytelling test has similar benefits, but for some clients, a unique story created by the assessor may be quite powerful. Working with metaphors and allegories is further elaborated in Allyn (2012), and she provides structured guidance on writing an allegory for an adult or adolescent (p. 188). A case study including the importance of metaphors and guidance for using them and allegories effectively in TA letters can be found in Engelman and Allyn (2012).

The Therapeutic Psychological Report

The term Therapeutic Psychological Report is used to describe several types of psychological reports that differ from a traditional report, in that they have a goal of continuing change. The sections that make up a Therapeutic Psychological Report may be the same as those in a traditional report (Table 10.1). However, given the client is considered a primary audience for the report, the language and style are different, and often the Summary section is written in a way that captures the client and their contribution in a more individualized and less technical fashion. Such reports are beneficial to the client, while typically containing information necessary for other professionals and meeting documentation requirements.

Allyn (2012) identified questions an assessor can consider when deciding between a traditional report, a Therapeutic Psychological Report and a TA letter, and we edited her language to match what we have used in this text (see Table 10.5). There are a variety of ways an assessor could structure a Therapeutic Psychological Report and assessors looking to implement such a document into their practice are encouraged to review the elements in the first column: "Questions to ask."

Table 10.5 TA Letter, Therapeutic Psychological Report and Traditional Report

Questions to ask	Traditional Report	Therapeutic Psychological Report	TA Letter
Who is the audience?	Third party	Both third party and client	Client
What is the goal?	Share assessment data	Aspects of both a TA letter and Traditional Report	Remind the client about the TA and support client change
What is included?	Traditional report sections	Aspects of both a TA letter and Traditional Report	Answers to the client's AQs structured in a similar way as the discussion session
What is the style and tone?	Professional	Aspects of both a TA letter and Traditional Report	In alignment with the language used with the client

The elements of a TA Letter presented above are likely to be beneficial when writing a Therapeutic Psychological Report. Many of these ideas were influenced by Fischer's (1985/1994) writings on individualized reports, which is an early example of a Therapeutic Psychological Report. She recommended organizing the report using sections such as those presented in Table 10.1, but decisions about what to include are made based on what intended readers will find beneficial. She believed in the importance of building the report around themes in the client's life, rather than presenting consecutive test results.

> Reports should *not* record all that the assessor saw and learned, nor even all that he or she went through to arrive at the ultimate conclusions. The assessor asks, 'What do I know now that is important for others to know in order make their decisions and to work with this person?' (p. 116).

Fischer also recommended that assessors avoid overly professional language and write in concrete terms. This thinking aligned with the growing guidance on writing reports that used simple and straightforward language (Ownby, 1997; Tallent,1993). However, Fischer's reports included examples "that bring the client to life, making concretely visible what you the assessor came to know" (1985/1994, p. 116). Given her emphasis on helping clients gain insights, often those examples were moments during discussions when a shift occurred, and the client came to understand themself in a new way.

When writing a Therapeutic Psychological Report, assessors can consider language and style elements that are described for the TA Letter to inform some of their choices. Given these documents are a hybrid of a traditional report and a TA letter, some of these strategies are included. One simple approach for a Therapeutic Psychological Report is to complete the document with the typical sections included, and then write the Summary section after the feedback session and incorporate the client's input. What follows is an example from a Therapeutic Psychological Report that includes two paragraphs from the Summary section and one example of a recommendation.

Shannon was 18 years old at the time of this evaluation and court ordered for an assessment at the suggestion of her probation officer.

Shannon and I discussed test results that suggested an impulsive and independent style. She recognized these aspects of herself and during the interview described herself as "stubborn" and "bossy." I shared with her the elevated scales on her self-report tests that showed a history of abuse and family conflict. We talked about how as a child she learned adaptive ways of dealing with those experiences by adopting a tough stance and dominating others before they dominated her. She acknowledged that occurs and described how she used to be a bully and was often cruel to her friends. She has been aware of this tendency, but also has struggled to make any significant changes. Within the context of this discussion, she recognized she struggles with authority figures, often pushes back, and she was concerned that she does not feel guilty about some of her actions. We talked about how a therapist may be able to help her with all these things, as they may cause her difficulties as an adult, particularly in intimate relationships. Shannon endorsed that this has already happened in her past relationships with boyfriends.

Shannon and I then reviewed the test results that show elevated levels of anxiety and mild-to-moderate levels of depression. She recognized her anxiety and made a correct connection between the anxiety and her abuse history, but she initially disagreed that she was currently depressed. We explored this further, and Shannon described a time when she was severely depressed (sad and suicidal). We talked about the possibility that she only sees herself as not depressed now because things are not as bad as they used to be, but there is still some lingering depression. She agreed that although she might not currently see herself as depressed, she may not be as happy as she could be.

Recommendation

Shannon would benefit from working with an individual therapist to address her mood and trauma symptoms, and a female therapist might be best given her history of sexual abuse. During our meeting, I discussed this recommendation with Shannon and she seemed interested, but stated a preference for a male therapist. I shared my thoughts of the pros and cons of a male versus female, and she agreed to think about her choice.

Common Mistakes in the Content and Process of Written Feedback

A few errors are common when writing the final document, and these are divided into mistakes related to the content of the letter and the process of writing the letter.

Content Mistakes

The primary mistake an assessor can make with the letter is including information that was not discussed during the Summary/Discussion Session. The final document should not contain new information and should capture the conversation that occurred during that session. Ideally, when a client is reading a TA letter, they will have the experience of remembering that discussion and think, "This feels like having another conversation with the evaluator." We prevent this mistake from occurring in our planning of the Summary/Discussion Session, and ensure that the most important information is in our written notes, and then discussed in that session and captured in the letter.

If, during the writing process, the assessor discovered that some information was not adequately reviewed during the Summary/Discussion Session but should be in the letter, two options may rectify the situation. Choosing between these two will depend on the importance of the missed information to the client's self-understanding. First, if the information is important and likely to be Level 2 or 3 Information, it will be best for the assessor to arrange another meeting with the client to discuss this information. Second, if the information is important, but likely to be Level 1 Information, it may be possible to present this information with transparency and some caveats. For example, "During our discussion about what might help with your depression, I shared the suggestions listed previously. However, while writing your letter I realized there is one more thing for you to consider. My ideas are below, but if what I share is unclear, let's discuss it in our Follow-up Session."

A second common content mistake is focusing on the tests and not the person. As described, we weave test data, conversations, and the client's experience answering AQs. This style differs from many traditional reports in which each test is fully interpreted on its own or test data from various domains is integrated. Sometimes a focus on a test makes sense, given the client's interest in the test or when a test captures an important part of the client. This aligns with method three of organizing data for the Summary/Discussion Session and letter. However, it is more therapeutic to write in terms of the person and their lived experience, rather than the test results. Clinicians who have been practicing the traditional, information-gathering approach to assessment often have difficulty with this difference in writing and may benefit from consultation if they struggle to make this shift.

A final content error that can occur is related to language choices. We agree with current guidance on writing psychological reports and the importance of not including jargon and unfamiliar clinical terms (Groth-Marnat & Wright, 2016; Wright, 2011). Given clinicians have their own professional language, we may not recognize jargon or how clients may define a term. A simple example is the term antisocial, which clinicians define in terms of criminality and self-focus on interests, while lay people often use the term to refer to not wanting to engage socially (i.e., being asocial). Clarifying important terms and language with clients during the Summary/Discussion Session can help ensure the language used in the letter is clear.

Process Mistakes

The clinician's process of writing a TA letter differs from completing a traditional psychological evaluation report. First, TA letters will take more time, given they are more complex and highly personalized. We have found that it takes 25–30% more time to write than a traditional report. Thus, TA assessors should plan for extra time and bill appropriately for their work, and not doing so are other possible mistakes.

Psychological assessors have debated the question of how long and how much should be included in the final document for decades. These discussions are influenced by the fact that certain settings and types of evaluations have different audiences and thus different expectations for that final document. Assessors' education and training experiences, as well as ethics around competent services and creating the "perfect" document often contribute to the number of pages written. TA assessors can make the mistake of writing a letter that is too long, as they hold templates of psychological reports from other experiences or to meet their own feelings of competency. We agree with the advice that "More is not better" (Schectman, 1979, p. 783), and that the "reports are for the readers, not the for the author" (Fischer, 1985/1994, p. 115). We encourage assessors to consider whether they are writing too much and if so, what is influencing those decisions. Here again, some consultation around these choices may be helpful.

Clerical errors can also contribute to process mistakes and attending to needed tasks throughout the TA helps in this regard. The writing of the final document begins when the TA commences and writing notes or possible parts of the letter after each session helps facilitate the final writing process. Tracking the timing of completing the letter is also important, as a delay in the letter's timing is another mistake, and ideally the letter arrives 2–6 weeks after the Summary/Discussion Session. In this way, its timing serves as another intervention after the client has lived what they learned in the last session.

Summary

We have presented various ideas about how to structure and write a final document following a TA. While the ideas presented are common practice for many TA assessors, we encourage those learning the model to use these ideas as building blocks and flex their creativity when writing to their clients. Ultimately, as long as we continue to empathize with our client and hold our TA values, we can ensure that we are meeting the goal of the written communication: Continued client change.

Those looking for examples of TA letters can see Finn (2020), which includes a full letter, including a mix of presenting major findings, specific test results, and answers to the client's AQs. A TA letter following method one can be found in Groth-Marnat and Wright (2016). Other examples of letters are in chapters 7 and 10 of Finn (2007), and in Kamphuis and de Saeger (2012).

Clinical Case

What follows is the TA letter sent to Emma after the Summary/Discussion Session. First, Hale describes a bit of his process and thoughts when writing the letter.

Hale's Approach to the Letter

I felt the Summary/Discussion Session had gone well and that we had put together important understandings that Emma seemed to take to heart. I heard from Jeanne afterwards that Emma had been a little shaken right after I left them, but that in their next therapy session, Emma seemed to have digested much of the Summary/Discussion Session and was realizing its value. Knowing this, I approached the letter and finished it about two weeks after the Summary/Discussion Session. I sent it about a week later. I like to write the letter and then sit with it some to make adjustments before I send it. I recognize it is potentially a very important and enduring summary that the client may read from time to time to be reminded of the understandings that had emerged. This was especially true for Emma. I knew the assessment had been a major endeavor for her and hoped that the insights we had reached would affect her world and be enduring. I also wanted to include hints that might lead to future growth.

Letter to Emma

Dear Emma,

As promised, in this letter I have written down the results of the testing that we put together in our last meeting so that you will have something to look back on. I believe we came to important understandings of your questions that will be helpful to you as you move ahead with your life. I hope this letter will serve as a good point of reference for the things we spoke about. As we agreed, I am also sending a copy of this letter to your therapist, Jeanne.

First, I want to reiterate how much I enjoyed working with you and getting to know you. Thank you for trusting me enough to collaborate in this important work we did. I also want to thank you for all the effort you put into the testing. I know I asked you to do a lot, but you always worked hard, even though you sometimes had had a hard day, and sometimes our work touched on difficult issues. I believe your willingness to extend yourself in difficult areas is a good sign for your future. I want to do the best I can to summarize the answers to the questions you asked of the assessment.

Opportunities for Assessment

Below I have listed the tests you completed. The first group are tests we used to figure out if you had ADHD or a learning disorder. The WAIS-IV was the test that we did together at table with the red and white blocks and other tasks, and during the WJA-III you completed tasks that felt more like school, such as vocabulary words and solving math problems. The CAARS is the rating scale you completed for ADHD, and your sister completed the BASC-2 and Conners-3, so we could gather her perspectives on you as a child. The MMPI-2 was the true/false self-report test that tells us about your personality and potential mental health symptoms. The AAP, Rorschach, and Wartegg test (WDCT) are all called performance-based tests; they also tell us about your personality, but they tap into areas that a person may have less awareness of. The Rorschach was the inkblot test where you told me what you saw on each card. For the AAP you told stories to drawings, and for the WDCT you drew pictures in different boxes with small marks. Last, for the EMP, you wrote about important early memories, which we then reviewed.

Tests to Help Determine ADHD or a learning disorder

- Wechsler Adult Intelligence Scale—Fourth Edition (WAIS-IV)
- Woodcock-Johnson Test of Achievement-III (WJA-III)
- Conners Adult ADHD Rating Scale (CAARS)
- Behavior Assessment System for Children, Second edition (BASC-2)
- Conners-3 Parent form

Tests that Help us Understand your Personality and Social/Emotional Difficulties.

- Minnesota Multiphasic Personality Inventory 2nd Edition (MMPI-2)
- Rorschach Performance Assessment System (R-PAS)
- Wartegg Drawing Completion Test, Crisi Wartegg System (WDCT/CWS)
- Adult Attachment Projective Picture System (AAP)
- Early Memory Procedure (EMP)

Overview of Test Results and Answers to Your Questions

As became apparent in our last session, and is often the case, the questions and answers stem from a bigger picture. Let me first give an overview of what we discovered, and then I will describe the specific answers we arrived at during our last meeting. A central factor among the answers is the difficult experiences you had as a child, which set a lot in motion.

One of the unusual results in your testing is that the self-report measures (those through which you described likes, dislikes, behaviors, etc.) showed very few problems, but the performance-based measures like the inkblots, the Wartegg test, and the picture story cards, as well as the ratings of you by your sister of when you were a child, showed issues under the surface. It appears you adapted to your early environment by focusing on the positives and telling yourself things were okay. Remember on the Wartegg drawing test you drew two beautiful butterflies in the box that pulls for reality testing and planning (while most people draw an organized rectangle or square figures like a window or television)? Your drawing fit with other test findings, showing that you work hard to put a good face on things, but we came to understand that there are ways this does not serve you well. Underneath the "butterflies" there is a lot going on in you that distracts and disorganizes you. This leads to several of your questions. As I did in our last session, I am grouping two of your questions together because the answers seem clearly related, and the answer to the first question bears on subsequent questions.

WHY AM I SO AFRAID TO COMMIT TO ANYTHING? WHY AM I SO AFRAID
TO FAIL OR SUCCEED?

The testing was clear that you are very cautious, particularly with your emotions, and that you have a lot going on inside—much more than meets the eye. It seems that this caution comes largely from your early experiences with a mother who had a problem with alcohol for a critical period of time during your development. She was normally a responsible mother, but, as you so vividly described, in your early formative years she regularly became rageful. At the "witching hour" of 5 pm, she often changed into a terrifying presence under the influence of alcohol. Your father avoided coming home to it, which left you unprotected and frightened. You and your older sister retreated to the basement to hide out. You described one time your mother threw away all your toys in her rage. The next morning you timidly asked her if you could dig them out of the trash—and she did not even remember throwing them away.

The worst part of these experiences is that you had little help with all the feelings they created. You were left to adapt to the situation largely on your own. This is a definition of trauma—being alone with overwhelming emotions resulting from terrifying situations and having no one to help with them. While your father was very protective in some ways, especially later in your life, he was not there to help you in your younger years. Perhaps he too was afraid of your mother's anger or didn't want to confront her drinking, and he didn't stop to think about how all this must be affecting you. Fortunately, your sister Tessa was there to make sure you were fed and bathed, but she was not old enough to serve your every need—especially your emotional ones. And she too was likely traumatized by the situation with your mother. The result was an unpredictable, confusing, and very scary world in which you felt you needed to be very cautious to stay safe. As we discussed, the anxiety you felt and the obsessive-compulsive behaviors you displayed as a child were likely the result of feeling unsafe and trying hard to control your world. It was powerful to hear you say in our last meeting how awful it was to have to leave the table in a restaurant with your family when you had a panic attack. These early experiences were no doubt traumatizing for you, and we see the fallout in the test data today. The results showed some of the effects of that early trauma, for example, that still today you keep a close eye on your environment for any signs of threat.

Thus, the answer to these two questions seems to be rooted in this fear and trauma in your childhood. Committing to things makes you vulnerable to unknown threats that you sense (not consciously think) may be overwhelming and potentially traumatic. The same sense causes a fear to succeed or fail. When you were explaining this question to me, you said that even succeeding led to fear that you may not be up to it and that you may let others down.

WHY HAVEN'T I BEEN ABLE TO HAVE A SUCCESSFUL LONG-TERM RELATIONSHIP?

As we discussed, this kind of early trauma affected your development at an early point, so it had a big impact on your growth from that point onward. Other aspects of your development were affected, especially your emotional development. The testing suggests you made the world safer by clamping down your emotions—the phrase you used in our last session was that you "bottled up" your feelings. You learned this so early that it became a natural way to be and not even a conscious action on your part.

Understandably, one aspect of development that did not happen ideally for you was learning to take an appropriate adversarial position. As we discussed this capacity develops gradually in life, usually in relationship to parents at first. It involves defining yourself in new ways that are at odds with powerful people in your life. How they respond to your difference of opinion and independence determines how you learn to be appropriately challenging with others, an important capacity in life. I suspect it was difficult to be effectively adversarial with your parents because you idealized your father and relied on his super-competence, and you were afraid of provoking your mother.

Furthermore, you learned from your mother that anger was a terrible thing, "very destructive," and you stayed as far away from it as you could. As your memory of confronting the man who was belittling the older gentleman in the grocery checkout line showed us, you tend to see two options to confrontation: Walking away trying to ignore it or seeing red and really laying into someone. Your description of becoming "Minnie Mouse" on the outside, while inside you were feeling "don't you dare'" captures this situation.

I thought an important insight occurred when you confronted your friend Bob for his superior attitude about you not being able to look out for your interests regarding your house sale. You were offended by his attitude and backed off that relationship. But when you confronted him in an honest and appropriate way, you told me it went surprisingly well—and it even renewed your friendship with him! Your being able to be appropriately adversarial really does have lots of important effects!

If you continue to develop the skills to be appropriately adversarial, this will lead to greater confidence in your ability to manage conflict and will allow you to explore relationship options more fully. Working with Jeanne on this would be a great way to learn these skills such as gradually escalating confrontation only to the level needed, without going overboard.

Other dangers of not being appropriately adversarial are that you may tolerate a lot of bad behaviors in the service of peace, which lets silent resentments build up toward your partner. Without a mechanism to address issues as they arise, the "bottled up" feelings can fester and detract from the intimacy you feel for your partner. When the resentments get too strong, you may explode with an intensity that is surprising to your partner.

Another critical element of close relationships is attachment status. I described to you the Strange Situation research that discovered four different attachment strategies, which a child learns to guide their relationships. The test we did where you told stories to black and white drawings assessed how you manage close relationships. Given your early experiences with a sometimes "rageaholic" mother, you seem to have developed two different ways to be close to others. When things are going well and negative emotions are not too challenging you can handle the stress by doing what you said you wish someone had done for you, like say, "let's sit down and talk about this." However, when close a relationship evokes strong negative emotions (like your mother yelling at you), you have the tendency to shut down emotions and protect yourself by distancing yourself in various ways. The really good news is this test shows that you got enough healthy intimacy as a child that you have achieved the underlying capacity for a secure attachment; this means you have the potential to have successful long-term relationships.

Because you didn't have the support to learn how to handle emotions as a child, you sacrificed an important skill that makes relationships work better (i.e., appropriate confrontation). Furthermore, not developing early emotional skills made it harder to have experiences of success when you were a child, and this further affected your development, as well as your self-esteem. So, there are a number of ripples from early trauma that have disrupted your life. These are things you can work on with Jeanne to break old habits and develop new skills. The incredible steps you took during the assessment show me that you are ready and able to make these changes.

The test results suggest other possible obstacles to your having a successful long-term relationship. First, the answers to the previous questions are relevant here. Your tendency to be very cautious may not only perpetuate a fear of commitment and of success or failure but may also affect relationships. Initially being overly cautious to avoid people who might get angry may limit your pool of possible partners, and lead you to people who maybe don't have other qualities you seek. Also, being careful to present yourself in ways that you don't antagonize others (like Minnie Mouse) seems like a big limitation in developing healthy relationships.

Finally, your tendency to see "beautiful butterflies" instead of more realistic situations puts you at risk of not fully appreciating the negative elements of a relationship. It may be that your detector of possible negative factors unrelated to anger and conflict is not well calibrated, so that if a person does not threaten anger or conflict, they pass your filter, even though there may be other shortcomings that limit that person's suitability as a good mate. This is an example of the downside of putting a good face on life rather than seeing the negative. The testing also suggested that your emotional judgment is not as perceptive as when you think things through. Thus, it seems like a significant problem is getting into relationships with people who are not good prospective partners. So, while you have lots of potential for a good relationship, there is a lot that gets in the way that you will want to work through. You may need to consider the judgments of other people you trust (like Jeanne or Tessa) about your potential partners—as well as your own deep gut feelings— until you can calibrate your own emotional judgment.

WHY HAVE I NEVER BEEN ABLE TO MAINTAIN A LONG-TERM POSITION IN A CAREER I AM PASSIONATE ABOUT, LIKE TEACHING?

As we discussed, the answer to this question is similar to the previous one in that some of the same factors may be in play. First, your self-doubt and fears make it difficult to commit passionately to a career—even if you suspect you would succeed. Some of your fear may stem from being very averse to anger and the threat of rage, especially when it is directed at you by an unhappy boss, disgruntled co-worker, or dissatisfied parent. I really liked what you said in our last session about your reactions when the child went out the gate at school. It sounded like you did the right thing, but we could see it was still very distressing to you. As you get more experience with those types of situations while feeling the support of important others around you, you may still feel uncertainty, but you will be able to put your self-doubts to rest quicker, so they take less of your energy and mental time.

Maintaining a solid career would also require some ability to be appropriately adversarial. As strange as that may sound (because part of keeping a job requires getting along with everyone), sometimes just having the confidence to stand up for yourself, if need be, causes others to treat you better. It's like you have a sign on your back that says, "I am friendly, but I can protect myself, so don't mess with me." As you mentioned in one of our sessions, your anger (and also its close cousins: Irritation, resentfulness, dissatisfaction, etc.) may "come out sideways," without you even being aware of it. If this happens, it can also interfere with work relationships.

Your deep negative view of yourself—which comes from your early experiences—may also play a role in limiting what you reach for. How you have been viewed in your family since you were very young—as someone who needs special care and may not be able to stand on your own two feet—probably affects your self-esteem and comfort level in being more autonomous. The fear that something was wrong with you likely comes from the way others saw you. And then you may have worked to maintain this stance because of your lack of confidence. There may have been some realistic early struggles that started and fed this concern that I will address in answering the question below.

Again, part of the issue may boil down to not having had–yet–enough successful experiences to allow your self-confidence to grow and be solidly grounded. A clearer understanding and greater comfort with all your feelings will allow you to express your full range of emotions. And being in touch with all your feelings will help you realistically appraise what you can do and what you need help with. Realizing your full potential will take some time, effort, and help from others, but again, from the work you did in the assessment, I have no doubt that you can do this.

DO I HAVE A LEARNING DISABILITY OR ATTENTION DEFICIT HYPERACTIVITY DISORDER?

The results of the testing showed that your cognitive abilities are certainly adequate, though I am convinced the results are underestimates of your true ability. As we discussed, there is strong evidence that your cognitive performance is impaired by emotional factors. This was clearly demonstrated in the very first testing session we had when we started with the subtest to arrange blocks to match a pattern. You quickly got very upset because you thought you were not doing well. That negative thought got in the way of you doing as well as you could have. We stopped to talk, you gradually calmed down, and then were feeling good again. Then we went back to the block design test, and to your surprise, you did better on it! We saw this kind of process play out often in the rest of the cognitive testing. I remember you telling me that you had just guessed at some things you think you actually could have gotten because you were feeling uneasy and just wanted to get the task over with so as not to feel vulnerable or humiliated. I wonder how often this happens in your real life and how much it leads you and others to believe you can't do more than you do?

I suspect sometimes pulling back from challenges is the result of several factors. First, you are uncomfortable when you are put on the spot, perhaps because of an old sense of not feeling adequate or big enough to manage what is thrown at you—just like you must have felt as a child at times when you had to handle situations no child could manage on their own. Your pulling back also is related to self-confidence, which you have not had enough opportunity to build yet. Second, as we discussed, your sense is that you are worse in math and its associated challenges. We suspected this is at least partly due to the fact that you missed a lot academically because of early turmoil/trauma. Math is one of those subjects that if you miss the early fundamentals, it is hard to catch up with, in part because we need the basics to understand what comes next in math, but also because we form a belief we are not good at math, and it intimidates us, so the problem grows. Finally, there was a significant difference in the test results between your verbal abilities and visual-spatial abilities. This discrepancy suggests there likely is an actual difference between these two areas of cognitive function. This is just the way your brain is made and is not that unusual. But these kinds of differences often create a lot of confusion in a student, as well as in teachers and other adults, and may lead a student to feel both "smart" and "stupid" at the same time. As we discussed, your visual-spatial scores are still in the average range even though they are lower than your verbal abilities. Your verbal abilities are a normative (compared to others) and personal (compared to your other abilities) strength for you. It is an ability that you can play to in your life and career.

In summary, there is no evidence of a traditional learning disability in the pattern of your scores, but it is difficult to say for sure because extraneous factors such as emotions affect performance so much. Similarly, the impact of your early trauma and the resulting emotions with which you wrestle also make it difficult to say anything definitive about ADHD. The results of Tessa's ratings of you as a child suggest inattention and hyperactivity, but also high anxiety, somatization, withdrawal, depression, and internalizing problems. These emotional factors can mimic the symptoms of ADHD. So, it could be that your problems paying attention and concentrating are due to emotional factors, or it is possible that ADHD is accompanied by the emotional difficulties. Interestingly, Tessa's ratings show below-average scores on aggression and conduct problems—A sign that you had inhibited your adversarial tendencies as a child.

Finally, Emma, given all we have figured out, here are some things to consider that might be helpful. It is clear to me that you are in good hands with Jeanne, and I suspect she'll be able to take some of this new information and make good use of it for your therapy. I won't provide many suggestions for that here, but I will include a few things for you to consider. I trust you and Jeanne can review these and then decide if they are helpful to prioritize or not.

- Continue to work on being appropriately adversarial, like you did with Bob.
- Continue communicating what you have previously kept inside with trusted others. Continue taking calculated risks. You are much more capable than you think.
- Remember that as an adult you are much, much more capable of handling whatever challenges come up than you were as a child.
- Remembering your concern about possible brain damage when we first met, if you continue to be concerned about this, you can contact me for a referral for a neuropsychological evaluation; however, I did not see anything in our work that suggests this would be necessary.

So, these are the best answers I see from all the work we did together, as well as some additional ideas for you to consider. Of course, you are the most important judge about how well all this fits you. We will have a chance to talk further at the Follow-up Session we discussed. Typically, that occurs 2 to 3 months after the summary-discussion session, but let's make sure we do it when it would be helpful to you. Let me know when you are ready to meet, and if I don't hear from you after a while, I will contact you to see if you are ready. These Follow-up Sessions allow us to see how you are progressing, clarify or deepen answers to your old questions, and address any new questions that have come up since the assessment.

Again, Emma, it was a great pleasure to work with you. Thank you for collaborating with me. I was touched by your honesty in the face of your fears and your earnest efforts to understand and improve. It is clear you have done a lot of work on yourself, and this is the best sign that you will continue to grow and become the best version of you. I hope this testing is helpful in your future work.

Let me know if you have any questions. Feel free to contact me directly by phone or email.

Best wishes for a bright future,
Hale
CC Jeanne...

Reflections on Emma's Letter

I devoted about eight hours to the letter over two weeks. I thought it was little long and a bit complicated, but all the information that ended up in it seemed important, and I thought Emma was capable of assimilating it over time. I also thought it worked well to start with the overall results rather than jump into the questions because many of the answers emerged from the root cause, her early trauma.

Throughout the letter, I worked to make the text personal to increase its meaning to her. I did this by including metaphors that Emma had used (e.g., "becoming Minnie Mouse," "the witching hour") in order to support findings in words that came from her own lived experience. I also referred to important moments we had experienced together that would illustrate and deepen meaning, such as her experience with the Block Design subtest of the WAIS-IV, drawing two butterflies on the little marks in

Box 6 of the WDCT, and her reparative experience with Bob. I included subtly hopeful comments and signs of support, such as "As you get more experience..." using "yet" at various points to imply she is on her way and even said "I have no doubt..." to show my confidence in her.

I also limited psychological jargon to make the letter accessible, except where I had introduced psychological concepts to Emma during the assessment, such as the strange situation (Ainsworth et al., 1978) and appropriate adversarial capacity (Wolf, 1988). I did this to let her know that our work was solidly grounded in psychology and that her intelligence was respected. It also gave her the opportunity to read more on the internet if she wanted, although I refrained from including an appendix of test scores, as is sometimes done with TA letters. Because of Emma's hypervigilance, I feared she would spend hours trying to decipher the tests on her own. Last, I further highlighted my respect for her by referring to the knowledge she had from being a teacher, for example, that kids need help learning about themselves. I did not include a long suggestions section as I thought Jeanne and Emma could effectively talk about Emma's next steps in therapy. After the Summary/Discussion Session, I connected with Jeanne to share some of my ideas and did not think it was useful to add more detail to the suggestions above or additional ideas.

Although—as I had mentioned to Jeanne in our meeting before the Summary/Discussion Session—I thought Emma recognizing how her father had failed her was important for future successful relationships, I did not take her father on in the letter. I felt that she was not ready for this, but I did plant some seeds for her work with Jeanne, such as mentioning her father's failure to protect her from her mother's rages. I also tried to support Emma's relationship with Jeanne, by saying Emma was in good hands and by suggesting areas they could work on.

Most important in my mind, was directly conveying my sincere appreciation for her. After being very vulnerable by all she had revealed to me, I wanted Emma to know I still held her in high regard. I also wanted her to know I was not abandoning her, by looking forward to the Follow-up Session and by letting her know she could contact me.

Note

1 Assessors can download the AQ from the Therapeutic Assessment Institute website (*www.therapeuticassessment.com/assessment_questionnaire.php*).

References

Ainsworth, M. D. S., Blehar, M. C., Waters, E., & Wall, S. (1978). *Patterns of attachment: A psychological study of the strange situation*. Erlbaum.

American Psychological Association. (2017). *Ethical principles of psychologists and code of conduct* (2002, amended effective June 1, 2010, and January 1, 2017). www.apa.org/ethics/code.

Allyn, J. B. (2012). *Writing to clients and referring professionals about psychological assessment results: A handbook of style and grammar*. Routledge.

Armengol, C. G., Moes, E. J., Penney, D. L., & Sapienza, M. M. (2001). Writing client centered recommendations. In C. G. Armengol, E. Kaplan, & E. J. Moes (Eds.), *The consumer-oriented neuropsychological report* (pp. 141–160). Psychological Assessment Resources.

Bagby, M. R., & Solomon-Krakus, S. (2020). Writing a psychological report using evidence-based psychological assessment methods. In M. Sellbom & J. A. Suhr (Eds.), *The Cambridge handbook of clinical assessment and diagnosis* (pp. 101–110). Cambridge University Press.

Brenner, E. (2003). Consumer-focused psychological assessment. *Professional Psychology: Research and Practice, 34,* 240–247.

Brown, E. C. (1972). Assessment from a humanistic perspective. *Psychotherapy: Theory, Research, and Practice, 9,* 103–106.

Bruhn, A. R. (1992). The Early Memories Procedure: A projective test of autobiographical memory (Part I). *Journal of Personality Assessment, 58,* 1–15.

Engleman, D. H., & Allyn, J. B. (2012). Collaboration in neuropsychological assessment: Metaphor with a suicidal adult. In S. E. Finn, C. T. Fischer, & L. Handler (Eds.), *Collaborative/Therapeutic Assessment: A casebook and guide* (pp. 69–91). John Wiley & Sons, Inc.

Finn, S. E. (1996). *A manual for using the MMPI-2 as a therapeutic intervention.* University of Minnesota Press.

Finn, S. E. (2007). *In our clients' shoes: Theory and techniques of Therapeutic Assessment.* Routledge.

Finn, S. E. (2020). Communicating the assessment findings to Madeline G. In C. J. Hopwood & Mark H. Waugh (Eds.), *Personality assessment paradigms and methods. A collaborative re-assessment of Madeline G.* (pp. 183–223). Routledge.

Finn, S. E., Schroeder, D. G., & Tonsager, M. E. (2000). *The Assessment Questionnaire-2 (AQ-2): A measure of clients' experiences with psychological assessment.* Unpublished manuscript, Center for Therapeutic Assessment, Austin, TX.

Fischer, C. (1985/1994). *Individualizing psychological assessment.* Lawrence Erlbaum & Associates.

Fischer, C. (1998). Th Rorschach and the life-world: Exploratory exercises. In L. Handler & M. Hilsenroth (Eds.), *Teaching and learning personality assessment* (pp. 347–358). Lawrence Erlbaum.

Fischer, C. T. (2011, March). Language matters: How to evoke life worlds. In C. T. Fischer (Chair), *Conceptual Developments in Psychological Assessment. Symposium Conducted at the Annual Meeting of the Society for Personality Assessment,* Boston, MA.

Groth-Marnat, G., & Wright, J. A. (2016). *Handbook of psychological* assessment (6th ed.). John Wiley & Sons, Inc.

Kamphuis, J. H., & Finn, S. E. (2019). Therapeutic Assessment in personality disorders: Toward the restoration of epistemic trust. *Journal of Personality Assessment, 101*(6), 662–674.

Kamphuis, J. H., & de Saeger, H. (2012). Using Therapeutic Assessment to explore emotional constriction: A creative professional in crisis. In S. E. Finn, C. T. Fischer, & L. Handler (Eds.), *Collaborative/Therapeutic Assessment: A casebook and guide* (pp. 133–156). John Wiley & Sons, Inc.

Klopfer, B., & Kelley D. M. (1946). *The Rorschach technique.* World Book Company.

Lance, B. R., & Krishnamurthy, R. (2003, March). *A comparison of three modes of MMPI-2 test feedback.* Paper presented at the annual meeting of the Society for Personality Assessment, San Francisco, CA.

Ownby, R. L. (1997). *Psychological reports: A guide to report writing in professional psychology* (3rd Edition). John Wiley & Sons, Inc.

Schectman, F. (1979). Problems in communicating psychological understanding. Why won't they listen to me? *American Psychologist, 34*(9), 781–790.

Schneider, W. J., Lichtenberger, E. O., Mather, N., & Kaufman, N. L. (2018). *Essentials of assessment report writing* (2nd Ed.). John Wiley & Sons, Inc

Tallent, N. (1993). *Psychological report writing* (4th Edition). Prentice Hall.

Tharinger, D. J., Finn, S. E., Wilkinson, A. D., DeHay, T., Parton, V., Bailey, E., & Tran, A. (2008). Providing psychological assessment feedback with children through individualized fables. *Professional Psychology: Research and Practice* 39(6), 610–618.

Wolf, E. (1988). *Treating the self.* Guilford Press.

Wright, J. A. (2011). *Conducting psychological assessment: A guide for practitioners.* John Wiley & Sons, Inc.

Wright, C. V., Beattie, S. G., Galper, D. I., Church, A. S., Bufka, L. F., Brabender, V. M., & Smith, B. L. (2017). Assessment practices of professional psychologists: Results of a national survey. *Professional Psychology: Research and Practice, 48*(2), 73–78.

Wright, A. J., Chávez, L., Edelstein, B. A., Grus, C. L., Krishnamurthy, R., Lieb, R., Mihura, J. L., Pincus, A. L., & Wilson, M. (2020, November 12). Education and training guidelines for psychological assessment in health service psychology. *American Psychologist, 76*(5), 794–801. doi: 10.1037/amp0000742.

Zuckerman, E. L. (2019). *Clinician's thesaurus: The guide to conducting interviews and writing psychological reports* (8th Ed.). Guilford Press.

11　Follow-up Session

The Follow-up Session is the final step of a Therapeutic Assessment (TA) and it was the last formalized step of the model, and for this reason and others, it has received the least emphasis in the literature. This step was added after Finn (2007) and others had a number of clients who did not go on to participate in therapy after the TA, but requested an additional session with the assessor after they received their TA letter. It became clear that these sessions served as a follow-up to the letter and helped clients consolidate their gains and further co-edit their new narrative. This session is not often mentioned in the literature because at times it does not occur. For example, clients who were not involved in psychotherapy at the beginning of the TA may now be engaged in treatment with the assessor who shifted to the therapist role. In such situations, the Follow-up Session may merge with the first session of treatment. Other times, the client is referred to a new therapist or continues treatment with the therapist who referred the client. When clients have begun the next steps in their therapy work with another professional, they may not need or want to engage with the assessor again.

However, we believe that most clients would benefit from re-engaging with the assessor, who considers how best to conduct this session given the client's specific characteristics and needs. In this chapter, we first describe the common topics addressed in the Follow-up Session, and then specific issues that may arise given different settings and client characteristics.

Common Features of the Follow-up Session

The Follow-up Session is typically scheduled from one to six months after the TA ends. As originally conceptualized by Finn (2007), it is a moment in which clients and assessors discuss the client's reactions to the letter, and any changes or lack thereof in their life after the TA. This session is also an opportunity to review questions that have arisen after the TA and formalize the conclusion of the assessment relationship.

We recommend including the Follow-up Session in the initial TA plan. We emphasize with the client that a Follow-up Session is part of the process from the first description of TA during the initial contact through the various discussions. Prioritizing this session is important, because once the other steps are completed (i.e., the client's letter has been sent), the idea of a Follow-up Session may recede from memory. Often clinicians finish one TA and then engage with other clients, and the client might also be focused on their next steps in life and less interested in attending. It is the assessor's choice about how much effort to put into scheduling a Follow-up

DOI: 10.4324/9780429202797-13

Session and choosing not to have that meeting will have less influence on the impact of a TA than missing other steps in the model. However, we recommend assessors include the Follow-up Session in the TA plan as that increases the likelihood of the client attending this session. For example, the Follow-up Session can be included in the cost of the TA, especially when the client is not paying after each session. Some assessors decide to offer the session for free as part of their pro-bono work and because they are interested in seeing the effects of the TA on the client. Importantly, in order to avoid the client failing to recall or attend this session, assessors may schedule it during the Summary/Discussion Session. Doing so means the assessor has a reasonable expectation of when the TA letter will be sent to the client. If that is not possible, when the letter is sent, the assessor can remind the client in the letter and through other communications about the Follow-up Session.

As in the other steps of TA, the assessor's goal during this session is to help the client feel "accurately seen and held in mind" and, for this session, also "remembered" by the assessor after time has passed. To do so, assessors review their notes and read the TA letter before the session, so they approach the meeting mindful of the general characteristics of the client, and the collaborative communication used during the TA.

At the beginning of the session, assessors welcome the client warmly,[1] demonstrating their appreciation for the opportunity to meet again. Applying a developmental metaphor to the Follow-up Session, it might feel like parents greeting their child who is coming home after a long trip. The parents are happy to see their child, interested in hearing about the trip, and can connect these experiences to their knowledge of their child's prior resources and difficulties. We recall what we learned about the client through conversations and the testing, and celebrate successes they have experienced while being prepared for any new challenges.

After initial remarks, the assessor asks the client if they have an agenda for the meeting. Some clients enter the Follow-up Session saying things like, "I have been able to improve my relationships, but I'm still struggling with how best to change things with my supervisor. It would be great if we could talk about that." When clients identify a personal interest or goal for the session, the assessor organizes the time to make sure it is addressed. We also prioritize asking the client about their reactions to, and questions about, the written feedback. Typically clients simply report that the letter was validating and captured what was discussed, but sometimes they have questions about certain parts, and we discuss their concerns.

The client may share their questions or provide an update, and the assessor uses their knowledge of the assessment to link important topics to the major findings from the TA. In this way, clients further process what they learned from the assessment and reflect on how it aligns with their current life functioning. Some clients enter the Follow-up Session with new Assessment Questions (AQS), and assessors use their knowledge of the client to provide answers, if possible. By the end of the TA, assessors know their client very well, and often can provide a meaningful answer. However, on occasion, clients identify a new concern and related AQ which requires additional testing to answer. In this situation, we provide as much information as possible and make suggestions about what else might be helpful. For example, 20-year-old Carmella initially posed AQs primarily related to her mood and relationships. During the Follow-up Session, she reported improvements in both areas and stated, "I really thought if my anxiety dropped, I'd be able to get more done at school, but I'm really struggling with focus." The assessor explored Carmella's experiences and provided psychoeducation about how additional testing could target attention or learning issues. Carmella decided she would first access support through her university, and if that did not lead to adequate changes, she would revisit the idea of more specific testing.

During the Follow-up Session, clients often report positive changes in their lives, and these accomplishments are validated and appreciated by assessors. In a meta-analysis on TA, Durosini and Aschieri (2021) pointed out that TA affects three realms: Symptomatology, self-growth, and the subsequent treatment process. In our experience, most clients report changes in the way they cope with their problems and symptoms, even if they are still present. Assessors validate these changes, or the new ways clients see themselves, which are often more accurate and compassionate. Clients with severe mental health issues who do not show major improvements in their symptomatology can be praised for their improved capacity to use the skills they developed during the TA or their increased compassion for themselves. We also hope that these clients are more fully engaged in treatment, and when clients share that is the case, we applaud their efforts. Conversely, when clients report continued difficulties, we review our suggestions and explore alternatives (e.g., increase the frequency of therapy, different treatment approaches, medication, or self-help strategies).

Finally, during the Follow-up Session, assessors have a final occasion to meta process the TA and learn from the clients what they experienced as useful and what they did not like. This information is valuable to the assessor, as such feedback helps them develop their self-awareness and improve their TA skills. Metaprocessing the TA experience is also a powerful occasion for clients to develop better awareness of their needs in meaningful relationships (such as the assessor-client relationship), and that awareness can be implemented in different relational contexts, such as with their partners or other mental health professionals.

Assessors close the session sharing appreciation for the meeting. Depending on the client and on the assessment context, assessors specify guidelines for future contact (see the following section) and say goodbye.

Unique Features of the Follow-up Session Depending on the Setting and Specific Client Characteristics

As mentioned, there are cases when the client begins therapy with the clinician who conducted the TA. In these situations, the TA letter may be given to the client after the beginning of therapy. When this happens, the "assessor-therapist" and the client review the letter to evaluate how the newly started treatment matches the suggestions developed during the TA, and how the therapy is addressing the client's issues. Devoting a therapy session to follow-up on the TA is an occasion for the assessor-therapist to evaluate the appropriateness of, or the need to change, how the treatment is unfolding.

When clients are referred to a new therapist after the TA, the Follow-up Session may be an opportunity to discuss how the client is experiencing the differences between the TA and the new therapy, and between the assessor and the new therapist. Often, clients use this opportunity to process their grief at the end of an important experience (the TA) and relationship (with the assessor). When this happens, it is not unusual that clients lament that their new therapist is less responsive and less able to "understand" them than the assessor. Assessors thank the client for their appreciation of the TA experience and of them as professionals and try to de-personalize the client's idealization by highlighting that the use of psychological testing was a fundamental ingredient for the rapid way they came to be understood during the TA. We also convey hope that the new therapist will use the TA letter to better understand the client, and encourage the client to allow some time for that relationship to grow.

When a Referring Professional (RP) initiated the TA and continues to provide therapy to the client, assessors plan a Follow-up Session after discussing this idea with the RP. Ideally, the assessor has consulted with the RP on how the TA affected the client's ability to work in therapy and on any therapeutic impasse that may have originally motivated the referral. When the RP is open to the assessor scheduling the follow-up with the client, this session is an occasion to explore with the client the effect of the TA on their treatment, and how the RP is using the TA results in therapy. The client's perspectives may represent a further contribution that the assessor can then discuss with the RP, as it is common for RPs to request further consultation from the assessor in the future. The assessor can also serve as a substitute therapist when they are on vacation or when clients are undergoing a period of distress during which they need extra support. A last viable option for the Follow-up Session is to meet with both the client and RP. In this scenario, the assessor typically "visits" a therapy session with the client and RP, and they can ask questions and the assessor can provide answers and lead a discussion of the client's progress and places the client is stuck. If the assessor has planned the session with the RP beforehand, both clinicians may agree on issues that will be discussed in the Follow-up Session and how the assessor can best assist in ongoing psychotherapy.

When clients who did not engage in treatment following the TA attend the Follow-up Session, the assessor explores the client's questions, how things have been going, and their current thinking about mental health support. Assessors—keeping in mind the client's AQs and answers—explore how the client has implemented what they learned from the TA, "fine-tune" new behaviors, and remain available to continue monitoring their growth with additional Follow-up Sessions.

Clinical Case: Follow-up Session with Emma

Because Emma was always busy, arranging the Follow-up Session with her took much longer than usual to schedule (5 months). I contacted her several times during this period to propose that we meet. She expressed interest but claimed she was too busy with her work and attending to her mother. This delay fueled my concern about how she was doing. I heard from Jeanne that Emma broke up with her boyfriend, moved out of the family home into a small apartment, and had been fired from her work as a teaching assistant. Had things gone terribly wrong? Had the assessment not really helped her? My conversation with Jeanne helped me feel a little better, but I was still eager to meet with Emma. Finally, we arranged a meeting for the three of us. Emma arrived on time and seemed to be in good spirits.

Hale: Nice to see you, Emma!
Emma: Nice to see you too, yeah.
Hale: It's been a little while.
Emma: It has been, I know. And it's probably a good thing. If we would've met sooner, it would have been same old, same old. But everything in my life has completely changed.

Hale: Wow! Really! Well, this is our opportunity to catch up, see how things have been going for you and see if the assessment we did might be of more use.

Emma: I think the last time we met I was kind of ... not upset, but sort of like, "I'm trying to understand and wrap my head around what my assessment meant." And what it meant is almost exactly what I was expecting, but it was hard for me.

Hale: Tell me.

Emma: When you and I and Jeanne met, I left a tad upset. So, she and I talked for a couple more minutes. What I was upset about, and it does make sense now, is the way that I handled things in a positive way instead of in whatever that adversarial thing was.

Hale: In an appropriate adversarial way?

Emma: Yes, in an appropriate adversarial way. And it does make sense to me that I didn't get it modeled from other people. I watched my mom get enraged a lot, and I watched my dad walk out the door a lot—not mad but avoiding. So, I didn't really have real good role models watching people say, "Let's talk about this before we do anything. What can we do about that? I know you're upset about that, what can we talk about." My mom used to get really angry, and she'd just slam doors and cupboards.

Hale: So that part hit you and it made you upset?

Emma: Yes, but it upset me because it was almost like new information even though it's old information. *[Emma describes that the new narrative about her past was somewhere between Level 2 and Level 3 Information.]*

Hale: It hit you in a different way.

Emma: Yes, it hit me in a different way, like I'm a new person now. I'm a totally different person from who I was when we first started noticing these patterns. Now, my mind is really wide open. Wow! That really hit me, I get it. When I do have a conflict, I want to run away, but I'm learning that it doesn't really help me in my life.

Emma went on to describe the messy break-up with her boyfriend. After she told him it was over, he started harassing her, calling and texting to tell her how stupid and ugly she was. She did not see red, but held her ground "appropriately," and she quickly had had enough of it and got a legal restraining order on him. She was talking with energy and confidence that I had not seen before—she did seem like a new person. She talked about "cutting the cords" to her fear and doubt and said she was moving into a new way of being. She told me that she had been let go from her old job but had quickly signed up to be a substitute teacher.

Hale: So, the substitute teaching, how has that been?

Emma: It's been busy and good, and I've even been subbing in the high schools. So, I am just trying different realms. I've been working in special ed classrooms and am totally confident. I mean I am like very confident. I am very good at this. Kids are really responsive to me. I'm good at all these skills, and all my life, I didn't believe I could do anything. It's like I'm a different person.

Hale: What do you make of that?

Emma: I just picked myself up by my bootstraps, and I don't think I'm supposed to be at that school anymore *(referring to her job at the time of the TA)*. I just felt like I had been demoted.

Hale: You didn't feel good there because you weren't appreciated?

Emma: Yes, really under appreciated. Not by the parents; the parents loved me. But by the teachers and the administration.

Hale: So, is that the difference between the two jobs, that you feel appreciated?

Emma: Yes, I mean they're like, "Oh my God, we are so glad you're here today. Thank you."

Hale: And you feel confident you said.

Emma: Yes. And they ask for me back. They're like, "Can you come in tomorrow? Can you come for the next three days?"

Hale: Oh my!

Emma: Yes, so I am totally valued.

Hale: And it sounds like you value yourself.

Emma: I do, yes. As a matter of fact, I had a bad day at one of the schools that I'm a regular at. It was a fourth-grade class, and they were not a very well-behaved class, so I ran into a lot of behavior problems and kids who were disrespectful to me and talked very rudely to me and stuff. So, in the middle of the day, I said, to the children, "I come to this school all the time, and this is a classroom that I'm choosing not to come back to. I'm not very happy. I don't like the way you're treating me today, and I don't have to come back to this classroom again." I wasn't doing it to punish them, but I was letting them know, "If you're going to diss me like that, I don't have to come here again." And they were shocked.

Hale: Were they?!

Emma: The kids were like, "But we like you." And I was like, "Well, you need to change it right now because you're not going to talk to me that way."

Hale: Wow! You really stood up for yourself!

Emma: You know, it's like I went down a rabbit hole in my life somewhere, and when I came back out of the rabbit hole, I popped out as this person that was like, "Yes, I respect myself. Yes, I am going to put a restraining order on this person. No, you're not going to talk down to me. No, I'm not going to sub for your classroom because your kids don't understand that they need to respect guest teachers." I'm just different.

Hale: What helped you get out of the rabbit hole? What changed?

Emma: I don't really know....

Hale: Something from the assessment do you think?

Emma: Maybe. Yes, maybe from the assessment. To me life is short, and I don't need to be treated like crap. No one is going to talk down to me.

Hale: You know, I wonder if one of the things the assessment did was to remove some of the doubt, the self-doubt that started a long time ago. Maybe that's part of the cord that you cut, to the self-doubt that held you back.

Emma: Oh my God, completely!

Hale: There was a part of you that worried, "Is there something wrong with me?"

Emma: Yes, I was worried, well and my sister was worried. She was really worried.

Hale:	She was, which made you even more worried. It was like, "People are worried about me? There must be something really wrong!" *[Hale adopted Emma's language, an example of collaborative communication.]*
Emma:	Yes. It was like, "What do you see that I don't see? Why was my father always worried about me?" After my dad died, I was kind of paralyzed. I was in the house. I was waking up in the middle of the night afraid someone was at my door or breaking in. I had so much fear and anxiety.
Hale:	That was unempowering.
Emma:	Yes, very unempowering, making me feel really scared.
Hale:	Now that you are starting to feel empowered—you have used that word about ten times now, which is wonderful to hear—things are different.
Emma:	Yes, well in the past if I heard a scary noise, I would be like, "Oh my God, what was that sound?" And then I'd be lying there, and my heart would be racing, and I'd be terrified. Now, there were some noises last night, but I'm getting familiar with them, and it's no big deal. Last night I said, "Emma, you know what that sound is, it's ok."
Hale:	So, you were able not to go where you used to go.
Emma:	Right, I didn't go there.
Hale:	Do you think that's related to some of the things we talked about that you experienced as a little girl? The caution, the uncertainty.
Emma:	Yes, I think so.
Hale:	The cautious approach you developed to the world, and now that you understand where that comes from, maybe it's a different experience for you.
Emma:	I think so, because when I was a little girl, I was afraid I was going to die every night because I had this fear. Every night I was, "What if I die, you know I might die." I don't know why, I just did, I had a lot of fear. But I also had a mom who was drinking, and I mean there was a lot of fear I used to have. I used to have really gruesome dreams about my mom. One time I dreamed she was so angry at me and Tessa that she was carving our rumps like rump roast.
Hale:	Wow, what a dream!
Emma:	Yes.
Hale:	So, there was a **lot** of fear!
Emma:	Yes, I mean I was really riddled with fear for a long time. A lot of anxiety.
Hale:	And maybe that is part of the cord you cut.
Emma:	The adult is taking care of the little girl inside me now, yes.
Hale:	Beautiful!
Emma:	Yes, I don't have to explain myself to people anymore. I don't care. I gave my ex-boyfriend two chances. The second time, it's done. "He's not going to get his act together, and I can't wait around, I don't want to wait around. You know I am a grown up. I need to be around grown-ups." And then, oh my God, the other thing you told me was um… and I don't remember it, and it's really important. I can't remember the other thing that you noticed.
Hale:	Are you talking about the self-doubt?
Emma:	Yes, that's it. Why that disappeared, I don't know.
Hale:	I wonder if it did because the assessment helped understand things that have long been in the back of your mind.
Emma:	Haunted me for years.
Hale:	Haunted you for years.

Emma: Years. I mean years and years and years of, "I don't know how to do that. I'm really stupid at math. I'm really dumb at explaining things. I'm never going to amount to anything. I don't know if I know how to do things. Am I capable at making it a living? Could I do that really?"

Later:

Emma: I know substitute teaching is a very good part-time job, but it's not a living, and I know that. So now, in the next few days, I'm going to start looking for full-time work with full-time benefits. But I also found out about some other ways I could get benefits in the meantime. Oh, another thing I found out about myself is that I'm one of the most resourceful people I've ever met.

Hale: Isn't that something—to be able to say that and to feel the truth of it in yourself? Good for you, I'm completely thrilled for you!

Emma: Well, thank you for all of your help with the assessments. I mean they were hard, they were scary, and they were intense. I was like, "Oh God, I'm the biggest moron. I don't know what I'm doing." But I realized, "No, au contraire. I've never been a moron." I was just a moron for calling myself a moron. It was sad that I did that.

Hale: It is sad, isn't it? But you weren't a moron for doing it. You had to think of yourself that way to cope with what was happening to you at the time. [*Hale seizes the moment to make a shame intervention.*]

Emma: You're right!

Reflections on the Follow-up Session with Emma

And so ended the Therapeutic Assessment with Emma. I was very happy about how she had turned her life around and had finally escaped the trauma of her early childhood. The assessment was also a deeply gratifying experience for me. I had learned so much from Emma about what it is like to be a terrorized child—and adult—and what courage it takes to overcome its effects. I developed a deep respect for her, and because of the way the assessment evolved, I expanded my capacity for both compassion and patience. I was grateful for my experience with Emma, and once again impressed with the power of TA to help clients make profound changes in their lives.

A Quick Postscript

In looking for a case for this publication (about five years after this assessment), I had a good excuse to contact Emma to see if she would grant me permission to write about our work together. She took some time to think about it and then consented, happy that others might learn something from her experiences. It was delightful for both of us to connect. She told me that her mother had died a couple of years previously and that she had handled the grief well, "like an adult." I also learned that she had a full-time job that she liked, and it provided good benefits. She had not found the romantic relationship she wanted yet, but she had high hopes, and in any event, she was happy and living a full life.

Note

1 An assessor's warm welcome may look different in different contexts and cultures. Assessors have to attune their emotional display to the cultural expectations of the client and to the context where they work.

References

Durosini, I., & Aschieri, F. (2021). Therapeutic Assessment efficacy: A meta-analysis. *Psychological Assessment*, *33*(10), 962–972. doi: 10.1037/pas0001038.

Finn, S. E. (2007). *In our clients' shoes: Theory and techniques of Therapeutic Assessment*, Erlbaum.

12 Learning, Practicing, and Marketing Therapeutic Assessment

Developing Your Competence in TA

Learning Tests

As you have seen throughout the book, Therapeutic Assessment (TA) assessors use a number of psychotherapy techniques and skills in their work with clients, and you will find that studying many different psychotherapies will help you practice TA. However, to be really good at TA you have to be competent enough with psychological tests that you can use them to understand clients' inner experience. Which tests to learn depends on your setting and the types of problems-in-living clients typically bring, and also on what tests are available and supported in your geographical area. If possible, we suggest that you become skilled with a broadband cognitive measure such as the Wechsler Adult Intelligence Scale-IV (WAIS-IV; Wechsler, 2008), one or more self-report measures such as the Minnesota Multiphasic Personality Inventory-3 (MMPI-3; Ben Porath & Tellegen, 2020), Personality Assessment Inventory (PAI; Morey, 2007), NEO-PI-3 (Costa & McCrae, 2005), or Millon Clinical Multiaxial Inventory-IV (MCMI-IV; Millon et al., 2015), and one or more standardized performance-based personality tests such as the Rorschach (Exner, 2002; Meyer et al., 2011), the Crisi Wartegg System (CWS; Crisi, 2018), or the Adult Attachment Projective Picture System (AAP; George & West, 2012). You can supplement these tests with non-standardized methods such as the Early Memory Procedure (EMP; Bruhn, 1992a, 1992b), Individualized Sentence Completions, or drawings. Importantly, TA can be practiced with any valid psychological test, and at times it is possible to perform an impactful TA with just a single test.

How does one learn tests? Hopefully, some tests were taught during your graduate studies and internship, and test publishers and professional organizations such as the Society for Personality Assessment (SPA) often provide trainings on tests. Beyond this, we recommend that you seek individual or group consultation with test experts as a way of furthering your competence and learning to integrate various tests into a case conceptualization. In our experience, there is no substitute for this kind of training, and it is the fastest way to become highly competent with tests. Also, because new knowledge is always accruing from research about the possible meanings of standardized test scores, learning tests is a lifelong pursuit and requires a commitment to ongoing training and continuing education. Last but not least, working with clients collaboratively over time will help you learn about the tests you use, as clients will give you words and phrases associated with inner experiences reflected in their test scores.

DOI: 10.4324/9780429202797-14

Such phrases are often highly meaningful and may be useful to subsequent clients you work with who have similar scores.

Learning TA

Begin Where You Are

As you learn psychological tests, you will want guidance in how to use them to create therapeutic experiences for your clients. Again, we hope that you may have received training in Collaborative/Therapeutic Assessment in your graduate studies, or at least have gotten instruction on how to give feedback to clients about their psychological test results. Wherever you are in your knowledge of TA, we encourage you to begin trying out with your clients some of the collaborative practices we have written about in this book. Many people find that gathering Assessment Questions in an initial session and doing Extended Inquiries after standardized tests are good places to start. These practices also don't add much time to your usual assessment sessions. Also, you can try out the Level 1, 2, 3 Information organizational strategy to see if it helps during your test feedback sessions. Start where you are, with those TA steps and practices that are easiest to implement in your setting, and do not feel that you have to use the whole model we have laid out to be doing TA. Remember, the core of TA is a set of values and principles that we aspire to implement in our interactions with clients: Collaboration, respect, humility, compassion, openness, and curiosity. If you remember these principles and look for ways to put them into action, you will find yourself "creating" many of the practices we have described in this book.

Studying TA on Your Own

We encourage you to read about TA, and besides this book, there are a number of published books, case studies, articles, and chapters describing the rationale and techniques of different aspects of TA. Many of these publications are listed under the Resources tab of the Therapeutic Assessment Insitute website: *www. therapeuticassessment.com*, and some articles can be downloaded from there. We find that the varied case accounts are inspiring in showing the many ways TA can be adapted to diverse clients and different settings, and we hope they will stimulate your creativity and free you up to try TA with your clients. There are also videos you can watch on the TA website, and we hope to be creating more of these in the future.

Another self-study tool, if your clients will allow you to do so, is to videotape your assessment sessions and watch them afterwards. This is how Steve Finn began to develop TA, and you may be surprised by how much you can learn by reviewing your own videos with TA in mind. Pay careful attention to clients' responses to your comments and interventions, and especially look for signs of shame (i.e., client's head lowered, silence, covering mouth or face), evidence of coping mechanisms (e.g., client changing the topic, laughing, becoming more intellectual), and moments of clients transforming (e.g., getting in touch with split-off emotions, being vulnerable with the assessor, finding more self-compassion). As you notice these different elements, look for the intersubjective (i.e., systemic, interactional) interplay of you and your clients that brought them into being. How did the client guide you to a new place of exploration or signal you to veer away from a certain subject? How did you respond?

Where did you miss a signal or cue, or bypass an opportunity for further exploration? Where did you follow a hunch or take a leap that worked out well?

Peer Consultation and Study Groups

One step beyond recording and watching your own videos is to get together with one or more colleagues who are interested in TA to read and discuss articles together, talk about clients, and (as trust builds) possibly even watch each other's session videos. Groups like this can be small (e.g., 2 people) or larger; they can meet for a fixed period of time (e.g., weekly for 3 months) or be ongoing (2 hours once a month); and they can be in-person or virtual. There is an understandable desire in all of us to learn from experts who can "tell us the right answers" and guide us in our development. We'll talk about this option below, but again, we think you might be surprised how much you can learn about TA simply by talking with good colleagues about its principles and practices as these apply to your clients.

Expert Consultation

An additional helpful learning tool is to seek consultation, either individually or in a group. The Therapeutic Assessment Institute (TAI) coordinates training and certification in TA, has a list of faculty and supervisors, and has established reduced rates (adjusted for different countries) for TAI members who desire consultation. In our experience, consultation is helpful in seven ways:

1   An expert consultant can help you understand the TA model better, for example, to answer questions like, "What are the major differences between an Extended Inquiry and an Assessment Intervention Session?"
2   An expert consultant can help you understand your client's test results better, integrate them into a useful and compassionate case conceptualization, and discuss the implications of test results for conducting a TA, for example, "What should I focus on in this client's Assessment Intervention Session?"
3   TA is an "open model" that must be adapted to every client and to each particular client context. A consultant can help you think about how to tailor TA to your setting and client population and how to inform referral sources about your work and develop and market for TA. (See more below about marketing TA.)
4   When we use psychological tests as empathy magnifiers, inevitably we feel a great deal for and with our clients, and it can be tiring and lonely to "hold" clients' life stories on our own. A TA consultant can support you emotionally and help you continue to work deeply with your assessment clients.
5   In our experience, while learning TA most people are confronted with personal growth challenges they have not encountered previously. As Finn (2000) explained, this is because as we work to get "in clients' shoes" and find empathy for their dilemmas of change, we must confront aspects of ourselves (for example, split-off affect states) that we would never have encountered otherwise. A trusted consultant can be a great help in this process of increasing self-awareness/personal growth.
6   The TA model of supervision/consultation is similar to the model for clinicians working with clients. (See Finn, 2019.) Thus, participating in consultation with a

TA-trained supervisor can give you a "feel" for what your clients experience when they take part in a TA.

7   If you are interested in becoming certified in TA (more below), a TAI consultant can help you achieve this goal.

Besides providing individual consultation, the TAI sponsors ongoing consultation groups in TA and can also provide a consultant if you wish to put a group together yourself.

TA Workshops and Trainings

The TAI periodically sponsors in-person and (especially recently) online trainings in TA, and we encourage you to attend as many of these as you can. These trainings are conducted by people certified in TA and are sometimes general (e.g., "Introduction to Therapeutic Assessment," "50 Ways to Do an Assessment Intervention," "Working with Shame in Psychological Assessment"), sometimes focused on a particular TA model or population or test (e.g., "Therapeutic Assessment of Adults," "Using TA with Severely Traumatized Clients," "TA with the MMPI-3," "Using the Crisi Wartegg System in Therapeutic Assessment"), and all typically involve workshop attendees as participant-observers. Another exciting type of workshop periodically sponsored by the TAI is the "Live Therapeutic Assessment," where participants observe over a video link while a TA-trained assessor conducts a TA with an actual client, family, or couple. Workshop participants serve as consultants to the assessor and help to interpret the testing, plan Assessment Intervention Sessions, and outline Summary/Discussion Sessions before they occur. They then get to observe and discuss these sessions afterwards.

Frequently, TA workshops are also featured at the annual meetings of the Society for Personality Assessment (*www.personality.org*) and at the periodic congresses of the International Society of Rorschach and Projective Methods (www. internationalrorschachsociety.com). Also, besides time-limited workshops, at times there are lengthier TA courses lasting 6 months to a year—often affiliated with a university—that are available to practicing psychologists. All TA-sponsored workshops and courses are listed on the TA website and offer discounts to TA members and to graduate students.

Internships/Post-docs/Apprenticeships

At this time, the European Center for Therapeutic Assessment in Milan, Italy accepts students for internships (*tirocini*). The Center for Therapeutic Assessment in Austin periodically accepts doctoral-level graduates for post-doctoral fellowships. And various TA practitioners around the world often take on licensed psychologists who wish to learn TA as employees/apprentices. All of these settings provide intense learning opportunities for people wanting to be certified and practice TA independently.

Finally, as we write, the TAI is collaborating with the Society for Personality Assessment to survey graduate training programs in clinical, counseling, and school psychology to discover which of these programs offer training in collaborative assessment and TA. This information will be posted on both the SPA and TAI websites when it is compiled.

Certification in TA

As we have alluded to, the Therapeutic Assessment Institute provides the opportunity for licensed psychologists to become certified in TA. Separate certifications are available for TA with adults, children, adolescents, and couples. Practitioners wanting certification in TA with couples must first be certified in TA with adults. All certified practitioners are listed on the TAI website.

Do I Need to Get Certified?

A logical question is, "Why would I want to get certified in TA?" This is reasonable because, as we wrote earlier, we encourage you to take whatever you find useful in this book and begin integrating it into your work with clients, and the most important elements of TA are its core values combined with excellent skills in psychological testing. The main reasons people seek formal certification are typically to: (1) know they are practicing TA with fidelity and competence, (2) take part in research on TA, (3) structure their TA training and learn advanced skills, (4) grow and learn more about psychological assessment, the human condition, and themselves, (5) advertise to clients and referral sources that they are competent in TA, and (6) become more involved in the TA community and help spread the knowledge and practice of TA. We understand that many wonderful and skilled assessment psychologists will not choose to undergo the certification process in TA, and we welcome everyone to be active members of the TA community.

Steps in Certification

The steps for getting certified in TA are explained on the TAI website under the **Training** tab. Briefly, in order to apply for certification, all candidates must be members of the TAI and have passed the Level 1 online certification exam available under the **Training** tab: *https://www.therapeuticassessment.com/level_1_certification_process.php*. The Level 1 exam is an online multiple-choice test of your knowledge of the theory, research, and techniques of TA. There is a list of readings you can do to prepare for the exam, and you may consult whatever materials you want while you are taking the exam.

Once you have passed the Level 1 exam, you can work on becoming fully certified. To do this, you must show videos of your TA sessions to a certifying TA faculty member who can judge that you have mastered a set of core competencies specific to each model. You may record videos of one case and send them in to be reviewed and rated (again, instructions are on the website), or show different sessions to a TA consultant/mentor who will rate them and accompany you through the process of certifying you on each step of TA. The TAI is committed to helping people who want to be certified in TA to achieve that goal.

Introducing TA into New Professional Settings

So, let's say you have become certified in TA or you have incorporated a number of TA practices into the way you do psychological assessment and you are hired for a new job in a hospital, clinic, or group practice. How should you go about introducing TA into your new setting?

Observe and Learn about Your Context

We recommend that you start by learning everything you can about your new work setting and how psychological assessments are currently conducted or have been done in the past. What types of clients are typically referred and what are the usual reasons for the referrals? What are the predominant theories/clinical models used by colleagues and staff to conceptualize clients? Have your bosses and colleagues heard about collaborative assessment or TA? Are any collaborative assessment practices already in place (e.g., feedback sessions, letters to clients)? Are there time and service constraints and requirements that must be met when assessing clients? Do the staff seem open to learning about a new method of doing assessment? This type of informal assessment will help you think about your next steps in educating your colleagues about TA.

Use Scaffolding in Introducing TA in Your New Setting

Once you get a feel for your new setting and colleagues, you can begin acquainting them with how TA works. We believe the same TA principles apply here that we use when working with clients:

1   Building trusting relationships with colleagues is the key to fostering collaboration and introducing new ideas or procedures. Be patient and don't try to introduce TA too quickly before you have established good relationships.
2   If you want others to change and accept new ideas about assessment, you must be curious and open to their thoughts also, and be willing to change yourself. Remember, your colleagues may understand your new setting and client population better than you do, and they can help you adapt TA to this next context.
3   Scaffolding is key—gradually introducing new ways of thinking about and conducting assessments and assessing how your colleagues react. For example, they may more easily accept you asking clients for Assessment Questions than you writing feedback letters to clients. Start where you can and let your colleagues see the results.
4   How fast you can go depends on what is Level 1, 2, or 3 information. If your colleagues practice from a psychoanalytic, "blank-slate" stance with clients, most likely you must go more slowly in introducing TA than if they work from an interpersonal, humanistic, and attachment-based perspective. And remember TA is not wed to any theory of human behavior. See you if can explain TA theory and practices in psychoanalytic (or cognitive-behavioral) language.
5   Provide information. If your colleagues have never heard about TA, consider giving a short talk over the lunch break or providing them with things to read about TA. Remember, they are busy, so don't overwhelm them. Perhaps construct a fact sheet of bullet points and let them ask questions.
6   Collaboration is key. To the extent you can, take time to look over test materials together with colleagues, discuss clients, and ask them to share their thoughts and expertise. Be willing to change your language and adopt their terminology to make your thoughts about clients more accessible to your colleagues.

Table 12.1 Referring Professional Feedback Form

1 Briefly, what were your hopes and expectations when you referred this client for a psychological assessment?
2 Did the assessment meet your expectations?
3 What part(s) of the assessment was most useful to you and the client?
4 What part was least useful?
5 What would have made the assessment more useful?
6 What would you tell a colleague who was considering referring a client to me for this type of assessment?

7 Pay attention to disruptions and make repairs. If a colleague seems to feel "shown up" by you or is upset by the strong alliance her or his client developed with you during a TA, think carefully about whether you were unconsciously competing with your colleague, and make an effort to talk things through with her or him. Again, start from the premise that you have as much to learn as you have to teach and share.

8 See any "resistance" to TA that you encounter as reflecting a dilemma of change—either of the individual colleague or of the system. For example, if your new boss rejects the idea of your doing Follow-up Sessions with clients, consider whether this stems from a concern about billing for such sessions or from trying to shorten an extensive waiting list. Be curious, ask questions, and don't get insistent or defensive.

9 Be open to and seek feedback about your work, both verbally and by asking referring professionals to fill out an assessment feedback questionnaire. (See Table 12.1.) Consider modifying your approach based on any feedback you get.

Establishing a Practice Specializing in TA

Let's say you don't work for a clinic or agency and are in practice on your own. You are confident in your TA skills (either because you are certified or have learned TA another way) and want to establish a practice that specializes in TA. How should you market your services?

Marketing to Professionals

At this point in the development of TA, it's very likely that you will have to educate referring professionals in your local area about what TA is and how it can benefit their clients. This can be done in a number of ways—by inviting individual colleagues to lunch or coffee to tell them about TA, giving a talk at a local psychological association or group practice (especially if you can show a video of your doing TA with a client), sending out an announcement of your practice with a brief TA fact sheet for referring professionals, or joining a peer consultation group where you gradually build trust and talk about TA. An important thing to remember is that colleagues may already have negative or neutral attitudes about psychological assessment because either (1) they have had experiences with unhelpful or damaging assessments or (2) traditional psychological assessment conflicts with their own values as practitioners and they have "thrown the baby out with the bathwater." If this is so, you will have to explain that TA is quite different from traditional assessment and is a humanistic, client-centered approach. Another common hesitation is the worry by other practitioners that TA will interfere with their current treatment plan. While this is not impossible, typically we reassure colleagues that referring professionals are involved as collaborators in their clients' assessments, and we share the evidence that TA is known to facilitate ongoing treatment. (For example, see the studies by Hilsenroth et al. (2004) and by Smith et al. (2014), discussed in Chapter 3.) Of course, we also encourage them to refer a difficult client and see how it goes.

Along these lines, as discussed earlier, TA can be used at many points in treatment, that is, before, during, or even towards the end of an intervention. But one way to build a TA practice is to assist colleagues with clients they find puzzling, difficult, or frustrating, and to market TA as a means of treatment consultation. This is how Steve Finn originally established the successful Center for Therapeutic Assessment in Austin. Finn found that many practitioners were eager to have a colleague collaborate with them in understanding and discussing challenging clients, and that beginning therapists or non-doctoral level practitioners were especially grateful for his input. Independent practice is a lonely enterprise for many clinicians, and even the most experienced clinicians end up wondering if they are doing the right thing for clients. If the TA assessor is willing to "team" with colleagues on difficult cases, show sympathy for colleague's doubts and struggles, and help plot a way forward, this often leads to a steady stream of referrals.

Marketing to Clients

In the USA it is considered ethical to market directly to clients, as long as the information in your advertising is accurate and not overstated. Years ago, Constance Fischer (see Chapter 2) periodically posted a small add in the local newspaper that read, *"Facing a major life decision? Puzzled about your life, career, or relationships? Get consultation from a psychologist who uses psychological tests to help people learn about themselves and figure out how to move forward. For more information, call Dr. Fischer at ..."* Apparently, Fischer never lacked assessment clients (Fischer, 2017.) Even if an approach like this would be frowned on in your area or country or is too bold for your liking, do consider that advertising TA directly to clients can be a service to them. It directs suffering people towards a process that has been shown to be helpful for many different types of contexts and problems in living, and the marketing you do may help clients avoid interventions that are less helpful. Other ways of reaching clients directly might involve giving talks at a church or Lions Club meeting, writing an article about TA for a community newsletter or magazine, or putting a flyer (with permission) in the waiting rooms of physicians with whom you collaborate. As discussed in Chapter 4, we recommend you also prepare an information or fact sheet, that can be in paper form and also on your website, for clients who inquire about TA.

We also want to affirm that in the experience of many TA clinicians around the world, satisfied clients and referring professionals are the best referral sources. If you do good work and you treat TA clients with respect and care, it seems that often they cannot wait to tell others about their encounter with TA. This does not mean that every friend of a former client who calls will be appropriate for or decide to do a TA. But, the "buzz" about TA will start getting around, and in less time than you might imagine, we predict you will have more referrals than you can handle on your own.

What to Charge and How to Bill

To successfully practice TA, you need to get paid for it, and here we address issues that seem to arise in a number of settings.

Don't Undervalue Your Services

Whether you work in a clinic or on your own, we urge you not to charge less for the time you spend on your TAs than you charge for your other professional services. We recognize that this may go against market trends, and that other practitioners may charge less for their assessments. Still, in our experience, if you explain to clients and referring professionals that TA is different than traditional psychological assessment, that it combines assessment *and* intervention, and that research shows TA can aid subsequent treatments, you will be able to reimburse yourself fairly for the time it takes to do TA. Of course, if a particular client truly cannot afford a full TA, you can consider offering a shorter TA involving only 1–2 tests and 2–3 sessions (Finn et al., 2017). This is a better course of action than offering to do a TA "on the cheap."

How to Bill

We recommend that you bill TA for what it is—a mixture of psychological assessment and of psychotherapy. Initial Sessions are typically billed as diagnostic interviews, standardized testing sessions as psychological testing, and lengthy Extended Inquiries as psychotherapy. Assessment Intervention Sessions are typically billed as psychotherapy, as are Summary/Discussion and Follow-up Sessions. Depending on the rules in your area, the time to write Therapeutic Psychological Reports or feedback letters to clients may be billed as psychological testing or as preparation of written feedback. David (2013), Finn (2007), and Finn and Martin (1997) have all published sample bills for TA, and David has written about how U.S. practitioners can effectively deal with managed care companies to get insurance reimbursement for TA.

Getting Support While Learning and Practicing TA

We close this chapter by encouraging you not to practice TA all on your own. Often, the clients referred for TA are complex ones that other clinicians have difficulty treating and who may be high in Epistemic Hypervigilance. (See Chapter 1.) Engaging challenging clients in TA, confronting their "inner worlds" and traumas as depicted in their psychological test responses, and aspiring to "get in clients' shoes," all the while collaborating with both clients and the complex systems that surround them (e.g., referring professionals, families, spouses) requires a great deal of energy and emotion regulation on the part of assessors. Above we discussed the usefulness of expert and peer consultation, and we emphasize here that we believe such networks of support are essential to practicing TA at a high level over time. In our experience clinicians who attempt to learn and practice TA in isolation—without help and encouragement from others—eventually burn out or end up "cutting corners" in their assessments to conserve energy and protect themselves emotionally, for example, by writing "boiler plate" reports, cutting out Extended Inquiries and Assessment Interventions, or spending very little time preparing Summary/Discussion Sessions. It is our hope that this book both inspires you to do TA and is a step in your joining the larger TA community, which will also help you feel less lonely and make practicing TA easier and more enriching.

References

Ben-Porath, Y. S., & Tellegen, A. (2020). *Minnesota Multiphasic Personality Inventory-3 (MMPI-3): Manual for administration, scoring, and interpretation.* University of Minnesota Press.

Bruhn, A. R. (1992a). The Early Memories Procedure: A projective test of autobiographical memory (Part I). *Journal of Personality Assessment, 58,* 1–15.

Bruhn, A. R. (1992b). The Early Memories Procedure: A projective test of autobiographical memory (Part II). *Journal of Personality Assessment, 58,* 326–346.

Costa, P. T., & McCrae, R. R. (2005). *NEO Personality Inventory 3 (NEO-PI-3) manual.* Psychological Assessment Resources.

Crisi, A. (2018). *The Crisi Wartegg System (CWS) manual.* Routledge.

David, R. M. (2013). Billing health insurance for Therapeutic Assessments. *The TA Connection, 1*(2), 13–17.

Exner, J. E. (2002). *The Rorschach: A comprehensive system.* Wiley.

Finn, S. E. (2007). *In our clients' shoes: Theory and techniques of Therapeutic Assessment.* Routledge.

Finn, S. E. (2000, March). *Therapeutic Assessment: Would Harry approve?* Paper presented at the Society for Personality Assessment annual meeting, Albuquerque, NM, as part of a symposium, "Harry Stack Sullivan and Psychological Assessment," F. Barton Evans, Chair. Reprinted as Chapter 3 in Finn, S. E. (2007). *In our clients' shoes: Theory and techniques of Therapeutic Assessment* (pp. 23–31). Erlbaum.

Finn, S. E. (2019). Supervision of Therapeutic Assessment. In A. J. Wright (Ed.), *Essentials of psychological assessment supervision* (pp. 221–242). Wiley.

Finn, S. E., De Saeger, H., & Kamphuis, J. H. (2017, March). *An ultra-brief model of TA with adults.* Workshop presented at the annual meeting of the Society for Personality Assessment, San Francisco, CA.

Finn, S. E., & Martin, H. (1997). Therapeutic Assessment with the MMPI-2 in managed health care. In J. N. Butcher (Ed.) *Objective psychological assessment in managed health care: A practitioner's guide* (pp. 131–152). Oxford University Press.

Fischer, C. T. (2017). *On the way to collaborative psychological assessment: Selected papers of Constance T. Fischer.* Routledge.

George, C., & West, M. (2012). *The Adult Attachment Projective Picture System: Attachment theory and assessment in adults.* Guilford.

Hilsenroth, M. J., Peters, E. J., & Ackerman, S. J. (2004). The development of therapeutic alliance during psychology assessment: Patient and therapist perspectives across treatment. *Journal of Personality Assessment, 83,* 331–344.

Meyer, G. J., Viglione, D. J., Mihura, J. L., Erard, R. E., & Erdberg, P. (2011). *Rorschach Performance Assessment System: Administration, coding, interpretation, and technical manual.* Rorschach Performance Assessment System.

Millon, T., Millon, C., & Grossman, S. (2015). *Millon Clinical Multiaxial Inventory - IV manual (4th ed.).* NCS Pearson, Inc.

Morey, L. C. (2007). *The PAI professional manual.* Psychological Assessment Resources.

Smith, J. D., Eichler, W. C., Norman, K. R., & Smith, S. R. (2014). The effectiveness of Collaborative/Therapeutic Assessment for psychotherapy consultation: A pragmatic re-plicated single case study. *Journal of Personality Assessment, 97*(3), 261–270.

Wechsler, D. (2008). *Wechsler Adult Intelligence Scale–Fourth Edition.* Pearson.

13 Forward!

This book was written during a time of great turmoil in the world, as the COVID-19 pandemic surged, and quarantines, vaccines, and social distancing became common human experiences. The efforts made to produce a vaccine and distribute it to protect humanity were commendable. Yet, one wonders what might have occurred if scientists and doctors identified a way of assessing and intervening with patients to meet two goals: (1) Achieve a more accurate assessment of the patients' symptoms, prognosis, and treatment needs, and (2) invite patients to take an active role in understanding and improving their health to lessen the impact of the symptoms on their functioning. Certainly, a medical assessment intervention that achieved both these goals would be beneficial to a wide variety of clients with various medical issues. However, within the medical model, assessment and treatment are generally considered separate procedures, and it is not expected that the assessment process will also be a treatment that affects both the symptoms experienced and their severity.

As validated by research, Therapeutic Assessment (TA) meets the above two goals. It is an empirically supported approach to psychological assessment that concludes with the same type of information and decisions that occur with a traditional psychological evaluation. In addition, in as few as two or three sessions, clients may experience a decrease in their symptoms, and an increase in confidence and self-esteem (Durosini & Aschieri, 2021). These improvements are accompanied by clients having a clearer picture of the salient issues they should address in future treatment if warranted, and clients are more likely to engage in subsequent treatment in ways that lead to better outcomes (De Saeger et al., 2014; Durosini & Aschieri, 2021).

If we recognize that TA can lead to improvements for clients, then we have an ethical responsibility to use the approach to enhance client care (Bersoff et al., 2012; Boilen, 2017). Bersoff et al. (2012) identified specific collaborative strategies that assessors should use to conduct assessments that are highly ethical. They argued in favor of contextualizing the evaluation, being transparent with clients, and inviting client input on findings. They also endorsed Fischer's (1985/1994) idea of having clients review a test report and offer comments before finalizing it. We see these ideas as aligning with what we have described in the previous chapters, and agree that a collaborative approach to assessment contributes to a more valid interpretation of test results that "promotes enhanced ethicality and heightens trust in the evaluator" (Bersoff et al., 2012, p. 60). The field of psychology has rightfully stressed the importance of competent and ethical practice. We believe TA aligns with these values, and leaders in the field have also endorsed adopting TA practices to enhance the

DOI: 10.4324/9780429202797-15

competent provision of psychological assessment (e.g., Kaslow et al., 2018). In fact, as Poston & Hanson first stated in 2010:

> Those who engage in assessment and testing as usual may miss out, it seems, on a golden opportunity to effect client change and enhance clinically important treatment processes. Similarly, applied training programs in clinical, counseling, and school psychology should incorporate therapeutic models of assessment into their curricula, foundational didactic classes, and practica … competency benchmarks and guidelines for psychological assessment practice should be revisited to make sure they include key aspects of therapeutic models of assessment (p. 210).

TA is also aligned with current trends in the field related to providing psychological services to diverse clients and, specifically, those who have been marginalized by society. TA assessors are in a unique position to help such clients. The TA values of respect, humility, and collaboration are synonymous with the values our pofessional organizations advocate for when it comes to providing diversity-sensitive care (American Psychological Association, 1993, 2003). Also, assessors trained in TA are highly attuned to the client's circumstance and context when conducting a TA (Martin, 2018). Throughout a TA, and especially during our moments of case conceptualization, we go beyond a simple interpretation of a test score to include the client's context related to current social, occupational, community, developmental, and life experiences. For clients from diverse backgrounds, this means those diversity elements are deeply considered and discussed with humility and openness, which aligns with best practices (Bersoff et al., 2012; Smith & Krishnamurthy, 2018). These skills are core to all TAs, but for marginalized clients who often experience shame connected to social stigma, it can be transformative to work with an assessor who is aware of that shame and who works to help them understand their shame and heal from it.

We also want to mention one other beneficial aspect of TA. Assessors that practice this approach often find it to be among the most rewarding work they do. At least one empirical study (Smith & Egan, 2015) and numerous published accounts from trainees (e.g., Miller et al., 2019: Miller et al., 2019; Peters et al., 2008; Tharinger, 2016; Turret, 2015) suggest that graduate students exposed to TA are moved by participating in the process and develop a heightened interest in psychological assessment. We believe there are several factors that contribute to those positive feelings. First, given the efficacy of TA, assessors often witness significant client growth, and our clients are grateful for the changes that have occurred. As noted by De Saeger et al. (2016), "Patients reported in various ways how they felt empowered by the TA experience, and became ready to get started with treatment." (p. 476). A client taking part in an empirical case study of Virtual TA stated, "There's been some pretty significant 'tectonic' shifts within me over the past 8–10 months and I think that a lot of the foundational work for this happened in the work [TA] we did together." (David et al., 2021, p. 9). To be witness to such growth and the impact on clients is highly rewarding.

Second, TA requires a high level of critical thinking, creativity, and relationship skills. We find it very fulfilling to review test results and build a collaborative understanding of what those results mean for the client. At the same time, we use our relationship and therapy skills to create deep and meaningful moments with clients, which often leave us changed for the better. Last, given the complexities of each client and their testing, the experience never feels rote or boring. Unlike some testing psychologists that feel burnt out by administering tests multiple times and writing reports that have a similar quality, when conducting TAs each experience feels novel and has its own unique challenges. We are continuously challenged and surprised by what occurs with clients and find that these ever-new experiences keep us engaged in our work. That being said, these benefits may also be challenging for clinicians. It can be difficult to connect deeply with clients without being emotionally impacted, which is why we believe consultation with others and connection to a community of like-minded assessors is crucial.

Connie Fischer's influence on the TA model is clear. When her students received feedback on their work, she often closed her comments with "Carry on!" We see this as capturing her support of their developing abilities as emerging clinicians. We also hold this idea closely as we practice TA and survey the evolution that has occurred. TA initially was influenced by core concepts from Sullivan (interpersonal theory), Swann (self-verification theory), Kohut (disintegration anxiety), and Vygotsky (scaffolding). Fischer was instrumental in explaining how to work collaboratively with clients towards their goals, and Handler continued those ideas by describing unique ways of "playing" with tests. The idea of using psychological assessment as an occasion to relate respectfully with clients, collaborate with them, and improve their life has a long history that extends beyond the authors explicitly mentioned by Fischer and Finn as inspiring their way of working. However, it was not until Finn & Tonsager (1992) demonstrated how a collaborative assessment could decrease client symptoms and increase hope, Finn published the treatment manual for the 1992 study (Finn, 1996), and then they clearly delineated how this approach differs from the traditional model of assessment (Finn & Tonsager, 1997), that the larger community of psychologists considered the potential of testing for both understanding *and* helping clients.

Core Concepts and steps of TA were identified and expanded to best serve clients (e.g., the addition of the Assessment Intervention Session; Finn, 2007). As the field evolved with the growing understanding of neuroscience, attachment, and the importance of emotion-focused interventions, these ideas were also added to the TA assessor's knowledge base and skill set. Fonagy and colleagues' (2017a, b) writings contributed to the recent Kamphuis & Finn (2019) article, providing researched concepts and theory to explain how TAs can be so efficacious with various types of clients, with different levels of psychopathology, and across various settings. A good example of the model's adaptability occurred during the COVID-19 Pandemic. As the world pivoted to the use of virtual video conferencing, so did TA. The initial experiences of TA assessors, and an empirical case study, demonstrated that a virtual TA can be efficacious (David et al., 2021).

Perhaps most important for the model's future development is the research of Durosini & Aschieri (2021), as their recent meta-analysis of well-defined TA suggests:

> that the most important aspects of Therapeutic Assessment may be its underlying philosophy and values, and—within certain parameters—not so much the exact way in which it is implemented. When collaboration, respect, compassion, openness, and humility are brought to bear in assessing clients, psychological assessment can be a life-enhancing experience in multiple ways (p. 970).

We believe that if you hold to TA values in your work, you are providing proficient and ethical care to your clients. We hope you are inspired to add some new TA elements to the various stages of your assessment process, even if currently it is difficult to implement the full model. We also hope this book continues the "forward" movement as the model grows further. We continue to learn from our clients, and from those practicing TA, and that collectively we learn how to best help our fellow human beings live their best life.

References

American Psychological Association. (1993). Guidelines for providers of psychological services to ethnic, linguistic, and culturally diverse populations. *American Psychologist, 48*(1), 45–48.

American Psychological Association. (2003). Guidelines on multicultural education, training, research, practice, and organizational change for Psychologists. *American Psychologist, 58*(5), 377–402.

Bersoff, D. N., DeMatteo, D., & Foster, E. E. (2012). Assessment and testing. In S. J. Knapp, M. C. Gottlieb, M. M. Handelsman, & L. D. VandeCreek (Eds.), *APA handbook of ethics in psychology, Vol. 2. Practice, teaching, and research* (pp. 45–74). American Psychological Association.

Boilen, S. (2017). Therapeutic Assessment in rural America: Our ethical responsibility? *The TA Connection, 5*(2), 7–13.

David, R. M., Carroll, A. J., & Smith, J. D. (2021). Virtual delivery of Therapeutic Assessment: An empirical case study. *Journal of Personality Assessment.* 1–11. Advance online publication. doi: 10.1080/00223891.2021.1929262

De Saeger, H., Kamphuis, J. H., Finn, S. E., Smith, J. D., Verheul, R., van Busschbach, J. J., Feenstra, D. J., & Horn, E. K. (2014). Therapeutic Assessment promotes treatment readiness but does not affect symptom change in patients with personality disorders: Findings from a randomized clinical trial. *Psychological Assessment, 26*, 474–483. doi: 10.1037/a0035667

De Saeger, H., Bartak, A., Eder, E. E., & Kamphuis, J. H. (2016). Memorable experiences in Therapeutic Assessment: Inviting the patient's perspective following a pretreatment randomized controlled trial. *Journal of Personality Assessment, 98*(5), 472–479. doi: 10.1080/00223 891.2015.1136314

Durosini, I., & Aschieri, F. (2021). Therapeutic Assessment efficacy: A meta-analysis. *Psychological Assessment, 33*(10), 962–972.

Finn, S. E. (1996). *A manual for using the MMPI-2 as a therapeutic intervention.* University of Minnesota Press.

Finn, S. E. (2007). *In our clients' shoes: Theory and techniques of Therapeutic Assessment.* Lawrence Erlbaum Associates.

Finn, S. E., & Tonsager, M. E. (1992). Therapeutic effects of providing MMPI-2 test feedback to college students awaiting therapy. *Psychological Assessment, 4*(3), 278–287.

Finn, S. E., & Tonsager, M. E. (1997). Information-gathering and therapeutic models of assessment: Complementary paradigms. *Psychological Assessment, 9*(4), 374–385.

Fischer, C. T. (1985/1994). *Individualizing psychological assessment.* Routledge.

Fonagy, P., Luyten, P., Allison, E., & Campbell, C. (2017a). What we have changed our minds about: Part 1. Borderline personality as a limitation of resilience. *Borderline Personality and Emotional Dysregulation, 4*(11). doi: 10.1186=s40479-017-0061-9

Fonagy, P., Luyten, P., Allison, E., & Campbell, C. (2017b). What we have changed our minds about: Part 2. Borderline personality, epistemic trust, and the developmental significance of social communication. *Borderline Personality and Emotional Dysregulation, 4*(9). doi: 10.11 86/s40479-017-0062-8

Kamphuis, J. H., & Finn, S. E. (2019). Therapeutic Assessment in personality disorders: Toward the restoration of epistemic trust. *Journal of Personality Assessment, 101*(6), 662–674.

Kaslow, N. J., Tyler Finklea, J., & Chan, G. (2018). Personality assessment: A competency capability perspective. *Journal of Personality Assessment, 100*(2), 176–185.

Martin, H. (2018). Collaborative/Therapeutic Assessment and diversity: The complexity of being human. In S. R. Smith & Krishnamurthy, R. (Eds.), *Diversity-sensitive personality assessment* (pp. 278–293). Routledge.

Miller, J. D., Shah, T. D., Brooks-White, C., & David, R. (2019). Implementation of Therapeutic Assessment in a community mental health training site: Potential barriers, implications, and benefits for adolescents and their families. *The TA Connection, 7*(2), 19–25.

Miller, L., Novotny, D., Cotas-Girard, A., & Gromoff, C. (2019). Therapeutic Assessment at Child Haven. *The TA Connection, 7*(2), 4–10.

Peters, E. J., Handler, L., White, K. G., & Winkel, J. D. (2008). "Am I going crazy, doc?": A self psychology approach to Therapeutic Assessment. *Journal of Personality Assessment, 90,* 421–434.

Poston, J. M., & Hanson, W. M. (2010). Meta-analysis of psychological assessment as a therapeutic intervention. *Psychological Assessment, 22,* 203–212.

Smith, J. D., & Egan, K. N. (2015). Trainee and client experiences of Therapeutic Assessment in a required graduate course: A qualitative analysis. *Journal of Personality Assessment, 99*(2), 126–135.

Smith, S. R., & Krishnamurthy, R. (Eds.) (2018). *Diversity-sensitive personality assessment.* Routledge.

Tharinger, D. J. (2016). Learning/practicing and participating in a Therapeutic Assessment: What can we learn from the voices of graduate students and clients. *The TA Connection, 4*(1), 4–8.

Turret, J. (2015). Assessment intervention: A doctoral student's perspective. *TA Connection, 3*(2), 15–17.

Appendix

Examples from the Literature of Assessment Intervention Sessions (AIS) with Adult Clients

Article	Client Characteristics	Primary Difficulties	Description of AIS
*Chudzik, 2016	male, age unknown	violent offenses; psychosis; drug and alcohol dependence	TAT cards help the client and assessor recognize the connections between loneliness, despair, and violence.
*Durosini, et al. 2017	51-year-old Male	complex bereavement; PTSD	Pictures from the internet of people interacting were used in a storytelling task that helped the client understand why it is difficult to assert himself.
Finn, 2003	28-year-old male	possible ADD; romantic relationship problems	Number recall tests like the Wechsler Digit Span subtest and select TAT cards were used to help the client see how, when he becomes emotionally overwhelmed, his concentration and attention are impacted.
Finn, 2007	24-year-old male	low self-esteem, achievement issues	The Bender Gestalt was used, emphasizing copying and immediate recall, to develop insight into the effects of the client's pattern of underperforming or wanting to give up due to self-denigration.
Finn, 2012	27-year-old male	sexual compulsive behavior	TAT cards were used to give the client an opportunity to experience negative emotions in session and gain insight into his compulsive need to act out sexually in response to those emotions.
*Finn, 2016b	44-year-old transgender woman	overconfidence to mask self-doubt and shame	The Thurston Craddock Test of Shame (TCTS) was used to help the client recognize tendencies towards being too confident and independent in her problem-solving.

(*Continued*)

Article	Client Characteristics	Primary Difficulties	Description of AIS
*Finn, 2020	55-year-old female	negative affective states and ineffective coping strategies	TCTS cards helped the client see how she could let down her "armor" and be more vulnerable.
Finn & Kamphuis, 2006	45-year-old female	depression, dissociation	TAT cards were used to bring into the room feelings of abandonment and resultant dissociation. Grounding techniques were employed, which helped the client gain new experiences and insight.
Finn & Martin, 1997	35-year-old female	anger, premature termination of therapy	TAT cards were used to induce feelings of frustration and the client's pattern of over controlling her anger due to a fear of hurting others. The client was then able to develop new stories which entailed assertive communication.
Finn & Martin, 2013	26-year-old female	childhood trauma, current alliance issues with therapist	TAT, Adolescent Apperception cards, and Family Apperception Test cards were used to evoke an increasingly intensive emotional reaction, in the hope of increasing the client's ability to control the pace of emotional experiencing in a therapy session.
Fischer & Finn, 2014	male, age unknown	anger and emotional abuse toward supervisees at work	To bring the client's anger into the room, WAIS-III Block Design was used to intentionally deceive the client to believe he should be able to complete the 9-block pattern with only 7 blocks. The client expressed his anger with this impossible task and the assessors' role. The client and assessor then discussed more adaptive ways of expressing anger with his work staff.
Hinrichs, 2016	55-year-old male	sedative dependence, narcissistic traits	The assessor asked the client to interpret his own test data, claiming he had nothing more to add, with the intention of bringing the client's independent style and tendency to constrict affect into the room.
Kamphuis & de Saeger, 2012	37-year-old male	work issues, unhappiness	Card one of the TAT was the focus, with an emphasis on having the client better understand his difficulties in accessing his feelings in the moment and being assertive.

(Continued)

Article	Client Characteristics	Primary Difficulties	Description of AIS
Martin & Jacklin, 2012	27-year-old male	possible learning disability, relationship issues	TAT cards were used to help the client develop ways of expressing needs and expectations in relationships that were being impacted by her feelings of loss and abandonment.
Overton, 2012	35-year-old female	experienced chronic childhood abuse	The Rorschach was given a second time with special instructions to help determine the client's ability to separate her previous traumatic experiences from present moment attention and awareness.
*Sapozhnikova & Smith, 2017	45-year-old male	inattention, disorganization, and planning issues; recent death of a parent	The Rey–Osterrieth Complex Figure Test was administered a second time to help the client change his approach to problem-solving with support from the assessor.
Smith & George, 2012	52-year-old female	depression and anxiety related to cancer diagnosis; unresolved attachment status	A personalized Sentence Completion Test was used in what is referred to as a "low intensity assessment intervention session" designed to help the client begin to see the connection between her trauma and her current difficulties.
Turret, 2015	30-year-old female	anger, depression, difficulty maintaining employment, volatile relationships	TAT cards were used to help the client have an experience of feeling supported, and not judged, for expressing her emotional pain.

Originally published in David & Bertucci, 2015.
*Articles added since that publication date.

Index